Diversity's Promise for Higher Education

❁

Diversity's Promise
for Higher Education

Making It Work

DARYL G. SMITH

The Johns Hopkins University Press

Baltimore

© 2009 The Johns Hopkins University Press
All rights reserved. Published 2009
Printed in the United States of America on acid-free paper

2 4 6 8 9 7 5 3 1

The Johns Hopkins University Press
2715 North Charles Street
Baltimore, Maryland 21218-4363
www.press.jhu.edu

Library of Congress Cataloging-in-Publication Data
Smith, Daryl G.
Diversity's promise for higher education : making it work / Daryl G. Smith.
p. cm.
Includes bibliographical references and index.
ISBN-13: 978-0-8018-9316-2 (hardcover : alk. paper)
ISBN-10: 0-8018-9316-X (hardcover : alk. paper)
1. Minorities—Education (Higher)—United States.   2. Minority college
students—United States.   3. Multiculturalism—United States.   I. Title.
LC3727.S65 2009
378.1'982900973—dc22   2008056093

A catalog record for this book is available from the British Library.

Special discounts are available for bulk purchases of this book. For more information,
please contact Special Sales at 410-516-6936 or specialsales@press.jhu.edu.

The Johns Hopkins University Press uses environmentally friendly book materials,
including recycled text paper that is composed of at least 30 percent post-consumer
waste, whenever possible. All of our book papers are acid-free, and our jackets and
covers are printed on paper with recycled content.

CONTENTS

I see the significance of diversity everywhere. And, perhaps because I have devoted my professional career to higher education as an administrator and faculty member, I believe that higher education must play a critical role if we are to achieve the promise of our democracy—developing a pluralistic society that works. While few of us have lived or worked in such a setting, this is one of the foremost challenges of our day. This book is an attempt to bring together several large bodies of research, along with lessons from the field of practice, to reflect on the status of diversity in higher education and, more centrally, on what we are learning about the conditions necessary for developing effective and sustainable strategies that work.

Today, diversity is no longer a projection—it is a reality. The challenge is that while the historic issues of diversity, which have occupied many in higher education over the past forty years, have grown in their urgency, new issues are emerging. The context for diversity is shifting, and the rhetoric about diversity is increasing. As a result of the research done in preparing for this book, it is now clear to me that understanding the conditions under which diversity works and addressing them institutionally—something we can now do—provides an opportunity to confront the unfinished business of the past even as we address the newer issues of today.

Indeed, the demographic shifts of our society and the patterns of immigration around the world create a critical opportunity. Our institutions will become more diverse. Arguing about the merits of diversity and defending its existence (as if there were a choice) may be necessary and, indeed, have been the starting point for a great deal of important research in higher education. But at the core, our challenge is to achieve the benefits of diversity for our institutions and for society. Simply acknowledging diversity will not be sufficient. We can see the difficulties inherent in creating truly diverse communities that work well. Fortunately, a reasonably robust body of knowledge from research and practice now exists and can help illuminate the conditions under which diversity works and the implications for colleges and universities—as institutions.

I have learned, however, that reframing diversity to focus on building institutional capacity is not an easy transition. Understanding the notion of "building capacity" requires a clear picture of the stakes for *institutions* concerning diversity. Here I want to suggest, as I do at greater length in chapter 3, a useful parallel with the imperative of campus efforts to build capacity for technology. Several decades ago, as technological shifts began, campuses all across the country understood that their viability as institutions would rest on building capacity for technology.

Technology was understood to be central, not marginal, to teaching and research. But more critically, technology was seen as central to the viability of every educational institution—that is, how the institution communicated, built infrastructure, spent money, and went about hiring. Because technology has been continually changing, institutions, almost without question, have been continually adapting as new technologies are introduced. Technology is now part of everyday life and every corner of institutional life. On some campuses, a new position has been created for a chief information officer, whose task is to develop strategies for incorporating future technological developments, for allocating resources, and for coordinating campus efforts. Building technological capacity has required that institutions develop adequate human, physical, fiscal, knowledge, and cultural resources.

We are now at a time when we must understand that diversity, like technology, is central to higher education. Will institutions be credible or viable if diversity is not fundamental? I believe not. Locating diversity as central to institutional effectiveness, excellence, and viability frames the orientation of this book. The diversity imperative goes far beyond student success, though student success remains critical. The issue today is fundamentally whether and how institutions are building the capacity to function in society in a way that is appropriate to their mission. In the next generation of diversity work, student success will be a necessary but not sufficient indicator of institutional effectiveness.

As I developed the approach I wanted to take in this book, it became apparent that I needed to focus on the concept of identity as well. While identity is a common framework for human development approaches to diversity, it is also essential in understanding diversity institutionally. More significantly, current research on the concept of identity and how it functions in both institutional and social contexts is extraordinarily useful for thinking about the conditions under which diversity can be established as a strength rather than encountered as a barrier in developing healthy institutions.

The book is organized into four parts. Part 1 describes the imperative of diversity in a national and global context. Chapter 1 seeks to establish that the significance of diversity in higher education is linked to many compelling issues in the world and in the United States, including immigration, continuing inequities, the formation of nation-states, histories of injustice, and creating effective workplaces. I hope it provides a convincing argument that diversity offers both powerful opportunities and serious challenges. These opportunities and challenges can no longer be framed in terms of pursuing diversity or not pursuing it. *Diversity is.* Rather, we must establish the conditions under which diversity works.

Because the notion of identity is central to the discourse on diversity, chapter 2 draws together current research and theory about how identity is developing as a concept, how it informs conversations about diversity, and how it might be understood to facilitate institutional thinking about diversity. Concepts of multiplicity, intersectionality, and context will challenge some of the static ways in which identity is understood while at the same time underscoring the need to engage complex notions of identity in institutional approaches to diversity.

Part 2, "Reframing Diversity," suggests a way of understanding diversity and provides an overview of the past forty years of diversity in higher education. In the early chapters, I use the term *diversity* rather broadly, to include all of the many identities that are salient to higher education and society today. In chapter 3, I address the issue of definition, challenging the idea of diversity as a laundry list of identities while also establishing the need to be inclusive. The chapter will describe a framework for diversity that I have been developing over the years, focusing on ways in which diversity can function as both inclusive and differentiated. Access and success of historically underrepresented populations remains the legacy and the soul of diversity work today. At the same time, campuses have struggled with a growing list of issues to be addressed. This has led to strong criticism of many diversity efforts as losing an essential focus on historic issues of inequity in favor of a long list of topics. How *can* a campus choose among legitimate issues expressed by diverse groups?

In response to such criticism, I have attempted throughout the book to make explicit the central relationship between diversity and equity and to suggest that institutions can make diversity be inclusive of the many and growing issues reflected on campuses across the country without losing focus. I will suggest that engaging the concerns and experiences of different groups and individuals must be differentiated so that diversity efforts in their inclusiveness don't become generic laundry lists. Historic and largely unfinished efforts related to race, class, and gender remain and must be addressed. Other concerns related to ability, sexual orientation, immigration status, religion, and so on also need to be engaged deeply. It is possible to move forward on multiple fronts. Moreover, current research makes clear that intersections of identities and multiplicity of identities will need to be addressed for traditionally underrepresented populations, in which gender and class, as well as other identities, are gaining in significance.

Chapter 4 gives an overview of the data for the past forty years of diversity in higher education and asks what has changed. Because so many books on diversity provide standard data on demographic shifts, I have tried to offer new ways of approaching these data and review the most current research in higher education during this period. Though it is not the centerpiece of this book, the chapter will also address admissions policies in select institutions and testing, topics that have been so important to much of the literature on diversity in higher education. Finally, because counting (i.e., how we count people and the role of classifications) is vital to the data on diversity, chapter 4 also describes the growing challenges to our ability to monitor progress.

The third part of the book, "Building Capacity by Interrupting the Usual," brings together research from different disciplines to address what we are learning about three important topics for building institutional capacity for diversity. The conclusions in each chapter suggest ways in which higher education will have to "interrupt the usual" to make the fundamental changes that are required. Chapter 5 focuses on the critical area of identifying talent in higher education, particularly with respect to faculty diversity. The chapter will explore the rationale for faculty diversity, the conditions of hiring, and the practices likely to lead to developing the diversity in leadership necessary for building capacity. How we identify talent and define excellence will most certainly need to change. However, the need for talent and excellence in the service of higher education should not change.

Chapter 6 synthesizes social science research from higher education, organizational theory, and social psychology that examines the conditions for successfully bringing together people from diverse backgrounds. The results of this synthesis have profound implications for practice on our campuses. While the higher education literature has focused on how to bring students together to realize the benefits of diversity, this chapter looks at the conditions necessary for establishing effective intergroup relationships at every level on a campus—from the president's cabinet to decision-making bodies to administrative units.

Chapter 7 then pulls together three related and complementary bodies of research on what we are learning about the conditions for student success. A review of the general literature on student success, the diversity literature, and the literature on special-purpose institutions, such as historically Black colleges and universities (HBCUs), tribal colleges, and Hispanic-serving institutions (HSIs), yields some important principles to guide institutional practices for student success.

Part 4, "What Will It Take?" summarizes, in both practical and conceptual terms, several approaches to building capacity for diversity over the long term. These final chapters make clear that sustaining efforts to bring about change to build capacity will require monitoring progress and engaging change in strategic ways.

Chapter 8 suggests an approach to monitoring progress that has emerged from research and projects across the country. The guiding question for this chapter is, how can an institution determine whether it is making progress? The reality on many campuses is that perceptions of progress on diversity are very much influenced by individual perspectives. Leaders often need to highlight positive changes even when others in the institution see little or no change. Talking past one another is common and frustrating. This chapter suggests ways to monitor progress and act on the information collected.

Chapter 9 provides a set of recommendations and conclusions. Building deep capacity for diversity will require the commitment of senior leadership. However, leadership at every level is required. Every individual and every group, wherever they are located in the institution, can be guided by this book and especially by this chapter.

One of my goals in writing this book was to recognize, and promote the further development of, a broad-ranging literature dealing directly with diversity in higher education or having implications for it. I hope the references will themselves serve as a resource. The bibliography also reflects my commitment to acknowledge (as I do explicitly below) that my work continues to benefit from the extraordinary work of many scholars. Each reference was added with an appreciation for how the particular article or book contributed to my own thinking.

Taking a transdisciplinary approach to the topic was essential. Too many of our fields exist in isolation from one another. Research on the conditions that either facilitate or impede the development of diverse institutions that work is not unique to higher education. My goal has been to draw from as many literatures as necessary to bring together what is known, or not yet known, about the topic. The diversity of research methods employed in different fields has also served a positive purpose. When the conclusions from a wide variety of studies, using different methodologies, begin to converge, we may apply the results with some confidence. That pattern emerged for many of the topics explored in this book.

The rhetoric about diversity as transformation has been used for quite some time. As we think about the future, however, I believe we will see that diversity, like technology, can both transform and facilitate the core mission of a campus. Some things will certainly need to change. But if we frame diversity as central to the institution, our campuses can become more vital to the health and well-being of their communities and to the issues that challenge society as a whole.

What drives me is the vision of higher education's role in building a pluralistic and equitable society that thrives because of diversity. What fuels my impatience is that too much of what we are discussing today has been discussed for forty years. At the same time, dramatic changes are occurring. Diversity is no longer optional. And if higher education cannot or does not build capacity for diversity, who will?

This book is not a definitive statement on diversity in higher education; the topic is far too dynamic. It does, however, seek to present findings from current research within a framework of promising practices and approaches. As I note in the final chapter, it is too soon to imagine what a truly equitable institution will look like in the future. How diversity and equity are understood and engaged today, however, will be critical for that future.

❁

Although I am the sole author of this book, it has benefited enormously from the powerful and inspirational colleagues with whom I have collaborated over the years. Through them, I have learned the benefits of working in diverse teams and the challenges of working alone. As I added each reference to the bibliography, I felt indebted to the contribution that that author or authors have made, and continue to make, to building a sophisticated body of literature on the topics of diversity in general and diversity in higher education.

Because their collaborations have been essential, I want to specifically thank Sharon Parker, Alma Clayton-Pedersen, José Moreno, and Daniel Teraguchi, the most recent team of co-authors I had the privilege to work with over a six-year period on the James Irvine Foundation Campus Diversity Initiative Evaluation Project. Our extended team of evaluators (Suzanne Benally, Susan Borrego, Mildred García, and Jennie Spencer Green) and our research associates (Belinda Vea, Mari Luna de la Rosa, and Jocelyn Chong) provided many opportunities to engage the topic of diversity and institutional change. That project would not have been possible without the efforts of Robert Shireman, Hilda Hernandez-Gravelle, James Canales, and Martha Campbell. Mildred García, Caryn McTighe Musil, Caroline Turner, Lisa Wolf-Wendel, Gwen Garrison, Nana Osei-Kofi, Sandra Richards, and Lee Tidball have been wonderful colleagues with whom I have worked on research and writing that contributed significantly to this book.

To my colleagues at Claremont Graduate University, I express deep appreciation for a culture that permits each of us to pursue our passions and encourages students to do the same. I also wish to express my appreciation to all the students with whom I have worked and written throughout the years, for continuing to teach me and to engage with me on this important topic. Without their support, some of the research would not have been possible.

I am grateful for many opportunities to participate in other foundation efforts and for foundation support. Early funding from the Spencer Foundation, the Ford Foundation, and the James Irvine Foundation made it possible to conduct some of the research that has informed my work and this book. I want to particularly acknowledge the Ford Foundation's support for the Tri-National project *Diversity, Democracy, and Higher Education*. The efforts of the late Edgar Beckham, program officer at Ford, to provide a unique opportunity to situate diversity in a more global context helped me see how domestic struggles for equity can usefully be linked to international efforts without losing the soul of U.S. diversity efforts. The work of teams from the United States, South Africa, and India showed how themes being addressed in the United States paralleled those in India and South Africa even as identity issues that were salient for their diversity work differed. The opportunity to visit South Africa after apartheid ended was humbling and forced many of us from the United States to appreciate the role of democratic aspirations perhaps even more.

The Association of American Colleges and Universities has played an important role. It has served as a resource for scholars and practitioners and provided ongoing resources to college campuses through its conferences and Diversity Web. It has also given me opportunities to share research with practitioners throughout the country. In addition, I have had the privilege of visiting many campuses to collaborate with committed individuals who have helped me connect academic research and practice. Their support for my work continues to motivate me.

Jacqueline Wehmueller, executive editor at the Johns Hopkins University Press, has been supportive throughout. Indeed, it was she who encouraged me to embark on this project, and without her this book probably would not exist. Jack Schuster gave important feedback on an early version of the manuscript, and Yolanda Moses reviewed the entire manuscript and provided thoughtful guidance. Hugo Garcia, my research assistant, was enormously helpful in creating most of the charts and tables for the manuscript and reading early drafts. Nancy Trotic did a masterful and thoughtful job editing the final draft.

Finally, I am grateful to my family, who support my work and believe in the issues of diversity, and who in their own lives fight for justice and equity in our society. I thank my partner, Barbara, for her support, love, encouragement, laughter, and life lessons; and I thank little Sage, who makes me smile.

PART I

The Diversity Imperative

CHAPTER ONE

The National and Global Context for Diversity in Higher Education

Diversity is a powerful agent of change. Indeed, diversity is an imperative that must be embraced if colleges and universities are to be successful in a pluralistic and interconnected world. While technology has long been recognized as a transformative element of society, the dynamics of diversity are reshaping the world and its institutions with equal impact. Like technology, diversity offers significant opportunities to fulfill the mission of higher education and to serve institutional excellence, albeit in new ways. By asking what we have learned about the conditions under which colleges and universities can maximize their capacity to function in a pluralistic society, this book sets out to frame the dimensions of diversity within an institutional context.

The question is not whether we want diversity or whether we should accommodate diversity, for diversity is clearly our present and our future. Rather, it is time to move beyond old questions and to ask instead how we can build diversity into the center of higher education, where it can serve as a powerful *facilitator* of institutional mission and societal purpose. Using a broad range of research from multiple disciplines, I hope to underscore not only the imperative of diversity, but also the conditions under which it is best approached to optimize and benefit institutional practice and strategy. This way of understanding diversity and its role for higher education goes significantly beyond individuals and the interactions between individuals and groups. It is centrally related to institutions—their mission, their capacity, and the ways in which they are designed and function.

More than ever before, the discussion about diversity in higher education needs to occur within a global and national context, adding greater urgency and complexity to the topic. Our challenge is that few examples exist of diverse societies that are successful. Sadly, there are far more examples of failure. We have only to look around us at the ethnic violence, religious conflicts, struggles for sovereignty, urban unrest, and challenges to nation-states to know that how we engage diver-

sity has profound national and global implications. At the same time, historic issues of race and gender and continuing concerns about access to higher education for underrepresented minorities and low-income students grow more and
more urgent. For American higher education, the question is whether our colleges
and universities can become models of diverse institutions that function well. Furthermore, can our institutions help build resources through scholarship and policy that will effectively address inequities that keep the world off balance?

The Context for Diversity

Engaging diversity in higher education requires an understanding of the national
and international concerns that set the context for campus approaches. While discussions concerning globalization commonly focus on commerce, it is essential
to look beyond market-driven matters to other domains as they emerge around
the world, because they introduce important perspectives to the topic of diversity in higher education. Should we choose to address these topics deeply, they will
provide us with opportunities to re-envision our questions and reconsider old
conclusions. The several topics outlined below reveal the urgency of diversity, the
inevitability of having to face questions associated with diversity, and the potential of diversity to create, as Knefelkamp and Schneider (1997) have said, "a world
lived in common," rather than a world lived in chaos and hate.

Changing Demographics

Throughout the world, immigration is transforming the face of nations. With
these changes, conflict—and some soul-searching—has emerged concerning increased violence against immigrants, the integrity of borders, national identity,
language, religion, cultural patterns, ethnicity, and race. Many of these matters
that develop in the context of large-scale immigration are not new. Historically,
racist incidents and concerns about the national language, the contributions of
immigrants, and assimilation have been common responses to immigration (Bennett, 1998; Giroux, 1998; Hartman, 2006; Macedo & Gounari, 2006). In periods
of large-scale immigration, however, especially when the vast majority of immigrants are persons of color, these issues increase in intensity. Furthermore, in the
United States, intensifying conflicts over immigration policy may detract from,
if not overwhelm, long-standing, unresolved problems concerning race and ethnicity (Frey, 1999).

These themes raise fundamental questions about how a society negotiates pluralism and unity, how communities already suffering from economic or political disenfranchisement react to the introduction of "newcomers," and in general how immigrants are received (Bean & Stevens, 2003; Gerstle & Mollenkopf, 2001). A recent controversy in France is a case in point. A law passed ostensibly to protect secularism in schools and ensure that everyone was "equally French" forbade "ostentatious" religious symbols on the grounds that they served as "propaganda" that "pressured, provoked, and proselytized." In order to abide by the law, Muslim women and girls could not wear headscarves in state-run schools, and other visible religious symbols, including crosses, were not to be worn. The sense of threat in a post-9/11 world has undoubtedly exacerbated tensions within and toward the Muslim community, but banning a symbol of culture and religion as a means of protecting secularism generated enormous controversy and has served only to polarize the society.

The United States, a country that since its birth has seen wave upon wave of immigrants, is experiencing another influx of new peoples. While the resulting changes in demographics are more visible and dramatic in places such as California, Arizona, Texas, and New York, they are occurring throughout the rest of the country as well. For example, the Southeast, traditionally viewed through a Black and White lens, has long been home to communities of American Indians, as well as increasing populations of Latinos and Asian Americans, many of them immigrants. Minnesota, a state generally thought of as being racially homogenous, has one of the largest Hmong populations in the United States (Asante & Min, 2000; Farley & Haaga, 2005; Hughes & Seneca, 1999; Smelser, Wilson, & Mitchell, 2001).

The large infusion of immigrants from specific regions within Asia, Latin America, and Africa to the United States has also created critical masses of people who wish to retain their unique cultural identity (Anderson & Lee, 2005; Chin, 2000; Espiritu, 2007; Lee & Bean, 2004; Lott, 1998; Nakanishi, 2001; Root, 1997). Although an overall Asian or African or Latino perspective can be useful in some contexts, homogenous notions of identity across these large regions quickly break down when serious consideration is given to differences in history, culture, and experiences within each group, as well as to generational status (Min, 2002; Rodriguez, 1994). As the Asian American and Latino communities have grown, it has become much more possible to consider the enormous diversity within them and much more likely that such diversity will be taken into account. Not only do Filipinos, Japanese, Chinese, Hmong, Vietnamese, and South Asian Indians (to name only a few groups) have different ethnic, religious, and cultural traditions, they are also characterized by dissimilar conditions of emigration. Such differences mean that experiences of entry—with respect to legality, visas, asylum, and so on—differ, as do the immigrants' economic and educational backgrounds and needs.

The same is true for Latinos from Central America, South America, Puerto Rico, and the various regions of Mexico. Although there has been great controversy about Mexican immigration, Cubans' entry to the United States has been facilitated by federal policies granting residency. A recent National Research Council study of "Hispanics" (2006) reminds us that the origins of the U.S. Hispanic population predate the founding of the United States and that Latinos are now the largest minority group, encompassing more than twenty nationalities, each of which brings its own history, culture, ethnicity, and experience in relation to the United States. The growing concern about undocumented persons has placed the issue of status and entry at the center of the recent immigration discussions in the United States.

While the influx of immigrants is the greatest contributor to the changing population of the United States, demographic profiles are also affected by age, birthrates, and the ways in which members of various racial and ethnic groups that are already part of the population are counted. In recognition of the increasing complexity of the category system of race and ethnicity, both the Bureau of the Census and the U.S. Department of Education have altered their surveys to permit individuals to check multiple categories indicating ethnic and racial identity. Although the numbers of multiracial individuals, according to the 2000 census, constitute only a small percentage of the U.S. population (estimated at 2.4%), the notion of multiracial identity increasingly challenges us to consider a more complex and dynamic conception of race and ethnicity than could be reflected through the static categories of the past (Farley & Haaga, 2005; Tafoya, Johnson, & Hill, 2005).

The reclassification of the census has been controversial, and the ways in which the new classifications are used will deepen the controversy. The existence of clear and distinct categories has long had economic, political, and social significance for communities and for identity groups (Perlmann & Waters, 2002). For example, if the Department of Education labels those who mark more than one box as multiracial, those persons would be removed from their specific racial categories, resulting in a decline in the counts for communities in which mixed-race identity is common. We would lose important information about patterns across and between racial groups. At the same time, research has documented that when multiple categories are available, some communities, such as American Indians and Alaska Natives, actually increase in their numbers, because individuals have an opportunity to claim more than one heritage (Eschbach, 1993).

Political Structures and Access to Power and Resources

Globally, diversity continues to play a significant role in relation to many political structures, irrespective of whether those structures are democratic. Access to power, government, voting, resources, and decision-making remains a major factor in conflicts around the world. Discord may arise from religious differences, as in Northern Ireland; from ethnic conflicts, as in parts of Africa; or from racial issues, as in the United States. Gender and class issues also emerge in nearly all of these situations. But whatever the external manifestations may be in terms of identity, underlying them all are themes of economic and other inequities, racism, and historic and continuing injustice, played out through struggles over access to power. These issues determine the identities that are salient in the local context— whether they are related to religion, ethnicity, race, gender, sexual orientation, or some other category (W. Brown, 2006; Cross, Mikwanazi-Twala, & Klein, 1998; Macedo & Gounari, 2006; Marx, 1998; Twine, 2005).

In the United States, poverty and race are impossible to disentangle. As Hollinger (1995) notes:

> Arguments will continue to rage over how racist this society is and the extent to which the degraded conditions experienced in American cities can be attributed ultimately to racism. But a society that will not take steps to help its poor citizens of all ethno-racial groups will have little chance to find out how successful have been its efforts to overcome the racist attitudes of empowered Whites. . . . The members of these groups . . . will have more and more reason to interpret as structural or institutional racism those policies that, even if devoid of prejudicial intent, have a disproportionately negative impact on them. (pp. 167–168)

After the dismantling of apartheid in South Africa, Nelson Mandela pointed out that the victors of revolution are too often transformed into oppressors themselves. He envisioned South Africa as a country that, rather than give in to desires for revenge and retribution, would be able to use its bitter history to understand and resist oppression. As the new constitution was being written, the intersection of race and gender was seen as vital to the country's rebirth. Indeed, representation for women and the rights of gay people were written into the constitution.

The Health of Democracy and Community

Increasingly, many of those who assess the state of society make a direct link between diversity and the health and well-being of democracy (Gutman & Thompson, 2004; Layer, 2005; Nussbaum, 2003). Structural inequity (embedded aspects of society that disadvantage some groups and advantage others), poverty, and uneven access to power structures in communities and institutions are now seen as indicators of ill health for a society. Scholars who study the intersection of politics, economics, and social issues have begun to document connections between inequality and institutional and societal instability more generally (Feng, 2003; "Hispanics," 2006; Lardner & Smith, 2005; Lipset, 1959). Although many of the blatant structural forms of inequity, such as racial segregation, no longer exist in the Unites States, few would posit that the ideal of a pluralistic democracy has been attained.

Just as race and ethnicity continue to be correlated with indicators of well-being in this country (Adams et al., 2003; Blank, 2001; Conley, 1999; Jacobs & Skocpol, 2005; Kessler, Mickelson, & Williams, 1999; Krieger, Rowly, Herman, Avery, & Phillips, 1993; Oliver & Shapiro, 2001; Orfield, 2004; Tilley, 1998; Valenzuela, 1999; Williams & Swail, 2005), evidence of racism continues to be linked to inequities in housing, banking, and employment (Bertrand & Mullainathan, 2004; Committee on National Statistics, 2004; Sidanius & Pratto, 1999). A recent study has documented inequities in income based on skin color alone (Hersch, 2007). Current data concerning education, health care, the criminal justice system, and income suggest that while there has been some improvement in recent decades, significant differences remain between racial and ethnic groups and between genders. In many domains, the extent and degree of inequity become an everyday challenge to the rhetoric of democracy and to the idea that constitutional and legal protections are available to all citizens.

Thus, part of the drive to engage diversity can now be critically connected to national interests (see, e.g., Institute of Medicine, 2004; Milem, Dey & White, 2004). In the introduction to *America Becoming: Racial Trends and Their Consequences*, Christopher Edley underscores the aspirational aspect of democracy in the United States: "Our secular catechism of equality and justice for all, authored at the nation's birth, was belied by practice at the time. Yet these remain the powerful ideals to which we aspire, at least in our nobler moments, and without regard to political party or social status" (Smelser, Wilson, & Mitchell, 2001, vol. 1, p. vii).

One of the challenges of democracy in the United States is that while inequity is strongly associated with differences among groups, the nation's core values are generally associated with individual rights (Ferdman, 1997; Huber & Form, 1973). There has been deep ambivalence about collective responses to inequality. Indeed, part of the reaction against affirmative action is due to the uneasy relationship between individual and group identity (Astin & Astin, 2000; Huber & Form, 1973; Sumida & Gurin, 2001). In contrast, in other parts of the world there are constitutions that provide special consideration to groups that have been historically excluded. For example, women have been granted minimum quotas for representation in the government in South Africa, in Ghana (Tsikata, n.d.), and in the new constitution of Afghanistan. In India, "set-asides" have been created for members of certain castes (although, as in the United States, there is increasing resistance and controversy about how to respond to the inequities among a growing number of "protected classes") (Gupta, 2006).

There are, however, contradictions and hypocrisy in the debate that is occurring in the United States around protection of individuals versus protection for groups. Much of U.S. history embeds privilege for Whites in general, and White upper-class men in particular, in voting, landowning, and access to higher education. While this privilege is no longer explicit, as it often was in earlier eras, there is a growing body of literature documenting that the pattern continues, though in subtler and less visible ways.

An additional question for some scholars has been whether the conflation of democracy and capitalism in the United States and around the world conflicts with efforts to address inequity and attend to the social well-being of groups in society. As an economic system, capitalism emphasizes individual achievement on the one hand and the greater significance of business interests on the other. For some, this connection makes achieving real equity close to impossible (Darder & Torres, 2003; Wood, 1995). For others, it suggests interrogating the balance among the distribution of social benefits, economic capitalism, individual and group equity, and society's well-being. Scholars such as Sunstein (1997) point to the limitations of markets in addressing injustice and suggest that capitalism, as practiced in the United States, clearly requires government involvement, not only to protect those with less access to power, but also to preserve the government's own power. It may be appealing to create a dualistic approach that is both for and against capitalism, but much of the scholarship in this area engages the challenge of balance and the reality that no "pure" system of government has solved the problem of inequality and injustice.

The link between the creation of healthy and thriving democracies on the one hand and diversity, equity, and changing demographics on the other is underscored by Building Toward Inclusive Communities, a project of the National League of Cities. Recognizing the increasing diversity of the society and the problems that have developed in cities because of the lack of engagement with diversity—and often explicitly acknowledging historic patterns of injustice—the program identifies successful inclusion as crucial to the viability, vitality, and health of cities.

Rather than moving quickly to a rhetorical claim of inclusiveness, the league's program recognizes that developing an inclusive community is an aspiration that must be achieved through intentional approaches, including an honest evaluation of, and taking responsibility for, historical injustices that have influenced the highly segregated and unequal cities we have today. Residential covenants that included clauses forbidding the sale of homes to persons of color are explicitly addressed in the work of many of the cities participating in this program. These covenants set in motion and sustained, for many decades, the segregated communities that exist throughout the country today. By telling the history of communities that were "White after dark," emphasizing class and racial demarcations, the program demonstrates a willingness to deal with both the past and the present. In addition, it encourages cities to establish policies to develop training programs, to require inclusive hiring practices, and to test whether there are practices that continue to limit access to housing and other resources.

The United States stands as perhaps the most racially and ethnically diverse country in the world. Its obligation to demonstrate both the power of diversity and the possibility of developing a pluralistic society that works is crucial in creating a model for what can be done. The tensions between the aspirations and rhetoric of democracy and the reality, however, have existed for a long time. Franklin Roosevelt's 1944 statement on inequity in society encapsulated this issue: "The nation cannot be content, no matter how high the general standard of living may be, if some fraction of our people—whether it be one-third or one-fifth or one-tenth—is ill-fed, ill-clothed, ill-housed, and insecure" (Sunstein, 2004, p. 12). Furthermore, after World War II, Truman's Commission on Higher Education produced a significant report, *Higher Education for American Democracy*, that expressed the urgency of expanding educational opportunities and affordability and increasing social understanding for the future of the nation (Thelin, 2004).

In the eyes of the world, the credibility of the United States as the longest-existing democracy is linked to its record on issues of equality and justice. Gunnar Myrdal, in his classic work *An American Dilemma: The Negro Problem and Modern Democracy* (1944), makes this connection explicit: "America for its international prestige, power, and future security needs to demonstrate to the world that American Negroes can be satisfactorily integrated into its democracy" (pp. 1015–1016). Dudziak (2000) powerfully develops the link between a domestic record on equality and racism and the international credibility of U.S. foreign policy during World Wars I and II: "As the United States held itself out as the leader of the free world, the nation opened itself up to criticism when its domestic practices seemed to violate the nation's principles" (p. 29).

Such connections continue to be salient today. After 9/11, policies to build up "homeland security" were scrutinized throughout the world as the question was asked whether the United States' commitment to democracy—to judicial process, free speech, privacy, and other fundamental rights—was being seriously eroded at home even as the rhetoric of the principles of democracy was being communicated abroad.

Nation-States and Indigenous Peoples

There have been ongoing tensions around the world between nation-states and indigenous peoples concerning rights of sovereignty. These tensions are being addressed—in the United States, Canada, Australia, China, and India, to name only a few countries—in such a way as to recognize historical injustices and present-day claims to identity and autonomy.

The outcomes have significance not only for the sovereignty of indigenous populations and the ability of community members to govern their own lives, but also for how individuals and peoples from indigenous communities are characterized from within and without (Champagne, Torjesen, & Steiner, 2005; La Duke, 2005; Short, 2003; L. T. Smith, 1999). As Champagne (2005) writes, "Contemporary native identities are to a large extent based on relations to nation-states. While native peoples have identities that predate the formation of nation-states, and many aspects of these pre-state identities continue to persist and make their weight felt in everyday life, native identity is largely defined in relation to colonizing cultures and state governments" (p. 3).

The issues raised, then, are not just political. They are about cultural survival—the survival of language, religion, education, values, and identity.

Dealing with the History and Legacies of Injustice

The question of whether past injustices to groups in society should be addressed and, if so, how to address them meaningfully is tremendously challenging. Increasingly, efforts are being made to engage history and to create ways to bring "victim" and "perpetrator" together to form a narrative that can be shared (Barkan, 2000, 2005; Lederach, 1997; Short, 2003). Through its Truth and Reconciliation Commission, South Africa took the stance that unless the past atrocities were acknowledged, it would not be possible to move forward. We have seen similar decisions in Germany's response to World War II, in the Catholic Church's attempts to address its response to the Holocaust, and in a pending legal case where U.S. courts are investigating the clear misuse of funds that the federal government had placed in trust for tribal communities. Even institutions, including college campuses, have begun to address history and injustice. For example, Brown University's attempt to understand its role with respect to slavery prompted a self-study and a formal statement and had some policy implications. It is hard to imagine that merely forgetting and moving on is going to be effective for those whose history has been shaped by these injustices, particularly when their current reality reflects continuing inequality.

In the United States, there is an uneven record in this area. It took decades to include even modest accounts of slavery and transgressions against American Indians in basic history texts. Indeed, making these histories visible continues to be challenged. While reparations to Japanese Americans and expressions of apology indicate some awareness of the need to acknowledge historical injustices, efforts to discuss reparations to African Americans and to monitor treaty rights for Native Americans remain controversial even under circumstances where there appears to be little risk in doing so (Rouhana, 2004).

Moreover, so much history has been ignored or omitted that contemporary ways of framing it can be distorted by ignorance. Robust historical information is needed in order to effectively understand history. For example, the history of school desegregation is framed almost entirely by the 1954 *Brown v. Board of Education* case. What is missing from this history is information that the struggle to end school desegregation for African Americans, Asian Americans, and Latinos had been occurring for a long time in many parts of the country (Aguirre, 2005; Chesler, Lewis, & Crowfoot, 2005). Thus, groundbreaking though the *Brown* case was, it created the impression that segregation was an issue only for African Americans.

Acknowledging a more accurate and just history has political and psychological value and is immensely powerful in the way it can directly and indirectly affect current experience. Increasing evidence suggests that the lower levels of well-being for many racial minorities in the United States, especially African Americans, are based not only on current practices, but also on experiences of discrimination and the fallout from prior decisions (Delgado, Stefancic, & Lindsley, 2000). For example, the weak implementation of *Brown*, along with the dismantling of Black schools and the firing of Black teachers and principals, had a profound impact on schooling that continues into the present (Bell, 2004).

In a well-documented analysis of the ongoing impact of discrimination and the limitations of color-blind policies, Katznelson (2005) argues that the ways in which some policies—particularly Social Security and the Servicemen's Readjustment Act of 1944 (the GI Bill)—were implemented preserved White privilege and were essentially affirmative action for Whites. The GI Bill in particular is described by Katznelson as "the most comprehensive public policy to that moment in American history" and "the most democratic of public policies because . . . no one was excluded" (p. 118). However, even though the GI Bill was color-blind in the sense that the policy itself did not exclude anyone because of race, the ways in which it was applied denied benefits to enormous numbers of African American veterans. At the time of its passage, White southern politicians exerted their influence to limit the implementation of these policies in such a way as to protect White power and limit African American access to education and home ownership, by insisting that policies be implemented locally, where practices could be controlled. There was deep concern in the South among Whites and their political representatives that providing too much opportunity to returning Black servicemen would alter employment and living patterns. Many Latinos were also denied full use of GI Bill benefits through discriminatory practices (MacDonald, Botti, & Clark, 2007).

Thus, while the GI Bill opened up higher education to hundreds of thousands of service men and women, rigid segregation, discrimination, and the limited resources in historically Black colleges and universities (HBCUs) in the South severely limited access for African Americans (Gasman, 2007; Turner & Bound, 2003). The GI Bill also facilitated home ownership for veterans. But here again, though African Americans and Latinos were not specifically excluded—and many did indeed benefit—the decision to implement the bill's provisions through local banks and local administrations meant that many were denied access to home loans, through "redlining" and bank policies. These practices were particularly evident in the South, although they occurred in other parts of the country as well. Most economists agree that the GI Bill and the growth of home ownership were instrumental in building the middle class and the subsequent affluence that Whites, especially, now enjoy. Yet in its implementation, the bill contributed to inequities that persist today.

By 1984, when GI Bill mortgages had mainly matured, the median White household had a net worth of $39,135; the comparable figure for black households was only $3,397 or just 9 percent of White holdings. Most of this difference was accounted for by home ownership. Nearly seven in ten Whites owned homes worth an average of $52,000. By comparison only four in ten Blacks were homeowners and their houses had an average value of less than $30,000. African Americans who were not homeowners possessed virtually no wealth at all. (Katznelson, 2005, p. 164)

Today, even as many scholars point to the increases in racial diversity in the middle class using current income as an indicator, others are pointing to racial gaps in wealth as a more powerful gauge of economic well-being (Oliver & Shapiro, 1997, 2001; Wise, 2006). For example, there is far less resiliency in a family that does not own property than in a family that can leverage assets to get through hard times. It is difficult not to speculate whether, if the GI Bill had provided as many African Americans with opportunities for home ownership and higher education as it did Whites, there would be more resiliency, stability, and equity within American society today.

These patterns underscore the need to scrutinize whether "race-neutral" or "color-blind" policies are intentional or unintentional strategies to maintain existing power structures. Katznelson (2005) describes clearly how calls for "color-blind" policies often maintain White privilege rather than opportunity for all. In this context, White privilege, as McIntosh (2008) suggests, is an unearned advantage of being White. One sees this inconsistency when critics of affirmative action suggest that increasing the representation of historically underrepresented African American, Latino, and Native American populations undermines *excellence*, while they present the *diversity* argument when Asian American populations gain access to higher education in great numbers. In each case, the argument furthers the status quo favoring Whites.

The same holds for antidiscrimination arguments concerning admissions. There is no controversy about privileging legacies (the family of alumni) even though the alumni were admitted during periods of segregation in which Blacks could not be admitted, but it is less permissible today to invoke special attention to those who are not able to claim legacy status as a special consideration (Minnich, 2005).

Thus, history lives on—and with powerful ramifications. It lives on in the values, language, and policies that intentionally or unintentionally privilege some at the expense of others. It lives on in the legacy of individuals and families, communities and societies. It lives on in covert and overt practices. If historical inequities are not interrupted, they will continue to cascade from generation to generation. Engaging history fearlessly and truthfully is fundamental to transforming institutions.

Institutions as Workplaces

The changing nature of our society, including its increasing diversity, has meant that topics concerning diversity are now visible in the workplace (Miller & Katz, 2002; Pfeffer, 1985). The most obvious examples are in the corporate arena, where "marketing" to diverse communities has become a business mandate. However, building the competence of all organizations to serve communities in areas of social services, education, health care, and religion has also become essential (Jayne & Dipboye, 2004; Johnston & Packer, 1987; Judy & D'Amico, 1999; Loden & Rosener, 1991; Morrison, 1992). The literature on the workplace also includes work on organizational justice and the conditions under which people perceive that an organization treats them equitably (Colquitt, Greenberg, & Scott, 2005; Deitch et al., 2003; Greenberg & Colquitt, 2005; Mowday & Colwell, 2003; Steers & Porter, 1979).

The "business case for diversity," as it is called, rests almost entirely on what is perceived as the relationship between changing demographics, credibility with diverse markets, and profit. It often includes the claim that diversity directly benefits the organization in terms of credibility, creativity, and productivity (Adkins, 2003; Cox, 1993, 2001; Hayles & Russell, 1997; Nemeth, 1994; Wright, Ferris, Hiller, & Kroll, 1995). Some studies indeed demonstrate a positive relationship between diversity and business outcomes (Catalyst, 2004; Hartenian & Gudmundson, 2000). A study by Catalyst (2004) shows that companies with higher percentages of women in top leadership performed better financially and, significantly, that companies with the highest performance had greater percentages of women. A study by Herring (2006) looking at the relationship between racial diversity and performance showed a consistent and positive relationship in environments in which racial minorities were *not* confined to token positions.

Other research, however, has suggested that while organizations need to engage diversity, the simple presence of diversity is not sufficient to manifest the benefits that are so often suggested and might in fact produce negative results in the form of conflict, lack of trust, and less productivity (Blau, 1977; Colella, 2001; Glaeser, Laibon, Scheinkman, & Soutter, 1999; Kochan et al., 2003; Riordan, 2000; Skerry, 2002; Triandis, Kurowski, & Gelfand, 1994; Williams & O'Reilly, 1998).

A growing number of studies state that it is essential to understand *under what conditions* diversity will enhance or detract from the effectiveness of the organization (Cox, 2001; Cox & Blake, 1991; DiversityInc, 2003, 2006; Ely & Thomas, 2001; Friedkin, 2004; Gardenswartz & Rowe, 2003; Gudeman, 2000; Harrison, Price, & Bell, 1998; Hayles, 2003; McMillan-Capehart, 2006; Milliken & Martins, 1996;

O'Reilly, Williams, & Barsade, 1997; Page, 2007; Pettigrew, 1998a; Smith et al., 1994; Sonnenschein, 1999; Sparber, 2009; Thomas, 1990, 2006; Tushman & O'Reilly, 1996; Williams & O'Reilly, 1998). For example, Ely and Thomas (2001), in a study of the factors that influence outcomes of diversity, found that when diversity is seen as essential to the organization for the variety of perspectives and contributions that can be made, the outcomes are much more positive than when diversity exists simply to increase representation or to gain legitimacy in outside communities.

In some literature on organizations, especially research with an economic framework, the costs associated with diversity are emphasized. Such studies point out that institutional change and transformation require a significant outlay of resources of time, energy, and money.

Rarely is this question studied from the reverse point of view: what is the price of *not* creating the conditions under which diverse institutions can thrive and reap the benefits of their diversity? Studies reveal a significant cost associated with a failure to address diversity at the societal level. What can be said about not engaging it at the institutional level? Less has been written here, though some studies look at the cost of discrimination suits, boycotts, and racism (DiversityInc, 2003, 2006; Feagin & McKinney, 2003). Increasingly, there are cases in which institutions are "embarrassed" by lawsuits, incidents, or public disclosures that expose blatant discrimination or an absence of diversity. Although such cases are relevant, the costs of ignoring diversity or engaging it in inadequate or unproductive ways are probably much larger. Everyday patterns of turnover, dissatisfaction, and conflict affect team-building work and institutional productivity. Success in changing these patterns is contingent on organizational approaches (American Bar Association, 2006; Cox, 1993; Cox, Lobel, & McLeod, 1991; DiversityInc, 2006; Dobbin & Kalev, 2007; Forman, 2003; Friday, Moss, & Friday, 2004; Hawley & Jackson, 1995; Wright, Ferris, Hiller, & Kroll, 1995).

Though a review of the research on the benefits of diversity that has been conducted in the field (e.g., in "business") suggests uneven results, research conducted with quasi-experimental or experimental approaches has yielded more positive conclusions. This may be due to the fact that college campuses are often used as experimental sites and the subjects are college students. However, it is also possible that in an experiment, one can control and/or study conditions such as critical mass, shared goals, and differing kinds of diversity, while field studies in existing organizations are often limited by the presence of larger institutional conditions and the absence of significant diversity in leadership teams.

Moreover, in the research that looks at the impact of the diversity of the group (in race, gender, age, tenure status, etc.) on productivity, diversity is most often understood to be a characteristic of the individuals in the group. In contrast, Page (2007), in his provocative book on diversity, stresses that identity concerns are not necessarily about the characteristics associated with the individuals but rather about the collective experiences and perspectives that emerge. Sommers (2006), in a study of behavior in juries, demonstrated that the benefits of diversity might emerge because of group composition, not necessarily group interaction. White jurors behaved differently in mixed juries than they did in homogenous ones.

Studying group dynamics in the absence of information about institutional context can influence the results in dramatic ways. Konrad (2003) suggests that many of the diversity issues facing institutions are associated with issues of power and equity related to the groups for whom access and inclusion are lacking. Similarly, Baugh and Graen (1997) point to the difficulty in studying one unit of analysis (the team) in the context of another unit of analysis (the institution). Without attention to structure and situation, the results of studies on group process may inaccurately be associated with the diversity of people, rather than the conditions of institutions (Baugh & Graen, 1997; Ely & Thomas, 2001; Fagenson, 1993; Konrad, 2003; Polzer, Milton, & Swann, 2002; Van Der Vegt, Bunderson, & Oosterhof, 2006; Watson, Johnson, & Merritt, 1998; Watson, Kumar, & Michaelson, 1993).

In addition, some of the findings suggest that it may be Whites in relation to minorities, and men in relation to women, in particular, that find the adjustment most difficult, especially when the numbers of those in the minority begin to increase (Aldefer, 1992; Baugh & Graen, 1997; Cohen & Swim, 1995; Ely & Thomas, 2001; Fagenson, 1993; Yoder, 2002). This is not hard to understand if increasing diversity is experienced as a loss of status, power, or privilege—topics to be addressed more fully in chapter 2.

Many approaches related to diversity in the workplace hinge on hiring and retaining diverse workers. The literature on hiring describes how institutional cultures reinforce the hiring of people like those already in power, how to hold managers and leaders accountable for hiring and retaining diverse talent pools, and the challenges of creating more pluralistic and inclusive environments. Questions of power, climate, institutional culture, privilege, and discrimination remain a fundamental part of this literature (Bertrand & Mullainathan, 2004; Committee on National Statistics, 2004; Cummings, 2004; Devine & Elliot, 1995; Elliott & Smith, 2004; Feagin, 2006; Kilian, Hukai, & McCarty, 2005; Kirkman, Tesluk, & Rosen, 2004; Niemann, 1999; Ragins, 1995; Sidanius & Pratto, 1999; Thiederman, 2003). Leadership development, removing sources of inequity such as certain requirements for experience and education, and mentoring each have a separate literature addressing the need to increase diversity and the means by which to do it (Ensher & Murphy, 2005; Kalbfleisch & Davies, 1991; Thomas, 2001).

Research thus suggests that in virtually every sector of work, engaging diversity, building diversity, and taking diversity seriously are imperative for organizations. Because of the need for diversity in leadership and the costs associated with training employees to work in and manage diverse institutions, more and more organizations are looking to higher education to provide not only diversity in leadership, but also people with the competence to work in diverse settings. A RAND study published in the mid-1990s suggested that many companies do not believe that higher education is meeting these objectives (Bikson, 1996; Bikson & Law, 1994). Whether that currently remains the perception of business will require further research.

Building Institutional Capacity

Much like the language of democracy, the language related to the benefits of diversity appears to be aspirational, with success of diversity contingent on *institutional conditions*. Significantly, this conclusion is consistent with fifty years of research in social psychology and management that concludes that simply putting people together from diverse backgrounds does not necessarily lead to positive outcomes. The key questions for research are, *What are the conditions under which positive outcomes emerge from environments in which diversity is present, and which forms of diversity are relevant in these situations?* These questions will be addressed in greater detail in part 2, but the emerging results suggest that success is contingent on context, on how diversity is framed, and on the capacity of the organization to build effective teams.

All of the issues identified in this chapter relate directly to building the *capacity* of institutions in the society to function in a diverse environment, to find ways to capitalize on the benefits of diversity, and to do so in contexts that are too often characterized by inequities. Institutional capacity-building requires the creation of structures that serve institutional purposes and that connect the institution's core purposes with the needs of society. It involves allocating financial and other resources, as well as strengthening human capital, expertise, and culture. An institution's capacity for diversity is measured in the way decisions are made, in how power is distributed, and in the characteristics of institutional culture. Though there may be a substantial cost in building capacity for diversity, there is also a substantial cost for neglecting it.

One of the most striking illustrations of the necessity of building capacity for diversity comes from the automotive industry. Naming a product is a very significant linguistic and symbolic event. Companies spend a great deal of time, effort, and resources to find the right name with the right associations. It is not hard to imagine the marketing appeal of connecting a new car with something new or with a nova—a brilliant star. Nevertheless, with all its resources, how was it possible that Chevrolet named a new model Nova even though *no va* suggests "doesn't go" in Spanish, Italian, and French? Undoubtedly, there were individuals within the company who recognized the misnomer but did not feel sufficiently empowered, or were not in a position, to point it out.

Clearly, diverse perspectives and cultural values can benefit institutions on structural as well as individual levels and can make the difference between effectiveness and failure. Framing the issue of diversity in this way has extraordinary implications for excellence, leadership, and performance in any kind of setting (Blackwell, Kwoh, & Pastor, 2002; Combs, 2002; Iwata, 2004; Slaughter, 2004).

The concept of identity is both implicit and explicit in each of the literatures that set the global and national context for diversity. Chapter 2 develops the relationship between identity and diversity and, in particular, how it is that some identities become salient for societal and institutional diversity. The next chapter also provides an overview of the recent theoretical and empirical research on identity that will be foundational for the chapters on making diversity work on campus.

❀

CHAPTER TWO

The Role of Identity in Diversity

The concept of identity is core to the issues surrounding diversity. While a fuller discussion of the definition and conceptualization of diversity in higher education will come in chapter 3, I want to make explicit the significant role that identity plays in virtually all conversations about diversity. Human diversity takes many forms—in personality, points of view, appearance, background, genetic makeup, biological origins, and culture, to name but a few. However, specific kinds of individual and group identity formed by race, ethnicity, gender, class, culture, religion, sexual orientation, and ability emerge as significant not only for individuals and groups, but for institutions and society as well. Questions about identity underlie virtually all diversity-related issues, and certain identities emerge as salient.

What is identity? Which forms of identity matter, and under what conditions do they matter? Is paying attention to identity good or bad for institutions? Is it necessary or optional? How should one address identities that have been historically stigmatized? Having constructive conversations about diversity in higher education and in society relies on informed and knowledgeable answers to these questions; but informed discussions are not common.

Emerging Developments in the Concept of Identity

The nature, importance, and role of identity cannot be fully addressed in this book. However, I provide here a summary of some emerging developments in our understanding of identity that will provide a foundation for the higher education context to follow.

Kinds and Sources of Identity

Scholars have categorized identities in different forms, often to make clear that these may have different meanings. Identities may emerge from personal qualities, such as roles and personality, or from voluntary associations, such as sports teams or interest groups. They may be rooted in culture or religion. Identities also emerge through ascriptive (i.e., nonvoluntary) characteristics, such as race/ethnicity and gender (Gutman, 2003). To demonstrate how complex even this form of categorization can be, there is still debate as to whether sexual orientation is ascriptive or whether it is a voluntary preference. Other scholars distinguish between *personal* identity and *social* identity, contrasting characteristics that connect the individual with the group (social identity) with those that distinguish individuals from others (personal identity) (Carter, 2008; Monroe, Hankin, & Van Vechten, 2000; Parekh, 2008).

The category of race, though static in so much of the literature, is clearly quite complex in its relation to culture, biology, law, and even religion (Brodkin, 2004; Cornell & Hartmann, 1998; López, 1996; Mukhopadhyay, Henze, & Moses, 2007; Sanjek, 1994; Smedley & Smedley, 2005). Further, race and ethnicity are conceptually both distinct and interconnected, especially in the U.S. context. Often, ethnicity is connected to issues of language, culture, and history (Adams, 2001; Ferdman & Gallegos, 2001).

While visible forms of identity are the most obvious and are studied more often, invisible forms are extremely significant as well. Invisible forms of identity can place people in jeopardy, as sexual orientation has been known to do in the workplace. It can create perceptions of inclusion or exclusion, as has happened to persons who have disabilities that are not seen (Beatty & Kirby, 2006; Clair, Beatty, & MacLean, 2005; Herek & Capitanio, 1996). Moreover, invisible identities, especially those that bear a social stigma, create a number of unique stressors and experiences (Preves, 2005; Quinn, 2006; Yoshino, 2006).

Multiple and Intersecting

There is a growing recognition that any given individual has *multiple* identities and that these identities must be seen as they *intersect* one another. The list of identities associated with an individual may be long and may include race, ethnicity, class, gender, sexuality, abilities, and so on. Early literature in psychology emphasized the development of identity as a single and coherent concept (Erikson, 1997). With the emergence of ethnic and women's studies and other fields, however, the literature began to make explicit the multiplicity of identities for any given individual (Ali, 2003; Anzaldúa, 2002; Collins, 1990; Espiritu, 1997; Frable, 1997; Hull, Scott, & Smith, 1982; Lott, 1998; Omi, 2001; Omi & Winant, 1994; Sleeter & Grant, 1988; Takagi, 1998; Torres, Howard-Hamilton, & Cooper, 2003; Wilson, 1996; Woodward, 2000).

Sometimes identities have been seen as competing with one another for significance in a social context. Early scholarship developed by women of color responded that framing identity in terms of gender *or* race was inappropriate and inaccurate. Higginbotham (1993) pointed out that "race only comes up when we talk about African Americans and other people of color. Gender only comes up when we talk about women, and class only comes up when we talk about the poor and working class" (p. 14). Shirley Chisholm, the first African American woman to run for U.S. president, was constantly asked whether it was harder to be Black or to be a woman, a choice she refused to make. One of my favorite book titles in the early literature in ethnic studies, underscoring the intersection of race and gender, was created by Gloria Hull, Patricia Bell Scott, and Barbara Smith (1982): *All the Women Are White, All the Blacks Are Men, but Some of Us Are Brave: Black Women's Studies.*

The term *intersectionality*, developed by Williams (1994) in the context of international discussions of human rights, captures the importance of understanding the interrelationships of (for example) gender and race. As Hall (1996) has noted, "The essential issues of race always appear historically in articulation, in a formation, with other categories and divisions and are constantly crossed and re-crossed by categories of class, of gender, and ethnicity" (p. 444).

The notion of multiplicity of identity and intersectionality most often refers to different kinds of identity, such as gender, race, class, and sexuality. The concept of biracial identity, particularly with respect to race and ethnicity, can suggest multiplicity as well and must be understood as the relationship of multiple racial identities to one another (Lee & Bean, 2004). This is clearly becoming a topic of great interest as a result of the new census classifications that allow individuals to check more than one racial category, even though, as mentioned earlier, only 2.4% of the population in the 2000 census chose a multiracial category.

Context and Saliency

There is a growing understanding that identity and the degree to which it is salient are influenced and even defined by context (Crisp & Hewstone, 2007; Friedkin, 2004; Horse, 2001; Marable, 1995; Raskin, 2002; Taylor & associates, 1994). The kinds of identities that have emerged as salient for diversity conversations around the world emerge in large part because of their context—historical, political, social, and economic. Some forms of identity are more *socially salient* than others, and we can identify what they are. Identities may have positive saliency because in a given context, they are seen as relevant to the values, history, and culture of a given society. They may add to the vitality of a community and engender solidarity in a community or group. These forms of salience underlie the language of multiculturalism—phrases such as *the celebration of diversity*—and the ways in which identity contributes to self and society.

Those same histories that produce positive saliency also introduce saliency of identity through stratification, in which some identity groups maintain positions of power and dominance over other groups. How and why group identification emerges in ways that exclude and that even escalate into discrimination and violence has been the subject of decades of research. However, as Inzlicht and Good (2006) comment, "Social Psychological research shows us that our environments can be threatening. They can remind us of our social identities, activate negative stereotypes, and otherwise communicate that our groups are marginalized, devalued, and not accepted" (p. 146). The existence of stratification requires that power, equity, and discrimination be addressed in any discussion of diversity and identity.

Adams (2001) describes the contextual significance of identity in the following way: "Interdependence of fate (or 'historical consciousness' as Marable calls it) grows out of a group's shared and acknowledged experience of social inequality and oppression, the salience of which hardly rests on whether race or ethnicity is the accurate term to explain the visibility that allows for persecution based on difference" (p. 210). Thus, while having blue eyes could form a basis of identity, it probably does not, because it has not emerged in any particular society as relevant for significant ways of organizing or stratifying people.

The interplay of context, multiplicity, and inequity illuminates why and how identity becomes dynamic, complex, and significant. As Symington (2004) suggests, "People live multiple, layered identities derived from social relations, history, and the operation of structures of power. People are members of more than one community at the same time, and can simultaneously experience oppression and privilege" (p. 2). This can lead to sometimes contradictory behaviors in society. Frankenberg (1993), for example, points to the ways in which White women experience gender and then do or don't address race, which suggests that gender can be an important factor in racial dynamics and that race can influence gender dynamics. As Espiritu (1997) notes, "for women of color, gender is only part of a larger pattern of unequal social relations" (p. 5). Such an analysis need not stop with race, ethnicity, and gender (hooks, 2000, 2003).

We often think of identity as primarily an internal process through which an individual or group comes to be known. However, identity is fundamentally shaped in interaction with others and through response from others. The situation can be highly individualized, as when a token woman in a meeting with a group of men finds gender issues emerging more prominently than other parts of her identity. In a society in which racism and race have long histories and impact structures, as in the United States, race surfaces as extremely salient but still shifts depending on context (López, 1996; McGuire, McGuire, Child, & Fujioka, 1978). It is widely acknowledged that all groups are classified into racial categories, usually for purposes linked to gaining power or maintaining the status quo. Brodkin's *How Jews Became White Folks and What That Says About Race in America* (1994) and Tuan's *Forever Foreigners or Honorary Whites? The Asian Ethnic Experience Today* (2005) document the dynamic ways in which race has shifted through law and culture and continues to shift in terms of how groups are treated and classified and how individuals identify. Concerns about depicting Asian Americans as the "model minority" underscore the interplay of identity and social meanings (Lee, 1996; Takagi, 1998).

Identity development is an individual, group, and societal phenomenon, described well by Ferdman and Gallegos (2001) in their study of Latino identity: "Latino groupness emerges both from external factors . . . and from within group factors, including common experiences and features among Latinos. . . . A third element leading to Latino groupness, perhaps combining the external and internal factors, has been sociopolitical. . . . In sum, this sense of identification as a group is based on commonalities, treatment by others and utilitarian reasons" (p. 38).

Context, then, strongly influences how individuals both experience and act on their identity. A large and growing body of literature in social psychology underscores the important role that context plays in both the experience and the dynamics of identities that are stigmatized. Goffman, in his classic book *Stigma* (1963), focused on identities that are characterized as negative in a particular circumstance. This literature has drawn attention to how individuals experience, respond to, and interact with others as a result of being stigmatized (Inzlicht & Good, 2006; Mendoza-Denton, Page-Gould, & Pietrak, 2006). Research has also emerged concerning the behaviors and attitudes of those who are in the more privileged, unstigmatized position as they interact with others (Crocker & Garcia, 2006; Crocker, Major, & Steele, 1998; Levin, van Laar, & Foote, 2006).

Marcus, Steele, and Steele (2002) describe *identity threat* as a situation in which an individual or group perceives his/her/its identity to be the cause of threat from others—the responses and fear that emerge from hate crimes or violence, including threat from society or government agencies. The notion of identity threat will become more significant in later chapters. Here I will simply point out that issues of stratification, inequality, and threat explain why the study of identities is not simply a study of the multicultural richness of diverse people. A person in a subordinate position experiences identity quite differently than a person in a dominant position.

When identity intersects with power, privilege, or inequity, the experience of identity is likely to be *asymmetrical*, depending on where one is positioned socially. Holland, Lachicotte, Skinner, & Cain (1998) describe this positionality from the following perspective: "Social position has to do with entitlement to social and material resources and so to the higher deference, respect, and legitimacy accorded to those genders, races, ethnic groups, castes, and sexualities privileged by society" (p. 271).

The experience of being the only White in a group of Latinos may make Whiteness more salient and may make the individual uncomfortable, but it is probably not the same as being the only Latino in a group of Whites. The mother of a friend of mine grew up in the South at a time when threats from Whites—even lynching—were common. To this day, this gracious and confident woman experiences profound anxiety when she walks into a room filled with White people. An African American applying for an apartment in our society may have a different experience than a White person. For many Whites, individual qualities such as appearance or credit rating might matter in looking for a home, but not group membership. That is less likely to be true for many persons of color and gays or lesbians, who anticipate they might be treated differently as a function of their group identity. Depending on one's social position, then, ordinary behaviors and activities can be experienced quite differently.

Identity can also trigger internal responses, with expectations of discrimination or fear that interactions will trigger negative stereotypes in others. This is especially true in environments where one is in a numerical minority and associated with a stigmatized group (Aronson, 2002; Crocker, Major, & Steele, 1998; Steele, 1997). The large body of literature that describes patterns of response to stigma would probably resonate with most people who are part of stigmatized groups. These patterns include vigilance, stifling complaints, withdrawal, and, if the stigmatized identity is concealable, concealment (Crocker & Garcia, 2006). As Crocker and Garcia (2006) note, "The stigmatized often feel caught between two alternatives—confront or overlook prejudice—each of which has undesirable consequences" (p. 288).

Identity today represents a paradox. With our understanding of its complexity, the meaning of any single dimension of identity becomes less clear. At the same time, identity has powerful meaning because of its social salience. Fried (1995) expresses this paradox with respect to race: "Biologically race is an illusion. Sociologically it is a pervasive phenomenon" (p. 6). Thus, the personal meaning of identity may be highly individualized at the same time that the social salience of race, gender, or sexuality emerges for groups as very significant.

Comprehensiveness

In addition to sources of identity, multiplicity, intersectionality, and context, the literature on identity recognizes (though practice often does not) that for any given individual, single—or multiple—sets of identities are not comprehensive descriptors for the person. Knowing that a person is a woman, Latina, lesbian, and working class does not tell us everything about the individual. Indeed, it may tell us very little, depending on the person.

Moreover, one can discuss African American or American Indian culture, but one cannot assume that any given person has all the attributes ascribed to the culture. In reading the literature on identity, one has to be careful not to essentialize the identity—to attribute to the individual the general descriptions associated with the group. Assuming all women are caring, empathetic, and collaborative is an example of essentializing. This distinction is important both for the language used in writing about identity and for avoiding the tendency to stereotype individuals, even when it is well-intentioned.

Institutional Identity

Identities manifest themselves as rich and critical aspects of the human experience of individuals. They become institutionalized as a function of the historical and social conditions under which institutions are formed. That is, institutional cultures take on norms, values, and practices from the people in the institution and the historical and social circumstances in which it was developed and in which it exists. Because of this connection, institutions also reflect the stratification and values of the larger society. How identity is introduced into an institution, therefore, is not simply a matter of the current membership of the institution and access to the institution. Institutional culture represents one of the deepest and most important elements of how institutions admit, value, and reward people. It is directly linked to identity.

Institutional Culture

Identity and culture are as dynamic and complex in institutions as they are in individuals and groups. As with identity of individuals and groups, described in the preceding sections, identity in institutions has many sources, takes multiple forms, is not comprehensive in capturing all characteristics of the institution, and is very much shaped by context. Institutional patterns in particular can be shaped by history, by location, and by mission. As with individuals and groups, the questions an institution asks often reflect deeply held values: How is excellence defined? What does beauty look like? What defines merit? How should selection be practiced? What defines a family? What kind of knowledge is important? What do different forms of expression mean, and what is appropriate? Thus, institutions can either develop in ways that reflect and reproduce the larger society or—as in the case of civil rights organizations, women's colleges, and historically Black colleges and universities—act as catalysts and challenge the inevitability of replication by creating environments that attempt to reduce inequities.

When an individual's identities align significantly with the cultural identity of an institution, there is usually a sense of comfort and a lack of awareness of certain salient features of institutional culture. Institutional and societal norms are taken for granted. The institution can appear to be a neutral, cultureless place whose values and practices are simply the way "one does business" and where "individuals are treated as individuals." As a result, many institutional elements related to identity can be rendered *invisible*. What is more, the alignment between an individual or group and the institution can translate into definitions of excellence that reward some groups and not others.

Acceptable ways of dressing, talking, and wearing one's hair, as well as patterns of working, can be translated from cultural norms into acceptable work norms quite easily. In some institutions, to be successful, people must align with dominant ways of speaking, dressing, or expressing themselves or their emotions. "People must not be 'too Black,' 'too Jewish,' or 'too gay'" (Goodman, 2001, p. 17). Bertrand and Mullainathan's study on hiring (2004) suggests that a name that is "too Black" or "too ethnic" can affect search processes. As Ragins (1995) suggests, "Organizational culture is shaped and supported by the power-holders of the organization. These individuals influence the values, assumptions, and ideologies of the organization's culture" (p. 97). Unsurprisingly, the research evidence is clear that most people in an institution tend to hire people like themselves and perceive that those most like themselves are the most qualified (Elliott & Smith, 2004).

Until Section 504 of the Rehabilitation Act was passed in 1973, most institutions were designed for people who could walk up stairs, read signs, and so on. All too often, persons without disabilities were unaware that they were enjoying a privilege that was denied to others—the right of access. Even today, architecture programs must intentionally raise the issue of physical access with students who take it for granted. In historically male-dominated environments, facilities for women have often been afterthoughts. Once women enter these environments, the ways in which gender has been privileged become apparent. Early generations of women elected to Congress were soon introduced to this issue when they saw the inadequate lavatory and gymnasium facilities available to them on Capitol Hill. No woman who attends a large event and finds herself standing at the end of an interminably long line to the ladies' room doubts that the design of public restroom facilities is gendered.

Early airbags were developed around an erroneous gender assumption that presumed passengers to be the height of the average man, an assumption that led to airbags being a danger, rather than a safeguard, for many women and children. One explanation for why so few women astronauts have done space walks is that one-size-fits-all space suits are too large for all but the tallest women. Recently, doctors announced the development of a female knee to be used in knee replacements. It turns out that the structure of the "generic" knee previously used was designed for men. The new knee was finally developed because women were having more difficulty recovering from knee surgery.

In the United States, Christmas and Easter are automatically built into institutional calendars, reflecting the centrality of Christianity to American society. Most Christians take the presence of these holidays on calendars for granted, while those who identify with other religions view the universality of the Christian holidays as a clear indication of embedded norms. Even today, the association of science with maleness continues to be an impediment to opening science up for women at all levels (Schiebinger 2006, 2008; Tobias, 1990; Tobin & Roth, 2007; Towers, 2008). Further, many elite institutions are associated with the practices, behavior, and trappings of groups that formed around privileges of wealth and Whiteness.

Power and Privilege

As Peggy McIntosh (2008) so aptly describes in her metaphor about wearing the "backpack of privilege," it is important for institutions to understand what is privileged and valued and accessible to some people, and what is not. Because terms such as *privilege* and *power* carry both political and emotional weight, they are often difficult to engage. Yet unwillingness to name privilege and power can communicate arrogance about the fairness of the institution and its practices (Chesler, Lewis, & Crowfoot, 2005; A. Hurtado, 1996; Johnson, 2001; Kendall, 2006; Maher

& Tetrault, 2007; Thompson & Louque, 2005). Indeed, one of the consistent themes in the research literature on identity, particularly in organizational and societal contexts, is the importance of recognizing the asymmetry of identity when power or stigma is involved.

The literature in social psychology dealing with ethnic conflict throughout the world and intergroup relations demonstrates that intergroup teamwork can be experienced quite differently by individuals depending on their positionality and the context. A number of researchers point out the tendency of those in power positions to view group efforts in terms of individual competence and to assume neutrality or symmetry with respect to context and power. At the same time, those whose identity is associated with stigma or discrimination often wonder whether what takes place is a function of their identity in a particular group or something else (Dale, 2004; Dovidio, Kawakami, & Gaertner, 2000; Levin & van Laar, 2006; Rouhana, 2004). As Dale (2004) notes, "Identity and the experience of the parties [in conflict] is constructed differently given their relative high or low power position" (p. 189). This concept will be central to the discussion of the design of institutional intergroup efforts in chapter 6.

Maher and Tetrault (2007), in their study of three universities, suggest that an important element in institutional transformation with respect to diversity is to name and address the forms of privilege that are embedded in institutional norms and practices—forms of privilege that may be invisible to some but are very visible to those on the margins of that experience. White privilege. Class privilege. Gender privilege. Heterosexual privilege. For those who find the institution comfortable, it may be uncomfortable to name them; however, it is essential that forms of privilege be confronted. While it often takes people on the outside of privilege to point this out, those on the inside must be willing to listen and to act.

Robert Merton described the "Matthew effect" in the 1960s as the process of "cumulative advantage" that accrues to people in already advantaged positions in science. He says, "the concept of cumulative advantage directs our attention to the ways initial comparative advantage of trained capacity, structural location, and available resources make for successive increments of advantage such that the gaps between the haves and have-nots in science (as in other domains of social life) widen until dampened by countervailing processes" (1988, p. 606). The concept of cumulative advantage can certainly be applied to the inequities that emerged from the implementation of the GI Bill described in chapter 1. Cumulative advantage also accrues when institutions conflate identity with acceptable norms and practices that privilege some over others.

It would be easy to assume, therefore, that to build cultures that are more inclusive, one must fundamentally change the culture of the institution in all ways. Indeed, it would be easy to imagine that the only way to build capacity for diversity is to create a new culture. Because cultures are not easy to change, and because the people who are in institutions are often drawn to them in part because of the institution's mission and culture, most scholars and practitioners of institutional change suggest a very different approach to cultural change. This perspective is expressed clearly by Edgar Schein, one of the major scholars who has studied organizational culture and change for years. He suggests, "Never start with the idea of changing culture. Always start with the issue the organization faces. . . . Always think initially of the culture as your source of strength. Even if some elements of the culture look dysfunctional, remember that they are probably only a few among a larger set of others that continue to be strengths. If changes need to be made . . . try to build on existing cultural strengths" (1999, p. 189). Ultimately, the culture must be defined and perceived in such a way that it is seen as empowering and inclusive (Banks, 1997; Darder, 1991).

Individual Experiences in Institutional Contexts

Apart from individual personality, the institutional context can dramatically influence a person's behavior and experiences. The following sections describe some of the adverse ways that an institution can influence individuals as a function of identity.

Threat

Depending on the environment and history of the institution, there may be the perception of threat. For instance, to be gay or lesbian in the military is to experience a constant fear of discovery. To be a Muslim after 9/11 is to wonder how one is seen. Many African Americans move through their days with heightened vigilance in institutions where racist incidents are common, just as those who are undocumented—as well as those who simply look like those who are undocumented—feel threatened in environments in which immigration and illegal immigration are being discussed with hostility.

Threat can also take the form of wondering whether the institution with its cultural norms and practices truly welcomes the perspective of someone from the outside. Is it really okay to criticize the assumptions behind a dress code? Will voicing a concern about breakfast meetings be welcome if one is a single mother?

Can a lesbian put pictures of her domestic partner on her desk? Will a person of color be viewed negatively if she or he reports racist incidents? Why is there a common understanding among women of the times when one speaks and no one seems to listen?

There are many examples, large and small, where even in spite of inclusive rhetoric, people experience their identity as not welcomed or valued and where efforts to participate may be invalidated. A robust body of literature addresses the experience of stigma, often associated with exclusion, harassment, and denial of resources (Konrad, 2003). Being stigmatized can have powerful implications for identity, for relationships with others, for feelings of competence, and even for performance (Davies, Spencer, Quinn, & Gerhardstein, 2002; Eisenhardt, Kahwajy, & Bourgeois, 1997; Inzlicht & Good, 2006; Levin & van Laar, 2006).

Microaggressions

The growing literature on microaggressions describes how many of the experiences associated with discrimination do not take the form of major affronts. Rather, they are smaller incidents that occur perhaps unconsciously on the part of the other person but are experienced by minorities as insulting, degrading, or potentially threatening. Any one incident can be seen as minor, but the accumulation over time becomes significant (Rowe, 1990). A recent review of the literature in *American Psychologist* reflects the growing salience of microaggressions and the patterns of interaction related to them (Sue et al., 2007). The authors point out that microaggressions can emerge from human interaction but can also be communicated in institutional environments, through what is not said and through how the culture is represented. To the individual experiencing the microaggression, there is the time and effort spent questioning whether the event occurred and then whether to avoid saying anything for fear of being called oversensitive or paranoid. Identity and position in the institution inform a person's perspectives on the institution and can have implications for institutional dynamics (Crocker & Garcia, 2006; Inzlicht & Good, 2006; Levin & van Laar, 2006; Solórzano, Ceja, & Yosso, 2000; Sue et al., 2007).

Simply claiming inclusiveness will not be sufficient. In an institutional context, there is a powerful intersection between identity and the power and influence that are aligned with identity. When an issue arises in an institution, many will discuss concerns associated with race or gender or class, but the underlying issue may have been triggered by power dynamics or negative experiences associated with identity more than with the characteristics of people.

Despite years of research suggesting that women are more collaborative, for example, it is not clear that collaboration is a product of being a woman; rather, it may be a reflection of the fact that women are often in an environment where they are less likely to hold power, making collaborative strategies necessary. I have been in discussions where persons of color are angry and where Whites will ask, "Why do *they* have to be so angry?" When a group is seen as angry, is it because the *individuals* are angry people or because anger emerges from disempowerment, racism, sexism, or heterosexism? In the contexts of identity in institutions, questions of where the characteristic should be attributed are critical. Power dynamics, rather than individual characteristics, can explain many of the dynamics with respect to identity in an institution (Konrad, 2003).

Tokenism

The intersection of an individual's identity with institutions and societies is particularly relevant when an individual is a token, one of a few in an organization who share a salient identity. Some important themes resonate through the literature on tokenism (Agars, 2004; Kanter, 1977; Yoder, 2002). For example, a person may be visible as a representative of the group but invisible as an individual. The first African American woman to lead a corporation is highly visible as an African American woman; as such, she will be studied and watched. Consequently, her successes and failures will often be attributed to the salience of race and gender in the corporate setting.

However, the fact that she is an individual who carries with her the same range of strengths, weaknesses, and characteristics that others carry, irrespective of race and gender, will be considered far less often. As a result, her failure or success will take on huge significance for the group (i.e., African American women) while placing an extra burden on her as an individual. How often has one heard comments like "We tried a Latina in that position and it didn't work out" or "Our last CEO was a woman. We won't do that again"? Such sweeping generalizations and conclusions are not made about White men because their sheer number in the upper echelons allows any one individual to be just that—an individual White man who possesses individual strengths and weaknesses.

Not only is there considerable stress in being the sole representative of a group, there is also difficulty in satisfactorily negotiating culture. A woman who tries to be "too male" will not be accepted, but being "too female" can place her at risk. Similar dilemmas occur in scenarios that involve race, sexual orientation, age, and class. Research has suggested that those in token positions may experience a limitation of roles and a restricted range of acceptable behaviors, increased pressure to perform, threats to performance, lack of access to important informational and social networks, and stereotypes (Inzlicht & Good, 2006; Kanter, 1977; Konrad & Gutek, 1987; Wharton, 1992). Moreover, there is some evidence that women in token positions may be less likely to mentor, in order to not be seen as favoring women (Yoder, Adams, Grove, & Priest, 1985).

In highly visible positions requiring significant leadership, individuals will find themselves negotiating identities not only from their own (and the institution's) perspective, but also from the perspective of the communities from which the individual comes. Take, for example, the multiplicity of identities carried by a Latina lesbian who comes from a working-class background. Add a college presidency to that picture. It would not be surprising to find these identity groups expecting her to pay particular attention to diversity agendas. Because she is also a token in the institution, this president will be challenged to demonstrate that her vision is broader than diversity and that she represents the whole institution.

While the research on tokenism is still limited, it is apparent from numerous studies that context matters. Research has consistently shown that the more one is outnumbered, the greater the likelihood that the environment will trigger negative stereotypes or awareness of one's marginal position (Agars, 2004; Kramer, Konrad, & Erkut, 2006; Thompson & Sekaquaptewa, 2002; Williams & O'Reilly, 1998). Being the token can occur for anyone—a White man in nursing, for example. However, Yoder and Schleicher (1996) have found that the impact on the individual and the dynamics in the organization vary considerably with gender role violations and are asymmetrical.

A man's experience in a traditionally woman's field is asymmetrical to that of a woman in a man's field. Here the status of the field and gender interact. Yoder and Schleicher's research results suggest a much more positive experience for a man in nursing than for a woman in engineering. In one study, women in engineering were seen as less likable, less attractive, and, significantly, more distanced from colleagues than men. In nursing, in contrast, men experienced little hostility and were more accepted as a "nontraditional person." Even so, some other research suggests that men may be unhappier in the minority than women and that Whites may be more uncomfortable in the minority than persons of color. Thus, while being "the only one" could apply to anyone, the dynamics vary and are asymmetrical depending on social norms, status, and expectations in society (Fagenson, 1993; Richard, 2000; Richard, Kochan, & McMillan-Capehart, 2002; Riordan & Shore, 1997; Yoder, 2002).

Critical Mass

Rosabeth Moss Kanter's early work on tokenism and the consequences of skewed demographics in an institution suggested that when a group constitutes 20% of the organization, the impact of tokenism is decreased (Kanter 1977). More recent research suggests that to limit the impact of skewed environments, 35% would be a better proportion for any group (Ely, 1994; Kramer, Konrad, & Erkut, 2006). With such representation, individuals are more likely to be seen as individuals, without the visibility and stress of being a token. At the same time, achieving a critical mass allows members of an identity group to come together and gain some measure of "voice" in an institution. Paradoxically, it also helps to dispel stereotyping. The larger the membership of an identity group, the greater the likelihood that there will be individual variation that will facilitate the breakdown of stereotypes. Greater proportionality can also create more positive views of the organization and more optimism about the possibilities for success for minorities in token positions (Ely, 1994).

Though it is clear that achieving a critical mass for a salient identity group is crucial for the individual and for the institution, the concept itself is not well understood. It may be that the complexity of critical mass reflects the complexity of identity itself. In determining a critical mass, how and when can we aggregate groups so that we look at the numbers and percentages of persons of color in general? When do we need to disaggregate groups and look at racial, ethnic, and gender groupings separately? Does the location of a critical mass matter? Is the unit of analysis the institution, or does a critical mass have to be achieved in the location where individuals work or study? Is achieving a critical mass in a department more essential than simply looking at a critical mass at the institutional level? On the other hand, achieving a critical mass may matter a great deal at the institutional level. We know little about when a critical mass is reached. Because so few institutions have attained it in terms of race, ethnicity, and gender, there have been few opportunities to study the dynamics surrounding the conditions for achieving a healthy critical mass.

Institutional Isms

While racism, sexism, heterosexism, and other isms are often described from a psychological perspective as the behaviors and attitudes between individuals and groups, institutional forms of isms highlight the ways in which institutional structures, like culture, come to embody forms of inequity. Indeed, some identities, such as race, gender, and sexuality, become salient and often essentialized in part as a function of racism, sexism, heterosexism, and so on (Darder & Torres, 2003). Some scholars therefore urge shifting from the language of race, for example, to that of racism, to capture the social meanings for race, as distinguished from individual meanings (Baum, 2006). "It is racism as an ideology that produces the notion of 'race,' not the existence of 'races' that produces racism" (Darder & Torres, 2003, p. 257). Similarly, Minnich (2005) suggests converting nouns into active forms—for example, shifting from *race* to *racializing* and *gender* to *gendering*—to show the processes and means by which inequity is maintained.

These structural elements are significant precisely because the consequences in terms of inequality are not generally explicit. Institutionalized isms are standards, policies, and practices that are embedded in the institution, that have a disparate impact on particular groups, and that are not essential to fulfill the institution's mission. This last point is very important. Decisions about what is essential to fulfill institutional purposes are a necessary task for any institution. What makes something a form of institutional ism is that it limits access, success, or participation by individuals or groups who would otherwise be successful.

When police departments and fire departments had height requirements, this criterion—developed because a minimal height was assumed to be a necessary qualification—limited the number of women who could apply. Eventually, it became evident that women and men who did not meet the height standard could still pass rigorous tests for becoming a member of the police or fire department. This is an example of institutional sexism, as was the design of the airbags described earlier. The implementation of the housing policies of the GI Bill is a perfect example of institutional racism under cover of states' rights. Indeed, Sidanius and Pratto, in a review of empirical evidence (1999), have concluded that "institutional discrimination remains a very significant feature of modern 'democratic' states" (p. 303). These patterns are reflected in the workplace, schools, health care, housing, and the criminal justice system.

Chesler, Lewis, and Crowfoot provide a framework for the institutional elements that conceal or reveal structural inequity. They look at the institution's mission, culture, power, membership, technology, resources, and boundary management as places to be studied. Institutionalized isms are often not explicit but implicit, buried in the context of rules and norms that allow processes to be named as fair even when they are not (Chesler, Lewis, & Crowfoot, 2005; Sidanius & Pratto, 1999).

An institution that seriously wants to engage these embedded assumptions will have to determine which assumptions are essential to the institution and do not inappropriately deny access and success to particular groups, and which assumptions need to be changed in order to create a more inclusive environment. Some changes will cost money. Certain changes will affect everyone, and some of these will benefit everyone. The increasing number of companies implementing family-friendly policies that were originally introduced as "women's issues" has been positive for men as well. Change requires resources of time, people, and money. The willingness of an institution to make these investments is directly related to perceptions of a commitment to diversity. It appears that unless an institution understands these investments as being in its best interests, there will be considerable resistance to making significant changes.

Diversity and Divisiveness

Does an emphasis on diversity cause the kind of divisiveness that one witnesses throughout history and today? Would it be better to downplay identity groupings based on culture and religion? Would it be better to minimize ascribed identities such as race, gender, and ethnicity? One can understand why, as identity becomes more multifaceted and complex, some think we should not pay attention to identity at the societal level. This is the appeal of color blindness. We are happy to appreciate and celebrate the diversity of individuals and groups as long as at the institutional or societal level, things are "neutral" (Bennett, 1998; Marcus, Steele, and Steele, 2002; Yoshino, 2006). Unfortunately, structural inequities in society make serious discussion of color blindness—that is, identity blindness—much more problematic than simply a call to consider individuals as individuals (Eagly, Baron, & Hamilton, 2004; Wise, 2006).

When identities are embedded in circumstances that are characterized by exclusion, inequity, discrimination, injustice, and lack of access to power, they assume significance beyond the functions they serve for individuals and groups. Most of the identities associated with diversity in society and on campuses are linked to these issues, and they are fueling the collective and individual actions that seek to produce institutional transformation. As Gutman (2003) points out, "Socially salient parts of people's identities—such as their color, gender and physical disabilities—shape their interests, and their interests in turn shape their identities" (p. 133). She notes further that "the fewer the alternative means of representation available to disadvantaged individuals, the more powerful an ascriptive association is" (p. 137). In such cases, organizations often develop to represent the group's interests and participation in society.

In the United States, the legacy of race and racism in society and continued evidence of inequity leave race a highly salient part of identity. Even as women— particularly White women—have made progress, there are many contexts in which gender remains extremely salient for women (Blau, Brinton, & Grusky, 2006). Sexual orientation, disability, and class, as well as the intersections among them, are also significant with respect to inequity. However, for each identity, the particulars of the saliency differ, as will be discussed in chapter 3. How one frames diversity and the conditions under which identity is developed have a great deal to do with whether identity will serve a positive or negative purpose.

When someone asks why we can't be color-blind and treat everyone as an individual, they are asking the wrong question. We should all be asking, instead, how we might create just institutions and societies that benefit from diversity and that embody a multiplicity of cultures and identities. Significantly, such a question moves beyond individuals and groups. It asks us to look at inequity and how those from specific identity groups are positioned to benefit from and experience institutions quite differently. Until these inequities that are built into the structures of institutions and society are addressed, the consequence of color-blind (or gender-blind, or ability-blind) policies is more likely to be the maintenance or exacerbation of inequity—as we have seen with the implementation of "color-blind" admissions policies in higher education, gender-neutral airbags, and so on. The view that identity needs to be understood, not hidden, will be echoed in the results of the empirical work in the field of intergroup relations reviewed in chapter 6.

Current research suggests that rather than downplaying identity, a more powerful strategy for society and institutions would be to build on the multiplicities of identities and allow individuals to look at the similarities and differences across them, as well as the social context in which identities emerge. To do that requires building institutions that signal and manifest diversity in their culture (Ibarra, 2000; Padilla, 2004; Ramirez & Castañeda, 1991; Sanchez, 2004). Amartya Sen (2006), a Nobel Prize–winning economist, notes, "The hope of harmony in the contemporary world lies in a clearer understanding of the pluralities of human identity, and in the appreciation that they cut across each other and work against a sharp separation along one single hardened line of impenetrable division" (p. xiv).

In the process of South Africa's emergence as a democracy, a former justice of the Constitutional Court, Albie Sachs, spoke eloquently about the relationship of diversity and community:

> Shared citizenship, far from being the enemy of difference, is the bedrock for the recognition of difference. It is only when culture, background, language and ap-

pearance become used as a means of controlling resources and political power—ethnic mobilization for the purpose of advantage—that culture in that sense becomes politicized and is precarious and antagonistic to the culture of others. Where common citizenship is profound and strong, then the expression of one's culture in no way requires the disrespect of another's. (Sachs, 1999, p. v)

The Challenges of Language, Labels, and Identity

The question of language arises the moment one sets out to write about diversity. Issues of language, especially naming, can be appropriately introduced in regard to every category and label used in this book. Like so many other aspects of diversity, the nature of language itself is dynamic and ever evolving. For example, naming has profound political significance and is critical to identity and self-empowerment. Yet it is not always easy to know what names to use, and in what context. In 1986, I was working on the final edits of a monograph I had written on diversity when I began to hear Jesse Jackson refer to Blacks as African Americans. There had been no vote, no announcement of any formal decision; but it was clear that how we referred to Blacks was about to change—and indeed it did. For any author, the best approach to naming and other issues related to language is probably to identify the issues, make a decision, and go forward.

Because words can be seen as ideological or politically correct—or politically incorrect—the use of certain words can be catalytic, if not inflammatory. It is important to be historically, socially, and politically sensitive to words and names and their impact on individuals and groups. For anyone interacting in diverse settings, it is probably useful to keep in mind that regardless of how any one author or body of literature refers to specific groups, signifiers are seldom set in stone, and it is always best to ask and listen before making assumptions. Where possible, I try to honor self-identification, to be specific when there are other issues that emerge, to disaggregate large categories, and to recognize that these issues change all the time.

Naming

The significance of naming challenges both individuals and institutions to critically examine language, to disaggregate groups, and to avoid labels that, while convenient, may not be adequate. However, some clarification about my own use of certain terms may be helpful in understanding the text.

RACE AND ETHNICITY

Throughout the text, I often combine the terms *race* and *ethnicity* (*race/ethnicity*). In the current U.S. census, race and ethnicity are not interchangeable. The census classifies "Hispanic" as an ethnicity because Hispanics may be of different races. At the same time, issues of ethnicity and culture are core to discussions about African Americans and Asian Americans. Race and facets of ethnicity such as language, culture, and history are inextricably intertwined, and scholars may use one term or the other or both to capture this complexity (Adams, 2001; Ferdman & Gallegos, 2001). Rather than choose one over the other, I have elected to use *race/ethnicity* to capture both elements together.

The phrase *women and minorities* is often used to deal with the intersection of race and gender. However, it has become clear to me that in many cases, women of color are included in minorities (especially with respect to institutional data) and "women" really means "White women." The use of "women and minorities" often reflects a reluctance to specify "White women" when that is what is meant. This is a perfect example of the discomfort in naming race. If I am referring to White women, I will be explicit in indicating that.

One word commonly used in virtually all scholarship on diversity is *minority*. While this word has relevance as a numeric reference, it also has great significance in regard to issues of power. As a result, there is an enormous amount of research on "minorities," with *minority* defined as the smaller part of a population with respect to a particular characteristic. In the United States, that characteristic may be tied to racial and ethnic groups, with Whites being associated with the majority and all groups of color being characterized as minorities. However, diversity within the United States has increased such that there are now some states, such as California and Texas, where Whites are not in the numerical majority. Most would agree, however, that even in those states, Whites still represent the majority of individual and institutional power, and non-Whites continue to be seen as minorities even though they are the majority.

While the term *minority* still has significance in some contexts, my feeling is that it is too generic when used to represent all non-Whites. Perhaps more importantly, its use places Whites at the center of the diversity discussion. Therefore, I use it only when necessary and prefer to use *persons of color* when referring to African Americans, Asian Americans, Latinos, and American Indians.

Another term that is used in federal information and appears pejorative is *nonresident aliens*. One wonders how long international residents and students will be referred to in this way.

Continuing waves of immigrants require us to pay attention to the suitability of those names that have become established and to use new or broader terms to include new groups. While the term *African American* has been used for the past two decades, there is a growing recognition that the ethnic and national origin of Blacks in this country is expanding. Blacks who trace their roots to places outside of Africa, such as the Caribbean, do not necessarily see themselves as African American. For the most part, I continue to use the term *African American* unless the context suggests that a different choice would be more appropriate.

Preferences for group names can vary from region to region. Because the term *Hispanic* was used by the U.S. census, some groups view it as a governmental label that was imposed on them. However, many people in Texas intentionally use the term. The word preferred by many Californians is *Latino*, while other people favor names that reference national origin (e.g., *Mexican American*) or historical and political positionality, such as *Chicano/Chicana* (González & Gándara, 2005; Zavella, 1994). Considering the history and significance of these terms, I have chosen to use *Latino/a*, unless reference to specific subgroups, authors, or book titles is warranted or when the data are developed from government information using traditional labels such as *Hispanic*.

American Indians have gone through similar transitions in naming, and I have tried to honor those changes. Increasingly, American Indian authors self-identify through tribal affiliation. This is useful in highlighting the tremendous diversity among tribes, with each bringing its own history, traditions, culture, and language.

The term *Asian American* evolved through efforts of the civil rights movement to address the fact that Asian American issues were largely ignored in many diversity dialogues. Recognizing that there is power in numbers, Americans with ancestries rooted in the enormous Asiatic sphere have achieved some political clout by being combined into one category (Hune, 1995; Hune & Chan, 1997; Takaki, 1993). However, as with other pan-ethnic groupings, there is great diversity within the Asian American community, and the differences often outweigh the commonalities.

In the political and social context of the United States, where Whiteness has been dominant and where so much of the history of race has centered on what has been called the Black-White paradigm, pan-ethnic identities provide political and social communities where important issues can be addressed. However, in recognition of the heterogeneity within such groups, there are increasing references to particularity. A growing academic literature has developed for many such communities. Some of these efforts are now emerging in higher education, as researchers begin to delve into the experiences of specific national or ethnic groups in higher education. This disaggregation is also occurring in literature on White ethnic communities (Phinney, 1990, 1996). Researchers must not lose sight of the particular, even as we talk about the general.

In education, the issues associated with race have historically focused on African American, Latino/a, and American Indian students (Anderson & Kim, 2006). The term *historically underrepresented minorities* (URM) has emerged as useful in speaking of issues related to these three groups, who remain the most underrepresented in higher education relative to their share of the population. However, with increasing immigration and diversity, other groups have been, and will be, underrepresented and underserved in higher education. The term *nonimmigrant minorities* (Marcus, Steele, & Steele, 2002) may be a useful way to distinguish domestic diversity from immigrant diversity. Some have suggested broadening the term *URM* to include underrepresented people such as the Hmong and other Southeast Asian communities.

I recognize that the term *underrepresented minority* is not entirely adequate, but it is useful enough that I will employ it to refer to African American, Latino/a, and American Indian groups, keeping in mind all the caveats that suggest its limits. In the context of this book, referring to specific groups as much as possible and attending to disaggregated data are perhaps the most useful approaches. Doing so permits greater attention to American Indians, who often get lost in the data of aggregated discussions about URM because their numbers are small.

In the naming of groups, even spelling can come to have meaning. As Gonzalez (2006) notes, the spelling *Pilipino* has come to signify something associated with the roots of the Filipino community; the use of the initial *p* connects the word to indigenous cultures, where *f* did not exist, and also to progressive politics.

SEX, GENDER, AND SEXUALITY

There is a lack of consensus around the terms *sex* and *gender*. I prefer to use *gender*, because it takes into account biological, social, and cultural dimensions and reflects greater complexity.

Gay and lesbian terminology continues to emerge through efforts to deal explicitly with the intersection of gender and sexuality. What has been one of the most stable dichotomies, the sex dichotomy between male and female, is shifting with the growing recognition of transgender and bisexual identities. *LGBT* (lesbian, gay, bisexual, transgender) is commonly used as a way of acknowledging the complexities of sexuality, complexities that go beyond naming to the fundamental nature of sexuality itself. On many campuses, we will see variations such as *LGBTQ*, where *Q* stands for "queer."

ABILITY GROUPS

Concerning the concept of ability/disability, I have elected to use *ability* terminology (Hehir, 2005). The complexity involved in defining "disability" can be seen in the passionate discourse within the Deaf community. Advocates of sign language square off against those who promote spoken language. Endorsers of cochlear implants clash with those for whom being deaf is a way of life, rather than something that should be changed. The discussion of ability grouping has evolved into a debate that is articulated around two perspectives. One prefers to emphasize an individual who has a disability rather than someone who is a disabled person. The other suggests that differential abilities are present in everyone and that notions of disability are therefore overly simplified.

The word *ableism* is often used to mean "a pervasive system of discrimination and exclusion that oppresses people who have mental, emotional, and physical disabilities" and that, when combined with norms of excellence, ability, talent, potential, or appearance, creates environments hostile to those who have such issues (Rauscher & McClintock, 1997, p. 198). The topic of ability is at times given short shrift in diversity discussions. It is, however, quite important and requires attention.

CLASS

The use of socioeconomic status (SES) has a long history in the social sciences, and there is no question that economic and educational markers continue to be critically relevant to scholarship. However, these markers are too limiting in the context of this book. Therefore, I use *class*, not only to capture these identifiers, but to indicate the cultural aspects that are emerging in research (Borrego, 2004; Chan & Goldthorpe, 2007; Zandy, 1996, 2001).

Zandy describes class as "an aspect of shared economic circumstances and shared social and cultural practices in relation to positions of power" (1996, p. 8). This conception of class evokes not simply a person's economic circumstances, but also one's social and cultural capital, norms, and values—concepts that will be addressed in the following chapters.

The Politics of Language

Issues of language are not only questions about how to "name" individuals and groups. They also involve questions about how language is used and how it is received. As I write this chapter, I am very conscious that words such as *privilege, power, racism,* and other *isms*, along with phrases such as *White privilege* and *het-*

erosexual privilege, have become part of the culture wars in our society. Unless one is willing to ignore stratification and issues such as institutional racism, it is impossible not to use language that describes these conditions.

For me, this is not a matter of being "politically correct" in the pejorative way in which this term is used. It is important to try to accurately depict and engage issues that reveal embedded phenomena and to suggest ways in which change can occur. Because diversity is fundamentally about these issues, they must be addressed. There are few ways to avoid the use of words or phrases that will evoke reactions or risk putting my work in a box. Nonetheless, I have tried to be clear and to use terms as precisely as I can, even as I invite the reader to engage in considering the significance of language.

Diversity, Democracy, and Higher Education

It is in the broad national and global context, and with identity holding a central place, that diversity's role at the core of higher education emerges. In the mid-1990s, Peter Drucker (1993) began to describe a major transition in society as he named and forecast the rise of the *knowledge worker* as central to the future social, political, and economic organization of communities. The knowledge worker assumes a role that requires informational expertise more than, for example, physical strength. Knowledge workers come to their role in society through education. In that context, education in general—and higher education in particular—are critical.

Indeed, the mandate of higher education in the United States and its relationship to the future of democracy are emerging as a core context for diversity. In *The Quiet Crisis* (2004), Peter Smith talks about the connections between education, the aspirations of democracy, and the future of society. "What's really permanent?" he asks. "What really endures is the soul of our democracy. And deep in America's soul lies the promise of opportunity, of liberty and freedom for every person. . . . With this commitment, we will survive. Without it, we will decline. . . . Education is the path to the table of opportunity in 21st century America" (p. 6).

In their report *Now Is the Time* (2005), the American Association of State Colleges and Universities and the National Association of State Universities and Land-Grant Colleges declare that "the promise of a just and truly multi-cultural democracy made possible through a more diverse academy cannot wait for another generation. The challenge for change within higher education must be taken up and addressed boldly. And it must be addressed today" (p. 3).

And in *Grutter v. Bollinger* (2003), the Supreme Court affirmed the relationship between diversity, democracy, and higher education when it stated, "the diffusion of knowledge and opportunity through public institutions of higher education must be accessible to all individuals, regardless of race or ethnicity. . . . In order to cultivate a set of leaders *with legitimacy in the eyes of the citizenry*, it is necessary that the path to leadership be visibly open to talented and qualified individuals of every race and ethnicity" (p. 20; emphasis added).

These statements speak to the relationship between diversity and democracy and to the need for higher education to represent the diversity of society. However, the complexities that surface through issues of identity and the strategies needed to create pluralistic communities that work are not discussed frequently enough or with sufficient depth at the policy level or within academe. These issues are not about changing individuals; they are about changing the institutions and structures that make identities salient. As such, they are deeply connected to the ways in which individuals interact and institutions function (Gutman, 2003; Putnam, 2007).

By extension, these issues are also deeply connected to the future of a democratic society. In "Culture, Identity and the Role of Higher Education in Building Democracy in South Africa" (1999), Cloete, Cross, Muller, and Pillay suggest that "a curriculum for common citizenship and sites for democratic practices could be a central role for higher education in South Africa's fledgling democratic practice" (p. 46). In the 1990s, a Ford Foundation–sponsored program called for a conversation about diversity, democracy, and higher education among teams from India, South Africa, and the United States. This three-year project underscored the importance of diversity for the vitality and viability of democracy and the role of higher education in this effort (Beckham, 2000, 2002; Cloete, Cross, Muller, & Pillay, 1999; Cloete, Muller, Makgoba, & Ekong, 1997; Cross et al., 1999).

While the focus of diversity has often been on people and their interpersonal relationships, diversity is manifested through our institutions and society at large. Higher education, then, rather than being seen as the elite terminus of the educational pipeline, can be seen as one of the *beginnings*. In addition to its crucial role in building the capacities of individuals from all sectors of society, higher education plays a strong role in defining knowledge, identifying and framing problems that need to be solved, allocating resources, developing and training teachers and faculty, and cultivating leaders for all sectors.

We might say that higher education is the source of a river that waters culture and society and has the potential to nourish as it rectifies. These are the purposes for higher education today, and they are centrally linked to the issues of diversity described above. This is the context that frames the chapters to come, in which we will see how institutions can build capacity for excellence and diversity.

PART II

Reframing Diversity

✿

CHAPTER THREE

A Diversity Framework for Higher Education

Inclusive and Differentiated

It may seem strange to begin a chapter describing a diversity framework with a discussion of technology. But in my view, our current discourse on diversity in the academy is narrow and static—so much so that it does not permit the change that is needed to build institutions' capacity to function in our increasingly diverse society. Considering technology allows us to take a look at another change in the environment that has transformed higher education. Because of its increasing centrality to institutional life, it serves as a useful parallel. Technology has been understood to be an imperative—a necessity that, despite all the challenges of change, must be implemented without excuses. Establishing diversity as an institutional imperative is one purpose of this book, so it is appropriate to begin with a perspective on what the technology imperative has meant institutionally, and how it might help illuminate how diversity might be considered.

Several decades ago, when technological changes were emerging in society in the form of desktop computers and word processing, campuses throughout the country began to accept the need to educate for a technological society, *and* they began to build their own institutional capacity to function in that society. Technology imperatives appeared in strategic-planning documents, capital plans, curricular discussions, and educational objectives. Research and development on many aspects of technology began, and partnerships with industry emerged. Although student learning and educating students were central parts of the discussion, a more overarching and largely unquestioned assumption was that institutions themselves would need to prepare their infrastructures for a new era in technology. There were major debates at the time about what computer literacy meant (including whether one had to know programming to be literate or whether word-processing skills were enough), but the institutional debates were focused on questions such as whether the platform that served the sciences could also serve the humanities, how much money needed to be spent, what vendors to use, and how to computerize payroll, registration, and admissions.

The debates about definitions of computer literacy quickly became moot. What emerged as important were institutional needs and developing the capacity of faculty and staff to work in this new context. Desktop computers were offered, and much time was spent introducing the new technologies of word processing and then e-mail to staff and faculty on the campus, even as many faculty and staff in science and engineering were using and developing much more sophisticated technologies.

In an important way, technology was no longer the sole domain of science and technical fields; it quickly touched all aspects of the institution. The curriculum in virtually all fields was changed to engage technological advances, including the arts, the humanities, urban planning, and architecture, as well as the traditional scientific and social science fields. Hiring shifted as new fields of expertise were seen as necessary for student learning and for keeping the disciplines current. Basic values of academic culture even shifted somewhat, to legitimate connections to industry and the technological partnerships that could be developed. Strategic-planning documents asserted the imperative of technology, and budget plans estimated how much would have to be spent to build the necessary institutional capacity. The mainstreaming of e-mail and the Web, and the ubiquitous presence of integrated information systems, has changed how institutions communicate and how the campus presents itself to the outside world. Many campuses have even introduced chief information/technology officers, whose job is to ensure that the relationships among all the technology initiatives across the institution are strategically coordinated.

There have been controversies, to be sure. Online courses have raised serious concerns about the ownership of ideas and intellectual property in general. Security and privacy are matters of concern. And to some degree, the infusion of technology suggested a cultural shift in which technology seemed not only to take over for people, but to suggest a value shift from people to machines. Significantly, while many of the shifts came with great costs and were not always easy to manage, there was virtually no question about the imperative to build institutional capacity for technology into every campus in the country. Rather, questions were framed in terms of how to minimize the risks, how "cutting edge" to be, or how far to develop different opportunities that emerged. Even those who hated the idea understood that technology was inevitable and essential if the campus was to remain viable and vital. It also became clear that the campus had to either identify or hire people who had the necessary expertise to manage the new technologies and to advise about the best strategies in the context of the institution's mission. The hiring of faculty and staff with technological competence increased, and professional development was designed, and continues to be used, to bring others "up to speed."

There have been, over time, issues of *definition* (are we discussing distance learning, digitizing information, new pedagogies?), *structure* (should the organization of technology be centralized or decentralized?), and what constitutes *excellence* (in hiring and knowledge). There has also been anxiety about what the changes will bring to the form of things near and dear to the academy. Will libraries disappear, or (as it appears) will they be reconfigured? Will books disappear, or (as it appears) will they come in multiple formats? Will technology make history and other disciplines irrelevant, or (as it appears) will it influence and make more accessible the significant knowledge of the classics?

Overall, technology has introduced new approaches and new knowledge; affected research, pedagogy, and communication; and created links that would not have been possible in an earlier era. Moreover, it has forced institutions to build capacity—the resources, expertise, and talent—to function and work in a technological world. What is seen as excellent and essential has also changed with the advent of the resources of technology. While there are some who are saddened by some of the changes and who long for a simpler time, few institutions would turn their back on what technology offers. As Friedman wrote in *The World Is Flat* (2005), "the experiences of the high-tech companies in the last few decades who failed to navigate the rapid changes . . . may be a warning to all . . . that are now facing these inevitable, even predictable, changes but lack the leadership, flexibility, and imagination to adapt" (p. 46).

Diversity, like technology, represents a powerful change in our environment. Like technology, it is an imperative that must be engaged if institutions are to be successful in a society that is ever more pluralistic and in a world that is both interconnected and challenged by diversity. Diversity, like technology, introduces significant strategic opportunities to fulfill the mission of higher education and to serve institutional excellence. And, as with technology, the challenges and changes keep coming at the same time that the institution must continue to function. This understanding of diversity begins at the institutional and societal levels. Nonetheless, diversity is far more contested than technology with respect to questions about the strategies for achieving change—or even whether it must be addressed at all. While technology, too, is about power, it is not nearly as contentious as race and gender or justice and inequity in our society. No one has had to "prove" the benefits of technology; no legal challenges have ensued over whether the people hired under job descriptions that focus on technology were hired unfairly; and so on. Technology is understood as an imperative to be engaged without excuses.

There is another potentially useful parallel between technology and diversity. When the technology was new, the changes fundamentally challenged existing ways of doing things. Converting existing registration systems, including hand-entered data, was not easy. The early format for the Web was cumbersome and not user-friendly. And the basic cultures of institutions did not support technology. Today, while conversions are still not easy, the fundamental framework for technology exists. Moreover, many of the changes have facilitated institutional functioning and have in fact turned out to be a "good thing."

Today, the Web facilitates research and is easily used because of the developments in search engines. Similarly, in the environmental movement, early technologies were designed to reduce the waste and pollution of old technologies, such as those built into cars and power plants. Doing so was cumbersome and expensive. With the advent of new technologies, there is the promise of machines that no longer need to be cleaned up; the new systems and technologies will be "clean" to begin with. At that time, the culture will have changed, and the costs of being "green" will diminish.

What does this mean for diversity? Current efforts are largely focused on interrupting and changing embedded patterns and practices that serve to exclude and devalue. This process is, by its very nature, cumbersome and expensive. It is possible, however, that efforts to transform the academy and scholarship to fully embrace diversity will ultimately, as happened with the acceptance of technology, produce new ways of proceeding that become part of normal practice and that reflect excellence. Florida, in his response to Friedman's *The World Is Flat*, suggests that the world is also "spiky": technology is important, but institutions, especially colleges and universities, have an opportunity to be hubs of creativity that build on diversity, places that are "open to new ideas, cultivate freedom of expression, and are accepting of differences, eccentricity, and diversity" (Florida, Gates, Knudsen, & Stolarick, 2006, p. 35). Institutions that are more diverse and that have developed new ways will be able to respond to change and will be more viable, as well as potentially more attractive to diverse groups of people.

A Framework for Diversity

Perhaps one of the most vexing dilemmas on campuses is how to define diversity. As discussions of diversity proceed on college campuses across the country, the question of defining it often touches on the question of who gets included and why (Levinson, 2003). In a diversity task force, do we restrict the conversation to race and ethnicity, especially for underrepresented persons of color (African Americans, Latinos, and American Indians), or do we present diversity as a long list of identities—a list that, while being more inclusive, might also mean that issues of diversity lose focus? In the previous chapters, I used the term "diversity" rather loosely to incorporate many different elements that are salient for institutions and are parts of an individual's or group's identity. The list included, among other identities, race, ethnicity, gender, class, sexual orientation, and ability. Today, however, we need to incorporate the complexity of diversity in such a way that the concept does not become watered down and generic. On the other hand, it needs to be inclusive. How can that be accomplished?

Historical Evolution

There are conceptual and historic ways of thinking about diversity that can reflect both inclusiveness and differentiation. Because the framework that I will suggest is aligned with the development of diversity over time, I offer here an overview of the evolution of diversity efforts over the past forty years. This description will necessarily be broad. It will be useful, however, as a way of connecting the past with a strategic future.

OPENING DOORS

The earliest efforts toward diversity were attempts to open doors to those who were excluded by law from educational institutions. While many of our current discussions about diversity take as their historical source the early stages of the civil rights movement and issues of access to higher education that gained momentum during that period, the struggle for access to education predates the 1960s. There were many other challenges to lack of access and to segregation throughout the country involving Blacks, Chicanos, Asian Americans, and American Indians (Aguirre, 2005; Chesler, Lewis, & Crowfoot, 2005; Ladson-Billings, 2006; MacDonald & García, 2003; Moreno, 1999; Valencia 2008). The landmark desegregation case involving Chicanos on the West Coast, *Mendez v. Westminster* (1947), is but one of many cases often overlooked; it would go on to provide an important precedent for the historic Brown case seven years later. Indeed, Chicano and Asian groups were fighting segregation in numerous locations, but especially on the West Coast. Nonetheless, much of the early work on diversity in higher education is centered on the civil rights movement in the South and, in particular, on the civil rights movement most visibly represented by African Americans and White women.

That era of struggle led to the Civil Rights Act of 1964 and various executive orders for affirmative action that focused on ensuring access to higher education for historically underrepresented minorities (African Americans, Latinos, and American Indians) and for White women in fields in which they were underrepresented. The struggle for access concerned not only student admissions, but hiring as well. Significantly, and a fact often lost in current discussions, affirmative action was not framed as a method to hire or admit people, but rather as a way to hold institutions accountable and to minimize discriminatory practices against protected classes for whom discrimination was documented.

Other pathbreaking legal and legislative mandates also pushed higher education to make changes. The 1965 Higher Education Act established need-based financial aid for the first time, along with the creation of TRIO early-intervention programs for underrepresented minorities and low-income students. In 1972, the Basic Educational Opportunity Grants (later renamed Pell Grants) were a long-overdue fulfillment of the recommendation of the Truman Commission report of 1947 to open access to higher education to people from all classes (Thelin, 2004). The landmark legislation of Title IX (1972) mandating access for women in athletics was important not only because it required equivalent support for male and female athletes, but also because it did not permit the excuse that women didn't want to do athletics. Section 504 of the Rehabilitation Act of 1973 and the Americans with Disabilities Act of 1990 required that campuses move to provide access and accommodation for persons with disabilities. Thus, legal and policy initiatives provided some of the framework and pressure for diversity efforts early on.

BEYOND OPEN DOORS

In the 1960s and 1970s, the prevailing notion was that by opening the doors to higher education, the inequities of exclusion would be remedied. While the focus on access did make a difference, it did not take long for the literature on higher education to reveal a shift from a concern solely about access to a concern about student success as well (García, 2002; Smith, 2005). Because so much research was designed to compare students who succeeded with those who did not, and because there was little systematic study of institutions, it is not surprising that the early research in this area directed attention almost entirely to students and the reasons for their failure. As a result, campus efforts targeted student preparation (almost certainly a part of the issue), the effect of family culture (much of which has been disputed), and motivation. Today, this deficit model, while still embedded in some research, policies, and procedures, is less credible (Blake, 1985; Walser, 2006). Nonetheless, the notion that students are "at risk" because of their background rather than "at risk" because of their experiences on campus continues to inform many campus efforts, even though, as we shall see in chapter 7, who is at risk and why varies wildly.

In the 1970s and 1980s, more topics of diversity were framed in such a way as to highlight the institution and the ways in which colleges and universities were and were not prepared to educate diverse students of color for success (Gándara, 1999; Gándara & Contreras, 2009; Nakanishi & Nishida, 1995; Sedlacek, 1999; Smith, 2005; Stein & Malcolm, 1998; Wright & Tierney, 1991). Nevertheless, even today, diversity efforts are largely focused, as they were in previous decades, on outreach, access, and success—mostly at the undergraduate level and mostly in terms of underrepresented-minority (URM) students. Gender issues for White women remain for certain science and engineering fields. And too often, concerns about access and success remain centered on issues of preparation at the K–12 level.

In more selective institutions, as we shall discuss in chapter 4, the focus has been on maintaining affirmative action as a tool for diversity. Although affirmative action became the mechanism for admissions in such institutions, it has been a contested one since the Bakke decision in 1978. Today, admissions remains a topic of huge debate and concern (Altbach, Berdahl, & Gumport, 2005; Gallacher & Osborne, 2005; Lowe, 1999; Massey, Charles, Lundy, & Fischer, 2003; Wilson, 1995a). There is still a heavy reliance on parallel processes to ensure diversity in admissions even as these approaches have been limited by recent legal and policy mandates and even though they have had only limited success. Increasingly, the basis for using race or gender as a factor is whether diversity is central to the institution's academic mission. Fundamentally, the concern in highly selective admissions will be an institutional one: how to develop the capacity to identify talent in students who might not look like the "traditional" student.

Although much of the national attention to diversity has emphasized the admissions debates, the role of community colleges, as the point of entry for many low-income and URM students, has also been important. Over the decades, the question of whether community colleges adequately serve as a bridge to the bachelor's degree or employment or whether they serve as a place that limits opportunity has put increasing pressure on these institutions to attend to issues of success, not just access.

Remedial education has also been a cause of concern in four-year public institutions, especially where there is great ambivalence about providing it. Despite research showing that remediation has been with higher education for centuries, there remains the belief that this is the responsibility of community colleges or high schools, rather than four-year colleges and universities. However, a growing body of research suggests that engaging remediation through attention to more advanced approaches, rather than basic skills, has greater potential for success (Merisotis & Phipps, 2000). Included in this research is a concern about faculty capacity to interrupt patterns of failure through effective pedagogy and classroom structures (Merrow, 2007). Student support services directed to academic and social concerns remain a high priority in trying to improve the experiences of students from diverse racial and ethnic backgrounds, especially those from underrepresented communities.

In contrast to the focus on undergraduates, the issue of diversity in graduate education has remained in the shadows. However, it has begun to emerge as an important topic—in part because of the need to build capacity in the sciences, ensure a diverse faculty, and improve graduation rates, time to degree, and the relationship between the PhD and the needs of society (Golde & Walker, 2006; Goldman & Massy, 2001; National Research Council, 1997; Nettles & Millet, 2006; Perna, 2004; Woodrow Wilson Foundation, 2005).

Thus, the literature on outreach, access, and success today parallels strongly the literature of thirty and forty years ago. However, access and success is now stressed with increasing urgency, given changing demographics, the central role of education for individuals and the society, and, perhaps, the time constraints placed on the Supreme Court's Michigan case. The difference is that today, access and success is more often (though not always) framed as something the institution needs to be accountable for. A strong alignment between the changing demographics of society and concerns about the economic future of society has made accountability highly relevant, particularly with respect to the achievement gap (Clotfelter, Ehrenberg, Getz, & Siegfried, 1991; Gándara, Orfield, & Horn, 2006; Haycock, 2006; Jaeger & Page, 1996; Kirsch, Braun, Yamamoto, & Sum, 2007; Swail, Cabrera, & Lee, 2004; Watson, Cabrera, Lee, & Williams, 2005). Student success or lack thereof is today more likely to be seen as a reflection of institutional success or lack thereof.

Moreover, a much more robust body of research and programmatic approaches illuminate the conditions under which success can be developed regardless of a student's background. More campuses are focusing less on remediation and more on academic success and excellence. The use of data, as with the Equity Scorecard (Bensimon, 2004; Bensimon, Polkington, Bauman, & Vallejo, 2004), and the development of new approaches to honors programs, gateway courses, and a focus on success in science, technology, engineering, and mathematics (STEM) fields have increased.

CLIMATE

Activists in the 1960s and 1970s understood that access and success was a function of institutional practices and environments. Sandler's term "chilly climate" (1983) became a central organizing concept to capture ways to describe institutions with respect to openness to race/ethnicity, sexual orientation, women's issues, and religion. The regular occurrence of hate crimes and racist, sexist, anti-semitic, anti-Muslim, and homophobic incidents even today keeps campuses responding and reacting as each event occurs.

The study of campus climate provides opportunities to reflect on the culture and values of a campus, how people are treated, and how they perceive the institution with respect to diversity (Hurtado, 1992; Rankin, 2003). Concerns about the climate for diverse groups of faculty and staff have also prompted studies of the climate in schools and departments, work with deans and department chairs, and staff development. Invariably, work on climate leads to additional programmatic and policy recommendations related to hiring, teaching and curriculum, admissions, town-gown relationships, and community health.

CURRICULUM

In the early work on diversity, the introduction of ethnic studies programs, ethnic centers for students, women's studies programs, and women's centers was central to strategies for adding a diversity element to the education and climate of the campus. Beginning through grassroots student and faculty activism, ethnic studies programs were developed to create locations for new scholarship and teaching and ultimately to challenge some of the core assumptions of the traditional curriculum (Hu-DeHart, 1995; McLaurin, 2001). At the same time, the development of women's studies programs introduced gender into the curriculum and into institutional practices. Although most colleges and universities claimed to be coeducational and included male and female students, new scholarship at that time tried to underscore the Eurocentric and male bias in the curriculum and scholarship. The absence of women in STEM fields and the limited access for women to many graduate programs were important topics, though implicitly, this was mostly about White women (Rosser, 1995). These efforts on ethnicity and gender were compensatory in nature, but at their core they were also trying to show how generic approaches to knowledge were not sufficient and how knowledge itself reflects existing power and social structures (see, e.g., Banks, 1997; Butler & Walter, 1991; Cortés, 2002; Darder, 1991; Espiritu, 1997; Greene, 2003; Hu-DeHart, 1994, 1995; Hull, Scott, & Smith, 1982; Hune, 2003; Minnich, 2005; Minnich, O'Barr,

& Rosenfeld, 1988; Nardi & Schneider, 1998; Perkins, 1983; Schmitz, Butler, Rosenfelt, & Guy-Sheftall, 1995; L. T. Smith, 1999; Winston, 1994).

Using the resources and scholarship developed through ethnic and women's studies programs and research, curriculum transformation became a huge effort in the 1970s and 1980s. Propelled by student activism and the efforts of a handful of faculty, especially faculty of color and White women, the goal was not only to develop pedagogy and knowledge appropriate for the increasing diversity of the student body, but also to critique the adequacy of knowledge that claimed to be generic. The theme of *invisibility* was important. Takaki (1993) asked, "What happens when historians leave out many of America's people?" (p. 16). Adrienne Rich (1986) captured the significance of invisibility: "But invisibility is a dangerous and painful condition, and lesbians are not the only people to know it. When those who have power to name and socially construct reality choose not to see you and hear you, whether you are dark-skinned, old, disabled, female, or speak with a different accent or dialect than others, when someone with the authority of a teacher, say, describes the world and you are not in it, there is a moment of psychic disequilibrium, as if you looked into a mirror and saw nothing" (p. 199).

Peggy McIntosh's curriculum-transformation scheme (1983) provided, and still provides, a heuristic tool for seeing the intellectual shifts that have occurred in many disciplines. While she initially used gender as the focus, the perspective of race quickly emerged. The model can be applied as well to any form of identity group, and also to the issues concerning intersections of groups. She uses history as an example of how curriculum has evolved. In this process, the first stage is history without regard to gender or race; it is the study of wars and kings. Social history, the history of people's lives and communities, is seen as peripheral.

The second stage focuses on history with exceptions. In this stage, history is still about wars and kings, but with an effort to find exemplars from absent groups—women and persons of color, for example. Here we might include Joan of Arc or find a lone African American general. The next stage involves studying why certain groups were not present, usually in terms of deficit characteristics. In this period, one attributes a group's absence to its characteristics—women's brains' being deficient for doing math and science, for example. One sees considerable research on why URM students are not successful, why women cannot do math, and why many diverse groups are not well represented in the disciplines or present in leadership positions. As ethnic studies and women's studies grew, they gave voice to a large body of literature focused not on comparing women to men, or Blacks to Whites, but on the study of groups in their own right. This period also gave rise to the early work on the intersections of race and gender, in particular.

This phase of research, which continues today, has allowed for the knowledge base that informs much of the current pedagogical, curricular, and scholarly work and that continues to push for the final stage in McIntosh's model—intellectual and curricular transformation for all.

By opening up fields of scholarship to new ways of understanding and thinking, many disciplines have changed. The study of race, class, gender, sexuality, and culture has transformed many fields. The field of history now legitimates social and educational history, which, if properly taught, includes many people from diverse backgrounds. It also makes the study of history connected to many aspects of society apart from war. The study of human development has been fundamentally transformed by the scholarship related to identity. Even the study of women in science has legitimized women's presence in science and points to the institutional and structural impediments to careers in science or to the advancement of persons of color and White women (Harding, 1986; Minnich, 2005; Rendón, 2005). As Minnich (2005) cautions, however, "to pluralize is to hold open the question of whom we really mean to include, and why. It is a beginning . . . .We cannot think better about all of us if we simply tack 'and women,' 'and disabled women,' 'and minorities,' 'and other people of color' onto the same old exclusive meanings" (p. 11).

Today, the change in the curriculum and an increasing body of scholarship related to diversity, especially in ethnic studies and women's studies, represent an important shift from forty years ago, when these topics were not even visible, let alone acceptable. A significant number of campuses now have diversity requirements (Humphreys, 1997) as core to the institution's educational mission. These requirements are most often located in the general education program. However, the lack of clarity and the laundry-list approach to diversity have left many—those who argue for the need to increase the cultural competence of all students—dissatisfied with the more generic or singular focus of many of these requirements. At the same time, many more disciplines have incorporated diversity to some extent into the core canon of the field. As the scholarship grows in breadth, depth, and complexity, many campuses are being challenged to do more to incorporate diversity into the curriculum and teaching at every level. Religion, race, gender, and class, to mention just a few identities, intersect in profoundly important ways and touch on societal issues that are pressing campuses to continue the intellectual transformation of the academy.

Although there remain tensions and questions about the legitimacy of scholarship on groups from diverse perspectives, there is no doubt that such work is closer to the center than the margin. That said, considerable concern exists as to whether these fields have had to abandon some of their critique of higher education in order to become more legitimate (Boxer, 2001; Rojas, 2007). For example, while ethnic studies and women's studies built in a link between praxis and theory as part of the development of the field, some would argue that in an effort to be more acceptable, they have had to develop a more scholarly orientation with fewer links to praxis (Soldatenko, 2001). To the degree that this is true, there is a certain irony, because at the same time we see exponential growth in the fields of community studies and service learning, in order to provide greater links between student learning and praxis off and on campus. Questions of pedagogy and engaged learning have also been informed by efforts to link academic work with its applications. Such efforts relate not only to service-learning initiatives, but also to problem-based learning, from engineering to medical education.

Most of the effort regarding academic change has focused on the faculty. As a result, faculty development has been a central part of diversity work. Indeed, there has been an increase in the number and percentage of faculty involved in curricular transformation (Morey & Kitano, 1997; Musil, García, Moses, & Smith, 1995; Musil et al., 1999). Thousands of faculty across the country have been involved in some level of curriculum-transformation work. Where they have been most successful, the approach has been linked to the academic mission of the institution, excellence in education, and building faculty capacity. They have been less successful where curriculum change seems to be a superficial effort to transform the appearance of the syllabus rather than engage the substantive perspectives that diversity raises for scholarship and pedagogy. A significant part of current diversity initiatives across the country continue to engage faculty in the scholarship related to diversity and to curriculum transformation. The aspects of diversity brought into these efforts are quite broad, because educating all students for a pluralistic society must inevitably be inclusive, and constantly developing.

The educational focus of diversity and the concerns about student success have also raised important questions about pedagogy. Many campuses have approached the topic of teaching and learning through the lens of learning styles. While this approach runs the risk of incorporating stereotyped ways of characterizing groups that do not reflect individual and group variation, it has opened the door to the consideration of variations in how individuals learn and how to incorporate those approaches for the benefit of all students (Lawry, Laurison, & Van Antwerpen, 2006; Tusmith & Reddy, 2002). The growing areas of service learning, learning communities, problem-based learning, and civic engagement are often not at all related to diversity but in fact have significant implications for classroom interactions, learning, and success. In addition, as diversity has increased and some of the issues related to diversity have grown more contentious, building capacity to use conflict to facilitate learning has emerged as increasingly important (Palmer, 2002).

INSTITUTIONAL-LEVEL CHANGE

Whatever the diversity issue, recommendations and challenges for change invariably require institutional changes (Martin, 2000; National Science Foundation Advance Project, 2002). In part as a result of legal challenges, but also because of the need to defend diversity as an important institutional imperative, more and more campuses have been placing diversity at the institutional level, beyond climate and beyond the curriculum. Diversity is discussed to some degree in terms of institutional mission statements, strategic-planning documents, and the need to try to build diversity in leadership. Faculty diversity, especially in ethnicity and gender, has been the object of numerous efforts on campuses all across the country in the past forty years. Rhetorical statements about the need for diversity throughout the leadership of the campus are common.

As a result of national conversations about the future of democracy and the changing demographics in society, even boards of trustees have begun to ask questions about how the institution is building its capacity and in what ways it is successful with respect to diversity. Most often, these conversations at the institutional level remain focused on undergraduates, undergraduate education, and undergraduate success. Recently, as a result of the growing numbers of programs and approaches, campuses have begun to appoint a chief diversity officer (CDO) whose task, in part, is to advise senior leadership and help coordinate efforts. The increasing number of people in this role is reflected in the development of a CDO national organization, an annual conference, and a journal, the *Journal of Diversity in Higher Education.*

We have some detailed information about what campus strategies have involved during the six-year period from 2000 to 2005 because of the Campus Diversity Initiative (CDI), funded by the James Irvine Foundation in California. This $29 million effort was designed to assist twenty-eight independent colleges and universities in California in strategically improving campus diversity, with the aim of increasing the access and success of low-income and URM students in higher education.

An important part of the initiative was to build in a strong evaluation component to help each institution focus its strategies and track progress. A team of researchers from around the country under the auspices of Claremont Graduate University and the Association of American Colleges and Universities, led by principal researchers Alma Clayton-Pedersen, Sharon Parker, and myself, worked with the campuses to build their capacity to measure success, to make corrections, and ultimately to broaden and sustain their efforts beyond the scope of grant-funded projects. Another purpose of the evaluation was to contribute to the field. There will be references throughout this book describing the results of the evaluation and the research that emerged.

One element of this work was to look at what strategies the campuses were employing. While the strategies developed were all located in the particular context of the mission, resources, size, and selectivity of the campus, there was considerable overlap. Virtually all the campuses with undergraduate programs used resources to increase access, and more than half focused on success. Three-fourths allocated funds to support faculty development in curriculum, teaching, and research, and more than half of the campuses focused on increasing faculty diversity. These efforts mirrored many of the efforts that have been developing nationwide over the past forty years (Clayton-Pedersen, Parker, Smith, Moreno, & Teraguchi, 2007; Parker, 2007; D. G. Smith, 2004).

EMERGING ISSUES

The early discussions of diversity began with issues of access and developed into discussions about student success, campus climate, curriculum, scholarly research, and institutional domains such as hiring. This way of framing diversity, however, was often reactive, focused on responding to events and being implemented primarily to serve specific populations. Diversity was not necessarily embraced as central to institutional functioning and the building of an inclusive institutional culture.

Today, we have a large (and growing) number of efforts and programs, focused on engaging the many groups and issues that have emerged. The list of identities that fall under the diversity umbrella has grown longer, in part as a function of historic concerns about rights and the growing identity movements in the United States that include issues of race/ethnicity, gender, religion, sexual identity, class, nationality, multiracial and biracial identities, differential abilities, mental health, age, weight, and so on. In part, the growth in the list of salient identities is a function of the very dynamic context in which the diversity discussions on campus take place.

Race, ethnicity, class, and gender remain central; indeed, many of the historic issues pertaining to these identities are still the core of diversity efforts. As will be clear in chapter 4, however, these issues are both the same as and quite different from the discussions of forty years ago. The understanding of class has moved beyond income to include cultural norms and values. Moreover, the intersections of race, class, and gender have grown in importance (Borrego, 2004; Frable, 1997; Langhout, Rosselli, & Feinstein, 2006; Sleeter & Grant, 1988; Teranishi, Ceja, Antonio, Allen, & McDonough, 2004; Zandy, 1996, 2001). After September 11, campuses became acutely aware of the issues regarding campus climate for Muslim students and questioned whether the standard curricular offerings dealt thoroughly enough with Islam and the role of religion in contemporary society. Furthermore, there are a number of groups that are clearly underrepresented on campuses, such as Hmong students and others from Southeast Asia (Chang, Park, Lin, Poon, & Nakanishi, 2007).

The increase in immigration and the concern about undocumented immigrant students have drawn more attention to immigrant students than one might have predicted forty years ago (Douglass, Roebken, & Thomson, 2007; Perez, 2009). Increased globalization has brought international issues to a higher priority as well. Also, while domestic discussions of diversity were clearly distinguished from international concerns forty years ago, that boundary is much more porous as a result of immigration. Today, domestic Latino students identify not just with Puerto Rican, Chicano, Hispanic, and Cuban roots, but also with Central America, South America, and specific nationalities within those regions. Similarly, as Asian American communities have grown, they have shown a greater desire to make distinctions among the vastly different nationalities and ethnicities captured under that large category. Korean Americans, Filipinos, Japanese Americans, and Hmong have different narrative histories, different locations and experiences within higher education, and different ways of engaging in the diversity conversation (Oliver and Shapiro, 2001).

As diversity has increased, especially among students, the rationale for diversity has begun to include its educational benefits. At the same time, concerns have emerged as to whether students are engaging one another deeply and often. It is unfortunate that on too many campuses, the problem is framed as self-segregation, primarily concerning students of color. This way of describing the problem prompted a wonderful book by Tatum, *Why Are All the Black Kids Sitting Together?* (1997), in which she summarizes the social, political, and psychological issues concerning patterns in which identity groups in a minority seek each other out. As we shall see in chapters 6 and 7, identifying self-segregation as a problem is itself problematic. It ignores the history of self-segregation among Whites and the continuing evidence that it is White students who have less contact with students of color, instead of the reverse. Self-segregation among White fraternities and sororities has existed since the founding of higher education, yet intergroup efforts today are too often framed as a concern about ethnic groups that stick together (Tatum, 1997). This formulation also assumes that the issue is with the students and not with the environment in the institution. And it focuses on undergraduates, as if there were no intergroup concerns between and within faculty and staff groups.

Some of these topics have been with us for decades, and others are newly emerging. In addition, as reviewed in chapter 2, our conceptual understandings of identity, once thought of as static and monodimensional, have expanded to recognize that identity is multidimensional and changing. Understandings of sexual identity, for example, now reflect the growth in discussions about transgendered persons and the increasing experience with diversity within the "traditional" discussion about sexual orientation. Indeed, the literature on sexuality shows the inadequacy of one of our last remaining dichotomies—the binary of male and female. Further, the increased visibility of multiracial students on campus and the census's introduction of multiple racial identities have more adequately captured the multiplicity of identity with respect to race and ethnicity and have served to add complexity to identity. Thus, the reality of the multiplicity and intersectionality of identities has emerged as important and inevitable (Collins, 1990; Omi, 2001; Wijeyesinghe & Jackson, 2001).

As a result, and to complicate matters further, it has become clear that many of our current category systems have to be questioned. Conventions that have proved functional for researchers and policy makers that aggregate groups have to be studied to see whether an aggregation still works. While many scholars in higher education, including myself, still find utility in referring to underrepresented minorities (URM) with respect to the *historic* underrepresentation of African Americans, Latinos, and American Indians, the data suggest that the experiences and trajectories of each group can be quite different and that aggregating data may mask important changes within them. The categories of Asian American, Latino, and even African American and American Indian have been and remain very useful, but there is a growing need to disaggregate data so as to differentiate the vastly different experiences for specific subgroups.

Dimensions of Diversity: Reframing the Focus

Institutional policy makers, then, are being faced with a great deal of diversity and with continually expanding notions of diversity. As a result, the number of potential programs and initiatives continues to grow. Diversity task forces around the country engage in uncomfortable discussions about the tension between being focused and being inclusive. "Plethorophobia," the fear of too many, seems to take over. I have seen many committed leaders throw up their hands in frustration with the implicit plea, "When will it stop?" At the same time, imagining a choice between picking the few identities that matter and defining diversity as a laundry list is not very satisfactory in most campus contexts. Conceptually, however, this is where most campuses seem to be.

To put in perspective the growing complexity in identities and diversity, it might help to think for a minute about the current growth in academic disciplines, fields, interdisciplines, subdisciplines, and, transdisciplines. While they may present administrative challenges, they are also seen as reflecting the cutting edge of knowledge and the intellectual vitality of the twenty-first-century academy. Similarly, higher education is being forced, mostly through the increasing diversity of individuals on campus, to engage issues of diversity in ways that reflect its complexity and significance. Moreover, as we have seen with technology, moving through this complex interplay of issues holds the promise of change that will ultimately benefit the institution. But the key strategy here, conceptually and in terms of excellence, is to use these changes and pressures to rethink the institution, its capacity, and its core functions in order to serve the purposes of the campus and higher education.

Thus, rather than engaging diversity as a list of identities or creating a uniform set of policies and practices, framing diversity in terms of how the institution's mission and goals can be improved through the lens of different groups or issues provides an opportunity for both inclusiveness and differentiation. For example, concerns in faculty hiring most often relate to race/ethnicity, gender (in particular fields), and the intersection of race and gender. In contrast, issues of sexual orientation more often relate to climate or to institutional policies for domestic partners than to admissions or hiring. Ability concerns can center on access, accommodation, climate, or scholarly work. Religious identity can develop as part of a curriculum conversation or because of an incident involving campus climate. Religion, especially in today's geopolitical environment and following 9/11, raises concerns about the campus's capacity to provide robust teaching and scholarship of non-Western religions and their role. By encouraging a differentiated look at the variety of identities, a campus is in a better position to engage diversity pluralistically and with greater equity and inclusiveness.

The framework presented here has emerged from diversity's historical roots and from current issues that have emerged on campus, but it shifts the focus from groups to the institution. The framework incorporates four dimensions. While these have changed over time and might well be described differently, as others have done (e.g., Bensimon, 2004; Hubbard, 1998; Hurtado, Milem, Clayton-Ped-

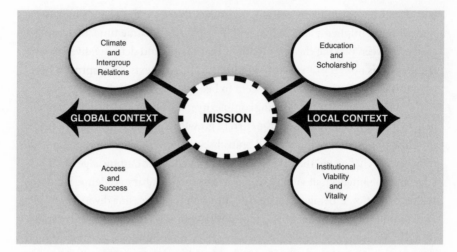

Figure 3.1. A framework for diversity

ersen, & Allen, 1998; Williams, Berger, & McClendon, 2005), they have been useful for capturing the work of diversity on campus and for helping to provide a
structure by which a campus can describe and evaluate its efforts. This framework
both engages the entire spectrum of identities and differentiates the concerns related to each. The four dimensions are access and success of underrepresented student populations, campus climate and intergroup relations, education and scholarship, and institutional viability and vitality (fig. 3.1). Together, the dimensions
provide a way of understanding what *institutional capacity for diversity* might mean
and what it might look like.

Because the history of diversity work on campuses began with a focus on access and success, beginning with that dimension—the heart and soul of much of
diversity work—would run the risk of continuing to avoid the centrality of diversity as an institutional imperative. On most campuses, access and success is
where diversity discussions start and remain. Fortunately, much of the research
available suggests that the institutional and group perspectives are not in conflict. More data on this will be presented in later chapters. But in order to make
sure that in this framework diversity is centrally identified with the institution, I
begin with the institutional dimension.

INSTITUTIONAL VIABILITY AND VITALITY

The dimension of institutional viability and vitality focuses on certain key domains that build the institution's capacity and structures for diversity. Building

capacity means developing the human and institutional resources and expertise to fulfill the institution's mission internally as well as to fulfill its mission for society. Earlier in this chapter, we talked about what it meant to have capacity for technology. Similarly, we can ask whether the institution has the people, resources, and expertise to fulfill its mission as it relates to diversity. While the tendency in the past has been to frame this dimension in terms of serving particular populations, my emphasis here is on the institution and how it fulfills its mission. In that respect, how well diverse populations thrive and succeed is important in part because it serves as the "miner's canary," providing an indication of the institution's health (Guinier & Torres, 2002).

Mission. Aligning diversity strongly with the institution's mission is a cornerstone of much of the research being done. While student success and the factors that influence it are part of the diversity agenda at virtually all types of institutions of higher education, the core work of campuses varies by their mission. The mission can be a function of institutional type, but it can also be a function of location and history. In any case, mission matters.

For a research university, diversity will remain marginal unless it is central to the core research and scholarly mission. Yet highly selective research institutions often find their diversity debates centering on admissions criteria. In public institutions, in particular, legal challenges have inevitably placed undergraduate admissions under scrutiny (Douglass, 2007). Nevertheless, while admissions is important from a student point of view as well as from the institutional point of view, the mission of highly selective research universities is much more about scholarship, research, and impact on society at large.

To be sure, one key role of these institutions has been to grant an elite stamp to graduates who go on to serve in many leadership positions in society. But another central role is to produce knowledge and scholarly advances for society. Identifying and understanding the relationship of diversity to these advances is important to whether diversity will be positioned as marginal or central. In other areas, numerous examples of institutional change, faculty hiring, curricular innovation, and even fund-raising have emerged in research universities that desire to engage cutting-edge research and policy. For example, developing a nanotechnology initiative results in new hiring, new building construction, industry partnerships, and huge investments, because it puts an institution at the forefront of science. In contrast, if the focus of diversity is on undergraduate admissions and general education, diversity will not be seen as core to what the institution deems important and thus not deserving of extensive attention and resources.

For community colleges, building institutional capacity to focus resources and attention on student success and career pathways is urgent, and it is central to their historic mission. That mission is about access, expressed through educational programs and connections with employers to help students develop skills and competencies in a wide variety of fields. A community college might also focus on serving local communities in a variety of ways. It would be appropriate in such a context to ask whether the institution has the necessary faculty and staff expertise to facilitate student success. For example, if students arrive with developmental needs in math, does the campus have the expertise to successfully educate those students to fulfill basic math requirements and to go on in fields that might require math?

For community colleges today, the concern about student success and the pathway to a four-year college is becoming urgent because so many students, particularly from poor or URM backgrounds, begin college there. Recent research on developmental education and the failure of students to successfully complete developmental education courses, especially in math, points to the need to interrupt patterns of failure with effective instruction (Clery & Solórzano, 2006; Dowd, 2007; Merrow, 2007).

What about an elite land-grant university? Such campuses also have a mission to serve state or regional needs, including serving communities. However, this mission is enacted not only through educating students, but often also through applied and basic research designed to address pressing needs of the state. Health care, urban planning, education, agriculture, and regional partnerships might all be central to the mission and receive high priority in fund-raising, grants, budget allocations, and strategic priority setting. The degree to which diversity is understood to be related to such topics will be significant for building institutional capacity.

In most states, comprehensive public institutions have a role in educating the citizens of the state. They are often seen as economic "engines" as well, because of the kind of education provided to graduates who go into the community. Increasingly, comprehensive institutions are playing other roles as well, such as developing an adequate teaching force for the state, contributing to policy and research, and serving local communities. Diversity might become an economic issue for the campus to the degree that tuition costs are related to access across all economic groups. Diversity might also become a political issue, as it has in some states, when policy makers note with alarm the glaring racial and ethnic achievement gaps among students.

Among the more than four thousand colleges in the United States are many small private institutions with a wide range of missions and selectivity. The liberal arts colleges often place their emphasis on the broadening of students' perspectives and preparation for leadership in a diverse society. In addition, an increasing cadre of for-profit institutions have emerged whose primary mission is providing specific and often applied educations to students. For many of these tuition-driven institutions, diversity is closely linked to institutional viability and survival. As the society becomes more diverse, the need to attract and keep students from diverse backgrounds in order for the institution to survive can place diversity conversations at the center.

While the descriptions provided here suggest distinct missions for each of these categories, the boundaries and distinctions among institutional types—as with identity and academic fields—are becoming less clear. What matters, however, is the ways in which a particular campus or system understands the relationship of diversity in its own context. Discussions of diversity from one campus to another too often look alike and undifferentiated. The discussions are often on tracks quite disparate from those of the strategic issues that really matter to the institution. A serious and deep look at the mission facilitates the process of embedding diversity more centrally and examining what it will take to develop the capacity to succeed strategically. A useful exercise is to look at core institutional documents—strategic plans, capital-campaign documents, accreditation self-studies, and so on—and ask whether and how diversity is engaged as a central element that grows out of the particular campus and the particular institutional type.

Culture. Culture and mission are related, but not the same. There is increasing work in the higher education literature on the important role that culture plays in an institution—in how the institution is perceived, its style, who is attracted to it, and who succeeds in it. Leadership and change can be dramatically affected by institutional culture (Aleman & Salkever, 2003; Crutcher, 2006; Kezar & Eckel, 2002a, 2005). This is especially true in relation to diversity. Roberto Ibarra (2003) draws attention to the embedded ways in which the culture of academe has developed from ethnic roots: "The cultures of our colleges and universities are permeated by cultural contexts forged from different academic roots. . . . While the ethnic markers disappeared long ago, the cultural contexts in higher education, such as preferences for individualized learning, as well as many gender preferences, have not. They have been incorporated into all academic disciplines" (p. 207).

Culture takes longer to change than climate, and it must be framed so that diversity can be facilitated rather than obstructed. Diversifying people in an institution can lead to greater turnover if the culture of the institution or the unit does not serve to validate and support them. The challenge, institutionally, is to scrutinize the culture so as to understand what is core and should not be changed and what must be changed in order to ensure that people from diverse backgrounds can thrive.

In many cases, campuses are not aware of the ways in which campus culture is transmitted. Cultures that have developed from particular customs, traditions, and values can create a sense of belonging and comfort for some but a sense of alienation and "otherness" for others (Johnsrud & Sadao, 1998). Padilla (2004), in thinking about the richness of Latino culture and what it offers, describes a form of alienation and also the loss to the institution resulting from the fact that most predominantly White institutions utilize an Anglo way of knowing—*saber*—that focuses on formal learning, measurement, and objectivity. He notes another potentially important form of knowing that is expressed in Spanish: *conocer* (if I understand it correctly) emerges from relationships and experience. Emphasizing multiple ways of knowing and learning is certainly at the forefront of efforts to develop service learning, problem-based learning, and other pedagogies that recognize and validate the integration of experience with learning.

Because disciplines and culture are intertwined, one can see how diversity might be perceived as a threat to the integrity of a discipline. The fact is that in different academic disciplines, certain methodologies are valued, certain ways of doing things are accepted, and certain ways of framing issues are expected. These elements become codified in a culture with norms and values that can limit the openness to new ideas and people but can also be seen as central to the excellence of the field. At that point, diversity is seen as threatening accepted notions of excellence, not just culture. Thus, conversations about diversity in science have to at some point address the core aspects of science. If science is seen as a largely White and male culture, it will not be open. It is important to sort out what in science has come to reflect maleness and what in science reflects good science. The maleness culture presumably can be changed; good science should not. Perceptions that science is isolating, separate from real-world topics, and linear have been recently challenged for these reasons. Because many of these elements of bias in culture are hidden and not explicit, the conversation about culture is often difficult, especially for those immersed in it (Jones & Young, 1997; Margolis, 2001; Margolis & Fisher, 2002).

Human Capital. Another key element in building capacity for diversity is whether the campus has the human capital—the expertise—to engage diversity. Diversity in the staff, administration, faculty, and leadership is critical here, as is the competence of people to engage diversity (Benjamin, 1997; García, 2000; Lindsay, 2001; Moses, 1997; Sagaria, 2002; Santiago, 1996; Turner, 2007). The rationale for diversifying a campus needs to be made explicit. Often, the assumption is made that the reason for diversifying is that the student body is diversifying. As will be clear in chapter 5, most campuses in the United States have too much homogeneity in decision-making to build human capacity—something that puts decision-making, perceptions of commitment, and credibility at risk.

There are, in my experience, seven important reasons for creating a more diverse community at every level.

1. Successful diversity in people represents one of the critical indicators of institutional equity and true inclusion. The absence of diversity can send powerful messages. It doesn't take long to look around an institution and see whether diversity is valued. If only White men are hired, it is reasonable to conclude that the institution does not seriously want anyone else to apply. One of the reasons that every hiring decision today is under such scrutiny for diversity is that diversity in leadership is so lacking that every new appointment is seen as one that matters.

2. Given the salience of many identities in the society and on campus, the absence of diversity puts the validity of decision-making at risk. It is not that identities each carry a prototype set of experiences, but in our society there are many perspectives held by diverse people that will enrich and inform decisions and policies.

3. People from different backgrounds bring with them different networks, connections, and associations with communities. Although communities can overlap, and people express their identities in many different ways, identity tends to bring with it networks of people. These networks can increase the campus's social and cultural capital.

4. Diversity in the community and especially in decision-making locations will increase the community's trust in the institution's decision-making.

5. True diversity in the institution is likely to increase the attractiveness of the campus to more diverse populations and decrease the negative impact of tokenism. In addition, Cameron (2005) poses the question of whether people are thriving; that is, do they experience "vitality, positive momentum, and learning" (p. 321)?

6. Diversity in all constituencies promotes the development of future leadership. Developing leadership among diverse communities is important, and one of the most effective ways to do this is to provide opportunities for people to get experience and to be successful throughout their career.

7. Diversity in leadership provides role models not only for those from a particular group, but for all. The absence of any diversity, especially, sends signals about lack of possibilities and lack of recognition and appreciation of talent in people from diverse backgrounds. The presence of diversity, on the other hand, creates a concrete sense of possibility.

Imagine that a campus president put together a senior cabinet composed entirely of physicists. There would no doubt be fear and outrage on the campus, as many constituencies would assume that the perspectives brought to decision-making would be narrow. Even if this group of physicists were broadly educated and aware of the need to take into account other perspectives, trust and credibility would become issues that would have to be engaged. Ironically, it would require more effort for this group of physicists to be conscious of what is not being said, of what perspectives are not being considered, than if there were diversity at the table. And in the end, there is no way that a group of physicists could become as deeply familiar with the concerns of the social scientists, the humanists, and those in professional fields as people from those fields.

Human capital in leadership is not simply a function of diversity in composition. It is also a function of competence and commitment among all groups. Indeed, without sufficient support and competence throughout the institution, leaders who are themselves tokens may find it difficult to succeed. While change in higher education is not accomplished through hierarchical mandates, there is often an expectation that a single leader, especially one who represents diversity, can generate great change.

Increasingly, not only in the higher education literature but in studies of organizations more generally, there is a recognition that leaders exist in a complex web in their institutions, that "followership" matters, and that success is a matter of building connections and capacity (Bligh, Pillai, & Uhl-Bien, 2007; Gilmore, 1997; Lipman-Blumen, 1998; Weick & Sutcliffe, 2001). Without knowledgeable and committed leadership at all levels, institutional change will flounder. I emphasize that I do not mean senior leadership alone (presidents, provosts, and deans). Leadership is important among faculty, in departments, in student affairs, among staff, and among students. Boards of trustees and community leaders play important roles as well. The critical capacity needed is the capacity to build synergies among the many efforts that most campuses are undertaking with respect to diversity.

While the literature on diversity frequently discusses leadership and its importance, the institutional record with regard to staff persons should also be considered. On many campuses, the only real racial and ethnic diversity is among lower-level, less well paid staff. An institution's commitment to diversity might well be understood according to how staff at these levels feel about the institution, the opportunities it offers for professional advancement, and whether staff concerns are considered seriously. Neglect of staff and their concerns also occurs in the research literature on diversity. But an institution's commitment to developing human capacity and the degree to which it engages staff are important elements for the institution's viability and vitality. Moreover, there are many stories about how staff members provide advice, support, and encouragement for underrepresented and first-generation students on a campus. This mostly invisible role needs to be strongly acknowledged.

Core Institutional Processes. A central element of institutional viability and vitality is whether diversity is a core part of regular institutional processes and plans. One good way to see where diversity stands is to take a look at strategic plans, ongoing reports to a board, accreditation documents, and proposals and see whether and where diversity is engaged.

An example of the significance of core processes and the degree to which key diversity constituents pay attention to them might illuminate this point. I was asked to work with an institution that was attempting to develop a proposal to a foundation regarding diversity. As is typical, a group of excellent people were brainstorming the kinds of diversity-related programs and initiatives they might undertake. I asked if I might see the strategic plan and talk to the president to understand more fully the status of diversity on the campus. When I read the plan that was about to be presented to the board of trustees for approval, I was struck to see that the only mention of diversity was related to the need for additional financial aid funds. I also had the opportunity to read the opening convocation address that the president had given. In it, diversity was central; it was invoked with passion and described as an imperative for the institution and the region. I met with the president and pointed out that if I were a person committed to diversity on the campus, I might be quite frustrated, even angry. His speech would have inspired me and affirmed my continued involvement, but the absence of any real engagement with diversity in the strategic plan would have prompted me to think that the commitment to diversity was more rhetorical than real. The president, who I believe was truly committed to diversity, was surprised by my observations but then sheepishly pointed out that he was scheduled to meet with an angry group of faculty the next day about the absence of diversity in the campus's strategic plan. Alignment of rhetoric, activities, and institutional goals is important in this dimension.

Perceptions of Institutional Commitment. One of the themes that emerge from research and from experiences on campus is that the morale of people, especially those in the minority on campus, is connected to perceptions of an institution's commitment to diversity and equity. Those perceptions have thus emerged as a significant predictor of satisfaction and success among students and faculty, and in the long run, they will probably be linked to alumni support and fund-raising. Work on organizational justice highlights the importance of perceptions about fairness, whether in terms of overall views of the institution or in specific domains such as allocation of resources, procedures, and interpersonal treatment (Greenberg & Colquitt, 2005; Mowday & Colwell, 2003). The issue of trust can also be an important mediating variable in considering how people feel about the institution and its fairness (Colquitt, Greenberg, & Scott, 2005). While we know less than we need to about what fosters these perceptions, it is partly related to diversity in hiring, how people from diverse groups are treated, the degree to which diversity is embedded in each of the dimensions we are discussing, and whether people feel the institution works at improving the climate for diversity.

The presence, absence, or role of diversity in all these elements—an institution's mission, culture, human capital, core processes, and perceived commitment—conveys a great deal about whether an institution has the capacity to engage fully in diversity efforts and whether these efforts are central or marginal. In our increasingly diverse society, an institution that relies on students for its existence will need to be diverse if it is to maintain its viability and vitality. But undergraduate student diversity, so often the focus of diversity conversations at the institutional level, is only one element for institutions with important research, policy, and community roles. In today's environment, a perception of commitment to diversity will, like a commitment to technology, increase an institution's vitality and attractiveness.

EDUCATION AND SCHOLARSHIP

The education and scholarship dimension focuses on the academic core of the institution. Questions about the research and teaching functions of the campus, in the context of the educational mission, frame this domain. Does the campus have the resources to give all students the experience of being educated to function effectively in a diverse society? What should that education look like in terms of curriculum, pedagogy, faculty expertise, and so on? In addition, for many campuses for which research and graduate education are central, this dimension brings attention to the production of new knowledge that addresses the intellectual and applied issues of the day. Is a land-grant institution that cares about health care studying the ways in which race, ethnicity, class, and gender influence access to health care and patterns of disease and health? What is the role of the campus in influencing educational reform, the production of teachers prepared to engage diversity in schools, the textbooks and knowledge being taught? How does a major research university position itself with respect to graduate and professional education, and how does it see its academic role with respect to diversity?

Framing the diversity imperative in academic and educational terms is critically important for the engagement of faculty and for moving diversity conversations to the center of institutional concerns. Indeed, supporting and encouraging opportunities for faculty to engage diversity deeply through their own scholarship and/or teaching has been very successful in getting faculty to be involved—leading curriculum-transformation efforts, undertaking new scholarly initiatives, and transforming the hiring process for faculty.

As described earlier, the development of ethnic studies programs and women's studies programs decades ago began primarily because of a need to engage what was missing in the curriculum and the scholarship of many fields. Without these developments, much of the exciting knowledge that informs the disciplines today would still be missing. While students and a small group of faculty led the movement for change, the issue of the adequacy of knowledge was at the core of this effort. This imperative for knowledge development continues and grows with respect to race, gender, sexual orientation, class, ability issues, age, ethnicity, and their intersections. In each area, there are new developments that not only inform the particulars for any given identity but also provide alternative ways of approaching traditional areas.

For example, the study of sexual orientation and sexual identity has informed our understanding of gender and heterosexuality (see, e.g., Preves, 2005). The study of ethnic and gender identity development has moved the work in identity forward from Erikson's early formulations (1997). As Fox, Lowe, and McClellan (2005) suggest, "The study of indigenous epistemologies, cultural traditions, and social structures also provides a richer array of options through which everyone can seek to understand and address the problems and opportunities that challenge them in the broad scope of their work and lives" (p. 3). International perspectives are important here as well; global work is often recommended because bringing in international perspectives not only educates about these perspectives, but also brings greater clarity to an understanding of the United States. In much the same way, the study of specific identities sheds light on other aspects of human development.

Thus, in this dimension we are asking about the educational experiences of all students and the scholarly focus of the institution. We ask about the adequacy of what is being taught. This is not for the benefit of a few, but for all students and for the advancement of knowledge itself. The advancement of knowledge needs to be the central concern for major fields, for graduate and professional education, and for faculty as well. Preparing doctoral students to be future faculty who are adequately educated in cutting-edge scholarship is critically important for their careers, but also for the institutions they will serve. Preparing students to be teachers, researchers, lawyers, and doctors who can function in competent ways for their professions requires engagement of diversity. Campuses throughout the country have had to initiate substantive professional-development opportunities in order to bring new perspectives to what the faculty teach and how they teach it. Addressing such competencies at the graduate level and underscoring their centrality to the discipline could limit the need for such remedial efforts in faculty development when graduate students become faculty.

While diversifying the faculty and the leadership will continue to be necessary, as will diversifying at every institutional level and constituency, the work of engaging all faculty and building the capacity of all faculty to address the pedagogical, curricular, and scholarly work of diversity is also critical. Indeed, it has become clear that curriculum transformation and building faculty capacity have been among the most successful efforts on diversity across the country. In part, this is because, as with technology, faculty are often excited when given the opportunity to engage the education and scholarship of diversity in their own fields (Musil, García, Moses, & Smith, 1995; Musil et al., 1999). Mini-grant and regranting programs have been reliably successful in engaging faculty.

The growing work on helping faculty facilitate the difficult dialogues that need to occur in classrooms will become more central as the complexity and breadth of diversity expand. Designing learning environments that make use of multiple ways of knowing and teaching will also help to increase student success and satisfaction and expand the kinds of fields in which students can succeed (Clayton-Pedersen, Parker, Smith, Moreno, & Teraguchi, 2007).

Where does science fit in this dimension? It is easy to imagine that science, broadly conceived, does not relate to the education and scholarship dimension of diversity at all, and indeed many scientists believe that. It is clear, however, that race, ethnicity, gender, and sexual orientation are increasingly salient for fields such as biology, genetics, and organic chemistry, and in many cases they challenge earlier assumptions in the field. Even in engineering, as a result of women engineers, there are new areas of bio-engineering where osteoporosis is being studied through a structural lens rather than a biochemical one. Researchers are trying to understand how racism impacts health. However, in fields such as physics and mathematics—except for the study of ethnomathematics and studies of history—diversity content might be less relevant (though there are many who maintain that the culture of fields such as math and physics affects the questions asked and the methodologies employed; see, e.g., Peat, 2002; Rosser, 1995; and Tonso, 2001).

But there are four very important ways in which diversity is relevant to science.

First, there is a growing concern about the diversity—and the domestic diversity—of people who become physical scientists, mathematicians, and so on. In many fields in science and mathematics, the number of U.S. citizens with a PhD has been declining over the past decade. A second central issue in the education of present and future generations of scientists is the development of engaging pedagogies that facilitate student success.

A third concern is creating a climate that invites students from diverse backgrounds to consider science as a field of study. A small but important body of research describes the culture and climate of science as fundamentally hostile, or at least nonwelcoming, for diversity (Ceci & Williams, 2007; Chubin & Malcolm, 2006; Moses & Cobb, 2001; Rosser, 1995; Seymour & Hewitt, 1997). Climate has implications not only for how open to diverse students the field seems, but also for the field's openness to differing perspectives for solving problems. Thus, while there has been substantial controversy about whether the diversity of the people sitting around the table informs the context and methods of science, there is sufficient anecdotal evidence to suggest a fourth role for diversity in science. The openness of science to diverse people and the cultures that are developed among them will affect the legitimacy, contributions, perspectives, and priorities of science.

CLIMATE AND INTERGROUP RELATIONS

The study of effective institutions often includes studies of individuals' perceptions about their institution. Is it inclusive? Is it welcoming? Is it fair in its treatment of people? There is a significant body of literature in organizational theory and social psychology, and to a lesser degree in higher education, concerning the impact of climate on morale, satisfaction, and effectiveness. The climate and intergroup-relations dimension focuses on the campus climate for students, faculty, and staff and the degree to which people are indeed interacting across diverse groups. This dimension includes looking at the institution through a variety of perspectives, including not only those of race and ethnicity for URM students, faculty, and staff, but the perspectives of all persons of color, women students, LGBT communities, religious minorities, and all other identity groups (McDonough, 2002; Rankin, 2003; Teranishi, 2002; Tierney, 1997).

As campuses have become more diverse, it has become increasingly clear that intergroup relations need to be addressed. While intergroup relations could be included in the education and scholarship dimension (because of their relevance to classroom discussions and faculty capacity), they are included here as a broader institutional concern. Work on intergroup relations these days most often addresses the amount and quality of interactions among students from different backgrounds based on race, ethnicity, gender, sexual orientation, or religion. However, campuses interested in building capacity for diversity should also attend to the quality and level of interactions among faculty and staff, and between faculty and staff as well. All these kinds of interactions have been concerns for a long time. As with so many aspects of diversity work, looking at intergroup relations doesn't cause problems; it just uncovers existing patterns and calls for their resolution.

With increasing demographic diversity, some campuses are beginning to build capacity to encourage dialogue among groups. There is an unfortunate tendency to frame some of the need for intergroup efforts in terms of the "self-segregation" of students of color; the issue of how best to achieve difficult dialogues without sacrificing the benefits of identity is less clearly understood on most campuses. As with other work on diversity, many of these intergroup efforts focus attention on undergraduates, rather than all constituencies. As we will see in chapter 6, there is a great deal that can be done that does not pit the significant role of identity or identities against intergroup dialogue.

In addition, campuses have begun to see that building a sense of community and truly educating students require the ability to engage in difficult dialogues that can range from discussions among racial groups to heated debates concerning the Middle East, religion, racism, and tensions over campus incidents. The topic of intergroup relations is a growing focus for twenty-first-century diversity efforts, as evidenced by a recent Ford Foundation initiative appropriately called Difficult Dialogues. In the foundation's call for proposals, a group of college and university presidents, along with the foundation's president, described the significance of the issue: "Colleges and Universities are on the front line in weaving together this unprecedented diversity of faiths, races/ethnicities, and cultures into a new American social fabric. . . . Diversity is simply a fact of our local and global world, but pluralism requires engaging that diversity with study, debate, and dialogue; and this constitutes a new intellectual challenge for colleges and universities" (Ford Foundation, 2005a).

A sense of urgency is emerging about the need to build the capacity of all members of the wider campus community to engage in difficult conversations. Succeeding in this effort will have an impact on the capacity of the campus to engage diversity both internally and outside in the community. While many campuses will start their diversity efforts by focusing on the dimension of campus climate, it is but one entry point into diversity; it is deeply connected to each of the other dimensions and cannot be understood apart from them.

ACCESS AND SUCCESS OF HISTORICALLY
UNDERREPRESENTED STUDENTS

The last of the four dimensions, access and success of historically underrepresented students, was historically the first. Its legacy is a focus primarily on African Americans, Latinos, and American Indian students and on White women in areas such as science and math. This is the historic heart and soul of diversity in higher education in the United States. But its history remains all too current. Indeed, a review of the literature today concerning student success for African Americans, Latinos, and American Indians reveals a chilling similarity to the literature of forty years ago. As chapter 4 will suggest, while there has been progress, issues of access and success remain all too pressing, especially in terms of the achievement gap and diversity in STEM fields. And while the focus has, here again, been on undergraduate education, this dimension of diversity must also incorporate graduate and professional education.

While access for URM students was the starting place of diversity efforts decades ago, the changing demographics of the society pose the danger that access will come to define diversity. I suspect most readers of this book will have heard a college president or campus leader instruct someone to appreciate a campus's success with diversity by inviting them to look around the campus and "see the diversity." While the changing "face" of a campus might be inspirational, diversity "by looking" says nothing about student success, campus climate, institutional effectiveness, or graduate-student or faculty profiles. Indeed, on too many campuses, equity, in terms of whether students are thriving, succeeding, or (in the case of community colleges) transferring, can be overshadowed by the presence of a demographically diverse student body (Bensimon, 2004).

Because early research on student success studied students themselves, the findings focused on characteristics of students who succeeded or failed, students at risk, and the inadequacy of K–12 preparation for college. In contrast, this dimension is meant to focus on students as an indicator of an institution's success, or at least as one key marker of its progress with respect to diversity. While student characteristics are, of course, issues in student success, focusing attention on them results in efforts to fix or remediate them. Using student success as an indicator of institutional capacity, on the other hand, directs attention to understanding students for the purpose of educational improvement. From an institutional perspective, access and success involves identifying talent, enabling student achievement, and studying which students are thriving and why. This is important, because framing access solely in terms of such things as grades and tests makes institutions vulnerable to legal challenges when those with higher scores get denied entrance in favor of someone with lower scores. Finding ways of identifying merit and excellence in broader terms has great potential for increasing diversity and excellence, as we shall see in the next few chapters.

Even as the focus on URM students must remain central, the recent demographic changes in society suggest that this dimension will need to expand its focus to others who are underrepresented, because nothing is static. Campuses will need to pay greater attention to, for example, Asian American groups such as Hmong and to some degree Filipino students, as well as historically overlooked groups from Hawaii, Alaska, and the Pacific Islands. The issue of class and whether higher education is truly accessible for poorer students is vitally important, as will be discussed more completely in chapter 4; recent research suggests that poor students who have academic potential equal to that of wealthier students have less opportunity for higher education than forty years ago, when access emerged as important (Carnevale & Rose, 2004; Ellwood & Kane, 2000; Heller, 2002; Kahlenberg, 2004). In part because of federal legislation and other civil rights initiatives, access and success is also important for students with a variety of ability issues. At the most basic level, the absence of ramps makes physical access impossible for students in wheelchairs. However, access goes much beyond ramps, as does the related question of whether an institution is set up to provide students with disabilities with the tools necessary to succeed.

Interconnected, Inclusive, and Differentiated

The dimensions of the framework I have described above are all very much interconnected. They provide a means to attend to an inclusive approach to diversity while differentiating where specific aspects of diversity might need to be addressed. Campus climate is very important for many specific groups, because it relates to the question of how they perceive the institution in the context of larger social, historical, and political experiences. The curriculum, of course, addresses the education of all students, but it must also attend to the adequacy of knowledge, whose story and experiences are included, and how new forms of scholarship change fields. We will see in later chapters how, for example, student success is related to institutional commitment, intergroup relations, and climate. Similarly, faculty, staff, and administrative hiring and retention must be attentive not only to racial and ethnic diversity and gender, but also to the climate, organizational culture, and institutional commitment.

Excellence in an institution, then, is defined by who succeeds, what is taught and what research is thought to be important, who feels as if they matter, and whether the institution has sufficient resources of people, ideas, and policy to successfully function in a diverse context. In chapter 8, we will see how this framework can provide the means to monitor progress in ways that are manageable and that facilitate organizational change.

Framing diversity as an element of building institutional capacity for educational excellence on campuses and for the society has enormous implications for institutional approaches. One of the dominant themes in the thirty years since Bakke has been framing diversity in terms of a response to legal challenges to affirmative action and more recently a response to public initiatives limiting the use of race and gender in campus decision-making. As a result, much of the work on campus and even in research is oriented toward this legal and public-policy context, often centering on admissions. The challenge moving forward is one of reframing the issue of diversity as an institutional imperative concerning education and excellence. To do so creates opportunities for new approaches and begins a conversation that focuses on the heart of the mission of higher education. While the legal and public-policy issues cannot be ignored, they move from being drivers of the conversation to being something that must be considered in the larger institutional context. How diversity is framed, then, becomes central to much of what follows in this book, and it is critical for the sustainability and centrality of diversity.

✿

CHAPTER FOUR

The Past Forty Years

A review of diversity in higher education over the past forty years cannot be done adequately in one chapter. Nonetheless, given the centrality of demographics to the national conversations about diversity, it is necessary to look at the numbers concerning institutions, students, faculty, and administration over the past four decades. I take away two important themes from this chapter's review of these basic data in higher education through the lens of diversity: great change and urgent unfinished business.

A Quick Look Back

The higher education literature of this forty-year period reflects the significant changes that have occurred with respect to diversity. A look back would demonstrate that, except in historically Black colleges and universities (HBCUs), the only students of color to be found in substantial numbers would have been international students. It was possible forty years ago to restrict the percentages of women on campus and in certain programs, including veterinary medicine, medical schools, and engineering. At some institutions, women still had curfews and were required to live on campus, and often they could not be married. It was not possible forty years ago to disaggregate student enrollments nationally by race and ethnicity (that practice began in 1976).

College presidents routinely traveled the country hiring faculty (mostly White males) because search committees were rarely, if ever, used. Faculties and administrators, except at HBCUs, were virtually all White and, except at women's colleges, mostly male. It was possible to set different salaries for men and women for the same job. Segregated fraternities and sororities were tolerated. The curriculum throughout higher education did not address race, class, or gender and certainly did not engage sexual orientation and other identity issues. The generic White male, like the generic pronoun *he*, stood for humans. Others were exceptions or were invisible. History was largely the study of wars; art history was the study of White male artists. Thus, race and gender, while invisible as an articulated form of study and invisible as a focus of institutional policy, were visible in their absence. Most college campuses—indeed, most other institutions as well—were not accessible for those with physical handicaps, and it was routine to discriminate against those with a variety of physical and other limitations.

At a national level, *Change* magazine, federal support for financial aid, and the posting of job openings as a common practice were just emerging. Forty years ago, the Cooperative Institutional Research Program began reporting annually on the backgrounds, attitudes, and behaviors of college freshmen. The *Chronicle of Higher Education* turned forty in November 2006. It developed as a particularly significant source of information for higher education in the 1970s when, for the first time, institutions were required by law to publicize positions and to actively seek to diversify pools. Partly as a result of the Civil Rights Act of 1964 and the executive orders that followed, and partly as a result of growing campus activism, higher education was forced to reevaluate who was hired, what was taught, and how students were admitted. Financial aid was implemented to open up access to higher education and to limit the restrictions placed on those from low-income backgrounds.

A review of the literature during that period would see a focus on opening up access to college campuses across the country. At that time, concerns about access attended to "minority" populations that were truly in the minority, not only on campus but in the society. African Americans were the largest minority population and were the primary focus of attention for race-related concerns, even though civil rights issues for Asian Americans, Latinos, and American Indians existed in many parts of the country where these populations were clustered.

Forty Years Later

How are we to interpret the status of higher education today with respect to diversity issues? Most often, when the literature describes changes in diversity on college campuses, the first and foremost indicator of that change is the demographics of undergraduates. To give a snapshot, as of 2005, 39% of undergraduates in the United States were twenty-five or older, and 62% of these were women. A significant percentage of students, 39%, were attending part-time. Forty percent were from low-income families; among this group, half were students of color (American Council on Education, 2005). Women were a majority at the undergraduate level in most institutions, though not in all programs within institutions.

Demographic changes are now visible in almost all parts of the country and show increasing numbers of people of racial/ethnic and cultural-minority backgrounds (Farley & Haaga, 2005; Johnston & Packer, 1987; Judy & D'Amico, 1999). These changes are reflected on campuses throughout the country—public and private, small and large, urban and rural. International students have continued to grow in number, in spite of the changing global context after 9/11. Indeed, the students who were characterized in the 1970s as "nontraditional students"—those who were *not* eighteen to twenty-four years old, White, and male—now clearly constitute the vast majority on many college campuses, especially outside of the four-year residential liberal arts colleges (American Council on Education, 2005). Forty years later, there are entirely new populations as a result of immigration; and there is a willingness to attend to issues that earlier would not have been discussed, such as undocumented students and issues of sexuality (McDonough, 2002; Perez, Coronado, & Ramos, 2007).

Community colleges continue to play a major role in higher education. Enrollment in that sector has quadrupled and now represents almost 40% of all enrollments, up from 20% in 1965 (see table 4.2). Tribal colleges were formally recognized, and the American Indian Higher Education Consortium was established in 1972 to facilitate coordination among tribal colleges and with the federal government.

Judicial and legislative mandates have played an important role by pushing higher education to make changes, and the current policy and legal landscape continues to influence higher education. The policy context that developed during the 1960s and 1970s remains important in terms of legal requirements for access, as well as federal support for financial aid. TRIO programs have provided both support and access to low-income and underrepresented students. The landmark legislation of Title IX mandated access for women in athletics. The executive orders and civil rights legislation that imposed affirmative action as a strategy for hiring remain federal policy. Section 504 of the Rehabilitation Act of 1973 marked the beginning of federal mandates to admit and hire persons with disabilities.

Yet virtually all of these historic policy and legal approaches have been challenged. Federal grants have been largely overshadowed by the use of loans and merit-based approaches at the state level. Title IX and affirmative action have been contested in the courts; and, of course, many of the policy and funding initiatives have been challenged or cut back (Olivas, 2005).

Indeed, we exist in a schizophrenic policy and legal environment. We open the morning newspaper to see a public-opinion poll that indicates support for diversity, and on the same page is an article reporting the passage of an initiative limiting the use of race/ethnicity and gender in decision-making at public institutions. Diversity is seen as central to corporate interests and political parties even as various groups attempt to limit its role. However, the current concerns about economic access, together with emerging data about the burden of loans on the poorest populations of students, have created new opportunities for a focus once again on access. Though it is hard to predict, the policy climate seems to be shifting in a recognition of the importance of diversity to society.

Along with the growth in scholarship itself, a number of scholarly publications focused on diversity issues have emerged in the disciplines and in higher education generally, including (to name just a few) the *Journal of Diversity in Higher Education*; the *Journal of Black Issues in Higher Education*; the American Council on Education's *Annual Report on Minorities in Higher Education*; the *Journal of Hispanic Higher Education*; the *Amerasia Journal*; the *Journal of Women in Psychology*; the *Journal of Lesbian Studies*; *Sex Roles*; *Psychology of Men and Masculinity*; *Cross-Cultural Research*; *Culture and Psychology*; and the *African American Review*. Magazines such as *Hispanic Outlook*, the *Tribal College Journal*, and *DiversityInc.* have also developed during this period. In addition, an analysis of the mainstream higher education academic journals, such as the *Journal of Higher Education* and the *Review of Higher Education*, reveals substantive engagement of diversity scholarship. A content analysis of topics related to diversity in the *Journal of Higher Education* over the past thirty years shows a change from about 3% in the 1970s to about 20% from 2005 to 2007 (H. Garcia, 2007).

A Look at the Numbers over Time

The remaining chapters will go into greater depth on building institutional capacity for diversity as we move forward. However, because the demographic changes in the society and the institutional changes in higher education are putting diversity more at the center of institutional conversations, it is important to look at these shifts more carefully. Indeed, the changing demographics reflect both the unfinished business and the newly emerging issues in higher education. Because these data are cited in virtually every document on the status of diversity in higher education, I am going to look at them, where possible, from several different perspectives so as to highlight multiple ways in which one can characterize change.

In the following sections, some important issues will be identified that form the basis for the chapters to follow. One of the important themes to emerge is the need to deal with multiplicity—of identity, of intersections, and of ways to look at change.

Higher Education Institutions

Higher education today reflects the significant growth over the past forty years in terms of both enrollments and institutions. An institutional perspective would show growth overall and in each of the two-year and four-year public and private sectors from 1965 to 2005 (see table 4.1). Higher education grew from 2,230 institutions in 1965 to 4,216 institutions in 2005, almost doubling institutional capacity. The two-year public community colleges have increased the most, particularly from 1965 to 1980, when their number doubled. However, every sector grew during this period—including the four-year private institutions, which many had thought would decline in number. These changes are visually represented in figures 4.1 and 4.2, which show the changes in percentage and number by sector during these two periods and during the past forty years as a whole.

The two-year public community college experienced its greatest growth (107%) during the first fifteen years, and private two-year campuses have grown the most during the past twenty years (66%). We can look at the profile of institutional types during this period through a slightly different lens as well. Using data derived from table 4.1, we see that the community colleges represented 19% of all institutions in 1965 (420 of 2,230) and 25% in 2005 (1,061 of 4,216). The proportion of four-year private institutions has declined from 52% (1,150 of 2,230) to 45% (1,894 of 4,216) even as they increased in number by 65%. This pattern of declining in percentage while increasing in number is a function of the larger number of institutions overall and is one that we will see in many of our analyses throughout the chapter. The profile of higher education now shows a larger proportion of public and private two-year institutions (37%) than forty years ago (31%). However, these changes are not as dramatic as one might think.

What about the intersection of enrollment and institutional type—public and

TABLE 4.1
Growth in Higher Education Institutions by Sector, 1965–2005
(by number and percentage)

	4-year public	2-year public	4-year private	2-year private	Total
1965–1980	(401–465)	(420–869)	(1,150–1,396)	(259–326)	(2,230–3,056)
	16%	107%	21%	26%	37%
1985–2005	(461–639)	(865–1,061)	(1,454–1,894)	(375–622)	(3,155–4,216)
	39%	23%	30%	66%	34%
1965–2005	(401–639)	(420–1,061)	(1,150–1,894)	(259–622)	(2,230–4,216)
	59%	153%	65%	140%	89%

Source: NCES, 2006, Table 248.

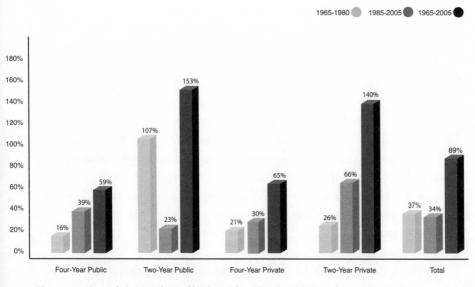

Figure 4.1. Growth in number of higher education institutions by sector, 1965–2005 (in percentages). (*Source:* NCES, 2006, Table 248)

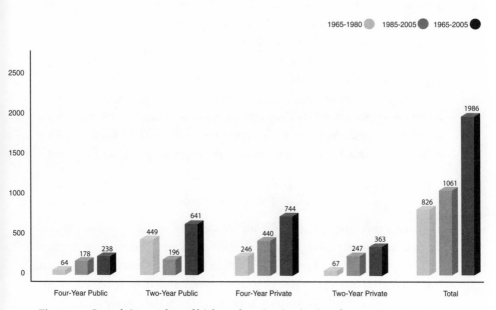
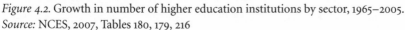

Figure 4.2. Growth in number of higher education institutions by sector, 1965–2005. *Source:* NCES, 2007, Tables 180, 179, 216

private, two-year and four-year? The total enrollment in higher education during this period almost tripled, from just under 6 million to 17.5 million students enrolled. As table 4.2 shows, 67% of students were enrolled in public institutions in 1965, 79% in 1976, and 74% in 2005. Enrollment in private higher education dropped from 33% of the total in 1965 to 21% in 1976 but increased to 26% in 2005. There has been consistent growth in each of these sectors during the past forty years. A major change has been the growth of the for-profit sector since 1976. For-profit higher education represented only 2% of total enrollments in 1976 and grew to 23% in 2005.

Enrollment grew in both two- and four-year institutions during this period. However, while students in four-year institutions represented 80% of total enrollments (including graduate and professional enrollments) in 1965, they represented 63% in 2005 (see table 4.2). This shift occurred mostly from 1965 to 1976. In 1965, 20% of students were enrolled in a community college; in 1976 the proportion was 35%; and in 2005 it was 37%.

The pattern of full-time and part-time enrollments, surprisingly, shows no appreciable shift between 1976 and 2005. About 61–62% of students were enrolled full-time in those years, down from 69% in 1965. Table 4.2 shows full-time status by race/ethnicity as well for 1976 and 2005. There are slight increases in full-time status for Whites, Asian Americans/Pacific Islanders (AA/PIs), American Indians/Alaska Natives (AI/ANs), and nonresident aliens. The percentage of Blacks and Latinos attending full-time declined slightly.

Part-time enrollments were, not surprisingly, mostly in the two-year public sector, where 61% of all students were enrolled part-time in 2005 (National Center for Education Statistics, 2005, Table 183). Perhaps surprisingly, the sector with the lowest rate of part-time students was private two-year institutions, where 15% were enrolled part-time. In the private, for-profit two-year institutions, only 11% were enrolled part-time. The four-year for-profit sector enrolled 80% full-time (ibid.).

Demographics of Students

The changing demographics of higher education can be clearly seen in a look at the racial and ethnic profile of campuses from 1976 to 2005. These data can be studied from a wide variety of perspectives, but the racial and ethnic changes over the past thirty years can best be seen in terms of overall growth in higher education, the demographic profile of higher education, and then the differences in enrollment in four-year and two-year institutions. Because racial and ethnic information was not collected until 1976, that is the earliest year for which data are available, although census data provide educational levels by race for earlier periods.

TABLE 4.2
Fall Enrollment in Higher Education Institutions, 1965–2005

	1965		1976		2005	
	Number	Percent	Number	Percent	Number	Percent
Total enrollment[1]	5,920,864	100	11,012,137	100	17,487,475	100
Public	3,969,596	67	8,653,477	79	13,021,834	74
Private	1,951,268	33	2,358,660	21	4,465,641	26
Not-for-profit	N/A	N/A	2,314,298	98	3,454,692	77
For-profit	N/A	N/A	44,362	2	1,010,949	23
Four-year[1]	49,447,912	80	7,128,816	65	10,999,420	63
Two-year	1,172,952	20	3,883,321	35	6,488,055	37
Full-time[2]	4,095,728	69	6,717,058	61	10,797,011	62
Part-time	1,825,136	31	4,295,079	39	6,690,464	38
Percent enrolled full-time[3]						
Total full-time	4,095,728	69		61		62
White	N/A	N/A		61		63
Black	N/A	N/A		64		60
Hispanic	N/A	N/A		55		52
AA/PI	N/A	N/A		60		63
AI/AN	N/A	N/A		57		60
NRA	N/A	N/A		73		78

Note: AA/PI = Asian American / Pacific Islander; AI/AN = American Indian / Alaska Native; NRA = nonresident alien (international).
[1]NCES, 2007, Table 180.
[2]NCES, 2007, Table 179.
[3]NCES, 2007, Table 216.

UNDERGRADUATES

Table 4.3 provides a broad overview of undergraduate enrollments over a thirty-year period. Besides the considerable growth in higher education during this period, there was growth for every racial group, ranging from an increase of 27% for Whites to 474% for AA/PIs. Even the number of international students grew substantially during this period, by 120% (the federal government continues to refer to these students as "nonresident aliens").

When studied in terms of the demographics of the undergraduate population, the changes are significant with respect to both race/ethnicity and gender. For example, White students made up 82% of the total undergraduate population in 1976 and 66% in 2005. During that period, the ratio of White men to women went from 1.1 to 1 to 0.8 to 1. Even so, both White men and women increased numerically—by 7% and 49%, respectively.

Black undergraduates increased from 10% to 13% of total enrollment, with the number of women almost double that of men in 2005. The number of Black

TABLE 4.3
Fall Undergraduate Enrolllment by Race/Ethnicity and Gender, 1976 and 2005
(in thousands)

	1976		2005		
	Number	Percent	Number	Percent	% change
Undergraduate total	9,419.0	100	14,964.0	100	59
Male	4,896.8	52	6,408.9	43	30
Female	4,522.1	48	8,555.1	57	89
White total	7,740.5	82	9,828.6	66	27
Male	4,052.2	43	4,330.4	29	7
Female	3,688.3	39	5,498.2	37	49
Black total	943.4	10	1,955.4	13	107
Male	430.7	4.6	697.5	4.7	62
Female	512.7	5.4	1,257.8	8.4	145
Hispanic total	352.9	3.7	1,733.6	12	391
Male	191.7	2	718.5	4.8	275
Female	161.2	1.7	1,015.0	6.8	530
AA/PI total	169.3	1.8	971.4	6.5	474
Male	91.1	1	448.1	3	392
Female	78.2	0.8	523.2	3.5	570
AI/AN total	69.7	0.7	160.4	1.1	130
Male	34.8	0.4	62.5	0.4	79
Female	34.9	0.4	98.0	0.7	181
NRA total	143.2	1.5	314.7	2.1	120
Male	96.4	1	151.8	1	57
Female	46.8	0.5	162.9	1.1	248

Source: NCES, 2007, Table 216.
   Note: AA/PI = Asian American / Pacific Islander; AI/AN = American Indian / Alaska Native; NRA =
nonresident alien (international).

men grew by 62%, but they remained just under 5% of the population; meanwhile, the number of Black women grew by 145% as they went from 5% to 8% of total enrollment. During this period, the ratio of Black men to women changed from 0.8 to 1 to 0.6 to 1. All other groups also saw growth in numbers and (except for Whites) in percentage of total enrollment, along with a growing ratio of women to men. Significantly, the data show that in each racial/ethnic group, women now outnumber men and account for a larger proportion of the undergraduate population than do men, even as men from every group also increased in both number and—except for Whites and American Indians—in enrollment share.

The Latino population in higher education grew from 3.7% to 12%, with the number of men growing by 275% during this time and women increasing by 530%. The ratio of men to women changed from 1.2 to 1 to 0.7 to 1 for Latinos. Asian

TABLE 4.4
Fall Undergraduate Enrollment by Race/Ethnicity and Sector, 1976 and 2005
(in thousands)

	1976				2005			
	2-year	4-year	Total	% 4-year	2-year	4-year	Total	% 4-year
Total	3,879.0	5,540.0	9,419	59	6,488.1	10,999.4	17,487.5	63
White	3,077.0	4,663.5	7,740.5	60	3,998.6	7,496.9	11,495.4	65
Black	429.3	514.1	943.4	54	901.1	1,313.4	2,214.6	59
Hispanic	210.2	142.7	352.9	40	981.5	900.5	1,882.0	48
AA/PI	79.2	90.1	169.3	53	434.4	700.0	1,134.4	62
AI/AN	41.2	28.5	69.7	41	80.7	95.6	176.3	54
NRA	42.2	101	143.2	71	91.8	493.1	584.8	84

Source: NCES, 2007, Table 217.
    Note: AA/PI = Asian American / Pacific Islander; AI/AN = American Indian / Alaska Native; NRA = nonresident alien (international).

Americans increased from 1.8% to 6.5% in share of total enrollment, as their numbers grew by 474%. Here the gender ratio shifted as well, from 1.2 to 1 to 0.86 to 1. The American Indian student population grew by 130%, and from 0.7% of total enrollment to 1.1%. The ratio of men to women in that group shifted from 1.1 to 1 to 0.6 to 1.

International students, officially designated as nonresident aliens (NRA), increased from 1.5% to 2.1% of the higher education population, with significant growth in the number of women (248%). As a result, the ratio of men to women also shifted here; men were twice as numerous as women in 1976, but women had a slight majority by 2005 (0.93 to 1).

Another perspective on demographics can be gained by looking at the kinds of institutions students attend. While the analysis could go much deeper by including different types of institutions, for this overview I look at the distribution within two- and four-year institutions (see table 4.4). Here the data look more stable over the past thirty years. Among White, Black, and Asian American students, 60%, 54%, and 53%, respectively, attended four-year institutions in 1976, as did 40% of Latinos and 41% of American Indians. The percentages for 2005 show increases mostly ranging from 5% to 9%, with noteworthy increases to 54% among American Indian undergraduates and 84% for international students. Overall, a slightly larger percentage of undergraduate students went to four-year institutions in 2005 than in 1976 (63% vs. 59%), including URM students (54% vs. 50%).

The undergraduate demographic profiles for both two-year and four-year institutions have also become more diverse. For four-year institutions in 1976, 12% of students were URM, and 2% were AA/PI. In 2005, 21% were URM and 6% AA/PI. The percentage of international students in four-year institutions more

TABLE 4.5
Graduate and First-Professional Enrollments by Race/Ethnicity and Gender, 1976 and 2005
(in thousands)

| | Graduate | | | | | First-professional | | | | |
| | 1976 | | 2005 | | | 1976 | | 2005 | | |
	Number	Percent	Number	Percent	% change	Number	Percent	Number	Percent	% change
Graduate total	1,322.5	100	2,186.5	100	65	244.1	100	337.0	100	38.1
Male	707.9	54	877.2	40	24	189.6	78	169.8	50	−10.4
Female	614.6	46	1,309.3	60	113	54.5	22	167.2	50	206.8
White total	1,115.6	84	1,428.7	65	28	220.0	90	238.1	71.0	8.2
Male	589.1	45	551.2	25	−6	172.4	71	125.6	37.3	−27.1
Female	526.5	40	877.5	40	66	47.6	20	112.5	33.4	136.3
Black total	78.5	5.9	233.2	11	197	11.2	4.6	26.0	7.7	132.6
Male	32	2.4	66.7	3.0	108	7.2	2.9	9.9	2.9	37.5
Female	46.5	3.5	166.4	7.6	258	3.9	1.6	16.2	4.8	314.1
Hispanic total	26.4	2	130.7	6	395	4.5	1.8	17.7	5.3	293.5
Male	14.6	1.1	47.5	2.2	225	3.5	1.4	8.6	2.6	145.2
Female	11.8	0.9	83.2	3.8	605	1.0	0.4	9.1	2.7	812.6
AA/PI total	24.5	1.9	118.4	5.4	383	4.1	1.7	44.6	13.2	987.9
Male	14.4	1.1	53.8	2.5	274	2.9	1.2	20.1	6.0	594.2
Female	10.1	0.8	64.6	3.0	540	1.1	0.5	24.5	7.3	2124.6
AI/AN total	5.1	0.4	13.4	0.6	163	1.3	0.5	2.5	0.7	90.2
Male	2.7	0.2	4.7	0.2	74	1.0	0.4	1.2	0.4	20.3
Female	2.4	0.2	8.7	0.4	263	0.2	0.1	1.3	0.4	534.5
NRA total	72.4	5.5	262.1	12	262	3.1	1.3	8.1	2.4	160.0
Male	55.1	4.2	153.3	7	178	2.5	1.0	4.4	1.3	75.3
Female	17.3	1.3	108.8	5	529	0.5	0.2	3.7	1.1	635.2

Source: NCES, 2007, Table 216.
Note: AA/PI = Asian American / Pacific Islander; AI/AN = American Indian / Alaska Native; NRA = nonresident alien (international).

TABLE 4.6

Doctorates Received by Race/Ethnicity and Citizenship Status, 1976 and 2006

	1976		2006		
	Number	% of total	Number	% of total	% growth
Total	33,126	100	56,067	100	69
Total international	3,747	11	15,975	28	326
Total U.S. citizens	29,379	89	40,092	72	36
Total U.S. citizens	29,379		40,092		
White	26,851	91	31,601	79	18
Black	1,253	4.2	3,122	7.8	149
Hispanic	522	1.8	1,882	4.7	261
AA/PI	658	2.2	3,257	8.1	395
AI/AN	95	0.3	230	0.6	142

Source: NCES, 2007, Table 280, Integrated Postsecondary Education Data System (IPEDS) Completions Survey.
Note: The federal IPEDS defines the doctorate as PhD and EdD.

than doubled, from 1.8% to 4.5%. White students declined proportionally (not numerically), from 84% to 68%. In two-year institutions, the pattern is repeated. Whereas 18% of two-year-campus students were URM in 1976, 30% were URM in 2005; in addition, 7% were AA/PI. There was little change for international students, who made up about 1% of the population at each point (NCES, 2007, table 217).

GRADUATE AND PROFESSIONAL-SCHOOL STUDENTS

Table 4.5 summarizes the changes since 1976 for graduate-degree (master's and doctoral) and first-professional-degree enrollments by race and gender. Dramatic growth overall, changes in the demographic profile, and faster growth among women for each racial and ethnic group are reflected at the graduate and first-pro-fessional levels, as they were with the undergraduate enrollment data. The num-ber and percentage of men increased for all racial/ethnic groups except White men. Most noticeable is the decline among White men in first-professional en-rollments between 1976 and 2005. Even so, White men represented 37% of the total enrollment, the largest ethnic/gender group. However, this is a significant change from their 71% share in 1976.

The doctorate is an important entry to the faculty, especially in four-year in-stitutions. Table 4.6 shows earned doctorates (PhD and EdD) in 1976 and 2006. Between those years, there was a 69% growth in total earned doctorates and a large increase in the diversity of doctoral recipients. The number of international students (non–U.S. citizens) earning a doctorate increased by 326%, representing 11% of all doctorates in 1976 and 28% in 2006.[1]

Among U.S. citizens, the percentage of African Americans earning the doctorate almost doubled, from 4.2% to 7.8%, as their numbers grew by 149%. The share of Latinos receiving doctorates grew from 1.8% to 4.7%, with a growth in numbers of 261%. American Indians / Alaska Natives received 0.3% of doctorates among U.S. citizens in 1976 and 0.6% in 2006, with a growth in numbers of 142%. Asian Americans / Pacific Islanders accounted for 2.2% of doctorates to citizens in 1976 and 8.1% in 2006, with a growth in numbers of 395%. Doctorates for Whites went from 91% to 79% but grew in number by 18%. These data underscore the critical importance of the intersection of race and citizenship, especially for faculty diversity. Among U.S. citizens, URM students earned 13.1% of the doctoral degrees in 2006. With the growth in AA/PI doctorates, students of color now represent almost 21% of all doctoral degrees earned by U.S. citizens.

The data for citizenship and race/ethnicity are often combined on campuses and certainly were combined prior to 1993, when federal data collection rules required their separation. Table 4.7 shows the racial and ethnic breakdown for earned doctorates (PhD's) by citizenship for 2006. The table illustrates the importance of the intersection of citizenship and race/ethnicity for doctoral recipients (see Moore, 2007). These data, based on the National Science Foundation's 2008 Survey of Earned Doctorates, have significant implications for faculty diversity. The demographic profile of doctoral recipients changes when citizenship is considered. Of all doctoral recipients in 2006, 61% were White, 28% Asian, 5% Black, 6% Latino, and 0.3% AI/AN. Overall, 63% of doctorates were earned by U.S. citizens, while 87% of the Asians receiving their doctorate were noncitizens. Among Latinos, 40% were noncitizens, as were 9% of AI/ANs and 24% of Blacks. Additional data from the National Science Foundation Survey of Earned Doctorates in 2005 show that among more than 43,445 PhD's granted, 38% of the recipients listed as Hispanic received their bachelor's degree at a foreign institution (not including institutions in Puerto Rico); that figure was 79% for Asians, 17% for Blacks, and 12% for Whites.

In the STEM fields, the issue of both access and success is important. In the past forty years, there has been considerable growth in the participation of students of color, especially URM students, in STEM fields. The growth among women of

---

1. The category of U.S. citizens, of course, would not include those who have permanent residency status in the United States. Federal data suggest that among noncitizens, only about 11% are permanent residents, while 89% are on temporary visas (National Science Foundation Survey of Earned Doctorates, 2005, Table 11).

TABLE 4.7
Doctoral Recipients by Race/Ethnicity and Citizenship Status, 2006

Race/ethnicity	Non-U.S.	U.S.	Total	% U.S. citizens
White	3,948	21,280	25,228	84
Black	515	1,659	2,174	76
Hispanic	919	1,370	2,289	60
Asian[a]	10,071	1,560	11,631	13
AI/AN	12	118	130	91
Total	15,465	25,987	41,452	63

Source: National Science Foundation Survey of Earned Doctorates, 2008, report tables. The survey includes the PhD only.
Note: Numbers do not include 4,144 recipients with race or citizenship unknown.
[a]Does not include Native Hawaiians or Pacific Islanders.

color is particularly noteworthy. In an important study of minority students in STEM fields, Anderson and Kim (2006) found that aspirations for STEM majors were quite high. Using data from the Beginning Postsecondary Students Longitudinal Study, which tracked twelve thousand students from 1995–96 through 2001 who began in four-year institutions, the researchers found that Latinos were more likely than any group except Asian Americans to declare a major in a STEM field. The percentages for Whites, African Americans, Latinos, and Asian Americans were 18%, 19%, 23%, and 26%, respectively. (They did not report data for American Indians.) Further, Anderson and Kim found that students of color were likely to persist through the third year and continue beyond six years—suggesting that completion was a more important issue than dropouts. According to Summers and Hrabowski (2006), background credentials are not the critical issue, because concerns about completion also appear for students with strong credentials.

AMERICAN INDIANS

Among students of color, and among URM students, the smallest population is American Indians / Alaska Natives, who often get lost in many analyses of demographics or student success (Pavel, Swisher, & Ward, 1994). From an institutional perspective, the numbers of these students are quite small, often amounting to no more than 1% of the total student population. In a paradox not lost on those in the AI/AN community, these small numbers could allow institutions to learn a lot about these students on their campus, should the institution choose to study them. Instead, the small numbers often mean that statistical analyses are limited and most often ignored. Nonetheless, issues of access and success for AI/AN students require continued engagement if this most underrepresented group is not to be ignored.

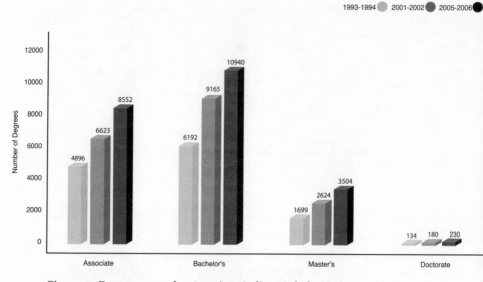

Figure 4.3. Degrees granted to American Indians / Alaska Natives, 1993–2006.
Source: NCES, 2007, Tables 271, 274, 277, 280

A focus on these students is most important in the many parts of the country where there are significant AI/AN populations—particularly in California and the rest of the Southwest, but also in upstate New York, Oklahoma, and parts of the South. These population centers for many are not rural, because many American Indians / Alaska Natives in California, for example, are urban and not reservation-based. Figure 4.3 shows the growth in associate, bachelor's, master's, and doctoral degrees awarded to AI/ANs from 1993 to 2006. The number of doctorates grew from 134 to 230, but this is still a small number.

GENDER

A gender analysis for each level of education would show the growth in number of women at many levels and for all racial and ethnic groups over the past thirty years. Nonetheless, the number of men also grew in each group, except for White men in first-professional or graduate-degree programs. Thus, although the gender gap—especially among African Americans—is significant, the concern about it is really an issue of the faster growth of women. The data presented clearly underscore the need to look at change from a variety of perspectives and also from a set of intersecting views.

There has been considerable discussion in higher education that seems to sound an alarm about "too many women." Disaggregating the data to look at where male participation and success should be monitored, where gender issues for women exist, and how gender, race, class, and other variables intersect is fast becoming an imperative. The concerns about "too many women" are reflected in national conferences and discussions about the feminization of the academy to the point that an institution may now try to make sure that its "face" is not too feminine (Eisenmann, 2006; Kimmel, 2000; Mortensen, 1999). At the undergraduate level, campuses have been known to add football teams, hire male admissions directors, and use other strategies to attract men—especially White men. This might not seem too alarming or suggest sexism and racism if it were not for the fact that the prevalence of men in science, and in athletics, did not inspire such concern and indeed required federal intervention to encourage change.

Interestingly, in a recent study looking at gender issues, Goldin, Katz, and Kuziemko (2006) show that in fact women and men were at parity in their enrollments from 1900 to 1930 and that the largest gender gap occurred right after World War II, when the ratio of men to women was 2.3 to 1. The dramatic growth in women's participation began again in the 1960s and is seen in terms of bachelor's degrees as well as graduate and professional degrees. In addition, the authors found that while class issues affected gender participation for high school graduates of the 1950s, there has been growth in women's participation at all economic levels and for all ethnic groups in recent years.

The gender gap among African Americans, and in particular the status of African American men, is cause for concern in the literature, with many scholars sounding an alarm (Cuyjet, 2006; Harper, 2006; "Half Century," 2006). Not only has the presence of African American men over the past thirty years been stagnant relative to all other groups (even as the numbers have grown), but deeper analyses also highlight concerns about where the African American men are. The increasing number of African American men in prison is regularly compared now to the number in college (Cuyjet, 2006). Harper highlights the disproportionate role of athletics in accounting for African American men's presence in Division I institutions. According to Harper's policy brief on African American men, they represented 30.5% of all male athletes in Division I sports, 55% of football teams, and 61% of basketball teams. The consequences of this are significant for issues such as stereotyping and retention. While it is easy to point to preparation issues in student success, the literature affirms the continuing themes of alienation, isolation, and incidents of racism at predominantly White institutions (Harper,

2006). Students report being one of the few African American students in class, and perhaps the only African American male; and those who are not athletes are required to continually explain and justify their presence.

A look at degree completion highlights the gender gap for African Americans. Though men still earn a majority of professional degrees, an analysis by Freeman (2004) shows that in 2001, African American women earned two-thirds of African American bachelor's degrees. Still, it is not clear whether the alarm that has been sounded is about the status of African American men in education or whether it is more about having "too many educated women." This issue requires more scrutiny than is evidenced in many studies on the topic.

If only to underscore again the important intersections of race, gender, and income, an American Council on Education study shows that for the half of all students who were dependent on their parents in 2003–4, the gender gap in undergraduate participation in higher education disappears (and slightly favors men) for the highest income quartiles across all ethnic groups. For example, among higher-income African Americans who were dependents in 2003–4, 54% were men and 46% were women. This stands in contrast to data from 1995–96, when this group was 41% male and 59% female. At the same time, among low-income students the gender gap has widened for Whites and Latinos, even as the percentage of African Americans and Asian Americans who are male increased (King, 2006).

ECONOMIC ACCESS

A great deal has been written about, and more attention is being paid to, issues of access based on income—for good reason. Access to college has long been associated with equity issues and the future of society (Advisory Committee on Student Financial Assistance, 2006). Here the data are a little more difficult to come by, because economic indicators are not routinely collected in higher education at the national level in such a way as to be integrated with other sources of data. Census data are most often used to study access by income and continue to demonstrate the significant relationship of income to college access. Quite often, eligibility for Pell Grants is used as a surrogate for low-income status, though many have pointed to the fact that this ignores the working poor (Institute for Higher Education Policy, 2007).

There is some indication that the income gap has shrunk a little over the forty-year period, but recent studies suggest its reemergence as a function of race and across race for persons from low-income backgrounds. A number of factors have been identified as important, including college-going rates, high school preparation, the increased use of loans and merit-based aid, and, importantly, the rise and fall of financial aid (Carnevale & Rose, 2004; Heller, 2002; Johnstone, 2005; Krueger, Rothstein, & Turner, 2006; Price, 2004; Vincent, 2005). New research is pointing to the difficulty in accessing information about financial aid as an additional factor (Fitzgerald, 2006; Luna de la Rosa & Tierney, 2006; Tomás Rivera Policy Institute, 2006).

A 2003 College Board study shows that the "chance of entering college is still closely correlated with family background though somewhat narrower than in the 1970s. Only 54% of high school graduates from the lowest income quartile enroll in college compared to 82% with incomes in the top quartile" (Bowen, Kurzweil, & Tobin, 2005, p. 74). Another study looking at the high school graduates who were qualified to go to college by taking a college-preparation curriculum in high school documents the problem. Among college-qualified graduates from low-income families, 20% attended no college, compared to only 3% of high-income graduates (Fitzgerald & Delaney, 2002). Further, a study by Ellwood and Kane (2000), in which family income and scores on a math test were compared, shows the dramatic differences in college attendance among high performers on the test based on family income. Whereas 84% of high performers from the highest-income families enrolled in a four-year college, only 68% of the high performers from low-income families enrolled. A direct relationship with family income continued for bachelor's degree completion as well. The study shows an even greater impact on college attendance when parental education is combined with income.

Recent research shows striking shifts in the allocation of aid funds. An Education Trust study from 2006 shows significant increases in aid awarded to students from families with high incomes in both public and private four-year institutions from 1995 to 2003. While the amount and percentage of aid increased for all groups, the significant growth in aid to students from high-income families reduced considerably the ratio of aid for others. For example, over this eight-year period, the average aid for a student in a four-year private institution whose family income was less than $20,000 went from $3,446 to $5,240—an increase of 52%. For a student from a family with income greater than $100,000, aid went from $1,359 to $3,447, an increase of 254%. Thus, the ratio of aid between the lowest- and highest-income families went from 2.5 to 1 in 1995 to 1.1 to 1 in 2003 in private institutions. The same pattern occurred in public institutions, where for low- and high-income students aid grew by 50% and 227%, respectively, and the ratio changed from 3.5 to 1 to 1.6 to 1 (Haycock, 2006). Data from the National Association of State Student and Grant Aid Programs (2006) show non-need aid in the form of state grants increasing from 13% in 1994–95 to 27% in 2004–5.

New data on class, using Pell Grants as a surrogate for low-income status, show the decline in economic diversity at the most selective institutions, both public and private. With notable exceptions such as the University of California at Berkeley and UCLA, where Pell Grant recipients constitute more than one-third of the student body, and Smith College, where they are 25% of the student body, most elite institutions have declined since 1983 in their percentage of students who are Pell recipients. For most institutions, Pell recipients are now hovering at 10–12% ("High-Ranking Colleges," 2006). Studies document the decline in federal aid relative to inflation, the increasing dependence on loans, and the increase in "merit" scholarships that overwhelmingly go to people who would have gone to college anyway (Vincent, 2005). Federal aid used to go entirely to people with need. In 2005, the proportion of students with need who received federal assistance declined to 60%; for state aid, it fell to 73% ("High-Ranking Colleges," 2006). From 2000 to 2004, the number of students on Pell Grants actually increased by more than 30% in four-year institutions; however, the amount of the Pell as a function of inflation and as a percentage of tuition has declined significantly (Moreno, Smith, Parker, Clayton-Pedersen, & Teraguchi, 2006).

In a provocative study looking at the intersection of race and class in twenty-two of the twenty-eight campuses participating in the James Irvine Foundation Campus Diversity Initiative (CDI), Moreno, Smith, Parker, Clayton-Pedersen, and Teraguchi (2006) found a complex relationship between class and race. Among URM students at these campuses, the percentage of Pell recipients was declining; at the same time, among Pell recipients, the percentage of URM students was increasing. This mind teaser emerged in the context of an overall decline in Pell recipients, in contrast to the national increases. Though the implications are not clear, these findings are important.

Recent research also suggests that in some cases, the issue is not the availability of financial aid, but rather that information about and access to financial aid are limited. A 2006 report by the American Council on Education documents that although there was an increase in the number of undergraduates who filled out the FAFSA (Free Application for Federal Student Aid, the government application that opens the door to federal, state, and institutional aid based on need), 28% of students with the greatest need did not file the FAFSA—a percentage that is increasing (American Council on Education, Center for Policy Analysis, 2006; Luna de la Rosa & Tierney, 2006). Limited resources in inner-city schools, the complexity of the FAFSA, and the lack of good information are all factors. As a result, public-service campaigns have been developed to reach students and their families directly about the process and the availability of financial aid. Discussions about simplifying the FAFSA are also under consideration by Congress.

STUDENTS WITH DISABILITIES

While there is a growing body of literature that engages the topic of differential abilities in higher education, demographic data are somewhat limited. Three primary sources of data exist that are relevant to higher education. The 2000 U.S. census estimates that persons with some sort of significant disability amount to about 18% of the total population. In addition, the National Center for Education Statistics (NCES), through the National Postsecondary Student Aid Study, asks about disability issues. According to these self-reported data, about 6% of undergraduates in 1995–96 reported a disability. Of these, 29% reported a learning disability and 23% an orthopedic impairment (Horn & Bobbitt, 1999). In 1999–2000, 2.5% of graduate and professional students reported a disability, with about 27% having a mobility-related disability and only 4% reporting a learning disability (NCES, 2000).

A third source of data is the National Science Foundation (NSF), which tracks earned doctorates, employment status, and disability. Its 2006 Survey of Earned Doctorates showed that 1.4% of all doctoral recipients reported at least one disability (NCES, 2007, Table 21). NSF data have also revealed that about 27% of doctoral recipients with disabilities (many of them invisible) were unemployed, in comparison to 10% of science and engineering graduates without disabilities (Harding, 2005).

Faculty Demographics

An important element of building capacity is diversity among leadership in higher education. Diversifying the faculty, in particular, has been an important component of diversity efforts across the country. It is also one of the key indicators of an institutional commitment to diversity, through its hiring practices. Chapter 5 will explore faculty diversity in greater depth, but here I examine the question of whether there has been change, and what kind, among the full-time faculty in higher education. The data here focus primarily on all full-time instructional faculty.

As with each of the empirical analyses presented so far, there are a number of lenses through which we can study progress on diversifying the faculty. Two of them will be employed here: growth of the racial/ethnic and gender diversity of the faculty; and change in the race and gender demographics of the faculty. Unfortunately, there are few available data disaggregated by ethnicity among these large categories. As many scholars have pointed out, while Chicanos are among the largest groups of Latinos in the United States, they constitute the smallest proportion of faculty

TABLE 4.8
Full-Time Institutional Faculty by Race/Ethnicity and Gender, 1993 and 2005

	1993	% of total	2005	% of total	% growth
Total	545,706[a]	100	675,624[b]	100	24
Male	363,430	67	401,507	59	10
Female	182,276	33	274,117	41	50
White	468,770	86	527,900	78	13
Male	313,278	57	313,685	46	0.1
Female	155,492	29	214,215	32	38
Black	25,658	4.7	35,458	5.2	38
Male	13,385	2.5	17,029	2.5	27
Female	12,273	2.2	18,429	2.7	50
Hispanic	12,076	2.2	22,818	3.4	89
Male	7,459	1.4	12,486	1.8	67
Female	4,617	0.8	10,332	1.5	124
AA/PI	25,269	4.6	48,457	7.2	92
Male	18,943	3.5	31,711	4.7	67
Female	6,326	1.2	16,746	2.5	165
AI/AN	1,997	0.4	3,231	0.5	62
Male	1,237	0.2	1,697	0.3	37
Female	760	0.1	1,534	0.2	102
International	10,829	2	28,057	4.2	159
Male	8,355	1.5	19,231	2.8	130
Female	2,474	0.5	8,826	1.3	257

Sources: NCES, 1996, Table 226; NCES, 2007, Table 239.
Note: AA/PI = Asian American / Pacific Islander; AI/AN = American Indian / Alaska Native.
[a]Includes 1,107 (0.2%) unknown for race.
[b]Includes 9,073 (1.4%) unknown for race.

by all estimates (Chapa, 2006; Delgado-Romero, Manlove, Manlove, & Hernandez, 2007; Garza, 1993). Considering international faculty separately is becoming important, not only to track the presence of such faculty, but also because prior to 1993, they were subsumed into the relevant racial and ethnic categories.

GROWTH IN DIVERSITY BY RACIAL/ETHNIC AND GENDER GROUPS

Table 4.8 and figure 4.4 show the growth in full-time instructional faculty by race/ethnicity and gender from 1993 to 2005. In that twelve-year period, there was growth in numbers and percentages for every racial/ethnic category.

The size of the faculty overall grew by 24% in this period; therefore, this was not a zero-sum game, in which the growth of one group necessarily came at the expense of another. White faculty increased by 13%, Black faculty by 38%, Latino faculty by 89%, AA/PI faculty by 92%, and AI/AN faculty by 62%. International faculty increased more than any other group, by 159%. And in each category, the

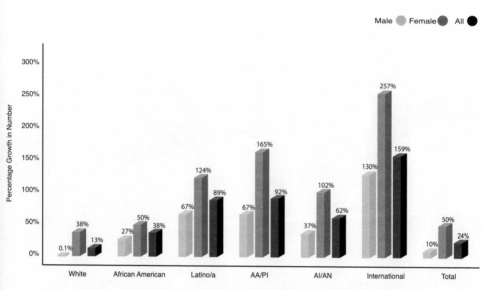

Figure 4.4. Growth in faculty by race/ethnicity and gender, 1993–2005. *Note:* AA/PI = Asian American / Pacific Islander; AI/AN = American Indian / Alaska Native. *Sources:* NCES, 1997, Table 226; NCES, 2007, Table 239

growth among women faculty outpaced that among male faculty. White, African American, Latina, AA/PI, and AI/AN women faculty increased by 38%, 50%, 124%, 165%, and 102%, respectively. The growth rate for international women was 257%. White men remained largely static, with only 0.1% growth. For African American, Latino, AA/PI, and AI/AN men, the growth rates were 27%, 67%, 67%, and 37%, respectively. The number of international men faculty grew by 130%.

This description, were we to stop here, would suggest aggressive and fairly successful efforts to diversify the faculty by race and gender, particularly gender. However, the percentage of growth in any population is a function of the size of the initial number. An increase from two faculty members to four represents a 200% growth rate, but it may not, from an institutional perspective, represent much demographic change in the total population.

DEMOGRAPHIC CHANGES BY RACE AND GENDER

How, then, has the configuration of the faculty changed during the 1993–2005 period? Figures 4.5 and 4.6 and table 4.8 show how, despite the growth by race and gender over this period, overall the faculty still looks White.

Figure 4.5 shows the racial breakdown of faculty in 1993 and 2005. White fac-

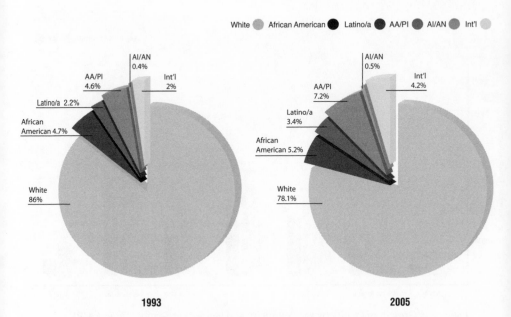

White ● African American ● Latino/a ● AA/PI ● AI/AN ● Int'l ●

AI/AN
0.4%

AA/PI
4.6%

Int'l
2%

Latino/a 2.2%

African
American 4.7%

White
86%

1993

AI/AN
0.5%

AA/PI
7.2%

Int'l
4.2%

Latino/a
3.4%

African
American 5.2%

White
78.1%

2005

Figure 4.5. Full-time faculty by race/ethnicity, 1993 and 2005. *Note:* AA/PI = Asian American / Pacific Islander; AI/AN = American Indian / Alaska Native. *Sources:* NCES, 1997, Table 226; NCES, 2007, Table 239

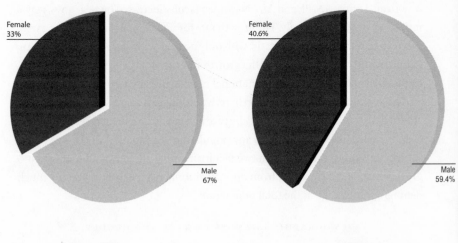

Female
33%

Male
67%

1993

Female
40.6%

Male
59.4%

2005

Figure 4.6. Full-time faculty by gender, 1993 and 2005. *Sources:* NCES, 1997, Table 226; NCES, 2007, Table 239

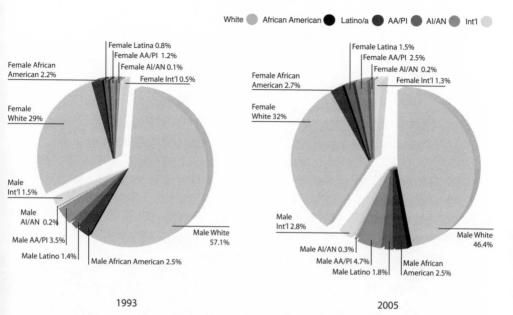

Figure 4.7. Full-time faculty by race/ethnicity and gender, 1993 and 2005.
Note: AA/PI = Asian American / Pacific Islander, AI/AN = American Indian /
Alaska Native. *Sources:* NCES, 1997, Table 226; NCES, 2007, Table 239

ulty went from 86% of the total faculty in 1993 to 78% in 2005, Blacks from 4.7%
to 5.2%, Latinos from 2.2% to 3.4%, AA/PI faculty from 4.6 to 7.2%, AI/AN faculty from 0.4% to 0.5%, and international faculty from 2% to 4.2%. URM faculty, as a group, increased from 7.3% to 9.1%.

From a gender perspective, as shown in figure 4.6, women increased from 33%
of the faculty to 41%. Figure 4.7 shows the intersection of race and gender. Clearly,
the largest demographic shift was the increase in the proportion of White women
and the decrease in the proportion of White men. White men are now just under
half of all faculty—still the largest of any group, but considerably smaller than
twelve years prior. In addition, the proportion of URM women went from 3.1%
to 4.4%, while URM men went from 4.1% to 4.6%. AA/PI women went from 1.2%
to 2.5% and AA/PI men from 3.5% to 4.7%. International women faculty increased
from 0.5% of the faculty in 1993 to 1.3% in 2005, while the share of international
men rose from 1.5% to 2.8%.

These demographic changes among faculty, however, do not reflect shifts in
faculty by sector, institution type, or tenure status. Such analyses can reflect different patterns. For example, a national analysis of tenured and tenure-track fac-

TABLE 4.9
Full-Time Administrators by Race/Ethnicity and Gender, 1993 and 2003

	1993	% of total	2003	% of total	% growth
Total	137,711		178,443		30
Male	80,014		88,405		11
Female	57,697		90,038		56
White	118,651	86	147,613	83	24
Male	70,303		75,072		7
Female	48,348		72,541		50
Black	12,232	9	17,228	9.7	41
Male	5,904		6,964		18
Female	6,328		10,264		62
Hispanic	3,580	2.6	7,006	3.9	96
Male	1,963		3,159		61
Female	1,617		3,847		138
AA/PI	2,243	1.6	4,813	2.7	115
Male	244		2,292		84
Female	999		2,521		152
AI/AN	726	0.5	1,064	0.6	47
Male	416		482		16
Female	311		582		87
International	279	0.2	719	0.4	158
Male	185		436		136
Female	94		283		201

Source: Cook & Córdova, 2006.
Note: AA/PI = Asian American / Pacific Islander; AI/AN = American Indian / Alaska Native.

ulty in 2003 showed, not surprisingly, that the percentage of URM faculty among this group was only slightly lower (8.6%) than the percentage of URM among all full-time faculty (9%) (Cook & Córdova, 2006). Any institution—two-year or four-year, public or private—might benefit from seeing how diversity in its faculty has progressed in the past decade or two, including the importance of the intersection of race and gender.

Administrative Demographics

Diversity at all levels of an institution represents true inclusiveness. If for no other reason than a symbolic one, diversity is one of the indicators of equity in institutional hiring. As was described in chapter 3, diversity in leadership legitimates and informs decision-making. The data on administrative diversity rely most heavily on information from the federal IPEDS (Integrated Postsecondary Education Data

System). Because each institution is permitted to define who is counted as an administrator, as opposed to a staff person, the data are only suggestive of the levels of diversity. Nonetheless, table 4.9 shows a pattern similar to that of the other data on diversity for the ten-year period from 1993 to 2003 (Cook & Córdova, 2006). There has been growth overall in administration (30%), with a larger share of this growth for women than for men. However, there has been growth—substantial growth, in most cases—for both men and women in every ethnic group, including White men, who increased in both number and percentage.

From a demographic perspective, however, there has been only a modest change overall. Whites accounted for 83% of administration in 2003, down from 86% in 1993. In recent studies (American Council on Education, 2008a, 2008b), the profile of chief administrators remained at about the same level, with Whites representing 84% of all administrators—and, surprisingly, very little variation by sector.

Because the presidency is the most symbolic leadership position in higher education, its demographics remain one of the most important indicators of change in leadership and in higher education itself. The diversity in leadership differs by institutional sector. Ruth Simmons was heralded as the first African American woman to lead an Ivy League institution after her appointment as president of Brown University in 2001, and Shirley Jackson was featured as the first African American woman to lead a major science institution (Rensselaer Polytechnic Institute). These firsts continue to emerge even for White women, whose growth in the academy has been noted for years. For women of color, these announcements are still few and far between. Nevertheless, as of 2008, four of the eight presidents of the Ivy League are women.

Overall, both presidential and administrative leadership, while becoming slightly more diverse, are still heavily White. As of 2006, 86% of college presidents were White; in 1986, that proportion was 92%. In 2006, 6% of presidents were African American (up from 5% in 1986), 5% were Latino (up from 2%), 1% were Native American (up from 0.4%), and 1% were Asian American (up from 0.4%). Women constituted one-third of African American presidents, 35% of Latino presidents, 22% of White presidents, and 26% of Asian American presidents. In total, the proportion of women among presidents rose from 10% in 1986 to 23% in 1996 (American Council on Education, 2007; Cook & Córdova, 2006).

Emerging Issues with Counting

With each of these studies of demographics in higher education, the reliance on broad racial and ethnic categories necessarily remains critical for tracking equity issues. At the same time, a number of trends are rendering these categories more difficult to interpret and in some cases are distorting institutional ability to track data over time. These issues are not surprising, given the changes in notions of identity suggested in chapter 2. However, they are important to engage and will become even more so. At present, they are most pressing with respect to the student data just presented, but they will become, and in some cases already have become, issues for tracking data for all groups. Whether the progress being made can stay ahead of the challenges that are developing in monitoring that progress is an important question.

Disaggregation

While federal data collection uses the standard category systems for race, the literature in higher education is increasingly focused on disaggregating by ethnicity and nationality. As previously noted, the importance of disaggregating data is most often discussed in regard to undergraduate demographics, but this issue will emerge more strongly with respect to all students, faculty, and administration over time. In addition, there is an increasing need to look carefully at not only ethnicity, but nationality and citizenship as well. This is true for graduate and professional degrees especially, because of the graduate pipeline to diversifying the faculty. The complexities of ethnicity and citizenship prompt scrutiny of whether change is taking place and for whom (Chapa, 2006; Delgado-Romero, Manlove, Manlove, & Hernandez, 2007).

Disaggregating ethnicity is important. For example, with respect to Asian American students, the legacy of academic access and success has led to the assumption that these students are the "model minority," with significant representation and success in higher education. As we have just seen with citizenship, the profile can shift when the data are disaggregated. Because disaggregated national data are often not available, analyses of specific Asian American groups have had to rely on institutional data and census data. Some recent studies document the large variation in representation, success, and experience in college among different Asian and Asian American students (Teranishi, Ceja, Antonio, Allen, & McDonough, 2004; Vea, 2008).

A growing body of literature focuses on Filipino students. The earliest of these studies pointed out that while Filipinos born in the Philippines were likely to be college-educated, this was less true of second- and third-generation Filipinos, whose college-going rates lagged behind those of the immigrant generation and other Asian groups (Okamura & Agbayani, 1997). The most recent data from the 2000 census suggest that this may be changing (Farley & Haaga, 2005). In 1980, for those twenty-five to thirty-four years of age, there was a thirty-point differential in college attainment between foreign-born and U.S.-born Filipinos, with those who were foreign-born showing higher levels of education. The gap was reduced to twenty points in 1990. In the 2000 census, the overall college-attainment rate for Filipinos was 43%, with no differential between foreign-born and U.S.-born. This rate is higher than that for Whites (30%) and Blacks (15%), but lower than that for Chinese (67%), Japanese (57%), Korean (59%), and Asian Indian (76%) students. The patterns for Filipinos may be changing overall, though data need to be looked at institutionally as well. It may be that the issues for Filipino students are less about access to higher education or graduation and more about time to degree, selection of major, family concerns, identity, issues of engagement, and so on (Maramba, 2008; Monzon, 2003; Vea, 2008).

There is some research emerging on Hmong students, and although it is still quite spare, it suggests important concerns about access and success (see, e.g., Hune, 2002). Institutions in regions where there are large Hmong populations are only now beginning to study these students more formally; and, as with American Indian / Alaska Native students, the small numbers might mean that students will be overlooked.

Data that disaggregate Latinos in higher education are limited, which means that within-group differences are rarely studied. In part because of the history of immigration, the experiences in higher education for Cuban Americans, Chicanos, and Puerto Ricans vary widely. Data on recent immigrants from Central and South America are even more scarce. National data tend to aggregate these many populations and thus probably underestimate the challenges for access and success already highlighted as a crisis in higher education. Institutions, which have the possibility of knowing more about who their students are, have opportunities to look at these patterns with a critical eye.

Though there has been little work in the higher education literature that disaggregates African Americans, some studies from other fields suggest the need to do so. The experience of Black students who immigrated from Africa or the Caribbean or students whose parents are from those backgrounds may well be different than the experience of African Americans whose roots are U.S.-based. A 2007 study by Massey, Mooney, Torres, & Charles illustrates this emerging line of research. Regardless, there is much we don't know, and we know even less when we take class, gender, and other identities into consideration.

Multiracial Identity

As mentioned in chapter 2, with the effort to identify and acknowledge the complexity of race, the U.S. Census Bureau and now the Department of Education have been developing multiracial categories, in which students can list more than one racial/ethnic background. A recent estimate using data from the Cooperative Institutional Research Program (CIRP) suggests that about 7% of college students (at least first-time, full-time freshmen) use a multiracial category (Pryor, Hurtado, Saenz, Santos, & Korn, 2007). A study by Smith, Moreno, Clayton-Pedersen, Parker, and Teraguchi (2005) found that the numbers of Latinos and American Indians increase among college students when the individual can check more than one category—a finding similar to that by Eschbach (1993).

The issue of multiracial identity is now mostly focused on undergraduate students, but it will no doubt begin at some point to affect the tracking of change at all levels. The challenge will be that with new requirements by the Department of Education, all multiracial students will be put into one category. While campuses can and should keep more detailed information, much will be lost under the new rules.

Unknown Students

Since the challenges to affirmative action began, institutions have noticed an increase in the number of students who do not state a racial identity, usually when applying for admission. Because the data collected at this time are what is reported to IPEDS, there has been growth as well in what has been called the "unknown" category—a significant enough rise to add even greater complexity to the racial and ethnic profile of a campus and ultimately of the nation. In 1991, 3.2% of students were listed as unknown in the IPEDS data. In 2001, this number grew to 5.9%—a large increase, though still a small percentage of all students (Harvey & Anderson, 2005). Who these students are has been the subject of a great deal of speculation. Some assume that unknown students are primarily multiracial.

In an effort to study this further, my colleagues and I conducted an exploratory study with three institutions that had race and ethnic data collected at entry and data collected early in the students' first term, using the Higher Education Research Institute's CIRP surveys of entering students (Smith, Moreno, Clayton-Pedersen, Parker, & Teraguchi, 2005). These three campuses had very high response rates, so that the population captured on the survey was almost identical to the population of entering students. This study revealed, first, that students were less likely to omit racial identity on the CIRP survey, supporting the notion that it is in the highly contested arena of admissions that race becomes salient. Second, it was clear that while a small proportion of students were multiracial, the vast majority of students in the unknown category were White.

These results had dramatic implications for the institutions' descriptions of their own demographic profiles. One campus that had eliminated the unknown counts from its racial profile went from 50% White to 72% White when the number of unknowns was included. This campus described itself as very diverse because of the omission of unknowns. To many students of color, however, it felt like the predominantly White campus that the study of unknowns revealed, rather than the very pluralistic campus that the institution had been describing. Thus, how a campus handles its unknowns and what assumptions it makes about who the unknown students are have significant implications for the campus's own sense of progress on diversity, its image, and its credibility.

The Achievement Gap

Affirmative action in admissions has dominated some sectors of the higher education literature and public perceptions about diversity. Increasingly, however, the achievement gap among URM students has grown in salience. This is in part as a result of the No Child Left Behind mandates in K–12 and also because of the growing accountability and assessment movements in higher education.

For years, the literature on achievement and success in higher education has focused on K–12 preparation and on factors associated with students. As data on the achievement gap have become more prominent, these results have also been used to suggest that admitting students to selective institutions does not serve them well (Nieli, 2004; Sander, 2004)—once again placing the burden of success on students, even though the data show much higher graduation rates than would be achieved at less selective institutions. All in all, this conversation is embedded in a deeply political process, with data being used to make a wide variety of cases. Nonetheless, the issue of achievement and success, especially for underrepresented and low-income students, is an important one with crucial implications for the society.

Data on the achievement gap take several forms in higher education. Several longitudinal databases at the federal level, including U.S. census data, provide some information on bachelor's-degree attainment for individuals (Adelman, 2006). The Higher Education Research Institute also has longitudinal data on entering freshmen. The continuing lag in bachelor's degrees for URM and low-income pop-

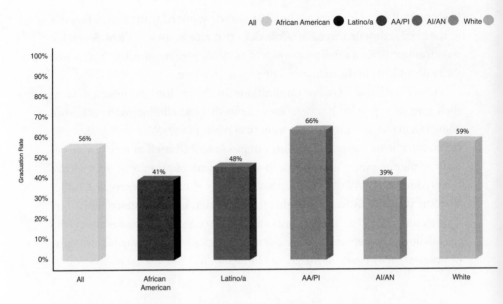

Figure 4.8. Six-year graduation rates at four-year institutions for entering cohort of 2000, by race/ethnicity. *Note:* AA/PI = Asian American / Pacific Islander; AI/AN = American Indian / Alaska Native. *Source:* Knapp, Kelly-Reid, Ginder, & Miler, 2008

ulations and the growing concern about educational attainment for men from certain groups are significant issues from a national perspective. Through an institutional lens, graduation rates and persistence rates from year to year disaggregated by race and gender are critical data points. While less information is available about income, the intersections of race, class, and gender are becoming increasingly important.

Using IPEDS data provided by institutions, the Ed Trust has begun to look at graduation rates in higher education disaggregated by race and gender. While the six-year graduation rate for first-time, full-time students does not capture adult and part-time learners, it is nevertheless useful to look at these data and ask about institutional capacity and success. Figure 4.8 shows the gaps in graduation rate by ethnicity for the 2000–2006 cohort of full-time students. The institutional six-year graduation rate was 56% overall. The rate was 41% for African Americans, 48% for Latinos, 66% for Asian Americans/Pacific Islanders, 39% for American Indians/Alaska Natives, and 59% for Whites.

Astin and Oseguera (2005), using data from 262 bachelor's institutions participating in CIRP, reported quite similar six-year graduation rates for students entering in 1994. Their data added an important dimension by including students who were still enrolled after six years. In addition, they show data for Latinos disaggregated by Mexican Americans/Chicanos and Puerto Ricans. Though the specific percentages vary somewhat from the Ed Trust data, Astin and Oseguera demonstrate the achievement gap and illustrate the importance of disaggregating. Puerto Rican students, along with American Indian students, had lower persistence and graduation rates than other groups. Astin and Oseguera's gender analysis also shows that women persist at higher rates than men.

These data provide a picture of the students who enter as first-year, full-time students and graduate from a single institution. It would not be difficult, though, for a campus to also look at the graduation rates of part-time and transfer students. In Adelman's work (2006) on graduation rates using a sample of transcripts nationally, he finds, not surprisingly, higher graduation rates if one tracks the rates for individuals across multiple institutions, rather than tracking graduation rates for institutions. His work takes transcripts from the entrance point to college and allows almost nine years for completion. He concludes that the graduation rates for individuals are higher than those often reported when IPEDS data are used. However, he affirms the existence of gaps by race/ethnicity. His data reveal that 45% of Latinos, 52% of African Americans, 65% of Asian Americans, and 68% of Whites finish.

The Ed Trust data reflect the concerns about the achievement gap nationally, although any given campus can have a very different profile. For example, one of our CDI campuses—not the most selective one—had eliminated significant racial gaps in graduation rates. Indeed, on seventeen of twenty-three campuses with sufficient data, the gap in graduation rates for Latinos had been virtually eliminated. On nine of those twenty-three campuses, the graduation rate for African Americans was equivalent to the rates for others on campus. These patterns were present at nonselective as well as selective campuses. While this is a significant accomplishment, very little data were available on whether students from various groups were thriving according to other indicators such as satisfaction, grades, honors, or persistence in STEM fields. Nonetheless, they were graduating (Smith, Parker, Clayton-Pedersen, Moreno, & Teraguchi, 2006).

There is growing frustration with the willingness of too many in the K–12 sector to accept dismal graduation rates and to feel satisfied in using excuses to explain them. Increasingly, the spotlight is being similarly placed on higher education. This began, interestingly, with attention to the graduation-rate gap for athletes in NCAA schools. Early data revealed that many athletes were not graduating, and, given the racial profile of many sports, there were questions raised about whether athletes were being used for the purpose of sports but discarded for purposes of academics (Harper, 2006). Over the past few years, regular monitoring and increasing attention on the part of institutions have led to real changes, with a significant reduction of gaps in graduation for NCAA athletes. Of course, whether these changes are a function of genuine changes in achievement or a matter of manipulation remains a concern and a matter to be addressed through processes within accreditation and institutions to ensure the integrity of these degrees.

Challenges to Traditional Admissions Indicators: What Counts as Merit?

Because there has been an assumed and unquestioned connection made by the public and in public-policy arenas between achievement, however it is measured, and traditional indicators of merit such as the SAT and other standardized tests, it is important to investigate how these traditional indicators of merit in admissions relate to success. Perhaps one of the most contentious areas of public debate in the past thirty years has been the use of affirmative action in admissions. Affirmative-action processes have been implemented to facilitate diversity in admissions among those underrepresented students whose performance on tests, in particular, might not lead to acceptance in highly selective institutions where the numbers form the core of the admissions process. With the passage of propositions in some states banning the use of race, gender, and national origin in decision-making in public institutions, the use of race as a means of assuring diversity has been curtailed (Holzer & Neumark, 2006; Orfield & Kurlaender, 2001; Orfield, Marin, & Horn, 2005; Tanaka, Bonous-Hammarth, & Astin, 1998).

While many criticize the focus of attention on those institutions with highly selective admissions as being relevant for only a small sector of higher education, the significance of these cases goes deeper. What is at stake is how merit and talent are to be identified when choices have to be made about limited goods and how outreach is to take place to communities that have not been part of the elite. Selectivity in admissions has become central to a broad range of institutions. Other, more comprehensive universities frequently have specific programs that have more applicants than places. With the legal challenges to affirmative action increasing, even programs at private institutions designed simply to reach out to underserved communities through information and support are being curtailed. Thus, even though the issue of admissions at elite public institutions may seem like a minor one, the impact of the current legal and public-policy debates is much more widespread.

If the fundamental discourse is not reframed, the battles are likely to continue to be resolved through voting machines and courts rather than in terms of educational and scholarly concerns. If diversity is to be more at the center of institutional efforts, a core element will rely on the meaning of merit and the indicators used to judge merit for any selection process. Many question whether the traditional indicators are adequate to identify talent for the twenty-first-century university and society (Alon & Tienda, 2007; Atkinson & Pelfrey, 2006; Pink, 2006; Sternberg & Grigorenko, 2002; Wheatley, 2006). This is not to suggest that those who perform well on tests, for example, may not bring a certain kind of intelligence, but it may be that this kind of intelligence is not the only kind relevant to academic excellence, achievement, leadership, and creativity.

In many large and selective public universities, the focus of attention has been on the SAT and other standardized tests, which, along with grades, have been seen as the best and most manageable indicators for college admissions. At their core, many policy discussions rely on the assumption that the tests are valid measures of academic merit and thus are a fair and important factor in deciding admissions. Indeed, most of the lawsuits that have been filed relied on differential scores on standardized tests, often of just a few points, to assert that students were unfairly denied admission. Most of these suits are brought on behalf of White students, suggesting that students of color with lower scores were given discriminatory preference (Margulies, 2002; Olivas, 1999). The Supreme Court cases in 2003 involving the University of Michigan rested on differences in test scores.

The arguments against affirmative action are posed not only in such a way as to condemn reverse discrimination, but also in a humanistic way that expresses concern for those admitted under affirmative action. The critics note that underrepresented students often have lower test scores and lower average retention rates than others. Thus, they state that ignoring scores not only penalizes those students who have worked hard and "earned" admission, it also sets underrepresented students up for failure—something that would be avoided, the argument goes, if these lower-achieving students were to attend less selective and "more appropriate" institutions (Nieli, 2004; Sander, 2004). These critics also point to the volumes of research that suggest that the SAT and high school grades are two of the best predictors of performance and that the focus of educational efforts should be on improving academic achievement and performance in high school, rather than on "lowering" admission standards.

Because selective public institutions have mandates to be inclusive, affirmative action in admissions has been the strategy used to diversify the student body, by creating either parallel or modified systems. With the legal challenges starting with the Bakke case in 1978, and with the passage of public initiatives barring the use of race in decision-making in public entities, the pressure on admissions has been to broaden the criteria so as to allow a wider set of factors to be considered. One of the responses by universities in California and Texas has been to use percentage plans in which top students in individual schools have opportunities for admissions, thus using high performance in local contexts as the indicator of merit. In some perverse form of justice, these plans only work to increase racial diversity, because of the highly segregated nature of public schools in these two states.

Significantly, however, the early research growing out of these plans shows that students who are among the top students in their schools do as well as or better than students admitted through the normal admissions process; this finding is true for underrepresented minorities as well. The research also reveals that this approach to admissions serves to increase the economic and regional diversity of entering students. The reality in both Texas and California, prior to the introduction of percentage plans, had been that only the high schools in the most affluent parts of the state routinely sent students to the flagship institutions. Percentage plans have opened access for rural students, who are now attending these universities in greater numbers. In Texas, in particular, this has generated a significant backlash among those who had a dominant claim on admissions in prior systems. The debate about solutions continues. Using percentage plans in highly segregated states and taking into account student hardships in a more holistic admissions process have been two significant approaches.

A look at the traditional academic index that was used by the university in California is extremely instructive. The classic indicator of academic merit involved a combination of three scores—high school grade point average, SAT scores, and the number of advanced-placement (AP) courses taken. What does this mean for equity and fairness? Historically, AP courses have only been available in more affluent districts. In many urban and minority districts in California, there were few, if any, advanced-placement opportunities. While a student in Beverly Hills might have a score of 12 or 13 for the number of AP courses taken, a student in Compton would likely have a zero. This would be problematic enough. But consider as well that taking AP courses affects the GPA. The highest grade in an AP course is a 5.0, whereas it is 4.0 in traditional courses. Despite their label and presentation as indicators of academic merit, these traditional indexes in fact revealed deep structural inequities. A student graduating from an inner-city school with few or no AP courses could be the valedictorian with a 4.0 GPA and not even be given serious attention because two of the three measures in the academic index would be structurally biased against her.

To make matters worse, recent research in California demonstrates that taking AP courses does not relate at all to later performance, even during the first year (Geiser & Santelices, 2006). Add to that the relationship between economic background and SAT scores, along with other factors that affect performance on tests, and we have designed a system that protects admissions for the privileged. Despite agreements by the state of California to address these disparities, the resources for advanced placement remain highly unequal, and the need to reformulate the role for AP has gone largely unaddressed. The most recent, and probably the most appropriate, approach has been to move to holistic admissions, where the student is evaluated individually and in context. I believe that there are, however, many programs, institutions, and departments that continue to rely on some version of the standard academic index.

Affirmative-action programs were designed to get around these disparities, but they did nothing to question core understandings of merit. Notice how this analysis shows the disadvantage that even an exceptional student would have in a school district with limited resources. Indeed, affirmative action has been a way to leave the core definitions of merit in place while opening the door to other students on the basis of nonacademic indicators such as hardship. This approach has two effects: it suggests that students are admitted for nonacademic reasons; and it leaves the existing notions of what constitutes merit unquestioned.

Besides grades and AP courses, the third leg of the academic-merit stool is, of course, the use of standardized tests such as the SAT, LSAT (Law School Admission Test), and GRE (Graduate Record Examination). These tests have been under scrutiny and controversy for years. It is widely understood and accepted that there is a significant correlation between test scores and economic background. Although some agencies suggest that the test scores reveal academic potential, there is considerable evidence of their weakness in determining academic potential, especially when one considers issues of race, gender, economic class, and age. Moreover, while the SAT was once presented as a "neutral" measure of aptitude and not open to being manipulated by preparation courses, the College Board has had to acknowledge that neither claim is true. The word "aptitude" has been removed from the name of the test, and test-preparation courses are now being made available to students from low-income backgrounds who might otherwise not be able to take advantage of them to improve their scores.

However, even if one removes economic background as a factor, differences remain. Women have historically performed less well than men on these tests, despite consistent and reliable data that they perform better in college. The recent research on stereotype threat consistently suggests that test performance is negatively affected when students are consciously aware that they are expected to do less well than others on an exam (Steele, 1997; Steele & Aronson, 1995). This is particularly true in high-stakes environments. What does this mean? It means that the test and the process of taking the test are vulnerable to factors other than academic merit (Helms, 2006).

This is not to ignore a large body of research that shows that the SAT and other tests are among the best single predictors of first-year grades—and another body of research that questions even this conclusion (e.g., College Board, 1997; Crouse & Trusheim, 1998; Duran, 1986; Sackett, Borneman, & Connelly, 2008; Zwick, 2007). However, the meaning of "the best" is often ignored in the policy debates. First, the "best" predictor is not necessarily a good or adequate predictor for individual academic success. Most research suggests that tests such as the SAT predict at most 20% of the variance of success (Beatty, Greenwood, & Linn, 1999; Schrader, 1978; Schwan, 1988). This means that 80% of student success or failure is explained by other factors, such as institutional efforts (Hurtado, Milem, Clayton-Pedersen, & Allen, 1998; Lowman & Spuck, 1975), noncognitive factors (Sedlacek, 1998), or psychological constructs (Steele & Aronson, 1995). Many studies show relationships much lower than 20%, and others show little or no relationship (Carver & King, 1994; Dalton, 1976; Fleming & Manning, 1998; Morrison & Morrison, 1995; Thacker & Williams, 1974).

Second, numerous studies suggest that the SAT's power as a predictor varies dramatically for different groups of students by race/ethnicity, age, and gender (College Board, 1997; Dalton, 1976; Duran, 1986; Guinier, Fine, & Balin, 1997; Rosser, 1992; Wightman, 1998).

Third, most research has focused on the role of the SAT in predicting first-year grades—leaving ultimate college success as measured by, for example, graduation, and success after graduation, largely unexplored (see, e.g., Burton & Wang, 2005; Geiser & Santelices, 2007; Sacks, 1999; Sternberg & Williams, 1997; Wallach, 1976; Wightman, 2000, 19).

Indeed, as measures of success look more at the long term and as race/ethnicity, gender, and age are considered, the power of the test often declines in significance. There are, however, few examples of such research, particularly at the graduate level. In a large meta-analysis of the relationship of the GRE to grades in graduate programs in psychology, Goldberg and Alliger (1992) found that the GRE accounts for at most about 5% of the variance. In one of the few retrospective studies, Sternberg and Williams (1997) asked faculty to evaluate the academic performance of students completing the PhD in psychology. The GRE was a significant predictor of success only for first-year grades. There was no validity after that (save a small relationship for men only between a subscore of the GRE and the quality of the dissertation).

Gough and Hall (1975) found that as medical students are evaluated for clinical competency, as opposed to academic performance, the role of standardized tests diminishes considerably. Guinier, Fine, and Balin (1997) found, in an analysis of grades in the first year of law school, that beyond a threshold LSAT score, there was no relationship between grades and LSAT scores. House (1989) found significant differences in predictive validity of the GRE for older and younger students in graduate programs in education, with much less validity for older students. In a review of studies of later life achievement, using indicators such as salary, professional esteem, and honor societies, Klitgaard (1985) found no relationship to SAT scores. In a retrospective study using grades in a first-year math course, Wainer and Steinberg (1992) found that women had lower SAT scores than men receiving similar grades. In another study of the relationship of the SAT to grades, Moffatt (1993) found no predictive validity for African Americans or for students over thirty. Similarly, Swinton (1987) found, in a study conducted by ETS, that women over twenty-five consistently outperformed predictors of first-year grades in graduate school.

Others have focused on the need to look at other factors and predictors: Sedlacek (1998) has demonstrated the predictive validity of "noncognitive" factors for African Americans; Sobol (1984) has documented the importance of admissions judgments; and various studies have demonstrated the impact of educational experience on performance (Lowman & Spuck, 1975; Steele & Aronson, 1995; Young, 1994). Bowen and Bok (1998) underscore the high graduation rates of students who attend selective institutions, regardless of their entering SAT scores—directly countering the notion that admitting students with lower scores necessarily jeopardizes their success. Sternberg and Grigorenko (2002) suggest the inadequacy of static testing such as the SAT.

In general, then, relatively few studies focus on longer-term success, and those that do point to a diminished capacity of tests to address admissions concerns. Indeed, few data outside individual institutions allow for the exploration of success looking back to entrance scores. Even fewer data sources are available that permit disaggregation by such factors as race/ethnicity, gender, age, and field of study. Finally, the existing research most often relies on the statistical terminology concerning "variance" to communicate the predictive power of tests, leaving open the very real possibility of misusing the results in policy and legal settings.

As mentioned earlier, one criticism of affirmative action is that it admits students without the necessary qualifications to succeed. These critics state explicitly that students would be better served by going to less selective institutions, where, presumably, they would perform better. This argument often relies on data showing an achievement gap by race in terms of graduation or GPA. This apparent concern for the well-being of students admitted under affirmative action ignores, of course, the dismal graduation rates for URM students at all but the most selective institutions, where these students, regardless of their test scores, are much more likely to graduate than URM students elsewhere. Moreover, it assumes that those who are not succeeding are those with the lower test scores at entrance.

A Retrospective Study of Success and Test Scores

In an effort to look at the relationship between student success and test scores, Gwen Garrison and I, along with a team of researchers, undertook a study (Smith & Garrison 2005) of indicators of academic success such as graduation and grades, looking back at the distribution of test scores for those with a range of success. This retrospective study showed not only how limited the relationship was between success and initial test scores, but also how little test scores meant for URM students in particular. Surprisingly, in most cases, there was not even a threshold point where students were likely to fail if their test scores went below a certain point. Even available data were limited, the results are significant.

This study was conceived because at a meeting concerning the use of testing in college admissions, a highly regarded and successful civil rights attorney commented that if the LSAT had been weighted heavily when she and Thurgood Marshall were applying to law school, neither of them would have been admitted. It was that comment that inspired the research. Clearly, finding ways to understand how standardized admissions tests identify or ignore talent is an urgent necessity. The study presented an alternative way of investigating the arguments for and against a test as an indicator of merit by looking at student talent identification retrospectively and empirically and asking the following questions: In an analysis that takes student success and looks backward at test scores, how well would the test fare in identifying talent? How many successful students, and which ones, would have been so identified at the beginning? How many of these would *not* have been admitted if the relevant standardized test had been emphasized?

An important contribution of this approach is that it retains an emphasis on academic merit and excellence while investigating the adequacy of standardized tests as indicators of excellence by using a variety of archival data sources to explore these issues. Legal and other policy debates ultimately rest on the validity of the tests.

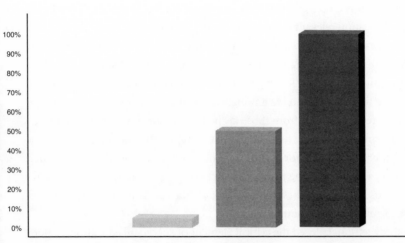

Figure 4.9. Expected relationship between success and test scores. *Source:* Smith & Garrison, 2005

However, rarely are validity studies carried out using anything more than first-year grades. A key component of any analysis, then, is the selection of success indicators that might more closely approximate genuine outcomes. For this study, several longer-term indicators of success were used. For undergraduate success, four-year GPA and graduation from college were appropriate. For law school, passing the bar was chosen as a reasonable proxy for access to the profession. Thus, this study does not explore other success indicators, such as professional success, for which tests might be an even weaker indicator (Klitgaard, 1985).

One of the challenges in looking at the data is the use of statistics in policy studies. The use of multivariate analysis in studying predictive validity is a perfectly valid approach. Indeed, it is the only way to look at a complex relationship among numerous factors. Nevertheless, the results of these analyses are often oversimplified when applied in legal and policy contexts. Even though testing agencies and others continue to state that the predictive power of a single test is quite limited, policy discussions and lawsuits continue to assume that merit and tests are almost synonymous (see, e.g., Mangan, 2002). The Smith and Garrison study (2005) attempted to depict the direct relationships between available indicators of test scores and academic success. Graphic illustrations were a powerful tool for demonstrating relationships relevant to the admissions issue. Indeed, Smith, Best, Stubbs, Archibald, and Roberson-Nay (2002) emphasize the important role of graphics in visually presenting information relevant to important policy and scientific questions.

The study was tailored to look narrowly at the relationship between a variety of success indicators and the test scores for various groups of students by illustrating graphically the predictive power or lack of power of test scores. In that context, one would expect to see among various indicators of academic success virtually no representation from those at the lowest score levels and total representation from those at the highest levels. Conceptually, one might imagine a stepped bar graph in which for any measure of success, few from the lowest scores would be present, continuing to greater percentages and perhaps total representation of those with the highest scores (fig. 4.9). Such a clean relationship would reflect a correlation coefficient approaching 1.0.

The study left unexplored the critical element of successful educational interventions that make test scores even less predictive and the many factors that influence performance outside of a student's background. It is clear that in all the data collected, tests were likely to have been one of the elements considered in admissions decisions. As with most studies, this research does not include students who were not admitted. The critical question here was the power of the relationship of tests and success and the implications for identifying academic talent and excellence.

One might also expect to find that there is a threshold score or range of scores that would be useful in facilitating the admissions process. Research might reveal that within a specified range at the lower end of the test scores, students are not likely to succeed. This study was designed to look at these questions and, in particular, to illustrate graphically the degree to which such distinctive relationships do or do not exist. Indeed, in some ways, the study provides a way of investigating levels of risk in admitting students whose scores range widely on a test, by focusing on the bivariate relationship between success and tests.

The study required identifying archival data that was longitudinal and included indicators of success and relevant test scores. A strong data set would also include information on race/ethnicity and gender. A search of existing data that would permit the required analysis revealed limited availability. By necessity, then, not all data were complete, nor could all questions be addressed. Some of the data were from single institutions (shared under assurances of anonymity), one source consisted of systemwide data, and another was a national database. In a few cases, we were able to disaggregate by race and gender, but in most cases such data were not available.

In some cases, the numbers were extremely small and possibly unstable. A subset of the results from the full study is described using the five data sources below.

1. *Systemwide data from a selective university system*. Information was available on SAT scores, successful graduation and retention, and dropout due to academic failure. More than thirty-seven thousand students were included, from the entering classes of 1989 and 1990. For this study, breakdowns by race and gender were not available.

2. *Admissions data for a selective public university*. The data included information about SAT scores, college grades, and graduation as indicators of success. No race and gender data were available for the study.

3. *"Baccalaureate and Beyond" data*. A license to access the Baccalaureate and Beyond data set was obtained from the National Center for Education Statistics. A subset of the data set focusing on selective institutions was developed. This data set for approximately two thousand college graduates of selective institutions allowed us to look at SAT scores, college grades, disciplinary fields of study, high school grades, and race and gender. The data did not permit a comparison of both "success" and "failure," since they included only college graduates. The study of college grades, however, permitted a look at levels of performance.

4. *Mean GPA and retention rates for a highly selective private science program*. The program provided math SAT scores, mean GPA, and graduation rate for its majority and underrepresented students from 1986 to 1995. The math SAT was used here because of its relevance to the science curriculum and its role in admissions.

5. *The bar-passage rate for a selective law school*. The data included LSAT scores, bar-passage rates, race and gender information, and whether the student was admitted on scores alone or by a committee's review and rating of the application.

The primary analysis looks at the percentage of success from each of the clustered test scores. That is, among those who were successful, what was the representation from the different SAT groupings? Here, threshold scores can be determined, as can the risk factor involved when students with various test scores are admitted. Even where differences among groups are noted, one can see the degree to which students do or do not perform according to what their test scores would predict. One sees in the analysis a variety of clusters for test scores. For most of the SAT data, we used distributions of SAT scores, since these are generally understood. However, the categories for the groupings of scores varied by data source. Because LSAT scores are less well understood, these scores were grouped by their overall distribution in the population such that we could look at students whose scores were one and two standard deviations above and below the mean. For the

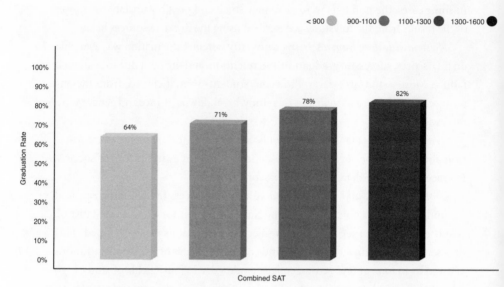

Figure 4.10. Selective university system: Combined SAT scores and graduation rates. *Source:* Smith & Garrison, 2005

Baccalaureate and Beyond database, because the ACT and SAT data were combined, quartiles were used.

SELECTIVE UNIVERSITY SYSTEM

The broad data on graduation and retention demonstrate, as expected, some relationship between SAT scores and graduation six years after entry for the entering classes of 1989 and 1990. Figure 4.10 demonstrates, in the aggregate, a linear relationship between the SAT and graduation rate, with a very gradual slope. Typically, these are the kind of data that would demonstrate the usefulness of the SAT. Nonetheless, we see that 64% of those with extremely low SAT scores (less than 900 combined) are still successful. The remaining three groups include success rates of 71%, 78%, and, 82%, respectively.

To exclude students in the lowest category from admission would have eliminated the 64% who were successful in order to avoid admitting the 36% who were not successful. Even in the highest SAT group, nearly 20% were not successful. How an institution evaluates this level of risk would depend on the institution's own view of the students in this lowest category and the other attributes these stu-

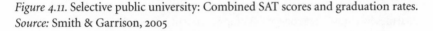

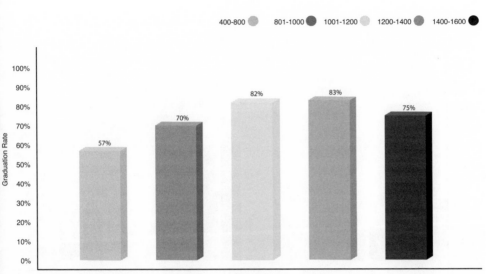

Figure 4.11. Selective public university: Combined SAT scores and graduation rates. *Source:* Smith & Garrison, 2005

dents might bring. For the data from this university system, a score of 900 could be considered a threshold.

It is important to emphasize that this study does not presume that admissions evaluations are not relevant or should not consider test scores. The results of the analysis suggest that the SAT alone is not pertinent to the ultimate success of students and that successful students are as likely to have lower SAT scores as higher ones. Moreover, basing lawsuits on discrepancies in scores, particularly from the midrange, would not be supported from these data.

SELECTIVE PUBLIC UNIVERSITY

In contrast to the results of the analysis for the system, the data for one of the most selective campuses in this system, displayed in figure 4.11, do not show a linear relationship between SAT scores and graduation. Indeed, the graduation rate for those with a combined SAT of 1400–1600 (the highest) is lower than for those with scores between 1000 and 1400.

BACCALAUREATE AND BEYOND: NATIONAL DATA

This rich data set permitted many analyses looking at how race, gender, academic major, and institutional selectivity mediated success. Data for the selective Liberal

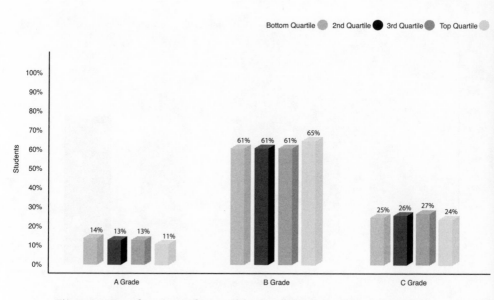

Figure 4.12. Baccalaureate and Beyond (national data): Combined SAT score quartiles by cumulative college GPA for all students at selective institutions. *Source:* Smith & Garrison, 2005

Arts I and Research I institutions are considered here. These data were examined according to levels of achievement as represented by grades and permitted some analysis by race/ethnicity.

Overall, as depicted in figure 4.12, there is little or no relationship between SAT scores and cumulative college grades in selective institutions. The students getting As are as likely to come from the lowest as the highest SAT quartiles. Indeed, for this population, students with low SAT scores are slightly overrepresented, and students with the highest scores slightly underrepresented, in the A grades. This is also the case for both men and women when they are considered separately. The relative lack of differences between test-score groups is the most important point here.

While the number of students of color is relatively small in this group of highly selective institutions, the data are quite revealing. Data for Latino students are presented in figure 4.13. The most important conclusion is that there is an uneven relationship between test scores and success. Among those in the A category, a higher percentage come from the bottom and second quartiles than from the top groupings.

Thus, these data from the Baccalaureate and Beyond set provide support for the weak relationship of the SAT to overall college grades. This study also reveals

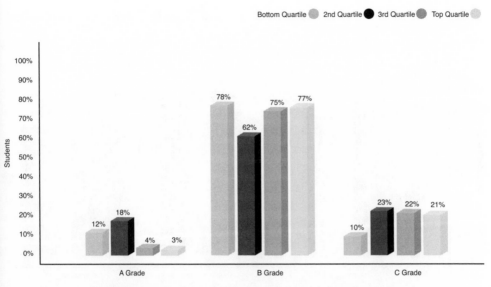

Figure 4.13. Baccalaureate and Beyond (national data): Combined SAT score quartiles by cumulative college GPA for Latino students at Research I institutions. *Source:* Smith & Garrison, 2005

that a loss of talent would occur if the SAT were weighted too heavily in admissions.

SELECTIVE SCIENCE PROGRAM

A highly selective science program provided data that allowed us to examine the relationship between students' SAT math scores and mean GPAs and the graduation rate for majority and underrepresented students. These data span a nine-year period, from 1986 to 1995, and involve 2,137 students. The data clearly reveal the limited range of SAT scores for students admitted; few have scores below 600 on the math exam.

Figure 4.14 displays the graduation rate according to SAT math scores for all students, for "majority" (White and Asian American) students, and for underrepresented students (African American, Latino, and Native American). The data suggest that there is a threshold score of 600 for the student body as a whole. The graduation rate ranges from 75% to 82% for all students with scores above 600. For underrepresented students with scores above 600, the graduation rate ranges from 65% to 83%. However, for the URM students, the highest graduation rates

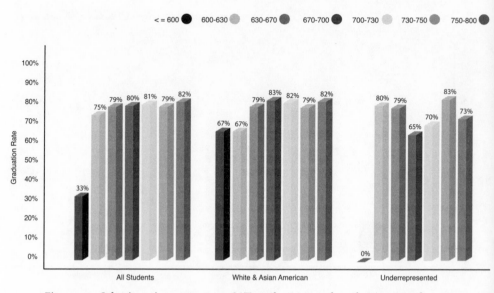

Figure 4.14. Selective science program: SAT math scores and graduation rates by student group. *Source:* Smith & Garrison, 2005

are in the second-lowest and second-highest SAT groups. The 65% graduation rate is from the middle of the range.

The figure shows that except for those with math SAT scores below 600, the graduation distribution for all students is relatively flat. For "majority" students, there is a slight threshold below 630–670 (though the graduation rate is still quite high below the threshold). One can see how variable the distribution is—in particular, for underrepresented students of color—and that URM students with scores above 600 succeeded as well as or better than students overall.

SELECTIVE LAW SCHOOL

The law school data focused primarily on bar-passage rate as the measure of success in relationship to the LSAT. For this analysis, the LSAT scores of all entering students were distributed according to standard deviations above and below the mean. For those not familiar with LSAT scores, the mean was 163, with the range being 141 to 178. In a pattern similar to that found in the other analyses, the data suggest limited relationships between bar passage and the LSAT for all students.

While the bar graph (fig. 4.15) shows a stepwise progression, the actual bar-passage rate varies from 63% to 100%. Here, too, the lowest LSAT group had the lowest pass rate, suggesting a potential threshold—though one at which the 63% who

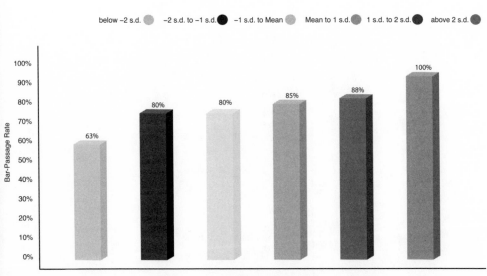

Figure 4.15. Selective law school: LSAT scores in standard-deviation (s.d.) distribution and bar-passage rates. *Source:* Smith & Garrison, 2005

succeeded might be eliminated. Indeed, there is little differentiation except for the lowest group.

The relationship between bar passage and the LSAT is quite unreliable for students of color. All Asian American students from the lowest LSAT groups passed the bar. For underrepresented students, the rates varied. While 60% of the lowest group (containing only five students) passed the bar, the rates for the other groups were quite varied (see table 4.10).

Data were also available for those who were admitted by their scores alone (usually undergraduate GPA and LSAT scores) and those who had to be reviewed by committee (see table 4.11). This analysis is important because the current notion is that those who are admitted by committee are most likely affirmative-action decisions—not admissible for purely "academic reasons." There are two significant findings here. First, there were no differences in bar-passage rate between these two groups. Of those who were admitted by their scores, 83% passed the bar, and 81% of those who had to be reviewed by committee passed. Moreover, forty-seven of the fifty-two underrepresented students of color were admitted by scores alone, not with committee rankings! Eighty percent of the five who were reviewed passed the bar, and 75% of those who were admitted by scores did so. Twenty-eight of thirty-two Asian American students were also admitted by their scores. Of these,

TABLE 4.10

Law-School Data: Distribution of LSAT Scores and Bar Passage by Race/Ethnicity

Standard-deviation distribution of LSAT scores	Whites			Asian Americans			Underrepresented students of color		
	Number of students	Number who passed bar	% who passed bar	Number of students	Number who passed bar	% who passed bar	Number of students	Number who passed bar	% who passed bar
Below 2 s.d.	1	0	0	2	2	100	5	3	60
Between −2 s.d. and −1 s.d.	5	3	60	3	3	100	12	10	83
Between −1 s.d. and mean	36	31	86	15	12	80	25	18	72
Between mean and 1 s.d.	69	58	84	11	11	100	7	5	71
Between 1 s.d. and 2 s.d.	28	24	86	1	1	100	3	3	100
Above 2 s.d.	2	2	100	0	0	0	0	0	0
Total	141	118	84	32	29	91	52	39	75

Source: Smith & Garrison, 2005.

TABLE 4.11
Law-School Data: Admissions Decisions and Bar Passage by Race/Ethnicity

		Admitted by scores				Admitted by committee review		
	Number of students	Number who passed bar	% who passed bar	% of ethnic group	Number of students	Number who passed bar	% who passed bar	% of ethnic group
Underrepresented students of color	47	35	75	90	5	4	80	10
Asian Americans	28	27	96	88	4	2	50	7
Whites	76	64	84	54	65	54	83	46
Total	151	126	83	67	74	60	81	33

Source: Smith & Garrison, 2005.

96% passed the bar. Of the four who were reviewed, 50% passed. In contrast, 46% of White students were admitted only after review. Of those reviewed, 83% passed the bar; of those admitted on their scores, 84% passed. These data support the usefulness of a review and also suggest that White students benefit more from these opportunities than is often presumed. Indeed, among the three ethnic groupings, the percentage of Whites who were admitted on the basis of their scores alone was by far the lowest (54%, compared to 88% for Asian Americans and 90% for underrepresented students).

Overall, one can see that there would be significant loss of talent if tests emerged as an overriding consideration in admissions. Though we might have expected some threshold point to be obtained for the data, we did not find this consistently, except in the case of the highly selective science school. In virtually all the data, there was some demarcation between those whose test scores were at the lowest levels and those just above. The advisability of admitting students from the lowest testing group would depend on institutional views about risk, intervention, and success. Even so, a high percentage of students in the lowest group were still represented in the success categories. One can only wonder what improved institutional practices would do to increase success. For all five data sources, successful students were as likely to come from the middle groups as from the top tier. We should note that the important findings of this study would have been masked in traditional validity studies.

Moreover, when looking at the distributions by race and ethnicity, one would want to use extreme caution when attributing significance to tests, given the lack of consistency shown in these data. Contrary to the views of many, it is clear that if there are differentials in performance, they may not be a function of test scores. While further exploration with larger samples of underrepresented students is needed, the current data underscore the need for caution in linking test scores and success. The lack of consistency among underrepresented students is one of the most consistent findings from this analysis.

In some policy and legal studies, we are led to believe that when we look at student success, we are only seeing students with higher test scores and that when we look at failure, we are seeing students with lower scores. This is particularly true when students come from an underrepresented group. These data suggest quite a different picture. The analysis, though not definitive and certainly limited, underscores the drawbacks of relying too heavily on tests in admissions decisions. It debunks the myth that performance in school is directly related to test scores. Finally, the study supports the power of using retrospective approaches to evaluate both policy and institutional efforts. The view of the relationship between tests and success described in the initial conceptual hypothesis is clearly not sustainable.

Concluding Thoughts on What Counts as Merit

Each of the recent challenges to affirmative action in admissions, whether through state propositions or legal action, rests on the argument that students are being admitted with "less merit" and that this approach works against students who have earned "merit." The results of the Smith and Garrison study suggest that if merit is defined by high scores on very traditional measures (a fairly conservative approach), standardized tests as pre-admissions indicators of merit are quite inadequate overall and are especially inadequate for underrepresented students of color.

In the absence of reliable indicators, holistic admissions and human judgment are likely to be the best approach. This is especially true for highly competitive admissions at elite institutions. In such contexts, there are many more people who are superbly qualified for admission than there are places available. Reducing the complex calculus of admissions to only one or two numerical indicators is likely to distort the range of talents wanted, needed, and admitted. The fact that many people who are not at the top of some entrance criterion perform better is not surprising, given the research on the important role of effort over "aptitude" (Dweck, 2000). Further, when standardized tests are used as the major criterion, this calculus will work against historically underrepresented students—the groups for whom affirmative action was initially created. It also does not take into account the reasons that high performers might not do well on high-stakes tests. As we shall see in chapter 7, there are factors that influence performance that, if not considered, will result in a significant loss of talent. Finally, it is clear that educators, policy makers, and lawyers must examine critically any argument that rests primarily on tests as indicators of merit.

Despite data such as those from the Smith and Garrison study, there has been considerable resistance to limiting the influence of high-stakes tests in many selective institutions. Indeed, a number of testing organizations, including the College Board and the LSAT group, have pushed to make sure that tests are not overused. Even in recent court cases, campuses have not taken the opportunity to show how weak tests are as a measure of merit and hence a weak basis on which to file lawsuits. As Klitgaard (1985) points out in his thorough analysis about the limits of using standard academic indicators to identify elites, tests and grades, regardless of their bias in whom they leave out, are far more efficient for the selection

process. Nonetheless, increasing numbers of institutions have minimized or eliminated the use of the SAT, both because of its limits in identifying talent and because the institution itself does not want to narrow the definition of merit to test-
taking at the expense of creativity, motivation, artistry, and other forms of
excellence that might not be captured by scores on tests. For that reason, many
private selective institutions have long relied on thorough and holistic readings of
student applications to find the diversity of talent and excellence required.

The fundamental issue in our current admissions process is that when one form
of criteria is used to the exclusion of others, who gets in and who doesn't has implications for equity in society. When these results are then linked to merit, the
discourse about equity, as we have seen in the Michigan case, will exist in contrast to merit (Alon & Tienda, 2007). As Atkinson and Pelfrey (2006) suggest in
their review of the admissions and affirmative-action dilemma, "UC's experience
with outreach, the four-percent plan, and comprehensive review show that students in these situations have often shown extraordinary academic initiative and
persistence. If our assumptions about merit are too narrow to include them, our
assumptions need another look" (p. 10). They go on to affirm that "one of the productive outcomes of the admissions debate is that it has led us to question some
of the long-held assumptions about academic merit and potential" (p. 11).

Looking Back and Looking Forward

For higher education—as for society—diversity is not only its challenge, but its
future. When we look over the developments of the past forty years, two themes
emerge. The first is the expansion and deepening of the domain of diversity. The
impact of changing demographics, the increasing calls for inclusiveness in higher
education, the expanding accountability mandates, and the growing understanding of the multiplicity of perspectives concerning identity all make it less and less
possible to simply add diversity to an institutional agenda. Rather, diversity will
become more and more central to institutional effectiveness. Moreover, simply
achieving a demographic mix on campus will not be sufficient. Creating the conditions under which diversity thrives will be critical to institutional success.

Second, there is an overwhelming amount of unfinished business. The current and past literatures often appear interchangeable in their discussions of the
access and success of underrepresented populations and a variety of institutional
issues such as curriculum, pedagogy, and faculty and staff diversity. As Peter Smith
(2004) observes in his reflection on the past fifty years in higher education:

In some important respects, we've succeeded beyond our fathers' and our mothers' wildest dreams. . . . In the last fifty years since that time [World War II], however, . . . our strides toward achieving the American promise of opportunity in higher education have shrunk. Although it is true we are graduating more students than ever, our success rates are flattening as a percentage of the total population. We are winnowing out the very people we need if we, as a nation, want to compete in a global market. We are leaving behind millions of Americans who have the capacity to learn and for whom the promise of opportunity was made but not kept. (pp. 9–10)

Our campuses appear more diverse if one allows the demographics of the undergraduate population to be the indicator. Diversity begins to disappear as one goes higher into the institution. Indeed, increasing diversity at the undergraduate level can often serve as a camouflage for the real issues that remain. Not only does it camouflage issues of student success, for example, it also suggests greater institutional capacity than is the case. A focus on undergraduate diversity can deflect attention from the issues of diversity in leadership, from the centrality of diversity to the core institutional values and strategies, and even from the need to prepare diverse leadership and future faculty to lead higher education in developing the kind of research and applications needed in society. With the increasing complexity of issues and identities comes the need for much more sophisticated forms of both theoretical and applied research that can inform institutional and societal concerns. A focus on undergraduate students and a focus on the most general of curriculum areas will not be sufficient. Moreover, the legal questions that appeared to be resolved in the 1960s and 1970s have become challenges to progress and have made fighting legal and public-policy battles central to much of the efforts on diversity.

At the same time, we will see some important lessons and strategies; these will be the focus of the following chapters. Central tenets of these lessons are that good education matters and can mitigate lack of preparation; and that institutional context matters as well. The conditions under which institutions function will affect the degree to which their approaches and strategies succeed. In each case, the success of institutional efforts will depend on whether diversity is framed as an issue central to the capacity of the institution, rather than as a marginal effort to "help" some groups. Even with respect to student success, the institutional context is central.

PART III

Building Capacity by Interrupting the Usual

❀

CHAPTER FIVE

Identifying Talent

The Faculty

Diversity in leadership is essential for building institutional capacity for diversity. Yet it remains one of the least successful areas, even as it becomes an increasingly urgent issue facing college campuses. Change has certainly occurred, but the question is whether the changes are sufficient.

This chapter addresses faculty diversity, especially in race/ethnicity and gender, because of their significance and because of the challenges associated with them that are reflected in the literature. These challenges are exacerbated by a limited educational pipeline and by a legal climate that has suggested that interrupting the usual is tantamount to reverse discrimination. The chapter will summarize the literature and some key research, present some mini–case studies that highlight the complexity of the hiring process and the need for careful attention to it, and suggest some strategies that can be helpful. While focusing on faculty, the themes and conclusions presented here apply to administrative hiring and retention as well.

The Rationale for Faculty Diversity

Existing research shows that greater clarity is needed about the rationale for diversifying the faculty. On many campuses and in much of the literature, a direct link is made between the increasing racial and ethnic diversity of the student body and the need for similarly diversifying the faculty. This link needs more development if it is to be compelling. At the same time, some of the limits of this connection must be acknowledged. Further, on other campuses, the kinds of diversity being targeted have been broadened to be all-inclusive. This undifferentiated approach to hiring can render diversity efforts meaningless, since individuals bring many forms of diversity to the institution. It is critically important, therefore, to clarify the role faculty play for higher education, why faculty are hired, and, in particular, why having a diverse faculty is significant.

For years, the *primary* rationale for diversifying the faculty that has been stated in the literature is the increasing racial and ethnic diversity of the student body. Indeed, faculty diversity is very important to students and student success. As the student body has grown more diverse, students have increasingly sought out faculty from similar backgrounds for advising and mentoring. Moreover, the presence of visible models of faculty from diverse backgrounds creates images of possibility in terms of career. In addition, the more diverse the faculty, the more opportunities are created for seeing faculty as individuals and making them less vulnerable to being stereotyped.

Though the significance of having a diverse faculty for the benefit of students cannot be underestimated, the reasons are often stated in terms that are open to some criticism and require some clarification. First of all, while students from diverse backgrounds do seek out faculty from similar backgrounds to a significant degree, it is always important to note that the correspondence between faculty and student identity is not one to one. That is, pairing students with a faculty member of one similar background may not be sufficient to ensure effective advising or mentoring. This is in part because, as I have shown in chapter 2, individuals bring many characteristics to their identity on which a student and faculty member may make a connection and other characteristics on which they may not. The mixed results on this question in the literature on mentoring may be explained by the multidimensionality of identity.

In addition, on most campuses, in most departments, it is not a matter of whether the diversity must match the diversity of students. Rather, it is a matter of the *absence* of significant diversity. In many departments, it is not unusual to have no faculty of color, let alone an underrepresented-minority faculty member. There may be no women, or only White women. The data are clear that there are significant numbers of students who have never been taught by a URM faculty member. The numbers of White women faculty have increased significantly; however, there are still many students who have never studied with a woman scientist, for example.

The absence of diversity places pressure on the token faculty from underrepresented groups to function as super mentors and advisors and also makes the lack of openness of the field extremely visible. If students never see an African American physicist, how likely is it that significant numbers of African American students will imagine themselves as physicists? Indeed, it is the presence of a diverse group of faculty that explains in part the significance of women's colleges and historically Black colleges and universities. If one goes to Spelman College or Bennett College to major in math or science, one will see a number of African American women mathematicians or scientists. Where else in the country might this be possible? In other women's colleges, the same holds true, except that in many of these institutions, the women are predominantly White. Nonetheless, the power of these institutions is in part a result of the visible presence of diversity in the faculty and also the presence of an entire faculty, regardless of their backgrounds, who are committed to the special mission and supportive of students entering academe. Much of the research on special-purpose institutions suggests that these two factors explain the impressive results that will be presented in chapter 7.

The significance of a visible presence of faculty of color and women faculty of all backgrounds is perhaps nowhere more challenged than in science, engineering, and other technical fields (STEM fields), where the lack of domestic diversity is emerging as a national crisis. Despite generations of students who have majored in these areas as undergraduates, the faculty in many departments are not very diverse, especially in terms of White women and URM faculty. Asian American faculty are more likely to be in STEM fields, and not uniformly visible throughout other disciplines.

Again, it is not that faculty of all backgrounds in these departments cannot be good mentors to URM students, all students of color, or White women; it is that the absence of significant diversity influences perceptions of possibility and openness. It puts pressure on any single faculty member to be the image of the field for whole groups of students. It suggests that the department does not believe that increasing diversity would strengthen the field or unit. It also suggests that the department does not believe that sufficient talent is present in those groups. The absence of diversity has significant implications as well for the quality of life for faculty and staff in the department, because being a token is not easy and is often quite impossible, both for the individual and for the department.

While there is no doubt that the increasing racial/ethnic diversity of the student body is significantly related to faculty diversity, emphasizing this reason to the exclusion of others will, in the end, undermine serious efforts at the departmental or college level to focus on increasing the diversity of the faculty. Faculty are hired primarily on the basis of field, department, or institutional priorities, *not* on the background characteristics of students. Even so, there are a number of very important institutional reasons to diversify a faculty. These reasons, already summarized in chapter 3, underscore the centrality of diversity for developing human capacity in colleges and universities. They are particularly important for faculty hiring.

First of all, diversity in the faculty represents the institution's values concerning equity in both hiring and retention. Any institution that describes itself as open and committed to diversity but has the faculty demographic common today could be seen as disingenuous and hypocritical. Thus, success in diversifying the faculty goes to the heart of whether an institution is seen as committed to equity and diversity.

Second, diversity is a central component of the academy's ability to develop diverse forms of knowledge. Partly in response to legal challenges to diversity, a body of research has been developed to study the impact of diversity in the faculty. The consistent findings from numerous studies demonstrate the role of URM faculty and White women, in particular, in bringing diversity themes to scholarship, increasing diversity in the curriculum, and introducing more and different patterns of pedagogy, including increasing the engagement of students in the community (Antonio, 2002; Astin, 2002; Hurtado, 2001a; Ibarra, 2000; Luna de la Rosa, 2005; Marin, 2000; Milem, 2001; Milem, Chang, & Antonio, 2005).

Whether through the vehicle of ethnic and women's studies, through emphases in mainstream academic departments, through cross-disciplinary institutes, or in programs related to specific communities in health, social services, medicine, law, and education, scholarly work has been influenced by the perspectives and experiences of women, persons of color, LGBT faculty, and faculty with disabilities. Most recently, one can see the important contributions of Muslim scholars and others from a variety of religious traditions, without whom many campuses would find their conversations about Islam restricted and inadequate. Indeed, if it had not been for the development of these new forms of scholarship over the past forty years, especially ethnic and women's studies, many campus efforts to diversify the curriculum would be difficult. It has produced the scholarly base, the books and articles, and the resources more generally to facilitate curriculum transformation.

The correspondence between scholar and field is not one to one: a number of faculty of color have had the experience of being asked to teach a course on race and/or gender even when their own expertise was not in that area. In this way, institutions can be guilty of pigeonholing faculty who do not emphasize diversity-related content in their own scholarship (Allen, Epps, Suh, & Stassen, 2002; Baez, 2000; Benjamin, 1997; Weinberg, 2008). One can make the case that until there is sufficient diversity in the faculty as a whole, there is the danger that faculty members from underrepresented backgrounds will not thrive as individuals, but rather as members of groups for which there is either student or institutional pressure to engage in diversity in ways that are often stereotypical (Baez, 2002; Villalpondo & Delgado Bernal, 2002).

Indeed, the presence of greater numbers of faculty who bring diverse perspectives to teaching and research decreases the likelihood that any individual faculty member will be stereotyped. With a critical mass of faculty from different groups, one may experience a woman who is caring and one who is not, a person who is effective as a teacher and one who is not, an Asian American who is a scientist and one who is a poet. Paradoxically, by paying attention to gender and ethnicity in hiring, a campus increases the likelihood of creating an environment where individuals can also be individuals (Jordan, 2006).

There is increasing recognition that one's position in society can help frame a set of perspectives or concerns that might not be introduced by someone else. This is true even in the sciences, where, for example, it has taken women scientists and supportive men to point out that the absence of women patients in clinical drug trials for treatment of breast cancer was not in the interest of women's health or good science. This practice, common up until the 1990s, resulted in federal legislation requiring that clinical trials include people from diverse backgrounds. By not including a variety of men and women from different racial and ethnic groups and by not addressing sexuality, many approaches to health care have been ignored or potentially misdirected.

A third benefit of faculty diversity lies in the development of vital relationships with diverse communities outside the campus. For both personal and intellectual reasons, many White women and faculty of color are more likely to cross a border between the academic institution and issues of practice outside. The early work in both ethnic and women's studies made boundary and border crossing an academic priority. In addition, when one experiences isolation in one setting, the tendency is to reach out to communities outside. This is true on campus as well, where one often sees campus groups and alliances formed around race/ethnicity and/or gender that bring together students, staff, and faculty, as well as community members in some cases.

Fourth, in what has been called the demographics of decision-making, faculty from diverse racial and ethnic backgrounds are essential to the capacity of institutions to make fully informed decisions at all levels. With URM faculty and Asian American faculty at low levels on many campuses, and with campuses increasingly engaging diversity as an institutional priority, those who bring diversity are spread thin, and the institution's capacity to make effective and credible decisions is hampered. In short, diversity is essential for the expertise, excellence, and perspectives required at the institutional and departmental levels. Participation by diverse faculty not only increases the likelihood of more informed perspectives, it also addresses power inequities on campus. As key decision-making bodies are diversified, power sharing in leadership increases.

I gave a talk once at an institution and asked the faculty and administrators present how they would feel if the provost or president only appointed physicists to his or her cabinet. The discussion that followed was energized by the understanding that both politically and rationally, this would not be a good thing to do. The faculty outside physics, or at least outside the hard sciences, would be alarmed that institutional decisions would be made without a deep understanding of and priority for their fields—and credibility and trust would thus be compromised.

Moreover, no matter how sensitive and broad-minded individual physicists might be, there would be a need to demonstrate—or perhaps overdemonstrate—how supportive they were of the arts and social sciences. In addition, the absence of diversity in academic affiliations would necessarily limit the information that emerges from being involved in relevant social networks. Thus, the importance of the composition of decision-making bodies lies not only in the qualities of the individual, but also in the perspective and position the individual is seen as representing and the quality of the perspectives around the decision-making table. Department affiliation is clearly a major source of identity on campus, and race and gender are as well. At least from the perspective of persons of color and all women, the profile around most leadership tables is remarkably homogenous. White women are sometimes present, though still often in token positions, but the presence of persons of color is quite rare. The implications for the content and credibility of decisions are profound.

We understand this when we think of global issues (or technology, for that matter). An interest in furthering internationalization as part of the institution's mission almost inevitably involves hiring international faculty, who bring the relevant educational and scholarly expertise. We also know that having people from international backgrounds represented on campus will enhance the institution's credibility and ability to connect to an increasingly globalized society. While this value commonly informs global discussions on campus, it is not always applied when hiring domestic faculty—even though, as mentioned earlier, recent research has documented that faculty from a diversity of racial and ethnic perspectives often bring new perspectives to the curriculum, to research, and to ways of engaging even traditional areas of the curriculum.

My examples here have focused on race and gender, but the issue of identity threat mentioned in chapter 2 should also be considered with respect to sexuality, ability, and even immigration status. Bringing diversity to the table requires, in most cases, a willingness to be public about the issues. While one can speak about concerns involving domestic-partner benefits, for example, without being gay or lesbian, the full benefit of that experience would only be realized if the environment in the institution made it possible and comfortable to be open.

Fifth, faculty diversity is essential for creating an environment that will be attractive to persons from diverse backgrounds as a place to work and to develop. The literature on the disadvantages of tokenism to the institution and the individual is quite sobering. Studies document the cost to individuals in terms of stress, overload, and visibility that would make working at such a place less desirable (Kanter, 1977; Smith, Yosso, & Solórzano, 2006; Thompson & Louque, 2005; Turner, 2002b; Yoder, 2002). The results can be damaging for the institution, too, if the dynamics on campus or in a department increase the likelihood of turnover, lawsuits, or decreased satisfaction.

It may be that despite the lack of diversity, higher education has managed up until now precisely because this is a condition true of most campuses. Moreover, the risks to any individual of suing a university are high enough to discourage lawsuits except as a last resort. Increasingly, however, lack of diversity may become a liability in terms of attracting candidates and the decisions of students to pursue faculty careers. I am aware of increasing numbers of faculty and administrators (of all backgrounds) who are basing decisions on where to work on the diversity of students, faculty, and staff on a campus.

Sixth, and perhaps the most overlooked rationale for faculty diversity, is the issue of the relationship between the faculty and the future-leadership pipeline. Because most academic administrators come from faculty ranks, a relatively homogenous faculty clearly limits the future development of diversity in leadership—something that is cause for great concern and is emerging as a significant issue in a number of sectors in higher education.

Finally, the most frequently mentioned rationale is to provide role models for all. Seeing individuals from diverse backgrounds function in faculty roles in all disciplines provides ways of envisioning oneself in such roles or experiencing others in one. The presence or absence of diversity sends strong signals about what is or is not possible and the degree to which talent from diverse groups is appreciated.

These reasons are both broad and deep in their implications for serious discussion of diversifying the faculty. While each probably applies to any campus, the process of engaging the rationale for diversity is best done in the context of a specific institution—with a focus on its mission, its academic purpose, and its culture.

The State of Faculty Diversity

Chapter 4 presented some figures on national changes in faculty diversity. These data can show change or lack of change in the aggregate, but they do not show patterns across sectors or regions, nor some of the factors involved in the results.

For example, in the study of the James Irvine Foundation Campus Diversity Initiative (CDI), which involved twenty-eight private campuses in California over a five-year period (2000–2005), faculty diversity was an important priority for the institutions. Yet on those campuses, the share of URM faculty among total tenured and tenure-track faculty only increased on average from 7% to 9%. This figure is similar to the five-year change in tenured and tenure-track faculty nationally, despite the diversity in the state of California (Moreno, Smith, Clayton-Pedersen, Parker, & Teraguchi, 2006; Clayton-Pedersen, Parker, Smith, Moreno, & Teraguchi, 2007).

The fast pace of hiring overall was perhaps one of the most significant and startling findings of the CDI study. For these twenty-eight campuses, not only had the overall size of the core tenured and tenure-track faculty grown by 5% during this period, but 31% of the faculty, on average, had been replaced. This rate of hiring is being replicated in many institutions across the country. Though it has taken longer than expected when Bowen and Schuster projected a generational change in 1986, there does now appear to be significant hiring because of retirements. This is an important era for faculty hiring and has created urgency to diversifying new hires. If one-third of a faculty is replaced during a five-year period, in ten more years the next generation will have been hired.

The Hiring Process

The question then remains, why has progress been slow? For the past few decades, there have been a number of conditions that have no doubt affected the hiring of a diverse faculty. The opportunities for hiring were limited by budget cuts and a relatively low rate of retirements. One could also point to the pipeline through graduate school as a factor that limited pools (though the diversity in the pipeline has been increasing) (Bowen & Sosa, 1989; H. A. Brown, 2006; Cole & Barber, 2003). In addition, changing the overall demographics of a population can be slow even if hiring is robust (Marschke, Laursen, Nielsen, & Rankin, 2007).

These factors led many to assume that supply and demand would place faculty of color, especially URM faculty of color, in high demand. Indeed, the prevailing explanations for lack of progress in diversifying the faculty included such statements as "There aren't any faculty of color," "They wouldn't want to come here," "We can't afford them," or "They are all going into industry." In the STEM fields, limited supply and significant demand has been the dominant explanation for the lack of diversity. It has been typical in campus reviews of diversity efforts, even in elite institutions, to find the following kind of statement:

> Although a concerted effort has been made, small candidate pools and intense competition between top universities has made growth in faculty numbers extremely difficult. . . . In disciplines such as engineering, mathematics and many of the hard sciences, the number of qualified candidates is extremely limited. In 1989, for example, of the 393 doctorates awarded in mathematics to U.S. citizens only six were earned by African Americans, eight were earned by Hispanics, while none were earned by Native Americans. Despite these problems . . . commitment to diversification among the faculty has not lessened. (Quoted in Smith, Wolf, Busenberg, & associates, 1996, p. 1)

At the same time, scholars of color and others—often employing qualitative studies concerning the experiences of faculty of color (and to some degree White women) in the recruiting and hiring processes—have been largely critical of such claims. The dominant themes have been the lack of effort on the part of campuses to recruit seriously and the existence of bias in how candidates are selected, in spite of a great deal of rhetoric. To those on the outside, institutional practices reflect continuing structural inequities, bias, and lack of commitment (Allen, Epps, Suh, & Stassen, 2002; Bronstein, Rothblum, & Solomon, 1993; Carter & O'Brien, 1993; Castellanos & Jones, 2003; Collins, 1990; Collins & Johnson, 1990; Cross, 1994; de la Luz Reyes & Halcon, 1991; Delgado, Stefancic, & Lindsley, 2000; Frierson, 1990; Garza, 1988, 1992; Graduate Employees and Students Organization, 2005; Knowles & Harleston, 1997; Harvey & Scott-Jones, 1985; Jacobson, 2006; Menges & Exum, 1983; Mickelson & Oliver, 1991; Misra, Kennelly, & Karides, 1999; Opp, 1994; Smith, 2005; Smith, Wolf, Busenberg, & associates, 1996; Staples, 1984; Tippeconic, 2002; Turner, 1999; Turner & Myers, 1997, 2000; Valian, 2000, 2005; Villalpondo & Delgado Bernal, 2002; Washington & Harvey, 1989; Wilson, 1995a, 1995b; Yale University, 1990).

Other empirical studies have documented the slow pace of progress in diversifying the faculty; the lack of any significant growth in the level of senior professors, despite the efforts at hiring assistant professors years ago; the growth in diversity among PhD's; and the presence of a significant percentage of African Americans in HBCUs, as places where serious hiring does occur (Beutel & Nelson, 2005, 2006; MacLachlan, 2006; Nelson & Rogers, 2004). Kulis, Chong, and Shaw (1999), in a large-scale statistical analysis of national data exploring institutional and statistical discrimination, conclude that "the allegedly escalating competition for black faculty labor . . . does not appear in our results to have markedly improved black faculty's prospects of securing positions in institutions with the most plentiful resources" (p. 142). In another article addressing supply-and-demand arguments, Olivas (1994) concludes that the credentials of Latino law-school faculty exceeded those of their White counterparts and suggests, "For most schools, White candidates with good (but not sterling) credentials are routinely considered and hired, while the high-demand / low-supply mythology about minorities persists" (p. 133).

Donna Nelson (Beutel & Nelson, 2005, 2006; Nelson & Rogers, 2004), in a continuation of her work on diversity in the top-ranked science fields, reported in 2005 that the racial/ethnic and gender diversity in faculty for thirteen fields in the "top-ranked" departments lags behind the national rate of PhD production in those fields. While it must be acknowledged that she is comparing total doctoral degrees to the "top fifty" (and presumably most selective) institutions for faculty hiring, the data are still important. In biology, URM graduates constitute 7% of the PhD's but are just 3% of the faculty. In psychology, where URM graduates are 11% of the PhD's, they represent just 6% of the faculty. This gap, true for all faculty of color and White women, is especially true for women from all racial/ethnic backgrounds. Moreover, an analysis of Nelson's data shows that in fields such as chemistry, physics, math, chemical engineering, political science, psychology, and biology, African American women and Latinas each make up a higher percentage of the PhD's than do White women.

One can look at these data in many ways. But a profile by department in each of these fifty institutions reflects the sense of isolation and tokenism that can result. Among the top-ranked chemistry, physics, math, chemical engineering, and psychology departments, for example, most have at least one woman, most often White. Thus, while White women have clearly made progress on faculties generally, their presence on faculties lags substantially behind their presence among PhD recipients, even in fields such as engineering and physics.

With respect to race and gender, the absence of URM faculty, especially URM women, is quite striking. Among the top fifty chemistry departments (with an average faculty size of 33), 33 have no Blacks (48 have no Black women), 30 have no Latinos (41 have no Latinas), and 47 have no American Indians (49 have no

American Indian women). There are 3 departments with no Asian Americans (34 have no Asian American women). Among physics departments (with an average faculty size of 40), 40 have no Blacks (50 have no Black women), 26 have no Latinos (42 have no Latinas), and 49 have no American Indians (50 have no American Indian women). There are 4 departments with no Asian Americans (33 have no Asian American women).

In social science fields, one typically sees more White women represented and more ethnic diversity. For example, among the top fifty departments in economics, with an average size of 28 faculty, 3 departments have no women. Thirty-three have no Blacks (45 have no Black women), 29 have no Latinos (43 have no Latinas), and 49 have no American Indians (50 have no American Indian women). Eight departments have no Asian Americans (36 have no Asian American women). Political science and psychology follow a similar pattern.

Trower and Chait's analysis (2002) of faculty at research universities results in similar conclusions. They report the progress for White women, at the same time noting that this progress does not reflect the growth in PhD's among White women and their rank and status in higher education. Similarly, while the number of minority faculty has increased, the percentage increase was less dramatic and mostly attributable to gains by Asian Americans or Asians. Indeed, in their study, the proportion of African American faculty at predominantly White colleges and universities has been relatively static since 1979. And in addressing the pipeline issue, especially for URM faculty of color, Trower and Chait conclude that "the pipeline is not the basic problem. In fact, even if the pipeline were awash in White women and minorities, a fundamental challenge would remain: the pipeline empties into territory women and faculty of color too often experience as uninviting, unaccommodating, and unappealing" (p. 34).

A look at the practice and the research reveals competing perspectives on why higher education is lacking in faculty diversity. The explanations by institutions and their leaders focus more on the situation, issues of availability in the pipeline, and academic preparedness, or the fact that progress is being made (which is somewhat true).

In an effort to study the strong competing explanations for lack of faculty diversity, I initiated a study (Smith, Wolf, Busenberg, & associates, 1996) of the hiring experiences of a diverse group of national fellowship winners. We chose national fellows for the interviews so that there would be no question about the quality of the individuals being studied. Through these fellowships, the scholars had been vetted at a national level for quality and competitiveness. Among 390 fellowship recipients, we conducted 298 in-depth interviews (76%) with those obtaining their doctorate between 1989 and 1994. Of those interviewed, 92% had received their degrees at Ivy League or elite research universities. The study addressed six myths.

> Myth 1: Because there are so few faculty of color in the pipeline, they are being sought out and bidded after.
>
> Myth 2: The scarcity of faculty of color in the sciences means the bidding wars will be even more intense.
>
> Myth 3: The nature of the pool of scholars in this study will mean they are only interested in being considered for positions in elite institutions.
>
> Myth 4: Individuals are continually being recruited by wealthier institutions, resulting in a revolving door.
>
> Myth 5: Faculty of color are leaving academe for more lucrative government and industry positions.
>
> Myth 6: Campuses are so focused on diversity that heterosexual White males have no chance. (pp. 4–5)

The results of the study highlighted that the supply and bidding arguments are grossly overstated and that the propositions offered above are indeed myths. While 70% of the candidates were employed in faculty positions, they were largely not hired with the frenzy or bidding that dominates the higher education "airwaves." Indeed, only 11% (including White and Asian American faculty) had anything like a bidding experience, and this most often amounted to offers from two campuses (not necessarily of the candidate's choosing), perhaps a course relief, and a summer research stipend.

A White male in the study, an art historian, reported that "there is a lot of talk about diversifying, but when push comes to shove, there is still a lot of hiring of White males, and I am a White male" (p. 117). Indeed, in this study, White males who had integrated diversity into their expertise were among those highly sought after. Many of them reported that although they brought the expertise of diversity, they also brought more comfort, because of the norms and cultures of their departments. One White male in classics reported that the institution "should have hired a woman. At that time, they had six men and no women. I was a man who did feminist scholarship. It gave them an out. . . . One more thing, . . . I didn't frighten the people" (p. 87).

This lack of bidding was especially true in the sciences and other technical fields, where, even after numerous postdoctoral studies, underrepresented-minority faculty reported such a lack of interest on the part of campuses that they began to consider industry positions, where they felt appreciated and where they felt that their credentials would be taken seriously. A number of scholars of color with elite backgrounds in highly technical fields, such as geophysics and biochemistry, had not found jobs after applying for dozens of faculty positions. They ended up in industry or in research labs.

Limited numbers in the pipeline can easily become an excuse for campuses when it comes to diversity in a way that is quite different than when a new program in nanotechnology or another "hot" field is being conceptualized. In such cases, limited numbers may indeed make the candidates even more desirable. Search committees or campus leaders are charged with finding and luring the candidates to the campus. During the era of growth in technology, for example, the limited supply of people with expertise was not offered as an excuse. Salaries rose, hiring strategies were creative, and campuses were proactive in identifying individuals to bring the necessary capacity to the campus. One had the sense that technology experts could name their price and write their own job description. In this case, supply and demand resulted in a very favorable job market for almost anyone with a reasonable level of technological sophistication. Costs were not very important, because the benefits were seen as critical and necessary for the institution. The contrast to hiring of diverse faculty suggests that while the supply of diverse candidates may be limited, the demand has not been there, in spite of rhetoric to the contrary. The absence of diversity is in many cases a regret on the part of the institution, but not deeply threatening to its credibility or viability—although this is perhaps becoming less and less true for White women.

The presence of more rhetoric than reality in the bidding-war myth is captured by a Latina interviewed for the 1996 study. A Chicana historian, she said, "I would say that I find it a little surprising that I do not regularly get phone calls, with respect to recruitment. We are so few, it's amazing that most universities will say 'We can't find anybody,' yet persons like myself are not recruited. I think I should be getting phone calls, and I don't get phone calls" (Smith, Wolf, Busenberg, & associates, p. 70).

The study also documented the wide range of institutions and regions to which candidates were attracted because of the location of offers, personal preferences, family circumstances, or institutional culture. There were a number of additional issues that emerged from the study. It affirmed the limited hiring during the early to mid-1990s. It also pointed to the significance of champions in the hiring process (either members of the search committee or mentors) who took a special interest in the candidate, assisted with the process, and even advocated for the person. The results also revealed the challenges of dual career hiring, the passive nature of hiring, and the importance of tenure for these candidates. Finally, a clear concern for the climate on campus emerged, including issues of fair treatment and isolation, as well as how faculty are very often prompted to consider alternative positions by unhappiness in the institution, rather than because they are offered more money elsewhere. Although this study did take place during a period of limited hiring, the results appear to echo continued concerns today, even as the pipeline and overall faculty hiring have improved.

Conditions for Faculty Hiring

While there are many studies using both qualitative and quantitative data on faculty hiring, there have been relatively few studies on the conditions under which faculty of color and White women have actually been hired. For the most part, such data are not readily available. A study titled "Interrupting the Usual: Successful Strategies for Hiring Diverse Faculty" was designed and implemented by Caroline Turner and myself, along with several colleagues, and was developed with the support of three major public research universities that provided relevant data on the conditions under which faculty were hired (Smith, Turner, Osei-Kofi, & Richards, 2004).

The study was designed to investigate the conditions under which a diverse faculty is hired and whether jobs that list ethnic or women's studies or special-hiring interventions would account for the bulk of the hiring of underrepresented faculty of color into tenure or tenure-track positions. In particular, the analysis tested the hypothesis that when underrepresented faculty of color are hired, (1) the field or department into which they are hired will more likely be related to race and ethnicity; or (2) a proactive intervention strategy, one in which the focus is on making diversity central, will have been employed—significantly more often than when White men or women are hired.

The results of the analysis of 689 searches over a three-year period, from 1995 to 1998, from these three large elite public research universities gave strong support to this hypothesis. Successful hires of underrepresented faculty of color at these predominantly White institutions were most likely to occur when a job description contained an educational or scholarly link to the study of race or ethnicity and/or when an institutional intervention strategy that bypassed or enhanced the traditional search process was used. The combination of diversity indicators and special hires was absolutely critical in the hiring of African American and American Indian faculty. Asian / Asian American and White faculty were almost always hired through regular searches, although they were in some instances hired through special hires and when diversity indicators were

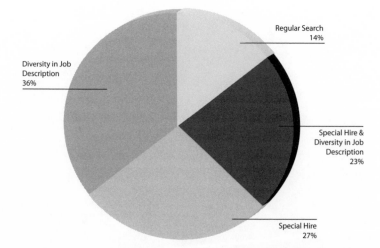

Figure 5.1. Hiring patterns for African Americans. *Source:* Smith, Turner, Osei-Kofi, & Richards, 2004

specified.[1] The difference was that Asian / Asian American and White faculty were hired with *and* without the use of the specific conditions that were the focus of the study.

Figures 5.1 through 5.5 show the percentage of hires, disaggregated by race/ethnicity, that were made through the regular search process, using job descriptions that focused on diversity, using other intervention strategies (special hires), or through a combination of job description and intervention by race/ethnicity. The findings are dramatic and sobering.

Among URM faculty combined, 71% were hired with a diversity indicator and/or special-hire intervention—24% using diversity in the job description, 24% as special hires, and 23% with a combination of special hire and diversity indicator. African Americans were hired almost entirely under the designated conditions expected (86%), divided among special hires and job descriptions (fig. 5.1). All (100%) of the American Indians were hired as a result of diversity indicators and/or special hires: 50% were special hires; 33% were hired with diversity indicated in the job description; and 17% were special hires for positions in which diversity was indicated (fig. 5.2).

For Latinos, the results showed a broader range of hiring circumstances, al-

1. Given what is known about the citizenship of Asian PhD's, it is likely that many of the Asian faculty are Asian, not Asian American. At the time of the study, citizenship data were not considered.

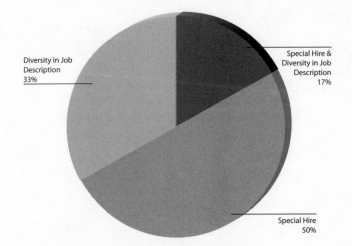

Figure 5.2. Hiring patterns for American Indians. *Source:* Smith, Turner, Osei-Kofi, & Richards, 2004

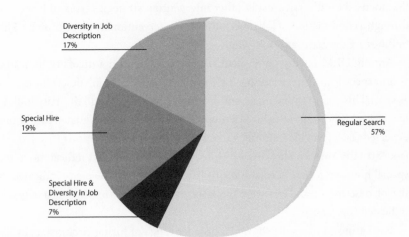

Figure 5.3. Hiring patterns for Latino/as. *Source:* Smith, Turner, Osei-Kofi, & Richards, 2004

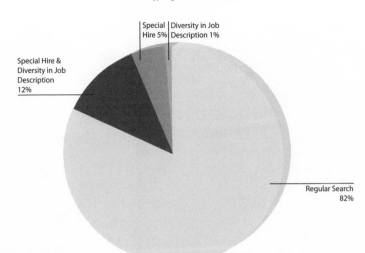

Figure 5.4. Hiring patterns for Asian Americans. *Source:* Smith, Turner, Osei-Kofi, & Richards, 2004

though 43% were hired outside of regular searches (fig. 5.3). Because the study's initial definition of diversity indicators did not include such fields as Spanish or Latin American studies, the data were reanalyzed to see how many Latinos were hired in these areas as well. This analysis revealed that an additional 14% of Latinos would have been included in hires resulting from a diversity indicator in the job description. Broadening the definition in this way would have brought the total proportion of Latinos hired using a diversity indicator and/or special hire to 57%.

A meager 5% of regular hires—that is, hires for positions without a diversity indicator and without the use of a special hire—resulted in the hiring of an underrepresented-minority faculty member.

In the case of Asians, 18% were hired with a diversity indicator and/or special hire (fig. 5.4). As with Latinos, broadening the definition of diversity indicators to include Asian languages and international studies would have resulted in an additional 7% of Asians being defined as hired under these conditions, bringing the total to 25%.

Overall, Asian faculty were represented in greater percentages in this hiring cohort than African Americans, Latinos, or American Indians. Nonetheless, the study revealed several challenges faced by Asians / Asian Americans in higher education. These challenges are compounded by the fact that many who are counted

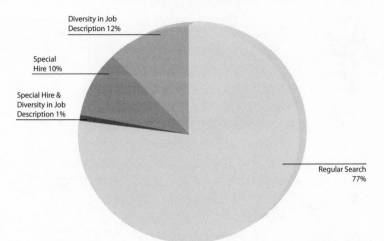

Figure 5.5. Hiring patterns for Whites. *Source:* Smith, Turner, Osei-Kofi, & Richards, 2004

as Asian Americans are actually foreign nationals. The data from chapter 4 illustrated how important this can be for Asians in particular. Contrary to the common misconception that Asian Americans are well represented in faculty ranks, the 2004 study shows that they were hired primarily into fields such as science, engineering, medicine, and Asian-language departments and were less commonly found in the social sciences and humanities. Moreover, Asian Americans were the least likely to benefit from special-hiring opportunities; Whites benefited substantially more often. Nakanishi (1993), Hune and Chan (1997), and Chang and Kiang (2002) argue that academic-pipeline issues are still critical to achieving greater representation of Asian Americans at all levels of higher education and throughout a range of disciplines. As suggested in chapter 4, the confounding of international and domestic faculty of color affects African American and Latino faculty as well (Chapa, 2006).

A total of 23% of Whites were hired under the designated conditions, with 12% hired for positions indicating diversity and 11% as special hires (fig. 5.5). While interventions and diversity indicators made a significant difference in the ethnic composition of the faculty, especially for underrepresented faculty, Whites maintained an overwhelming majority position throughout. Indeed, 65% of those hired with diversity indicators and/or special hires were White. This finding is worth emphasizing. The strategies that resulted in increased hiring for faculty of color were most often used to hire White faculty.

Because of the concerns about hiring in the sciences, the data were also disaggregated to pull out the STEM fields. The results mirror the larger findings, except that special hire was the condition most often employed. For African Americans, special hires were used 75% of the time; for Latinos, 36%; for Asians, 4%; and for Whites, 13%.

Special hiring was an important strategy for departments throughout the three campuses. They often took advantage of institutional resources to make a case for a special hire of talented individuals who were identified through the search process. Often the candidates did not fit an existing job description precisely but were otherwise well suited to strengthen the department. For example, at one institution, an exceptional-hire search was used to advance the departmental goal of increasing diversity among faculty after the usual search did not yield a diverse hire. A statement in the letter of support from a department chair in family studies articulates this goal more fully: "Senior faculty are of a single race. It is imperative in today's world to provide students with faculty that reflects, at least in some degree the ethnic diversity of the families they study and one day hope to serve. . . . Infusion of new blood is essential to the future vigor and robustness of the department. Beyond the obvious need to continue support for the graduate and undergraduate programs of the department, they will bring the new perspectives and scholarly priorities that will keep the department alive and current" (quoted in Smith, Turner, Osei-Kofi, & Richards, 2004, p. 151).

In this case, the departmental faculty gave unanimous support to the hiring of an African American female into a tenure-track assistant professor position. Within the letter of support, faculty outlined the ways in which the hire would promote the department's diversity goals:

> This exceptional hire will impact the academic priorities of [department name] in the following ways:
> - Provide a crucial element of diversity among an all Caucasian faculty
> - Allow for further diversity in the curriculum and the department research programs, responding to the needs and demands of our graduate and undergraduate students
> - Assist in the recruitment and retention of graduate and undergraduate students of color
> - Numerous opportunities for federal grants earmarked for faculty of color will increase the likelihood of external funding. (p. 152)

Such qualitative data support the hypothesis that institutional interventions or diversity indicators can be important strategies in the hiring of diverse faculty.

This example also demonstrates that the rationale for hiring involves substantive scholarly, institutional, and pedagogical reasons. In many cases, we observed that the department itself took the initiative to put forth the candidate. This suggests that these conditions become important tools for department faculty as additions to search-committee options and approaches. Moreover, it suggests that despite concerns in the field that persons hired though special interventions might not have the support of the department, most special hires were initiated by the department—with enthusiasm.

The study also permitted an analysis of the intersection of race and gender. For each ethnic group, with the exception of American Indians, more women than men were hired with diversity indicators or intervention strategies. All African American women, 62% of Latinas, 100% of American Indian women, 37% of Asian American women, and 36% of White women were hired under these conditions, in comparison to 77%, 34%, 100%, 8%, and 17%, respectively, for men. Thus, while the presence of White women on the faculty has grown much more robustly than for women of color, this study pointed out that interventions were important conditions for hiring women across all groups, as well as for hiring underrepresented men of color.

The study included an examination of the effect of search-committee composition on faculty hiring, but almost all the search committees were entirely White; there was little or no racial/ethnic diversity on any of the committees except in ethnic studies areas. The study also investigated the impact on faculty hiring when finalist pools contained some diversity and found a modest positive relationship here.

Hiring faculty for subject areas that contained some form of diversity yielded the most reliable hiring of underrepresented faculty of color. However, as others have pointed out, the potential for marginalization and restriction of scholarly range is significant enough to suggest that overreliance on these searches to secure faculty diversity is a mistake (Baez, 2003; Konrad, 2003; Smith, Yosso, & Solórzano, 2006). Indeed, such an approach would not be interrupting the usual but would, rather, be relying on a form of "barrioization" or "ghettoization." Introducing a diversity indicator in a job description, however, does create the potential for expanding the role of diversity in faculty searches throughout the institution. Even in science searches, adding an explicit criterion in the job description for experience and success in working with diverse groups of students has significant potential to broaden the qualities being considered. Moreover, there are many areas in science, medicine, and engineering that would benefit from a diversity of perspectives. Our data suggest that this strategy in the sciences is rarely considered. Reliance on diversity indicators in the job description to increase the likelihood

that faculty of color will be considered and hired requires that program considerations also be introduced to clarify why and in what ways diversity is important to the department and for a particular hire.

Campuses need to pay close attention as well to the diversity of faculty throughout fields and disaggregated by ethnic group and gender. Overall numbers of faculty of color might well increase because of the addition of Asian faculty in STEM
fields, but underrepresented faculty of color could well be declining at the same
time. Hiring of White woman may be increasing, but hiring of women of color
may not be improving. Such situations yield binary demographics, in which most
of the women hired are White and most of the minorities hired are men.[2]

Moreover, with the recent surge of lawsuits challenging affirmative action, it
is important to note that the approaches described in this study were largely directed to the notion of bringing the scholarship of diversity to searches as opposed
to only representative diversity, making these interventions a much more robust
strategy from a legal perspective. In this context, it is also important to note that
65% of those who benefited from special-hire interventions were White, which
limits the ability to charge that special hires are limited to minority hires.

Retention

A large volume of both quantitative and qualitative research over the past several
decades documents the challenges faced by underrepresented faculty, faculty of
color, women faculty, and gay and lesbian faculty. Even with the considerable
strides that White woman have made, recent studies of women in science at elite
universities reveal the continuing issues concerning sexism, tokenism, and marginalization on campuses and in fields where women, including White women,
have not achieved anything close to a critical mass and where institutional practices place women at a disadvantage (Chesler, Lewis, & Crowfoot, 2005; Lawler,
1999).

Numerous narratives describe the challenges and fears experienced by gay and
lesbian faculty in terms of discrimination, harassment, and the entire coming-
out process (Mintz & Rothblum, 1997; Tierney, 1997). Nonetheless, the bulk of
the research has focused on the challenges facing faculty of color and women faculty of color (Aguirre, 1995, 2000; Allen, Epps, Suh, & Stassen, 2002; Benjamin,
1997; Chesler, Lewis, & Crowfoot, 2005; Garcia, 2000; Gregory, 2001; Hagedorn,

---

2. Such demographics are echoed in the title of a now-classic book, *All the Women Are White, All the
Blacks Are Men, but Some of Us Are Brave* (Hull, Scott, & Smith, 1982).

2000; Hopkins, 2006; Johnsrud & Rosser, 2002; Smart, 1990; Smith, Yosso, & Solórzano, 2006; Thomas & Hollenshead, 2002; Tierney & Bensimon, 1996; Turner, 2002b, 2003; Turner & Myers, 2000).

The explanations given on most campuses for the turnover of faculty of color, especially, focus on aggressive "hiring away" or the lack of productivity. However, most of the research in which faculty of color and White women are studied contains powerful and emotional descriptions of climate, fairness, treatment, tokenism, and inequity. Studies report environments that are alienating and in which faculty report feeling that they don't matter. They mention having few mentors and few others who believe in their capacity.

The themes that scholars such as Laura Rendón have suggested for student success reappear in the literature on faculty of color. What is required is that the culture, perspective, language, and values that individuals bring are appreciated and are seen as being important for the department or institution (Antonio, 2002; Lawler, 1999; Moody, 2004; Rendón, 1992, 2005; Thompson & Louque, 2005; Turner, 2002b, 2003; Turner & Myers, 2000). A theme that emerges regularly is the classroom as contested terrain, in which students challenge the competence, position, and role of faculty of color and women faculty (Harlow, 2003; McGowan, 2000; Pope & Joseph, 1997). For many faculty and administrators, however, such issues are exacerbated by their being the only person of their racial/ethnic group or gender in the department. As MacLachlan (2006) suggests, it may be no coincidence that two-thirds of the 150 African American physicists work in HBCUs, partly because of climate and partly because of a recruiting process that takes their potential seriously. The same is true for African American women mathematicians.

Even as we talk about achieving some level of critical mass so that a faculty member may be an individual rather than a representative of a group, it is rare that any form of critical mass exists at the department level, except perhaps in women's studies or ethnic studies, and then only for the identity connected to the program. Scanning the tables in Nelson's study (Beutel & Nelson, 2005; Nelson & Rogers, 2004) of faculty at the top fifty departments in science, engineering, and social sciences, one sees many zeros and ones in columns, especially for men and women of color. This not only has implications for students and their exposure to diversity, it has huge implications for faculty and their ability to thrive and focus energy on teaching, scholarship, and service (Allen, Epps, Suh, & Stassen, 2002; Cooper & Stevens, 2002; Garza, 1993; Moody, 2004; Smith, Altbach, & Lomotey, 2002; Stanley, 2006; Tierney, 1993, 1997; Weinberg, 2008).

In the Campus Diversity Initiative study (Clayton-Pedersen, Parker, Smith,

Moreno, & Teraguchi, 2007; Moreno, Smith, Clayton-Pedersen, Parker, & Teraguchi, 2006), my colleagues and I attempted to understand why, in these twenty-eight campuses, the overall change in faculty demographics did not move faster, given the rate of hiring that was occurring and the increased diversity in new hires. While few studies have access to campus data for turnover, we were able to look at this for these campuses. It became clear that some of the new URM hires were going to replace URM faculty who had left. Thus, a campus might hire three new Latino faculty, but if all three of them simply served as replacements for Latino faculty who had left, it would not increase the net number of Latino faculty.

To study this more carefully, we developed a quantitative indicator, the turnover quotient (TQ), using three readily available data points—the number of URM faculty in 2000 (the baseline year), the number of new URM hires, and the number of URM faculty in 2004. In the example above, a campus with no turnover would expect to have six Latino faculty in 2004—three in 2000, plus three new hires. A campus that both hired and lost three Latinos would have a TQ for Latinos of 100, meaning that all new hires went to replace people who left. Such a campus would see no change between 2000 and 2004. The formula presented below can be easily used to compute a turnover quotient for URM faculty for any campus.

$$TQ = [1 - (\frac{2004URMFac - 2000URMFac}{New\ URMHires})] \times 100$$

In our study, the average campus TQ was 58%. What this means is that, on average, three of every five new URM hires went to replace URM faculty who had left. There was considerable variation among the campuses. Indeed, eleven of the twenty-eight campuses had a turnover of zero—all new hires added to the existing diversity. In contrast, the remaining campuses had turnover approaching 100%, meaning that most new URM hires were replacing URM faculty who had left.

While there are many factors involved, there was a dramatic relationship between the changes in faculty diversity on a campus over the five-year period and the TQ (fig. 5.6). Knowing its TQ can help alert a campus to issues of retention along with hiring. Many of the CDI campuses had no idea that retention was a significant issue and had little information on the sources of their turnover, whether through departure or retirement. However, when trying to explain a high TQ, campuses, in the absence of data, often reverted to the largely debunked myths discussed earlier. This is a cycle that is easily interrupted if campuses engage their institutional research capacities for "research" and organizational learning.

On many campuses, progress from year to year was often erratic, so that a campus that had a "good year" would, upon further analysis, find that it had had only

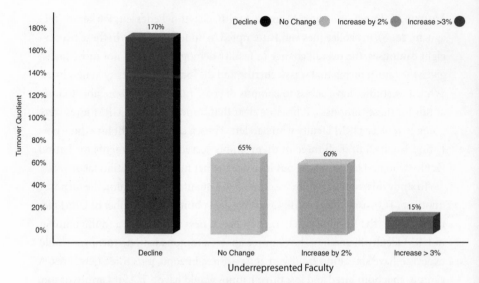

Figure 5.6. Change in percentage of underrepresented-minority faculty and turnover quotient. *Source:* Moreno, Smith, Clayton-Pedersen, Parker, & Teraguchi, 2006

one good year. Interestingly, such campuses often referred back to that single year's successes as typical when discussing progress. This served to demoralize faculty and staff who were working daily to support the campus in its efforts. It is important that campuses be willing to engage the lack of progress, as well as the successes, through empirical data assessed on a regular basis, rather than through anecdotes.

Some Examples

In this section, I want to describe three cases of faculty searches that actually occurred. In each case, the campus was deeply committed to diversity and especially concerned about faculty diversity. Yet the efforts that took place during the search process failed with respect to diversity and resulted in deep regret and frustration. These examples can serve as an opportunity for reflection on ways to anticipate and interrupt an unsuccessful process.

The first case occurred at a large comprehensive university that had succeeded in diversifying its pool of candidates in terms of both ethnicity and gender. When the search committee met, a number of White women and faculty of color with strong but ordinary credentials were not placed in the final pool of three to be brought to campus. Of the final three, one was a White woman with Ivy League credentials. The committee was impressed by this woman and felt that by placing her in the final three, they had exercised "due diligence" for diversity. The other two were White men with strong but ordinary credentials from similar comprehensive institutions. After coming to campus, the White woman withdrew, and in the end, the candidate hired was the third choice of the committee. While he had been included in the final three, it turned out that his credentials were no more impressive than those of a number of the other women and candidates of color in the original pool. It is not uncommon to have campuses place all their efforts on one "diversity" candidate. Then, if the person doesn't work out, the campus is left with no diversity to consider.

What is involved here is not unusual. Many campuses restrict their finalist pool to perhaps three candidates; in a set of three, the amount of diversity and the range of options are restricted. In this case, there were other candidates who had ranked near the top but did not make the top three. Had they been included, the likelihood of making a diverse hire would have increased. A number of campuses have offered this option to search committees who find themselves with more than three very positive-looking candidates. In some searches, committee members have found themselves the most enthusiastic about a candidate who on paper may have been ranked fifth but who excelled in person.

For my second example, we visit a small liberal arts college in the Midwest that has been known for its commitment to diversity. The campus had done a lot of work on diversity in the curriculum, in admissions, and even in staff hiring. Yet there was a palpable sense of frustration with regard to faculty hiring. The administrators expressed regret about the lack of progress, stating that their institution's location and budget meant that there were few candidates who would want to live in the area and that they couldn't afford to hire people who were being lured away by wealthier institutions. The president documented this by telling the story of a senior African American faculty member who had been hired away to a nearby research university three years earlier.

At the same time, the African American faculty and staff were quite frustrated about the increasing rhetoric of diversity and the lack of hiring, and they had a competing example to offer. Three years prior, the dance department had hired, on soft money, a part-time African American instructor to teach jazz and modern dance. This dancer had worked for a national dance company and had a background in ballet. Her presence had revitalized the dance program, increased enrollments, and built enthusiasm for dance. There was general agreement that she was an extraordinary teacher and also brought significant connections to the arts world. She very much wanted to stay on the faculty, preferably full-time, but her time was coming to an end and there had been no word.

As luck would have it, the dance department had a retirement in ballet. Because the chair of the department was so enthusiastic about the role this dancer had played and about the significance of introducing new forms of dance, she proposed a job description that would be broader than that of the prior ballet position; it would include some teaching of ballet but also jazz and modern dance. There was considerable agreement and enthusiasm in the department and among students for this new approach.

This chair, however, was a bit controversial on campus. Thus, before approving the new position, the campus curriculum committee suggested to the senior leadership that a program review in dance be conducted to see what the future directions for dance should be. That review was conducted with a nondiverse team of outside reviewers, who concluded that while broadening dance was "nice," ballet should be the core of this new position and that any dance department without ballet was not a "quality" dance department. As a result, the job description was rejected, and a new search was mounted for which the part-time faculty member was not a serious candidate, even though she had a background in ballet.

At the end, there was considerable regret on the part of the senior leadership, who felt compelled to explain the reasons for what had happened. And there was considerable frustration and anger within the African American community on campus about what had happened. Regardless, this incredible resource, who was universally viewed as an extraordinary teacher and contributor to a revitalized dance program, left. Had the original position been advertised, would this candidate have been hired? That cannot be known, but what could have been a wonderful scenario of fortuitous timing and good planning instead unfolded to a sad end.

This revealing case illustrates many issues central to hiring—what is considered excellence, who gets to decide what is considered quality, and institutional practices that, while having little to do with diversity, end up undermining diversity efforts.[3] Moreover, even though the institution was following its governance process, the senior administration did not make the connection between the process that was unfolding and its diversity efforts and thus did not see the results com-

---

3. Pressman and Wildavsky (1984) call this impeding change by a "thousand cuts."

ing. What was happening was ostensibly an argument about the curriculum, but what was really happening was an argument about the "canon" of dance—something that was determined by the group of people brought in as experts.

The third example occurred at a religiously affiliated small liberal arts institution in an urban area, very committed to diversity and with an extremely diverse undergraduate student body. Little progress had been made in faculty hiring, however. Again, the leadership and many faculty felt that there were few candidates "out there" and that they were being recruited by more affluent institutions with which this campus could not afford to compete. A Latino theologian had been hired in the religion department as a non-tenure-track, full-time faculty member. There appeared to have been universal agreement that he was an incredible teacher, as well as a very prolific scholar. Moreover, he loved the campus and, although concerned about his lack of a tenure-track position, wanted to make his career there. A retirement in the department led to the development of a position description that aligned well with the areas of expertise held by this faculty member. A search committee was formed, chaired by a somewhat controversial chair of this small department.

As the process unfolded, the Latino theologian emerged as one of three finalists for the position, and there was excitement for his candidacy among students and colleagues. In the meantime, a nearby research university began to contact him about a full-time, tenure-track position in religion. As the small college's search unfolded, it became apparent that the chair of the search committee preferred one of the other candidates, a White man, and championed this candidacy strongly. No one, including other members of the search committee, felt able to confront the chair. As a result, the offer was made to the chair's candidate. The Latino theologian went to the research university with great regrets and sadness, because he had wanted to be at this college. In the end, even though many on the search committee and in the senior administration were upset, no one interrupted this story as it unfolded. The failure to interrupt or to at least challenge what was happening was also a failure to attend to the ways in which diversity efforts can be undermined.

In the last two cases, the candidates were on campus, highly regarded, and well qualified, and almost miraculously, there were relevant positions open. Yet in both processes, campus dynamics and politics unfolded in ways that led to what everyone recognized as a regrettable outcome: a valuable member of the community left. The highly decentralized departmental structure, the impact of a single person left unchallenged to champion someone else, and the failure of anyone to interrupt led to these outcomes. From an institutional perspective, there were reasons for the outcomes. To members of the community committed to diversity, these were examples of lack of commitment. These are not isolated examples; similar ones can be found throughout the country. Such things happen in all searches. But if we are to take seriously the limited pool, then each time something like this happens and a faculty member either doesn't come or leaves, the consequences are more significant to the campus's diversity efforts.

Many others have documented in detail factors that influence the hiring process and that systematically undervalue minority and White women faculty (Moody, 2004; Turner, 2002a, 2002b). Too often, however, these patterns go unacknowledged until it is too late. Creating search processes that build capacity to evaluate and carry out effective searches requires commitment and training.

Issues to Consider for Interrupting the Usual

Higher education is quickly hiring the next generation of faculty, who at this rate will not be diverse enough to provide institutions with the expertise and competence to serve the needs of the institution, the students, or society. Not only must hiring practices be altered, but turnover must be understood and engaged so that all the efforts going into hiring and identifying talent will not go to waste. In addition, myths continue to create self-fulfilling prophecies and to allow excuses to explain the lack of progress, such as lack of diverse pools, "hoarding" of minority faculty by other universities, lack of competitive salaries, and slow rates of hiring.

A number of themes emerge from the material presented in this chapter. These themes are echoed widely in the literature on faculty diversity. While the focus of this chapter has been on core tenured and tenure-track faculty, the demographics and hiring of part-time faculty, full-time faculty, and "off-line" faculty also have implications for students, administrative hiring and retention, decision-making, and scholarship on campus (Schuster, 2003; Schuster & Finkelstein, 2006).

What Counts as Excellence: Identifying Talent

Epistemology and the definitions of knowledge and excellence in a field are very much framed by the field itself. For some, this is a struggle for the canon of the field and what counts as core knowledge. While some of the controversies about excellence are characterized as culture wars, there has been sufficient experience in higher education over the past forty years to demonstrate the fundamental changes that have occurred in many fields related to the impact of knowledge of race, class, gender, sexuality, and religion. There has also been significant change in the creation of new knowledge informed by these developments. What counts as excellence will not only affect who is hired and retained, but will also relate to the climate of a department and the success of the person hired. It will determine how seriously the faculty member's work is taken and whether it is appreciated. While taking new scholarship seriously was once a critical issue, more and more mainstream journals and presses are giving serious attention to diversity perspectives. Nonetheless, this can be a serious concern for a given department and for a particular set of scholars.

The search process can also be the site of struggle over priorities in developing job descriptions. In some areas of the hard sciences, one often hears, "We would be happy to add a woman or minority, but we simply hire the best." This assumes that there is a unidimensional ranking system based on a single criterion. Most job descriptions include a number of competencies that the search committee is looking for—expertise in an area, teaching experience, publications, grant awards, and so on. Here again, the issue of multiplicity emerges. I have been on enough search committees, including those in science, to know that most committees look at a number of candidates and wish they could take this quality from one and other qualities from others. There are many characteristics that are desired in a faculty position, and it is rare to find one person who fills all of them. Thus, in the end, the issue is where diversity ranks in the mix.

Academic elitism also plays a role. Even at a diverse comprehensive university emphasizing teaching in science and concerned about the lack of diversity among STEM graduates, how many search committees have been dazzled by the resume of someone from an elite research university who has had two postdocs but not significant teaching experience or success in working with diverse groups of students going into science? How many campuses use institutional prestige as surrogates for merit, regardless of whether this disadvantages those whose route to a faculty position might be different? In such cases, there is both an allure and a preference for prestige, rather than clarity about the excellence needed and how to identify it—questions that must be answered at the institutional and departmental levels.

Myths

The myths concerning faculty diversity with respect to availability, interest in faculty careers, bidding wars, and the lure of industry continue and serve as self-fulfilling prophecies—excuses—for the slow pace of change. Scrutinizing explanations for failure to make progress often reveals these assumptions, and making progress requires that they be debunked.

Rationale

Practices in the hiring and retention of faculty and the criteria for excellence have all changed over the years with the introduction of new technologies. Thus, it will be important for faculty search committees to pay attention to the rationale for diversifying the faculty and to see diversifying as essential, rather than simply optional. This is especially true for the STEM fields, where the obvious rationale concerning broadening the content of scholarship does not always apply (Brown, 1988; Chubin & Malcolm, 2006).

Decentralization and Silo of Faculty Hiring

One of the clear tensions at the institutional level is the decentralization of faculty hiring, which is located at the level of the department or search committee. Many agree that it is at the departmental level that most decisions about hiring are made. There is indeed considerable power at this level. Department heads and senior faculty develop recruitment plans and decide what constitutes "quality," including how scholarly "productivity" is measured, how publications and research are credited, and the areas of scholarship to be emphasized (Busenberg & Smith, 1997; de la Luz Reyes & Halcon, 1991; Gainen & Boice, 1993; Steinpreis, Anders, & Ritzke, 1999; Swoboda, 1993; Turner, 2002a; Turner & Myers, 2000; West, 2000).

The ability of departmental faculty to define what is important and to hire someone who contributes to department goals is a strong value of higher education in many institutions. With respect to diversity, it can give the department the freedom to change, but it can also inhibit the *institutional* efforts to diversify. The answer involves engaging the department in the institution's diversity efforts and helping and encouraging departments to locate their searches in this larger context. Through program reviews, strategic planning, or some other process, the department can come to see a connection between diversity and its own excellence, future, and place in the university. If this connection is not established, hiring will replicate what has always existed. If it is established, departments can create new job descriptions and position requirements for hiring that reflect changes in the field and the needs of the institution.

The Problem of "One"

At the institutional and departmental levels, search committees often lament the low percentage of URM doctorates vis-à-vis a national labor pool, even though at the department level, the need is to hire only one or two persons, a small fraction of the available pool. Ironically, the hiring of "one" often impedes hiring rather than facilitating it. The reality is that departmental searches often occur one at a time, making each hire significant and often placing a burden on a single search to capture all the needs that the department wishes to address. In such circumstances, moving in new directions, or hiring people who bring new perspectives, may be seen as "less comfortable" or may require having to give up something people have held dear.

Moreover, a single search can become a zero-sum game with respect to priorities concerning race, gender, and global and other perspectives. In contrast, hiring a group of ten, or even three, creates more opportunity for diversity and for different kinds of expertise, skills, and talent. Most departments are not hiring in this cluster fashion, although the new efforts to build interdisciplinary programs with a cluster of hires create a model for approaching searches. Even without cluster hiring, the need for increasing the domestic diversity of faculty is urgent, while many other aspects of diversity may need to focus on climate or policies. The experience of White women may first be an issue of satisfaction and climate. The experience of LGBT faculty may also be one of climate or campus policies.

Another problem of "one" is that in a typical pool of finalists, there is often one person who represents "diversity"—either an underrepresented person of color or, in some cases, a White woman. There are many factors that result in a successful search, and the likelihood that some problem or issue will arise increases when there is only one chance to add diversity. If there are five candidates and only one of them brings diversity, there is a much better chance that one of the other four will come through the search positively: there is room for one to give a bad talk and one to decide not to take the position, and two of the four will still be left. For the one candidate, there is only one chance. Extensive checking, prior interviews, and adding to the number of finalists increase the likelihood of a diversity hire.

The problem of "one" when the person is the only member of a group in his or her department or school also has direct implications for satisfaction and for retention. Being a token member of a group, as discussed earlier, has profound implications for the professional and personal experiences of the faculty member in this position. The challenge is that the development of a critical mass is not easily accomplished at the most local of sites—the department—and is often not engaged fully even if it exists at the institutional level.

Job Descriptions and Cluster Hiring

Perhaps the most important step following a review of diversity at the level of program or school is the development of a job description (Caldwell-Colbert et al., 1996; Light, 1994; Opp & Smith, 1994; Smith, Wolf, Busenberg, & associates, 1996; Turner, 1999, 2002a). This process can be quite controversial. Conflict about what is important can escalate unless a decision is made to keep the position description broad. In addition, because job descriptions are often developed within a discipline as understood by existing faculty, the group may not consider new developments in the field or new opportunities. So many of the almost seven hundred job descriptions reviewed for the 2004 study (Smith, Turner, Osei-Kofi, & Richards) looked as if they could have been written in the 1950s, and, except for positions that built in global or technology priorities, most did not appear to have been written in the context of program or strategic planning. The development of a good description requires some articulation of what skills and competencies are needed, including the competence to engage diversity and perhaps to successfully teach a diverse group of students. Moreover, the job description should not be pulled from an old file and developed, as it often is, apart from a review of the program or institutional priorities. Drafting a job description must be one of the core parts of a newly conceptualized hiring process in which the job description is linked to strategic plans, program reviews, and institutional priorities.

There are examples today where campuses are using a single job description to hire a cluster of faculty, either within a single department or within a school, who can address a particular area for research and teaching from different disciplinary and methodological vantage points. This approach broadens the job description, reduces the problem of hiring one, and increases the likelihood that persons bringing diversity to the department or school will be hired. It also has implications for retention. Pfeffer (1985), in a classic study concerning hiring, demonstrated that cohort hiring can be extremely effective with respect to retention and satisfaction.

Job descriptions are significant in another way. They signal to candidates something about the degree to which diversity really matters in the conduct and mission of the campus, in contrast to the pro forma "We are an equal opportunity employer" language. Statements about mission, student body, and community are often important in communicating the centrality of diversity and the potential attractiveness of the campus to a diverse pool.

A word about essentializing scholars and job descriptions is needed here. There is no question in the research that job descriptions that engage diversity more centrally are more likely to produce diverse pools and diverse hires. What does that mean for persons who bring diversity of background and experience but whose areas of scholarship—physics, accounting, Shakespeare, opera—are not directly related to diversity issues? I am not suggesting that all strategies should be focused on job descriptions and fields that explicitly address diversity. This is an important cautionary note. A campus needs to make some explicit statement about its commitment to diversity, through its mission statement, and about its need to hire people in all fields who have competence in teaching diverse groups of students and other skills linked to diversity. Such a statement also speaks to the willingness of a campus to be proactive in identifying diverse pools in fields whose content is not directly related to diversity. Without attention to this, campuses may be more diverse institutionally yet end up ghettoizing faculty in content-related fields.

Proactive and Careful Searches

Being on a faculty search committee is not a task that most faculty seek out, and chairing one does not always represent anything more than another major demand on an already overloaded schedule. Moreover, the highly sophisticated search processes now common in recruiting senior administrators are not common knowledge or practice in faculty searches. The pattern for faculty searches is to develop the job description or change dates on an old description and then place ads and send out letters. Applications are received and reviewed, and a group of finalists are selected based on their paperwork and sometimes on preliminary interviews at conferences. This is a fundamentally passive process, and it has often yielded sufficient numbers of applications—except when it comes to diversity. Having advertised in the major ethnic journals that announce positions, the department or campus feels it has done its job of advertising and opening up the pool.

Sometimes, when a campus is serious about proactively creating a diverse pool, members of the search committee are encouraged to network at the relevant professional meetings (after all, faculty hiring is often done from a bounded group of people located in programs or disciplines). However, it is not clear that professional societies are any less segregated by race than our schools and communities. One scientist told me in a moment of candor, "I know there are African American, Latino, and American Indian scientists at my meeting, but I don't know them and I feel awkward approaching them." Faculty tell people they know about searches they have. If those networks are de facto segregated, then the network serves those who are most like those in faculty positions already.

In contrast, by actively networking, members of a search committee have a chance to acknowledge the significance of a scholar's research, not just his or her ethnicity or gender. It became clear in the 1996 study concerned with debunking the myths about hiring for diversity (Smith, Wolf, Busenberg, & associates) that faculty of color, especially URM faculty, were reluctant to apply simply on the basis of advertisements, because they thought that they would not be taken seriously or that they might serve to diversify the final candidate pool but not really be a serious contender for the position. One participant in the study, an African American chemical engineer, highlighted the delicate relationship between affirmative action in hiring and her own accomplishments: "The first thing that somebody says to me when they find out I have a PhD or that I'm interested in an academic position . . . doesn't have anything to do with my research area or my research ability. It's 'Oh, you're Black and female, you'd be great.' After you work really hard for years you want to say, 'yeah, but I did some research'" (p. 108).

Fundamentally, the search process is about identifying talent. When affirmative action was introduced as a strategy at the federal level, colleges and universities were on the defensive. The lack of diversity with respect to gender and race on most campuses, and the resistance to change, prompted the federal government to pass affirmative-action legislation that mandated that search processes be open, that campuses work to diversify the pool, and that criteria for hiring be appropriate to the particular search. The underlying message was that there was talent available but that campuses had been unable or unwilling to interrupt their usual and often closed processes to find and consider that talent. That is still the issue. To what degree do campuses seriously engage finding talent from different pools of people, and to what degree do campuses have the competence to identify that talent when it looks different to search committees and campus groups? One of the important strategies, then, is the aggressive development of a diverse pool.

Overscrutiny and Bias in the Search Process

Most search processes put heavy emphasis on the initial review of paper applications. This is often felt to ensure objectivity. But the fact is that the paper presentation of candidates affords numerous opportunities for bias, either implicit or explicit. The bias toward privileging people who have attended elite institutions is common and often explicit (Knowles & Harleston, 1997; Smith, Wolf, Busenberg, & associates, 1996). Other biases are more implicit, involving where people have published, whether having explicit scholarship on issues related to race or gender is viewed as a strength or a weakness, whether a person's early experiences in community college are viewed as a strength or a weakness, and whether the person has done work in the community (Moody, 2004). Indicators such as where one went to school can become surrogates for merit and thus bias the process away from those who have not followed an elite educational trajectory (see, e.g., Busenberg and Smith, 1997; McGinley, 1997; Merritt & Resken, 1997).

Bias has been documented in a number of reports. Studies looking at letters of reference for women candidates and evaluations of resumes have found bias favoring male candidates even when the records are identical (Trix & Psenka, 2003; Valian, 2000, 2005). Such studies should be sobering and should provide an impetus to interrupting the usual when it comes to screening candidates. Though I have not seen formal research on this, more and more people who participate on search committees have begun to talk about the overscrutiny of women and minority candidates, including scrutiny of their tenurability, their degrees, their research, and so on (Kulis, Chong, & Shaw, 1999; Kulis & Shaw, 1996; Misra, Kennelly, & Karides, 1999). This would be consistent with the literature on tokenism, in which such a candidate is visible as a representative but invisible as an individual. Regardless, overscrutiny has devastating consequences for the equitable review of applications and the likelihood that even one "qualified" candidate will emerge from the paper review.

My own research suggests that champions on search committees play a valuable role in watching out for how individual applicants are reviewed (Smith, Wolf, Busenberg, & associates, 1996). But there is greater likelihood that underrepresented candidates will find themselves without champions and more likely to be questioned. The only way to guard against bias is to ensure that there is sufficient awareness in the search committee, through training, and sufficient diversity on the committee to avoid it.

Special Hires

Research results suggest that special hires (along with other strategies such as diverse search committees, relevant job descriptions, linking departmental hires to institutional priorities and processes, and proactive searches) may be required in order to promote success in the hiring of most underrepresented faculty outside of ethnic studies and women's studies departments. Such practices are referred to with a variety of expressions: exceptional hires, search waivers, spousal hires, special-hire intervention, expanded job descriptions, modification of usual search requirements to meet program needs, shortened search process (truncated process), cluster hiring, or out-of-cycle hiring. Special hiring will remain significant as long as regular searches result in hiring faculty of color only in expected fields. Significantly, such strategies yield hiring across all racial and ethnic groups, suggesting that they would not violate current restrictions in the use of affirmative action and legal challenges.

However, an important caution should be noted. Because faculty success is dependent on department support and mentoring, continued research and vigilance are needed to monitor the success of faculty appointed with such interventions. Special hires should be made with the enthusiastic support of the department and with high regard for the scholarly contribution of the person hired.

Leadership and the Timing of Interventions

It is common in the research and practice literature on this topic to talk about the need for senior leadership to stay involved. Some suggest that leaders should be willing to turn back final candidates if there is no diversity present. It appears to me that while this is a potential strategy, it is not the best one. By the time search committees have come to agreement about the final group to bring to campus, a great deal of compromise, effort, and frustration have already been expended. (This also shows how untrue it is that there is one dimension of excellence and that one candidate simply rises to the top.) If we are to break down the silos of hiring and build the potential for institutional, school, program, and department synergies, leadership has to be engaged early on in the process: the discussion of what is important as revealed in recent program reviews, formulating the job description, creating a competent search committee, selecting a chair, ensuring that the candidate pool is diverse, monitoring that outreach has taken place, supporting efforts to ensure that relevant people have been encouraged to apply, and working to have the department see the institutional and program imperative. As the search proceeds, it is critically important that someone in the administration know what is happening and that the necessary supports be in place to facilitate an effective search.

The very decentralized nature of faculty hiring, sometimes down to the level of the search committee, has important implications for the role of deans and department chairs. The leadership in schools and departments becomes critical in facilitating the development of job descriptions, organizing the search, structuring the search committee, and facilitating proactive networking strategies. Senior leadership, however, has a clear role to play in identifying the curricular, research, and hiring priorities for the institution. When there is alignment between institutional-level efforts and more localized efforts, then change can occur. Intervention strategies such as creating extra faculty lines have been effective and often involve departmental and senior leadership. Chairs of search committees, deans, and department chairs can also be oriented as to how to conduct effective searches that are intentional about identifying biases, overscrutiny, and other patterns that emerge (Moody, 2004).

Linking to Central Processes

The relationship between the need for diversity in core institutional processes and faculty hiring has been both implicit and explicit throughout this chapter. It is important enough to warrant some special attention. As technology became central to every sector of college campuses, it emerged as an important factor in many searches. This occurred in part because there was a recognition that these new developments were, or were going to be, central to program, school, and institutional needs. In these searches, there was often a recognition of the gaps in programs that needed to be filled. While often not as clear in matters of diversity, this connection between hiring and core institutional elements is critical to ensuring that diversity in hiring is a consideration. Otherwise, the rhetoric will be present and the words will be written, but in the end, the reasons for failure will be more common than the evidence of success.

Faculty hiring is so central to departmental autonomy that diversity has to be linked to or embedded in these cultures to really emerge as a priority. For campuses that have a well-developed program-review process or program-planning process that is linked to academic planning or institutional priorities, program plans can be an important vehicle if the structure is provided to facilitate the understanding of how important the diversity imperative is to the department.

The dimensions of diversity can be readily built in to most of these processes through the employment of disaggregated data. A number of questions can be included in program reviews: Who are our students (undergraduate, graduate, professional)? For whom are we successful (undergraduate, graduate, professional students)? What is the relationship between the mission of a department (program, unit) and the mission of the campus? What resources do we have, and what resources do we need? What are the new developments in the field that relate to diversity, and how well do we engage them? What are the curricular and/or scholarly needs of the institution, and to what degree are we prepared to meet them? How do we relate to our external communities? What societal needs should we be addressing? Many of these questions are being addressed in institutional plans that incorporate diversity. Asking departments to engage them at the local level will provide a much stronger basis for developing job descriptions and identifying faculty needs as units face hiring opportunities. Institutions can also use the priority of diversity as a way to prioritize the allocation of searches to units.

Legal Issues

Because the current environment may put campuses on the defensive about legal matters in hiring, the hiring and retention of faculty, as in other areas, needs to be understood as being focused on expertise, talent, skills, and institutional and departmental requirements (Alger, 2000, 2005a, 2005b). Locating diversity at the center of an institution's mission and educational and scholarly priorities is both effective and legal. An approach to special hires that focuses on levels of expertise and skills but that opens the application process to all persons is both narrow enough and clear enough to increase the likelihood of diverse pools while staying within legal limits. In contrast, the debates about affirmative-action practices are often framed today in a legal context, and often with a defensive posture. Approaching the hiring and retention of faculty in ways described here makes this very important institutional function a scholarly and educational one—proactive and central to the mission.

Many people critical of affirmative action suggest that there is nothing but diversity hiring occurring, thus leading to reverse discrimination. The data do not support such allegations. Indeed, the counterevidence is that in many fields and departments, there is a total absence of persons of color. The research suggests that the impetus for affirmative action—putting campuses on notice to diversify their hiring—remains a current issue that should leave campuses vulnerable to charges of continued bias, rather than the reverse. These data, along with evidence that diversity is central to the institution's mission, are critically important from a legal perspective. Moreover, while the focus here has been on race and gender, every campus must consider its own context in looking at the ways in which other forms of diversity are important.

Evaluation and Monitoring of Successful Practices

The need to evaluate and monitor progress is significant in faculty hiring and retention. Tracking patterns for faculty diversity over time, looking at turnover, gathering information about the reasons faculty stay and leave, and identifying locations on campus where success has been achieved can provide a manageable and useful store of information. In understanding promising practices and what works, institutions themselves will have to assess if, why, and how strategies worked, and for whom the strategies worked or didn't work. Research in the field now indicates significantly different results by discipline.

Departments and fields whose content is closely linked to diversity continue to be the most likely places for hiring of underrepresented faculty of color, while science and math fields are hiring Asian and Asian American faculty through the use of regular searches. Over time, this could result in distorted and potentially stereotypical placements. Campuses are often in a position to examine examples of successful departments and to share information. Such knowledge can inform all campus hiring processes. Significantly, context does matter. Each institution has to craft and characterize its interventions in ways that are congruent with its departments, campus environment, and mission.

The studies reported here have focused primarily on tenured and tenure-track faculty. It will be increasingly important to look at whether people who bring diversity, and which ones, are being hired—both "online" and "off-line." It has been well documented that, along with the recent growth in the number and percentage of tenured and tenure-track faculty, there has been much more significant growth in positions "off-line." While more data are needed, preliminary studies, including those by Trower and Chait (2002) and Schuster and Finkelstein (2006), suggest that a much higher percentage of URM faculty and White women are being hired in such positions than in tenure or tenure-track positions.

Graduate Students

It is not uncommon to discuss graduate-student diversity as part of an analysis of student diversity. Through the work with the James Irvine Foundation Campus Diversity Initiative, the important link between graduate-student enrollments and faculty hiring emerged. There is not yet sufficient diversity in graduate enrollments to create the robust pipeline necessary for "easier" faculty hiring. Higher education is not only hiring the next generation of faculty, it is also producing the pipeline for the next generation of faculty (Golde & Walker, 2006). Olivas has asked why schools "do not see their responsibility to recruit and graduate more Latino lawyers" (1994, p. 131). The national data suggest that despite the fact that undergraduate enrollments in doctoral-granting institutions are significantly more diverse, graduate enrollments are not moving fast enough (Congressional Commission on the Advancement of Women and Minorities in Science, Engineering and Technology Development, 2000; White, 1989; Woodrow Wilson Foundation, 2005).

There has been progress in diversifying students in doctoral programs by race and gender, but the rate of progress is not yet sufficient. Doctoral education and the development of future faculty are closely tied to faculty concerns, and they need to be part of the strategy for diverse faculty—especially with the robust hiring that is under way.

❀

The prevailing findings from research and practice suggest that *interrupting the usual* and *challenging myths* will be very important if colleges and universities are to achieve excellence in developing the necessary knowledge, capacity, expertise, and success in the very diverse society that the United States has become. Given the speed of current hiring on many campuses throughout the country, and the presence of significant turnover, we are running out of time to succeed in building institutional capacity in the form of faculty resources.

Moreover, what is done now will send a powerful message to students about the potential opportunities in faculty careers. Higher education really does produce its own labor pool. It has the ability to decide who will be hired and who will not. While providing excuses for failure may be convincing to some, the failure to succeed will have repercussions for years to come. Hence, there is today both urgency and opportunity.

NOTE

Parts of this chapter were drawn from Smith, Wolf, Busenberg, & associates, 1996; Smith, Turner, Osei-Kofi, & Richards, 2004; and Smith, Parker, Clayton-Pedersen, Moreno, & Teraguchi, 2006.

❀

CHAPTER SIX

Working with and across Differences

Intergroup Relations and Identity

The intrinsic connection between diversity and identity was described in chapter 2. Though identity is core to diversity issues, deep ambivalence about the role of identity emerges in many contexts. The question is whether identity is simply divisive and ought to be eliminated, if at all possible, from institutional strategies. The deep concerns about identity in an institutional context manifest in a number of ways:

- a concern about self-segregation directed almost entirely at the perception that students of color are clustering together on campus;
- a fear that the growing list of identities under the diversity "umbrella" will reduce diversity to simply the celebration of difference and will overshadow societal issues of inequity;
- the sense that emphasis on identity undermines institutional shared values; and
- the deep concern that is expressed throughout higher education about the challenges of having conversations about difficult issues related to diversity.

In the introduction to a very useful book on intergroup dialogue efforts on college campuses, Schoem, Hurtado, Sevig, Chesler, & Sumida (2001) underscore the relationship among democracy, diversity, and dialogue:

Democracy is a powerful but fragile political arrangement, requiring careful maintenance, regular nurturance, and continuing advancement in the areas of social justice and equality. The American ideal, that people from all backgrounds can join together to live in a just and democratic society, will become even more of a necessity for our democratic survival. . . . If we can't talk openly with one another in a sustained way, we have little hope of achieving our national ideal, let alone maintaining the progress we have made thus far. (pp. 14–15)

This chapter addresses what we are learning about the conditions under which people from diverse backgrounds within the faculty, staff, administration, and student body can come together for the work of the university. While the chapter is framed in terms of *intergroup* relations, the recognition that individuals bring multiple and intersecting identities and live in the context of these identities should make it clear that *intragroup* issues are relevant as well. There are gender issues that emerge in the context of race, ethnicity, religion, and so on. There are racial, class, and sexuality issues that emerge within groups of men or women.

It is also important to note that while the issue of intergroup relations and difficult dialogues is an important element of building institutional capacity, much of the research in higher education and the programs that result have focused to a large degree on undergraduate students. That is not true of the larger body of literature on which this chapter will draw, which uses experimental, theoretical, and applied approaches to address the question of the conditions for bringing people together and the role of identity throughout the institution.

One of the most compelling arguments for the importance of diversity has framed it as an educational opportunity for groups from different backgrounds to learn from and with one another. As a result, the educational benefits of diversity have become an important part of many campus efforts and an important focus for research in higher education (e.g., Hurtado, 2001b). While this approach sounds ideal as an aspirational effort, the fact is that intergroup efforts, as we shall see, cannot be based on a naïve notion that contact produces good results.

What is clear is that there is urgency (sometimes more indirect than direct) for building the capacity of the campus in the area of intergroup and intragroup efforts. Moreover, campus context affects the outcomes of programmatic approaches (Chang, Denson, Saenz, & Misa, 2006). It is important, therefore, to consider the question of design. How do we design opportunities for intergroup encounters in such a way that everyone benefits? Well-designed programs can add significantly to the climate and learning on campus. They also have the potential to engage faculty, staff, and students in building the kind of pluralistic campus the rhetoric now envisions.

Intergroup-Relations Research

A large body of research focusing on intergroup relations has emerged. The results suggest important theoretical, conceptual, and empirical strategies for reframing the discourse of identity in the context of diversity so that diversity can truly be both inclusive and differentiated. While one has to be cautious about drawing definitive conclusions from academic research of this kind, the results are quite robust and the consistency of conclusions quite impressive. Moreover, the lessons for this chapter are deepened because they are drawn from very different methodologies and from a variety of disciplines, including social psychology, organizational development, sociology, and political science. The research is also quite instructive for explaining contradictory findings and providing some insights into what campuses might consider for building capacity to foster intergroup efforts, as well as for program design. It illuminates some of the challenges of creating environments that support those from diverse backgrounds while also creating institutions where individuals and groups can benefit from the diversity that is so valued, at least rhetorically, by many.

While much of this research grew out of a desire to reduce prejudice and stereotyping in contexts around the world, it is fundamentally about building relationships across difference and thus is potentially very significant on college campuses today. Moreover, as we shall see, college campuses have more of the conditions that facilitate intergroup contact, or are in a better position to create them, than can often be achieved in the larger society. It is through this body of theory and research that we have, I believe, an exciting opportunity to both validate and reframe identity to serve diversity and institutional purposes.

Conditions for Contact

A significant body of research addresses the question of the best conditions under which people from different backgrounds can be brought together. This research tradition had its origins during the unrest due to large migrations of "minorities" to formerly primarily White cities in the United States in the 1950s. While much of this work focused on migrations of African Americans from the Southeast to the North, Zúñiga, Nagda, Chesler, and Cytron-Walker (2007) point out that this also occurred in the Southwest with large migrations of Mexican Americans after World War II. These migrations, rather than leading to prejudice reduction, often led instead to increased stereotyping. The large body of research that emerged during that era, beginning with the seminal work of Gordon Allport (1954), continues today with a focus on the conditions under which intergroup contact leads to the reduction of prejudice on the part of those in the majority. While attending primarily to race and ethnicity, studies have also looked at prejudice based on age, sexual orientation, and disability.

Significantly, with a wide variety of methods used and different identity groups considered, the results are remarkably similar. They suggest four important conditions under which intergroup efforts will work best, conditions described by Allport in 1954. They are equal status, shared goals, cooperation, and institutional support. Most of the work in social psychology has used as the outcome of interest individual attitudes toward "the other" in the minority, such as prejudice and stereotyping. Studies have demonstrated positive affects toward racial and ethnic minorities as well as positive attitudes toward gays and lesbians (Brewer, 1996; Dixon, Durrheim, & Tredoux, 2005; Pettigrew, 1998a, 1998b; Pettigrew & Tropp, 2000). In the fifty years of this research, conducted in work settings as well as on college campuses, using field but mostly experimental designs, these same conditions have continued to emerge as important for successful intergroup relationships.

Equal status. Equal status in stratification has been a key condition for achieving the benefits of intergroup contact. The research suggests that while equal status before the contact would be optimal, the conditions can be created in a particular setting. What is critical is that equal status must be perceived and experienced by those in both the majority and minority positions.

Shared goals. A common goal is perhaps best represented in settings such as athletics. However, it can be achieved through shared goals in organizations or in specific settings.

Cooperation. Intergroup cooperation suggests that the group must assume a collaborative approach to achieving the goals, rather than a competitive one. It is this pattern that led to the development of Aronson's jigsaw-puzzle approach to learning through collaboration in diverse classrooms (Aronson & Patnoe, 1997; Johnson & Johnson, 1987; Slavin & Cooper, 1999).

Institutional support. The supportive role of the institution through customs, laws, leadership, and clear commitment has remained an important condition throughout the generations of research. The relatively successful integration of the military is often cited—an effort that combined institutional mandates and increased diversification of leadership. In contrast, Pettigrew (1998b) notes that the relative lack of success in higher education, especially with regard to racist incidents, might be attributable to the absence or weakness of a strong institutional ethos to change power dynamics and structures of inequality on campus. A living mission with respect to diversity is one vehicle for setting a tone of institutional support and intention.

Researchers have tried to understand the underlying dynamics that inform these conditions. Studies suggest that this is a multidimensional phenomenon that includes learning about the group, changing behaviors in order to change attitudes, generating emotional connections, and, finally, creating an openness to broadening the understanding of the other (Pettigrew, 1998a).

In a series of contemporary meta-analyses, Pettigrew suggests that the only real modification to be made to these four conditions is that the design of intergroup efforts should occur in settings where there is an opportunity for long-term interactions, ideally leading to the possibility of friendship or other affective ties (Pettigrew, 1998a; Pettigrew & Tropp, 2000). In addition, Pettigrew and Tropp note that because much of this research focuses on changes in attitudes of the majority, more significant results are found there. They point out that the design of any approach must take into account the perspective of both high-status and lower-status groups if the outcomes are to benefit everyone. That is, as we shall see later, the impact on those in the minority is important and needs to be considered.

The results of this research are quite relevant to the design of intergroup efforts on campus. The internal design of the approach (ensuring perceptions of equal status, shared goals, and collaboration) and an institutional context that is supportive and that creates the likelihood of longer-term connections are critical. The asymmetrical impact of such efforts must also be considered; those in the minority or lower-status position must perceive institutional support and feel able to participate fully.

Social Identity and Intergroup Relations

A second body of research has emerged from social identity theory, one that had its origins in Europe (Tajfel, 1978). This work focuses on the notion of identity and the tendency for individuals to organize their perspective of themselves in the world on the basis of identities that carry inherent in-group and out-group significance. With identities, then, there is a tendency to view those in one's in-group as more like oneself, more trustworthy and likable, and to position oneself in competition with those outside one's group. For social identity theory, these cognitive representations of the world have deep significance. The core of social identity work relating to intergroup relations focuses in part on ways to alter the cognitive structures of identity from a simple frame in which there is a single in-group versus out-group to one in which the recognition of the multiplicity of identities is used and developed.

Over the years, a number of approaches have been studied and tested, both experimentally and in the field (Hewstone, Rubin, & Willis, 2002). Three will resonate with many on today's college campus. The first is *decategorization*, in which the attempt is to have everyone seen as individuals rather than as representatives of groups. This approach attempts to reduce, or even eliminate, any group identity and to highlight the commonalities of values and virtues of individuals. The challenge with this approach is that even in experimental conditions, where people have been encouraged to think of others as individuals and not group members, the effect does not seem to generalize to other group members. That is, negative or stereotyped attitudes toward the group might remain even if one becomes close to an individual. At the time, the individual becomes the exception (Crisp & Hewstone, 2007; Hewstone, 1994).

The second approach, *recategorization*, subordinates smaller identity groups to a single superordinate identity. One campus that I know of attempted to deal with race by suggesting that the only color that mattered on this campus was the campus color—purple. Following 9/11, there was a great deal of publicity across the country featuring people from diverse racial and ethnic backgrounds saying, "I am an American." Because these approaches attempt to reduce the salience of identity groupings, they have been identified as assimilationist. The research is reasonably clear, however, that for those for whom identity is salient, attempts to eliminate it may *increase* rather than reduce the salience of identity, in part because such an attempt constitutes a threat (Brewer, 2000; Hewstone, Rubin, & Willis, 2002). In a number of experiments, efforts to build a superordinate identity by eliminating salient group identities tended to increase ethnic tension, especially among those in the minority position in the society (Crisp, Stone, & Hall, 2006).

When the salience of a social identity is rooted in issues of equity and when historic injustices are important for that identity, calling for a community to ignore identity can be seen as a call to ignore equity issues. Indeed, campus efforts to encourage the reduction or elimination of identities in favor of institutional identities often do create a backlash. While we normally think of this research in terms of hot-button issues such as nationality, race, or religion, Hornsey and Hogg (2000) found the dynamic to hold even among university students in math and humanities when schools were being reorganized to form one unit. When I hear campus leaders calling for unity and the target (either explicit or implicit) is identity groupings, I can see the negative impact that this message has on groups on campus.

A third approach, described as *mutual differentiation*, is characterized by acknowledging identities but stressing their mutual interdependence. This pluralistic approach leaves identities intact while emphasizing connections across them. While the approach has been shown to reduce intergroup tensions under specific conditions, its usefulness has been found to be limited in contexts in which there is a great deal of inequality associated with these identities, where segregation among groups provides little opportunity for contact, and where there are significant gaps in access to resources and in presence in an institution. Under such circumstances, it is difficult or impossible to reduce the salience of identity (for those in the lower-status position) or for there to be true interdependence (Crisp & Hewstone, 2007; Hewstone, Rubin, & Willis, 2002).

Scholars in the field continue to explore other approaches for designing intergroup efforts, such as those that emphasize identity with one's ethnicity and with the nation. That approach is probably best captured in the United States by the motto *e pluribus unum*. One of the issues with this model is how the superordinate identity is created and whether there is genuine participation by minorities and majorities (Dovidio, Gaertner, Isen, & Lowrance, 1995; Dovidio, Gaertner, & Validzic, 1998; Dovidio, Kawakami, & Gaertner, 2000; Gaertner, Dovidio, Nier, Ward, & Banker, 1999; Guarasci, Cornwell, & associates, 1997). Social identities emerge from historical, cultural, and political contexts. If the superordinate identity is developed by the group that has a larger share of power and resources, then dual identity is not likely to emerge easily. The current debate as to whether the United States is at its core a Christian nation and should function that way has significance for whether non-Christian groups in the country can and will develop a national identity with the same commitment as that to the local identity. Research by Dovidio, Kawakami, and Gaertner (2000) underscores the fact that for both Whites and racial minorities, favorable intergroup contact contributes to satisfaction with an institution. However, they caution that

> strategies and interventions designed to enhance satisfaction need to recognize that Whites and people of color may have different ideals and motivations. Because White values and culture have been the traditionally dominant ones in the United States, American Whites are likely to see an assimilation model— in which members of other cultural groups are absorbed into the "mainstream"—as the most comfortable and effective strategy. For people of color, this model, which denies the value of their culture and traditions, is likely to be perceived as less desirable but also as threatening to their personal and social identity—particularly for people who strongly identify with their group. Thus, efforts to create a single superordinate identity, although well intentioned, may threaten people's social identity in terms that can intensify intergroup bias and conflict. (p. 157)

Thus, a fundamental asymmetry in perception emerges as an important factor to be considered in any intergroup effort. Considerable evidence from social psychology has emerged suggesting that those in power tend to focus on the symmetry of conflict without regard to differential power (Rouhana, 2004). As Tropp describes in her analysis of the intergroup literature (2006), most of that work focuses on the impact of intergroup efforts on the dominant group, since the underlying assumption has been that the goal of prejudice reduction relies on changing the attitudes of the dominant group. Some of this work has indeed demonstrated that intergroup efforts result in stereotype reduction, the ability to engage structural inequities, and the development among Whites of a more positive approach to conflict and a willingness to work toward social justice (Gurin, Peng, Lopez, & Nagda, 1999; Lopez, Gurin, & Nagda, 1998; Nagda, Gurin, Sorensen, Gurin-Sands, & Osuna, 2009; Zúñiga & Sevig, 1997).

Fewer studies have focused on the impact of such efforts on minorities in those contexts. Some of the research highlights how the experience of intergroup efforts can cause stress, distrust, and threat unless the differential experiences of minority groups are considered (Dixon, Durrheim, & Tredoux, 2005; Dovidio, Kawakami, & Gaertner, 2000; Major & O'Brien, 2005; Treviño, 2001; Tropp, 2006). Troy Duster (1992) did a study of students at Berkeley and found that while the desire for contact with people from diverse backgrounds was almost universal, White students simply wanted to get to know others as individuals (and share pizza). Students of color wanted to come together to engage in work concerning social justice and issues on campus. Ostensibly, it was the same shared goal, but there were very different perceptions about the conditions under which the groups of students wanted to come together.

In an approach that appears quite promising in its ability to combine the advantages of multiplicity of identity with the findings of contact theory, several researchers have proposed thinking about the issue of identity in terms of alternative multiple identities and crosscutting categories (Brewer, 1997, 2000; Brewer & Brown, 1998; Crisp & Hewstone, 2007; Crisp, Walsh, & Hewstone, 2006; Rosenthal & Crisp, 2006). In this approach, individuals are encouraged to think of the multiple groups with which they identify. The societal or institutional strategy is to encourage multiple identities and then to build meaningful participation in each of them in order to increase the likelihood that, rather than having a single in-group and out-group, one will find oneself connecting with individuals from many groups over time.

Studies done in anthropology, sociology, and political science suggest that countries organized in this way have reduced potential for conflict that would have been based on politically salient identities (Monroe, Hankin, & Van Vechten, 2000). As Brewer (2000) describes, using multiple identities and crosscutting categories makes systems of categorization more complex, blurs boundaries, and makes outgroup distinctions more difficult, especially if a positive affect can be developed

(Crisp & Hewstone, 2007). This pattern of results is consistent with the research to be discussed in chapter 7, which shows that engaging with diversity facilitates complex thinking. Overlapping group membership also makes it possible to develop relationships with individuals who share some of one's characteristics but are at the same time different from oneself. Central to this approach is acknowledging identities rather than diminishing them. This model has been tested successfully in a number of experimental settings (see, e.g., Crisp & Hewstone, 2007; Crisp, Hewstone, & Rubin, 2001; Marcus-Newhall, Miller, Holtz, & Brewer, 1993; Wittig & Molina, 2000).

Essential to this model is the notion of meaningful participation, belonging, or (as will be described in chapter 7) mattering. Brewer (2000) has a cautionary note, however, regarding the potential limits of models that emphasize overlapping identities. Gender and ethnicity are indeed multiple and crosscutting identities. But if an African American woman is in the minority among White women and perceives that for the other women race cannot be engaged, and if among men she feels like the token woman with respect to whom gender should be ignored, then experiencing connection across two crosscutting identities is not likely to be achieved. She is likely to feel that she identifies most with other African American women. Does this not sound very much like the dynamics on our campuses with respect to race and gender, whether among students, faculty, or administration (Brewer, 2000; Cole & Guy-Sheftall, 2003; Crisp, Hewstone, & Rubin, 2001; Levin, 2003; Simpson, 2003)? Thus, building the capacity of individuals and groups to meaningfully engage the multiplicity of identities requires that asymmetry is acknowledged and that the person or group feels acknowledged in meaningful ways. In this example, if the woman were not a token in each of the groups, then her ability to be seen and to participate as herself would not be limited.

The possibility of implementation of many of these conditions is often constrained in the larger society by patterns of societal segregation, which, of course, provides little opportunity for contact. This is true on campuses as well. Researchers have found that when little contact between groups is possible (as in highly segregated circumstances), attitudes can be shifted by cognitive approaches in which people actually imagine new ways of approaching people and learning about people from other groups (Crisp & Hewstone, 2007). This work relies on increasing knowledge and information about identities with which an individual is not familiar and linking these identities to institutional identity. This approach has important implications for the curriculum, especially in institutions where diversity is limited. Teaching about the complexity and multiplicity of identity in an institutional context in which diversity is seen as a commitment has significant potential for learning and the classroom. And as our campuses become more diverse, teaching without experiencing should become less and less an issue.

Programmatic Approaches

Among the thirty-seven campuses that received funding from the Ford Foundation's Difficult Dialogues initiative, described in chapter 3, most of them expressed concern about incidents on campus, about the difficulty of having open discussions on controversial topics, and about how the curriculum and the campus environment might build this capacity for students. Wegner's description (2006) of the context at the University of North Carolina at Chapel Hill underscored the urgency of the concerns: "The events . . . helped us to recognize the need to face the fact that we now live in a deeply divided society whose sharp differences often spill over onto our once-tranquil campus environment" (p. 49). Because of how the Ford project was described, religion emerged as central in many of these proposals. At the same time, virtually all the campuses named issues related to multiple identities, including race, religion, gender, class, and sexuality. Some even mentioned the issue of silence—that which was not being discussed (Ford Foundation, 2005b; O'Neill, 2006).

Faculty and staff development were core parts of the effort to build capacity to facilitate dialogues, engage conflict, and understand relevant content and scholarship on related topics. At least two campuses had placed this effort at the heart of their teaching and learning centers, where faculty development was central. A few of these campuses framed the difficult-dialogue imperative in the context of the campus and all its constituencies, not just in the context of undergraduate education, by building the capacity for difficult dialogues among staff and faculty. Southwest Minnesota State University built its efforts around opening dialogue between indigenous peoples in the surrounding community and the White population that dominates the campus. This project intended to "strengthen faculty capacity to deal with political, religious, racial, and cultural issues specific to the region" (Ford Foundation, 2005b).

Because so many have identified the challenge of intergroup relations as important, a number of programs have been developed throughout the country that build on and use the results of these volumes of research for the purpose of facilitating intergroup dialogue—the capacity of people from diverse backgrounds to engage one another. In higher education, many of these programs, such as the ones at the University of Michigan (Nagda, Gurin, Sorensen, & Zúñiga, 2009; Zúñiga & Nagda, 2001) and Arizona State University (Treviño, 2001), focus on building the capacity of students to engage in the dialogue process. Others, such as the National Conference for Community and Justice (Winborne & Smith, 2001), the Worlds of Difference Program of the Anti-Defamation League (Tiven, 2001), the Study Circles Resource Center (McCoy & McCormick, 2001), and Hope in the Cities (Greisdorf, 2001), have been developed in and are used in cities and communities throughout the country, as well as on campuses (Schoem, Hurtado, Sevig, Chesler, & Sumida, 2001). In 2007, the University of New Hampshire developed a network with the explicit goals of building institutional capacity and the capacity of higher education in general to foster deliberative democracy and to change the decision-making culture in the academy and society. This network has incorporated the use of Study Circles.

In the Ford Foundation's Difficult Dialogues proposals, besides the use of the intergroup-dialogue approach (Schoem & Hurtado, 2001), a number of national resources on dialogue were employed, including Study Circles, the Kettering Foundation's work with public forums, the National Issues Forum Network, Centers for Conflict Resolution, National Conference for Community and Justice (NCCJ), and peace-building initiatives (Gomez, 2006; Saunders, 1999). Emory University took its model from the South African Truth and Reconciliation Commission, where "the process demonstrated that public acknowledgement of deep hurts and heinous crimes can go a long way toward healing community fissures that many believed could never be resolved peacefully" (Harris, 2006, p. 32).

Schoem, Hurtado, Sevig, Chesler, and Sumida (2001) describe the dialogue process as an ongoing one designed to facilitate face-to-face interaction among people from different identity groups, using skilled facilitators. In a useful overview, Stephan and Stephan (2001) point out that while there are many intergroup programs, the specific designs and approaches reveal a variety of purposes, including staff training, managing group conflict, and multicultural education, as well as fostering intergroup relations. Some programs will focus on action and collaboration for change, some are more oriented toward healing relationships, and others aim to build capacity in the community as it develops. In most cases, however, "intergroup dialogues cross the boundaries of individual and group identities and experiences. It is important for each participant (1) to acknowledge his or her social group identities and those groups' roles in society and, (2) at the same time, to affirm his or her own individuality within and across social groups, and (3) to recognize commonalities across social groups" (Schoem et al., p. 11).

A review of these approaches across the country suggests some common elements. The orientation includes the use of identity, and especially multiplicity of identity, to encourage engagement across difference. Each program has a well-defined process, with trained facilitators to encourage difficult dialogues and the negotiation of conflict. Virtually all attempt to place the understanding of dialogue in historical context and in the context of social structures, inequity, and issues of power and justice. This is important. In our society generally and in some of the multicultural and intercultural approaches, we have used phrases such as "celebrating difference" to suggest that diversity is simply about learning about "the other." There is a danger that the language of *inclusion*, while not intrinsically problematic, could indeed be problematic, if it implies that we are all individuals coming together with a requirement to ignore history and context.

Because so much of the work has emerged from social psychology, the focus is not simply on understanding individuals and their differences. The goal is also to begin to develop conceptual and affective understandings of the different positions that groups occupy in the society and that impact individuals. The notions of privilege cross many identity boundaries, but they are probably among the more difficult to teach and to have people internalize. Survey research suggests that, in part because of the individualism of American society, many people attribute inequality to individuals, not to structural factors (Sumida & Gurin, 2001). People in subordinate positions may see those structures more clearly than those in dominant positions. Developing a pedagogy to help people understand these dynamics is critical to many of the intergroup efforts, even as they also engage individuals and individual experiences of identity (Collins, 2000; Johnson & Johnson, 1987).

Over the long term, an important question will be whether these efforts have been institutionalized—whether they are sustainable and central to the entire institution's capacity to function in pluralistic contexts, not just wonderful programs designed for a limited group of participants. Most of them seem linked to core institutional priorities. At the same time, they were also reacting to immediate and urgent concerns.

Principles for Building Intergroup Capacity

The results of the research from the field and the use of experimental designs suggest some powerful themes that have very practical implications for our campuses. In contrast to the society at large, campuses have the potential to create the conditions in which intergroup contact can be nourished. But these designs cannot ignore the issues of threat, stigma, distrust, fear, and histories of injustice that people experience, especially in minority positions. Using the new developments with multiple identities described here and in chapter 2, we can move out of the current framework that pits ethnic identities against one another, suggests that ethnic or other identities undermine institutional commitment, asks people to choose identities, and neglects the important inequalities that harden the salience of identity. In my judgment, building on multiple identities and the conditions for intergroup contact provide a kind of road map to the building of institutional capacity on our campuses. These principles emerge from a synthesis of the available literature, as well as from observing some highly successful efforts on campuses and in communities.

Not Just for Undergraduates

Building intergroup capacity is not just for undergraduate students. In staff meetings, office interactions, faculty meetings, and strategic-planning committees, and in all the myriad groups and interactions that occur on a college campus, paying attention to these issues and opportunities will be important for building the capacity across the campus to develop healthy intergroup and intragroup relationships. While building the capacity for dialogue is an important educational goal, it is also critically important for all constituencies and for the definition of competent leadership itself.

We can name the identities that are salient at the present time, but this approach provides a broad framework for intergroup and intragroup issues that may not be obvious today. Imagine how staff and faculty orientations might be approached, how leadership training would be conducted, and how campuses would introduce new members of the campus to the values of the campus under such a framework.

Institutional Context

There must be an institutional ethos that expresses how it values diversity and the multiplicity of identities with not only rhetoric, but policies and practice as well. An institutional identity that incorporates multiplicity of identities and addresses the political, social, and historical roles of diversity on campus and in the society has the potential to facilitate engagement for multiple groups. It is important that those in marginal positions on campus also perceive an institutional commitment. It cannot simply be rhetorically declared by those in leadership positions.

Shared Goals and Multiple Identities

Out of this institutional ethos, the campus needs to develop the kind of overarching goals and mission that matter to all communities on campus and around which there can be common identification. Strategic-planning processes, attending to diversity throughout the institution, and dialogues all facilitate the creation of shared understandings. In addition, in smaller units such as faculty meetings, research labs, classrooms, and residence halls, shared commitments and efforts, combined with the contributions of a variety of experiences, facilitate the conditions under which diversity enhances institutional effectiveness.

In this process at its best, one would see, for example, collaborative faculty research, team efforts among staff, and civic engagement of students. Fundamental to such results are a reasonable level of collaboration and the development of shared goals in which diverse groups feel some ownership. Only then can the broad range of identities be fully developed. Campuses seeking to maximize the benefits of diversity can build on the multiplicity of crosscutting identities both programmatically and through academic and social networks on campus. In addition to the traditional identities of diversity, such as race, gender, class, and sexual orientation, one can then also build in significant affiliative identities, such as athletics, extracurricular groups, and academic departments.

Acknowledging Asymmetry

The asymmetrical experience of intergroup issues must be recognized and incorporated into any approach. Publicly identifying self-segregation as a significant problem signals that ethnic identity groups are part of the problem, not the solution. A campus can, rather, fully address the degree to which it is building the capacity for engagement across and through difference for all groups on campus—including the board, faculty, administration, staff, and students.

A focus on intergroup efforts, however, must be joined with support for and recognition of the specific diversity groups on campus. As we have seen in the research, to act as if there were no differences among identity groups in resources, standing, and experience of the campus is to exacerbate the salience of identity and create additional separation. What allows the campus to fully benefit from diversity is the combination of a shared goal, the building of effective ways to bring people together, and the recognition of ongoing diversity efforts. The less diverse the campus is—the smaller the proportions of various racial and ethnic groups, for example—the more the institution will need to make sure that such groups matter while working toward shared efforts.

Mattering Matters

Feeling that one matters must be achieved in all groups for which there can be crosscutting identity. In chapter 7, mattering will be discussed in the context of student success, but its importance holds true for faculty and staff as well. If individuals do not experience that they matter, true inclusion cannot be achieved. In Brewer's example (2000), African American women must experience that they matter in a group of women—not that just White women matter—and that they matter in a group of African American men as well. There are many behaviors that are used to signal mattering. Who is tapped for leadership positions, for example, conveys a great deal about being taken seriously, as does being listened to and engaged.

Increasing Diversity

If we consider the principles outlined above together with the issue of tokenism, it becomes clear that achieving real diversity in crosscutting groups will be essential if the members of the group are to develop real commitment and ownership. Women's groups need to be diverse ethnically, for example, and the structures and culture of a group need to be developed so that the societal experience of stigma and powerlessness can be reduced and so that no individual or subgroup feels marginalized or essentialized. A campus choir could serve a crosscutting role, but only if it achieves diversity among its active participants and creates an environment in which the diversity that individuals bring matters.

Historical Context

The context for intergroup interactions on a college campus often includes a history. It could be a racial-discrimination suit, the residential or educational-achievement patterns in the region, a string of sexual-harassment incidents, or a history of no hiring for diversity. More often than not, the participants, or groups, have a social and historical context with which they enter the dialogue, a context that must be understood. Conflict-resolution and peace-building efforts around the world emphasize the importance of acknowledging and telling the stories that relate to those histories. While this can be very difficult, it is one of the opportunities created in an educational setting and one of the important roles for research and teaching.

Negotiating Conflict, History, and Perceptions

Intergroup efforts necessarily involve creating the capacity to deal with conflict. A rich and robust literature has developed concerning conflict, negotiation, and dialogue, which are all relevant to the important task of engaging across difference for the sake of institutional capacity (see, e.g., Cloke, 2006; Johnson & Johnson, 1987; Sturm & Gadlin, 2007). Avoiding conflict, while sometimes appealing, is rarely effective. At the same time, allowing conflict to develop without intervention can often strengthen notions that diversity is divisive. Sadly, the divisive aspects of dysfunctional conflict occur in many domains.

Intentionality

Well-designed efforts to encourage people to dialogue and act on difficult issues will not occur without intention. Avoidance and silence are much more common approaches. Moreover, like most things on campus, these efforts will not be sustained unless they are core to the mission.

For student-affairs units, placing difficult dialogues as an educational imperative in and out of classroom locations and working with faculty to facilitate lectures, discussions, theater events, and other programs that strengthen these efforts can be both exciting and significant. For the professional development of graduate students as future faculty, building capacity for dealing with conflict and dialogue is an important skill. Academically, these programs can directly affect teaching, learning, research, and the climate of the institution.

From a leadership perspective, good working relationships on a campus are going to influence the capacity of the institution to engage difficult issues as they emerge. Good relationships also have the potential to locate the campus at the center of positive approaches to change. But they will not develop and will not be sustained without effort and intent. Sharon Washington (2007), in *On Campus with Women*, makes the case for engaging conflict:

For the most part, we move through our lives in fairly homogeneous environments; we may enter the workplace poorly prepared to interact in an authentic manner with those different from ourselves. Frequently what we have learned about those different from ourselves is fraught with misinformation based on generalities and stereotypes, and often members of a minority group know more about the dominant or majority group than vice versa. Unless we pay conscious attention to the system of advantages in the U.S., higher education will continue to perpetuate misinformation that advantages some groups over others. This level of engagement asks individuals and groups to see some conflicts as a healthy part of group interactions. (p. 2)

The Role of Identity Groups

In the absence of critical mass, identity groups that support individuals who are in the minority will be important. For some efforts, bringing together identity groups rather than individuals can help ameliorate concerns about tokenism and can, paradoxically, facilitate the ability of people to be individuals. Groups can be encouraged to work together for both group and institutional goals. On a number of campuses across the country, there are intergroup programs that build on the resources of groups on campus and that operate as extensions of institutional priorities and with serious institutional support.

While many identity groups are focused on students, there is no reason they cannot be extended to bring together faculty and staff as well, for the benefit of all. Such programs facilitate crosscutting identities while strengthening the ethnic, gender, and LGBT groups on campus and encouraging them to work together. In addition, the best of these programs geared to students utilize the formal structure of classrooms to facilitate the kind of relationship-building envisioned in these models. Such programs are increasingly engaging faculty as well, so that they have the capacity to deal with issues in their classroom and to use research and teaching for building knowledge about multiple identities and helping people learn about others in contexts where diversity is limited.

Building Capacity for Alliances

For individuals and groups in an increasingly pluralistic society, being able to work in alliances across identity groups, disciplines, and status in the institution in the service of institutional success, engaging issues of justice, working with communities, or serving the needs of particular groups and individuals will only increase in significance (Blackwell, Kwoh, & Pastor, 2002; Kendall, 2006; Tatum, 2007). Alliances that invariably include multiple identities and the intersections of identities require significant skills and commitment on the part of their members. The benefits to the institution and to the participants can be immeasurable. Mildred García (2007), talking about a particular multicultural alliance of women, describes the personal benefits of such collaboration:

> I was able to see the world through several different lenses. How does a White woman feel when she works for diversity issues and people of color question her sincerity? How does an African American woman experience the pressure of being president of a college in an urban city? How do we ensure that the voices of Puerto Ricans are not lost as we educate others that Latino is not a homogenous term and that there is rich diversity within as well as between groups? How can we speak about class and the intersection of our multiple selves? As we addressed these questions, we had deep and difficult conversations; we walked away enriched by what we had learned, able to bring a new understanding to our profession and our communities. (p. 2)

The Role of the Classroom

For students on campuses throughout the country, classrooms hold enormous potential as a site in which intergroup dialogue and relationships can be built. Students from diverse backgrounds will find themselves in classrooms chosen because of majors, requirements, or subject matter. In such contexts, patterns of isolation can be interrupted. The challenge, however, is that most faculty have not developed their expertise and capacity for designing and implementing a context in which intergroup discussions can take place.

Framing Intergroup Efforts

To truly build institutional capacity, diversity on campus needs to be understood as contributing to the institution and its mission in fundamental ways. A belief that people from diverse backgrounds contribute to creativity, to new ways of approaching issues, and to learning provides an environment that suggests that diversity really matters. Framing diversity in this way is more likely to create an orientation to diversity that is not only about avoiding discrimination or bringing in people whose identity is different, but is also likely to provide the institution with ways to do things differently and consider alternative approaches. In addition, from an institutional perspective, a learning orientation directed to a larger goal must be combined with the recognition of other essential elements that create the conditions for fully benefiting from diversity. These include appreciation of what individuals bring, acknowledging the challenges, naming instead of disregarding history, and recognizing inequities, stereotype threat, and so on. This orientation will also affect the criteria used to identify talent and leadership on campus.

While these conditions can be developed for specific intergroup programs or initiatives on campus, they are also qualities that can be built into institutional practices to create an environment in which individuals can participate and contribute to their maximum. Thus, although this chapter has engaged issues of intergroup relations, these conditions also have the potential to create healthy institutional environments and climates in which individuals, no matter what their role, can thrive and be their most productive and in which effective alliances, coalitions, and work teams can be developed and sustained. Supporting a variety of identity groups and building their capacity to engage across identities can only facilitate communication, boundary-crossing, and the development of relationships that are so important today and so underdeveloped in most institutions.

In the next chapter, a discussion of factors related to student success will underscore the importance of effective intergroup relations and identity.

✿

CHAPTER SEVEN

Student Learning and Success

Reviewing the literature on student access and success over the past forty years can lead to a disheartening question: What progress has been made, if any? A recent report from the Educational Testing Service, *America's Perfect Storm* (Kirsch, Braun, Yamamoto, & Sum, 2007), reflects a sense of urgency, highlighting the significance of the changing demographics and the need for improvement in the educational system and suggesting that the future health and well-being of society will rest on access and success (Altbach, Berdahl, & Gumport, 2005; Carey, 2005; Hersh & Merrow, 2005; Miller, 1995; Puraskin & Lee, 2004; Rendón & Hope, 1996).

Chapters 3 and 4 provided an overview of the current state of progress and a description of the kinds of efforts being made. These efforts touch on each of the dimensions of diversity and, when done well, connect these dimensions to each other. From an institutional perspective, there are ways to approach student success by drawing out some key principles that seem to emerge from what is known and from the relationship between diversity and success. While the bulk of this chapter will refer specifically to undergraduates, the principles and themes are relevant as well for the experience of students in graduate and professional programs, where graduation and persistence remain concerns as well.

Reports such as *America's Perfect Storm* and other discussions about student success rightly express alarm at the patterns for first-generation and underrepresented students; however, it is vital to stress that the patterns for student success, and whether students are thriving, vary from campus to campus. Indeed, some campuses, and not just the most selective ones, have eliminated achievement gaps in terms of graduation rates (Clayton-Pedersen, Parker, Smith, Moreno, & Teraguchi, 2007; Smith, Parker, Clayton-Pedersen, Moreno, & Teraguchi, 2006). In our work with the James Irvine Foundation Campus Diversity Initiative, we witnessed that on some campuses, Latino students were graduating at rates ahead of those of their classmates. On others, African Americans were graduating at rates above those at most other campuses. On a few campuses, we noticed that White students and Asian Americans were beginning to lag. While these patterns varied and did not take into account other identities, such as gender and class, they point to the tremendous opportunity to interrupt patterns of failure and move to patterns of success.

This chapter will bring together three literatures on what we are learning about the institutional conditions for student success. These literatures provide a powerful set of examples and research that, when taken together, hold significant lessons for campus practice. The first literature comes from research on special-purpose institutions, primarily women's colleges and historically Black colleges and universities. The research here is instructive not only as it relates to these populations, but also insofar as it demonstrates the central role of institutions in facilitating success. The second body of literature is defined by its general concern for student success and the evidence that is accumulating on the institutional conditions for it. The third body of research highlights the role and experience of diversity in relation to student success and student learning. In part out of a response to legal challenges, in part because of educational philosophy, and in part as a result of the increasing student diversity on campus, a large body of research in higher education has been developed in this area.

Fortunately, there is a great deal of alignment in the results emerging from these three areas, so as to suggest some powerful themes for student learning and success. Moreover, the findings reveal patterns that are also in alignment with the latest in scientific research on learning. The results of the research suggest a number of principles for the twenty-first-century classroom and institution. A description of these themes will be developed in the final section of the chapter.

Special-Purpose Institutions

What does the literature on special-purpose institutions suggest about the conditions for student success? Though the bulk of the research to date has focused primarily on women's colleges and HBCUs, there is a growing body of work on tribal colleges, primarily in the context of two-year institutions (American Indian Higher Education Consortium, Institute for Higher Education Policy, & Sallie Mae Education Institute, 2000; Boyer, 1997; Carnegie Foundation for the Advancement of Teaching, 1989; Carney, 1999; Falk & Aitken, 1984; Martin, 2005; Wright & Head, 1990). Less work has been done on Hispanic-serving institutions (HSIs), although with their growing number, research is beginning to emerge (Dayton, Gonzalez-

Vasquez, Martinez, & Plum, 2004). However, the considerable body of research on women's colleges and HBCUs describes their success and factors associated with success.

For me, perhaps the most dazzling work on women's colleges and HBCUs has been a body of research called baccalaureate-origins studies (Smith, 1990; Smith, Wolf-Wendel, & Morrison, 1995; Solórzano, 1993, 1995; Tidball, 1976, 1980, 1986; Wolf-Wendel, 1998). In these studies, the focus is on looking at some student outcome of interest in relation to the profile of where the students received their bachelor's degrees. In the best of these studies, the entering characteristics of the students and institutional size are controlled. Xavier University in New Orleans, for example, an institution of about three thousand students, is known for producing a significant percentage of the African American medical doctors in the country ("Xavier University," 1996). Moreover, for the 25,400 African Americans who have completed medical school since 1950, there have been eleven top feeder schools. Of those, five are HBCUs that have accounted for almost two-thirds of the African Americans graduating from medical school ("Half Century," 2000–2001). Furthermore, a review of the baccalaureate origins of the twenty-one hundred African Americans who received their PhD's in 2005 reveals that more than 20% got their BA at an HBCU. Of the top twenty-five producers, regardless of size, fifteen (60%) are HBCUs, and most of these are small institutions (National Science Foundation Survey of Earned Doctorates, 2005).

Similarly, a large body of research by Tidball (1976, 1980, 1986) has documented the role of women's colleges in producing PhD's, especially in STEM fields. Studies of women in Congress point to the disproportionate role of single-sex education in their backgrounds. In a groundbreaking study, Wolf-Wendel (1998) looked at the baccalaureate origins of African American, Latina, and White women and found that the top ten baccalaureate institutions producing PhD's (when controlling for size) reflected the important role of women's colleges and HBCUs and, in the case of Latinas, the role of women's colleges and a set of small Catholic women's colleges. Significantly, this study looked at data through the 1990s, long after the admissions barriers for women had been ended at other institutions. Moreover, a follow-up study by Wolf-Wendel, Baker, and Morphew (2000) showed that in the case of HBCUs, resources were *negatively* related to success; that is, institutions with fewer resources were among the most successful—doing more with less.

Research has demonstrated the educational, personal, and social benefits that are associated with these special institutions, often in contexts with few resources

(Allen, 1992; Allen, Epps, & Haniff, 1991; Drewry & Doermann, 2001; Ehrenberg & Rothstein, 1994; Fleming, 1984; Garibaldi, Dawson, & English, 2001; Miller-Bernal & Poulson, 2004; Pascarella & Terenzini, 2005; Smith, Morrison, & Wolf-Wendel, 1994; Smith, Wolf-Wendel, & Morrison, 1995; Tidball, 1976, 1980, 1986; Tidball, Smith, Tidball, & Wolf-Wendel, 1999; Wolf-Wendel, 1998, 2000; Wolf-Wendel, Baker, & Morphew, 2000). Though HBCUs and other special-purpose institutions have demonstrable records of success, many of them also struggle with graduation rates and attrition. The summary to follow does not ignore the struggle these institutions have. Yet while few would suggest that all women should attend a women's college, that all African Americans should attend a historically Black institution, or that all African American women should attend Spelman or Bennett (the only two women's colleges that are also HBCUs), there is a great deal that can be learned from the research that has been done on these institutions. In many ways, this research and these institutions point the way to good educational practices and to establishing environments that facilitate student success in general. There are a number of themes that emerge from this literature.

High Expectations, Belief, and Support

If I were to describe a pattern that emerges in special-purpose institutions concerning student success, it is that faculty, staff, and the institutional ethos convey a belief in students' ability to succeed and excel, regardless of their background. At places such as Bennett College, a nonselective institution, students are assumed to be able to move from where they are when they enter to where they need to be when they leave (Tidball, Smith, Tidball, & Wolf-Wendel, 1999). At Xavier, the standards for students applying to medical school are very high. The strategy involves a strong commitment to support, excellence, and belief in students, even when they might not believe in themselves. One hears on these campuses numerous examples illustrating that students are taken seriously, that advising and mentoring take an active form in both academic and personal issues, and that there are numerous and visible role models among students, faculty, staff, alumni, and board members (Fries-Britt & Turner, 2002; Hubbard, 2006; Tidball, Smith, Tidball, & Wolf-Wendel, 1999). Moreover, students are regularly encouraged to go to graduate or professional school, and many forms of intervention assist in that process.

This approach is consistent with a large body of research on social learning, motivation, and cognitive approaches to learning (American Educational Research Association, 2006; Donovan, Bransford, & Pelligrino, 1999; Dweck, 2007;

Mueller & Dweck, 1998). Dweck's work is particularly relevant here. She has demonstrated in a number of contexts that when people believe, and a learning environment conveys, that intelligence is fixed, such beliefs reduce the amount of effort people make. Conversely, when individuals believe they can learn and that learning is a flexible aptitude, not an inherited one, behaviors associated with effort and engagement are likely to increase. This approach is also consistent with studies of successful programs such as Treisman's use of an honors model, the Meyerhoff Scholars Program, and other initiatives that incorporate characteristics of high expectations, belief, support, and an institutional ethos that suggests that effort and hard work matter (Hrabowski, Maton, Greene, & Greif, 2002; Hrabowski, Maton, & Greif, 1998; Thompson, 2007; Treisman, 1992). This orientation also has significance for interrupting the patterns of stereotype threat discussed later in this chapter (Aronson, 2002; Inzlicht & Good, 2006; Steele, 1997).

Education for a Larger Purpose

One of the findings about special-purpose institutions that relates to their success is that they convey a common message to graduates that education is for a purpose beyond themselves—for their families, for their communities, or to give back on behalf of the institution. This purpose is communicated through the mission, through the active involvement of alumni, through role models, and through programmatic approaches that involve service to the community. Though many institutions incorporate service learning, many special-purpose institutions link that with the purpose of learning and student success.

Thus, students who may not come with all the educational preparation needed to succeed are encouraged to persist and work because their success or failure has implications beyond themselves as individuals. This approach may place added pressure on the student, but it also provides a motivation and a sense of community support that can make a difference. While it can be expressed in specific programs, it is extraordinarily powerful when it is embodied in the institution, a characteristic common to many special-purpose institutions.

Institutional Purpose and Mission

In each of these institutions, there is a fundamental purpose embodied in the work of the campus, one that is devoted to student success and student education. At special-purpose institutions, this commitment is not generic but is explicit for the specific population served—women students, African American students, American Indian students. This sense of purpose permeates the culture, the sense of the place, the values, the stories of success, the alumni, and the icons.

Not only do these institutions have more diversity represented in the leadership and the faculty, but research suggests that the commitment to the mission and to student success is deeply held throughout. This characteristic first emerged when Tidball and her colleagues found that male faculty teaching at women's colleges believed in women's success overall and women's success in such fields as math and science more than did male faculty at coeducational schools (Tidball, Smith, Tidball, & Wolf-Wendel, 1999). Such a shared set of beliefs affects faculty behavior and also communicates itself in powerful ways to students.

Critical Mass at All Levels and Places

While the student bodies of most special-purpose institutions are made up largely of the group or groups to which the institution is dedicated, the faculty, staff, and boards of trustees are, ironically, more balanced than on other campuses in the country. Women's colleges have high percentages of men on faculty and on the board. HBCUs have many White faculty and board members. At the same time, there is a critical mass of women or African Americans or African American women in these positions. This is also true in tribal colleges. The pattern is not yet consistent in Hispanic-serving institutions, although research suggests that it is emerging as one of the factors that distinguish successful HSIs from others (Bridges, Cambridge, Kuh, & Leegwater, 2005).

Having a critical mass means that there is no sense of being a token or being marginalized in the institution. But it also means that, as a professor at Bennett said, "here you have a group of students who look like you, who come from similar backgrounds, and who all have the same high achievement goals" (Tidball, Smith, Tidball, & Wolf-Wendel, 1999, p. 99). If stereotype threat emerges in environments where negative societal assumptions are manifest, then special-purpose institutions provide the ideal context to break stereotypes, at least for the single identity represented (Aronson, 2002; Marx & Roman, 2002; Thompson & Sekaquaptewa, 2002).

On these campuses, students are scientists, athletes, artists, leaders. At a women's college, those achieving honors in physics are as likely to be women as those majoring in English. The athletes and the artists are women, as are the tech people. At HBCUs, the same is true. The athletes and the scientists are as likely to be African American as are the musicians and the philosophers. The pictures on the wall of leaders and outstanding alumni look like the students. In such contexts, success or failure is not attributed to race or gender, because of the wide variety of people participating. It is the ideal environment to combat stereotype threat and its invidious impact on student performance.

The visibility of alumni and other role models on campus facilitates this dynamic of success. Such an environment, contrary to one that is "out of touch with the real world," demonstrates what the real world ought to be and provides an opportunity for students and others to witness success.

Spaces and Places for Voices to Be Heard

In most special-purpose institutions, there are locations and places where issues are voiced and are heard. There is no concern about self- segregation of women on a campus that serves primarily women students. There is no sense of apology for meeting to discuss concerns, and in the best of these institutions, the campus leadership encourages student voices and perspectives.

Moreover, there is less likely to be a concern that mentioning group-specific topics will be threatening to the community at large. One of the challenges as our institutions become more diverse is that there appears to be reluctance to attend to one group out of concern for offending others. Ironically, many HSIs today find themselves both seeking out the federal support that comes from being an HSI and being concerned that those on campus who are not Hispanic will find this threatening.

Acknowledging the History

Because special-purpose institutions grew out of a society that closed doors to certain students and that still does not allow them full engagement and participation, students and others at these institutions are usually more fully conscious of the contexts of race, ethnicity, and gender. Special-purpose institutions today engage the histories of race and gender and build these topics into the curriculum. While the status of race or gender was not always explicitly addressed early on, it was always part of the understanding of these institutions' founding and mission. Many of these campuses have built this core identity into the rituals of the institution, from orientation to graduation to alumni relations. As higher education moves forward and there is recognition of the complex interplay among identities, all institutions are being challenged to find ways to express recognition of multiple identities and to address history.

Implications for Higher Education in General

Each of the qualities described above goes far beyond the characteristics of the student body; they describe the institution itself. Having an undergraduate student body that is primarily African American facilitates some elements of, and provides the rationale for the development of, the mission and culture of the place. It also results in a faculty and staff that are more explicitly committed to the success of students in these groups that have not always thrived in other educational institutions.

The challenge, of course, is what lessons emerge for the rest of higher education. For example, what does it mean for Hispanic-serving institutions? It would seem that simply having a critical mass of Hispanic students is not in and of itself sufficient to achieve institutional success with diverse students. Indeed, some recent findings suggest that success varies among HSI institutions, with some of the difference being accounted for by the presence of Latino faculty (Bridges, Cambridge, Kuh, & Leegwater, 2005). Unlike with HBCUs, tribal colleges, and women's colleges, the mission of the HSI was not necessarily established as a minority-serving one, with all the characteristics that follow. Many are predominantly White institutions that have achieved a critical mass of Latino students. But this is unlikely to be sufficient, suggesting again that these institutions, like the rest of higher education, will need to pay attention to the institutional characteristics that create an environment that facilitates success for each and every group being served.

How does one translate these characteristics, especially those unique to special-purpose institutions, so that they might be usable by the rest of higher education? It is not easy. Special-purpose institutions that understand the identity that makes them unique do not necessarily find it easy to translate that learning to engage other identities. I often think that while women's colleges "get" gender, and HBCUs "get" race, it takes a Spelman or a Bennett to "get" race *and* gender. Such specialization is not an adequate answer, given the multiplicity of identities in any institution. However, the potential advantage to special-purpose institutions is that their own histories of understanding exclusion and being committed to equity can provide a deeper understanding that can be broadened to include other salient identities. Presumably, if one understands the history of race in the context of an HBCU, one could begin to similarly look at gender, class, sexuality, and their intersections. By understanding the ways in which such institutions have been successful, another institution might identify the qualities that could be incorporated for other identities throughout its campus. By extension, all institutions could incorporate these elements in ways that speak to diverse groups on campus. Laura Rendón (1992) posed the challenge well:

It is my belief that institutions must consider past experience, language and culture as strengths to be respected and woven in the fabric of knowledge production and dissemination, not as deficits to be devalued, silenced and overcome. We need to validate students' capacities for intellectual development at the beginning, not at the end, of their academic careers. . . . We must set high standards, while helping students to reach them. Most faculty fail to give students the support they need in order to break free from belief systems that stifle their creativity. (p. 62)

Research on Institutional Qualities That Foster Student Success

A very large body of research now exists on the institutional factors that foster student success in general. Though very early research tended to focus on student-background characteristics to the neglect of the institutional environment, that is no longer the case. For nearly four decades, the thematic thrust of this research has documented the importance of student involvement in education. While the definitions of involvement (see Wolf-Wendel, Ward, & Kinzie, 2007) have changed and evolved, they all point to the opportunities for students to be actively connected to their education. The most recent literature has focused on the concept of engagement, and in particular engagement in educationally purposeful activities (Kuh, Kinzie, Buckley, Bridges, & Hayek, 2006; Kuh, Kinzie, Schuh, Whitt, & associates, 2005). While early research did not always disaggregate the student experience by race, gender, or class, much of the current literature is more likely to ask about the students for whom institutions are successful, thus framing the issue in terms of institutional accountability rather than student background (Barnhardt, 1994; Blake & Moore, 2004; Pascarella & Terenzini, 2005; Smith, 1995; Swail, Cabrera, Lee, & Williams, 2005; Swail, Redd, & Perna, 2003; Thompson, 2007).

In addition to research that has emerged from individual campus studies of student success and from smaller studies, there are several data sources that have shaped the research on students for the past few decades. The first data source was developed by Astin at the American Council on Education in the 1960s. Housed at the Higher Education Research Institute at UCLA, the Cooperative Institutional Research Program (CIRP) is the longest-standing study of college freshmen. It includes longitudinal studies of seniors and other studies of the college experience that have been a vital source of data on college students' attitudes and behaviors and on the impact of college.

Federal studies, especially the longitudinal studies—for example, the National Educational Longitudinal Study (NELS) and Baccalaureate and Beyond (B & B)— have also provided rich amounts of data on college-student trajectories. The federal transcript studies (Adelman, 2006) provide information on course-taking patterns and the relationship between course-taking and student success. A multi-institutional, collaborative longitudinal study under the direction of Pascarella and Terenzini (2005) focused on student learning. Two large national projects under the leadership of Kuh have studied the qualities of institutions that engage and involve students. The first, Involving Colleges, studied institutions that were widely considered successful in involving students in their learning (Kuh, Schuh, & Whitt, 1991). That study, while not looking at student outcomes, did include a variety of institutions in terms of size, location, and type. It concluded by describing a number of qualities that characterize highly involving institutions.

Kuh's most recent effort (Kuh, Kinzie, Schuh, Whitt, & associates, 2005) has been to use the data from the National Survey of Student Engagement (NSSE), distributed on hundreds of campuses across the country, to study levels of engagement in educationally meaningful activities as a way of approaching student learning. Parallel forms of the NSSE have been done for community college students (CCSSE), for law students (LSSSE), and for faculty (FSSE). A large number of studies have emerged using these data to look at differential engagement as a function of student characteristics, institutional factors and qualities, and faculty approaches. One of them is an important study called Project DEEP (Documenting Effective Educational Practice), in which twenty very different kinds of institutions were identified for their relative success with respect to student engagement and retention. Case studies were conducted to try to determine the institutional qualities that facilitated student learning.

The overall qualities that have emerged are quite consistent with the qualities described for special-purpose institutions, and it appears that the data on success also apply to underrepresented students of color. The six qualities identified by Project DEEP were a mission linked to student success, a focus on student learning, environments created for educational enrichment, clearly marked paths to student success, an improvement-oriented institutional ethos, and shared responsibility for educational quality and student success. These qualities—combined with faculty-student engagement, peer support, engagement of diverse ways of learning, integration of learning and experience, and relevant support programs—constitute Kuh's list of significant institutional criteria for student success (Kuh et al., 2005). A synthesis of findings from this and the rest of the literature suggests a number of important elements describing the conditions for student success.

Mission

The schools identified in the DEEP study, while having very different missions, were all found to have a "lived" mission and philosophy concerning student learning and success that was deeply connected to the culture of the institution. Moreover, the mission informed practice and policy in a very observable way. In all but the most selective institutions, and even in those institutions to some degree, the institutional focus was on student learning and engaging students in learning, more than on finding students who would succeed regardless. In the DEEP study, as with the Irvine Foundation's CDI study, campus mission and ethos emerged as germane (Clayton-Pedersen, Parker, Smith, Moreno, & Teraguchi, 2007; Kuh et al., 2005; Pike, Kuh, & Gonyea, 2003; Smith, Parker, Clayton-Pedersen, Moreno, & Teraguchi, 2006; Umbach & Kuh, 2006).

Campus Environments Focused on Learning

There is, and has been for some time, a significant body of research suggesting that an environment on campus that supports learning is critical. This environment is created not just through programs such as advising and learning centers. At every level, from the physical to the cultural, pedagogical, curricular, and program levels, student learning and assumptions that students can learn are encouraged and supported.

From a diversity point of view, the campus environment can be interpreted in many ways, depending on the identity issue that is relevant for students and others on campus. Thus, how the campus communicates its commitment to learning and success for all students has implications for how and for whom excellence is perceived. Campuses convey messages through, for example, the images of people selected for honors programs, the dean's list, and other recognitions of academic success, as well as through pictures of campus leaders—who are often not diverse in terms of race, ethnicity, and gender. A lack of diversity in these images conveys a powerful message to the campus and to individuals about who succeeds on this campus. Part of the significance of special-purpose institutions is that the images from these campuses that send messages about student success and about the leadership often stand in stark contrast to the images in mainstream institutions.

The Impact of Institutional Culture on Learning and Pedagogy

In general, research suggests that an orientation toward cooperative learning as one pedagogical strategy fosters success. An ethos of competition works against efforts to promote, for example, collaborative learning communities or peer-to-peer support and engagement. Something as modest as grading on a curve inevitably pits students against one another—suggesting that, whatever the rhetoric, students are on their own. On such campuses, study groups and other outside-of-class activities may be difficult to organize or may only emerge among students who think they are the "brightest." Moreover, this environment is more likely to trigger intergroup tensions that may be nascent in the environment (Aronson & Patnoe, 1997; Johnson & Johnson, 1987; Worchel & Austin, 1986).

Institutions whose mission and organizational structures are aligned with student success tend to have better records in that area. As Berger noted in a very provocative study (2002), higher student retention was associated with institutions that were focused more on students than on marketing or external constituencies. These environments were constructed to be rich in terms of learning and reflected cooperation among academic affairs and student affairs. In such institutions, one could often find engagement by many constituencies, including staff.

The institutional culture can also reflect inclusion or homogeneity. Is diversity visible, or is it visible by its invisibility? Does diversity seem salient in the symbols, values, and feeling of the campus? Are there certain styles of learning and approaches to research that are clearly valued over other forms? Are narrative approaches to knowledge valued for what they contribute as much as quantitative representations of knowledge? Does identity seem to be salient to the institution, as it is salient to individuals?

Clearly Marked Paths to Student Success

Much of the research on institutions that are successful with first-generation and low-income students underscores the importance of making the hidden curriculum explicit through clear paths to success. It is imperative that students be given information about how to negotiate the campus, through a variety of approaches that are often redundant. These include constant communication, peer programs, and robust advising. These messages provide vital information about procedures, rules, steps, and processes and also communicate that the institution is committed to student success.

Data-Informed Decision-Making

More and more of the relevant literature stresses the importance of having relevant data that provides information to the institution about its successes or areas of concern. Data on disaggregated persistence rates, grades, honors, success in gateway courses, persistence in STEM fields, engagement, satisfaction, and so on are all important. Understanding that students from different groups may encounter challenges at different points in their college career mandates collecting basic data longitudinally and using the information to guide institutional decision-making.

Faculty-Student Engagement in Educationally Purposeful Activities

While the historic literature on college impact consistently found peer relationships to be strong factors in student success and perhaps more important than faculty-student relationships, this pattern has shifted in the past twenty years (Astin, 1993b; Kuh, 1993; Pascarella & Terenzini, 1991, 2005). A clear and consistent finding in the research now is the positive academic impact of faculty-student engagement in *educationally purposeful activities* both in and outside of class (Antonio, Astin, & Cress, 2000; Kuh, 2003; Kuh & Hu, 2001; Kuh, Kinzie, Buckley, Bridges, & Hayek, 2007; Kuh, Laird, & Umbach, 2004; Pascarella & Terenzini, 2005; Terenzini, Springer, Pascarella, & Nora, 1995; Umbach & Wawrzynski, 2005; Whitt, 2005). These findings are significant because they also emerge on campuses that are not the four-year residential liberal arts campuses that have traditionally emphasized faculty engagement in and out of class.

The research also underscores the growing importance of the classroom and the activities associated with classes (Marin, 2000; Tinto, 1997). With more adult learners, part-time students, and nonresidential campuses, engagement with faculty is desirable. Educationally purposeful activities—that is, activities that support academic success and learning, as distinguished from nonacademic extracurricular activities—are increasingly vital for the success of large percentages of students. Faculty-student engagement in educationally purposeful activities has emerged as very important in affecting student success and satisfaction. Moreover, faculty from underrepresented-minority backgrounds and women faculty are more likely to engage in such activities (Antonio, 2002; Hurtado, 2001a; Luna de la Rosa, 2005; Milem, 2001; Milem & Astin, 1993; Umbach, 2006).

Patterns of active learning, research opportunities, mentoring, service learning, community partnerships, and many other approaches that emphasize engagement are vital to success. Such approaches also include writing, team projects, and discussions—activities that, while seen as traditional, may no longer be the pattern on campuses, especially those with large classes, part-time faculty (Umbach, 2007), and commuter students. Approaches that promote high expectations, in contrast to remediation, and engagement of peers have facilitated success in the STEM fields, for example (Hrabowski, Maton, Greene, & Greif, 2002; Hrabowski, Maton, & Greif, 1998; Maton & Hrabowski, 2004; Treisman, 1992).

There is significant evidence that what happens in college can diminish the negative impact of lack of preparation. Whether it is using a pedagogy of high expectations or fully engaging students from all backgrounds, it is clear that good education matters, and that it can interrupt background factors that militate against success (Bonsangue & Drew, 1995; Hrabowski, Maton, & Greif, 1998; Treisman, 1992). Too often, however, there has been reliance on remedial approaches, whether or not remediation is the best strategy. While remediation has been present in higher education since its founding, it has come under increasing scrutiny in terms of purpose, cost, appropriateness, and effectiveness (Merisotis & Phipps, 2000).

Shared Responsibility for Educational Quality and Student Success

Because our tendency when thinking about student success is to think about the design of programs, it is harder to imagine how to build an institutional culture in which responsibility for student success is shared and where concerns for students cross all constituencies. The power of such an ethos is that it creates robust and strong webs of the support and connections that are so necessary for success. This should not be too surprising (see, e.g., Aguirre & Martinez, 2007; Astin, 1993b; S. Hurtado, 1996; Kuh, Kinzie, Buckley, Bridges, & Hayek, 2006; Kuh, Kinzie, Schuh, Whitt, & associates, 2005; Pascarella & Terenzini, 2005; Rendón, 1999; Thomas, 2000; Watts, 2004). The connections and information that are central to knowing how the system works and who is available for help and information are often missing for first-generation and other students.

The challenge of single programs is that they provide one thread of support. If that doesn't work—for example, if there is not a good mentor or peer advisor—then that thread is broken. Students who enter higher education with family and peer knowledge or who are deeply connected to a variety of institutional resources are less likely to fall through the cracks and are more apt to be able to pick up a phone (or e-mail someone with a question) and to find ways through or around the problems they will inevitably confront. Stanton-Salazar (2001) writes, "The very texture of an individual's daily existence (and ultimately his or her life chances) is fundamentally shaped by structural and accumulated opportunities for entering multiple institutional contexts and forging relationships with people who control resources and who generally participate in power. An individual's social class, racial assignment, and gender play a decisive role in shaping these structured opportunities" (p. 17). Providing networks to those who don't bring them requires more than single programs or single individuals. It is a complex process and one that is at best difficult to negotiate, for individuals and institutions alike.

Part of the social and cultural capital possessed by those who have familiarity with higher education is all the knowledge and resources to negotiate the system in the form of family members, friends, or the individual's own belief in his or her right to have access to the system. Most of this information is, however, hidden to many. The hidden curriculum of any institution is just that—hidden. Moreover, in my judgment, it cannot be written down. What it takes to navigate are relationships where students *feel* free to ask for assistance; where there are a variety of connections, so that if one doesn't work, another one will; where people take an interest and are trusted. Thus, building a culture of shared responsibility involves multiple programs (ideally, where there is good communication between them); an institutional culture that supports, encourages, and believes in shared responsibility; an environment in which the student *perceives* that these resources and values are real; and links between the campus on the one hand and the larger community and the student's own off-campus community on the other (HeavyRunner & DeCelles, 2002; Perna & Titus, 2005; Pike & Kuh, 2005).

The Impact of Diversity on Student Success and Learning

A third body of literature, largely motivated by legal challenges to diversity, has focused on the impact of diversity on student success. The research, with a special focus on experiences that engage diversity or where students from different groups interact, consistently shows benefits in terms of student satisfaction, increased openness to diverse ideas, intellectual engagement, critical thinking, greater tolerance, and personal development (Antonio, 2001b; Antonio et al., 2004; Astin, 1993a; Bowen & Bok, 1998; Chang, 1999; Chang, Astin, & Kim, 2004; Chang, Denson, Saenz, & Misa, 2006; Chang, Witt, Jones, & Hakuta, 1999; Cole, Bennett, & Thompson, 2003; Gruenfeld, Thomas-Hunt, & Kim, 1998; Gurin, Dey, Hurtado, & Gurin, 2002; Hurtado, 2000, 2001a; Laird, 2005; Laird, Engberg, & Hurtado, 2005; Milem, Chang, & Antonio, 2005; Orfield & Whitla, 1999; Pascarella, Edison, Nora,

Hagedorn, & Terenzini, 1996; Pike & Kuh, 2006; Smith, 1997; Smith et al., 1997). Studies in institutions where students are randomly assigned to roommates have also found positive outcomes between roommates of different racial backgrounds, though the small numbers of minorities at the institutions severely limit the number of pairings that can be studied (Boisjoly, Duncan, Kremer, Levy, & Eccles, 2006; Sidanius, Levin, van Laar, & Sinclair, 2004; van Laar, Levin, Sinclair, & Sidanius, 2005).

One of the most significant bodies of research has emerged as a result of the University of Michigan's need to demonstrate these benefits empirically before the Supreme Court in the Grutter case. This research focused not simply on satisfaction or attitudes toward others, but also on the cognitive benefits of diversity. Gurin and her associates embarked on a series of studies to see whether greater cognitive complexity would develop from students' interactions with "diverse others." The theory behind this research was centered on student learning. The hypothesis was that diversity experiences, because they are challenging and sometimes difficult, would interrupt habituated thinking that is likely to interfere with learning (Langer, 1997). They further hypothesized that these experiences would lead to an increase in cognitive complexity (Gurin, 1999a, 1999b; Gurin, Dey, Hurtado, & Gurin, 2002). Thus, these studies made a link between the experience of diversity and a core academic learning outcome—cognitive complexity.

The results of these and other studies, not surprisingly, supported the notion that one of the benefits of diversity in the student body is to interrupt habituated modes of thinking (Gurin et al., 2002; Hurtado, 2006; Pascarella, Edison, Nora, Hagedorn, & Terenzini, 1996). From a pedagogical point of view, the research underscored the importance of environments that are sufficiently destabilized to encourage attention and focus. The results also highlight the central role of the curriculum, the opportunities outside of classes, and the links between the two.

Because many of these studies grew out of the need to demonstrate the benefits of diversity for *all* students (rather than serving only students of color), the emphasis of the results has been on the aggregated findings. Because the campuses studied are mostly White, the research has been most powerful in showing the benefits to White students, though this is rarely articulated. In some of these studies, where data were disaggregated, an underlying pattern suggests that while White students very clearly benefit, the benefits may be more conditional or uneven for students of color, especially underrepresented students of color (Gurin, Dey, Hurtado, & Gurin, 2002; Gurin, Peng, Lopez, & Nagda, 1999). This asymmetry is not surprising if one considers that White students are the vast majority of students on these campuses and are more likely to be segregated among other White students; they thus stand to benefit more from interactions with students of color. It is also true, however, that opportunities for cross-racial engagement can serve to further alienate already marginalized students, who in these settings feel they must educate Whites or defend themselves. The design of learning conditions and intergroup programs needs to take into account this asymmetry, as was discussed in chapter 6.

Benefits of Ethnic Support Services

While the research by Gurin and others focused on the effect of interacting with those different from oneself, another body of research has emerged that looks at the effect of interacting with people like oneself. Many have noted that as campuses become more diverse, there is a pattern of students staying in identity groups. Most of these concerns are expressed in terms of the self-segregation of students of color and ignore the self-segregation of White students. Indeed, most of the available evidence (e.g., Cole, 2007) suggests that on many campuses, White students have less interaction with those from other racial and ethnic groups than the reverse. This is likely to remain true as long as the proportions of students of color and especially underrepresented students of color are skewed. Some of the research also suggests that for White students more than for students of color, the result of self-segregation can be negative, especially in terms of tolerance, prejudice reduction, and behavior (Pascarella, Edison, Nora, Hagedorn, & Terenzini, 1996; Smith et al., 1997).

Beverly Tatum's 1997 book *Why Are All the Black Kids Sitting Together in the Cafeteria?* was a strategic attempt to bring together all the research on explaining and reframing the issue. Numerous reviews of the literature have suggested that for underrepresented students of color in particular and students of color in general, support groups and experiences in racial or ethnic groups have contributed to student satisfaction, retention, and less alienation (Hurtado, 2002; Milem, 2001; Milem, Chang, & Antonio, 2005; Moran, Yengo, & Algier, 1994). These results have been especially powerful in the research concerning African American students, where the relationships among in-group friendships, ethnic studies, and support centers are consistently positive in terms of measures of student success. For other groups, the relationships among same-group friendships and interactions, integration with the institution, and academic success have been more mixed (Antonio, 2004; Chang & DeAngelo, 2002; Levin, 2003; Levin, van Laar, & Sidanius, 2003; Sidanius, Levin, van Laar, & Sears, 2008; Sidanius, Levin, van Laar, & Sinclair, 2004). For example, Levin, van Laar, and Foote (2006) found that while African American students benefited from intraethnic friendships even if they were less engaged with the institution, disengagement from the institution was more problematic for Latino students.

A careful reading of many of these studies suggests that some of the differences may emerge because the conditions, both interpersonal and institutional, under which these interactions occur may not be optimal. Chang, Astin, and Kim (2004) suggest that the presence of a diverse student body is one of the conditions required for facilitating cross-racial interactions. Also, these studies have framed the self-segregation question in binary terms such that greater within-group friendships compete with academic success and engagement with the institution. Less has been done to look at the outcomes from engaging within one's racial or ethnic group while also being engaged institutionally. A good example of such a study is one by Hurtado (2002). She found that Latinos who were both engaged in Hispanic clubs and organizations *and* socializing with White students were much less likely than others to report racial tension and a hostile campus climate. Earlier research likewise suggested that while students of color joined ethnic groups for both support and identity enhancement, such students were also more likely to participate in racial and cultural awareness workshops (Hurtado, Milem, Clayton-Pedersen, & Allen, 1998).

Another issue rarely addressed is how "institutional engagement" is defined. In most research, the operational definition of institutional engagement rarely includes multicultural or ethnic functions. Institutional involvement is generally defined as involvement in "generic" activities such as athletics, fraternities, sororities, and student government. Engagement in rainbow coalitions or the development of the Martin Luther King, Jr., celebration on campus might not be so defined. As was apparent from the findings on intergroup relations, the fundamental *asymmetry* must be considered. That is, individuals or groups who are in a distinct minority on campus will benefit from support functions in ways different from how majority groups benefit.

The Impact of Climate

Connected to each of these findings about student success is the question of the presence of racial tension and alienation on campus and its impact on educational outcomes and adjustment to college (Hall & Allen, 1989; S. Hurtado, 1992, 1994a, 1994b, 1996; Hurtado, Carter, & Spuler, 1996; Nora & Cabrera, 1996; Ogbu, 2003; Olivas, 1986; Padilla, 1997; Smith, 2005). Discrimination has been linked to a sense of alienation and lack of belonging for Latino students (Hurtado & Carter, 1997).

While racial and ethnic student organizations mediated the alienation and resulted in an increased sense of belonging in Hurtado and Carter's 1997 study, Levin, van Laar, and Foote (2006) suggested that for Latino students, in-group affiliations may have exacerbated their perceptions of hostility and were thus linked to less institutional engagement. In general, however, experiences of alienation and disengagement result in lower academic achievement (Levin, van Laar, & Foote, 2006)—though, again, these findings sometimes vary with the particular outcome being studied.

Thus, the consequences of college experiences for different racial and ethnic groups represent a complex interaction between how the campus environment is experienced, the presence and quality of interactions within one's own group, and the quality, context, and amount of interaction between groups. In most studies, the educational outcomes of both intergroup and intragroup interactions for students of color are positive. However, the underlying findings suggest that without intragroup support, some intergroup experiences could be detrimental to students of color.

Perceptions of Institutional Commitment

The current literature suggests that institutional diversity initiatives have a positive impact on student learning and success. Perhaps surprisingly, one of the most important institutional qualities to emerge as related to student success is a perception that the institution is committed to diversity (Astin, 1993a; Smith et al., 1997). The perception of commitment, along with other variables, affects student satisfaction and retention. This finding was not expected, but it has been replicated in a number of studies. We still know less about how such perceptions are created, but it is clear that commitment to diversity is expressed through decisions that are made, visual cues about what is important, responses to incidents, language developed for a wide variety of purposes, and everyday behavior. Students and others from more marginal groups can be quite vigilant about what campuses do, and they are attentive to any gaps between what people say (the rhetoric) and what campuses do (the practice; Berger, 2002).

Mentoring and Advising

Mentoring and advising remain significant elements in creating opportunities for student success (Campbell & Campbell, 1997). The literature is usually framed in terms of the role of mentoring and advising in guiding and supporting students, early-career faculty, and graduate students and providing access to social and cultural capital. I also want to link it here to its potential to interrupt stereotype threat, as well as to a small literature on "feeling like a fraud," discussed in the next section.

Stereotype Threat

Because the achievement gap has been the subject of so much attention, it has become increasingly urgent to rethink how the gaps are explained. Lack of preparation remains a prominent explanation, especially when test scores are used as indicators of academic qualifications. Given what we know about the unequal education in K–12, and given the different patterns of course-taking in high school for different racial groups, this explanation should not be denied.

An important line of research, however, demonstrates another perspective on what happens to interfere with student success from a social-psychological perspective. It has implications for institutions and students alike. In one of the most elegant uses of experimental methodology in education that I know of, Steele and colleagues have been studying the concept of *stereotype threat* (Steele, 1997; Steele & Aronson, 1995). This work is worthy of fuller explanation. Based in the literature on social psychology, the research hypothesizes that people who are highly motivated to succeed and are from a group that experiences widely known negative stereotypes with respect to performance are more likely to underperform when attention is drawn to the salient identity. This research has special meaning in the context of African Americans, whose test scores tend to *overpredict* success; that is, they don't perform as well as tests would suggest they should. This sense of perceived inferiority was expected to impact both short-term performance and long-term engagement. That is, there is the additional vulnerability of disengaging from situations as a form of self-protection.

Steele's research sought to study this underperformance by varying the condition of stereotype threat for groups that are vulnerable to stereotyping. His initial research involved African American students in a highly selective context. His hypothesis was that students would underperform in environments in which they were vulnerable to stereotype threat and not in environments in which stereotype threat was removed. His manipulation usually took the form of telling participants that the test they were to take was diagnostic and showed no racial differences. In the stereotype-threat condition, the participants were asked to list their race. Striking results in numerous studies show that underperformance was eliminated when stereotype threat was removed (Spencer, Steele, & Quinn, 1999; Steele, 1997; Steele & Aronson, 1995).

Significantly, the findings have been replicated in numerous settings, including stereotyping of women in math and White men's performance in basketball (Inzlicht & Ben-Zeev, 2000; Marx & Roman, 2002). A recent study in Canada showed that women's performance on a GRE-type math test was influenced by reading essays that suggested that math performance was affected either by genes or by experience. Women who read essays suggesting a genetic basis to underperformance did much less well than women who read that experience affected performance (Dar-Nimrod & Heine, 2006). Another study showed that stereotype threat could affect the degree to which women correctly answered questions about political knowledge, an area in which they have traditionally underperformed (McGlone, Aronson, & Kobrynowicz, 2006).

In a related study, Pinel, Warner, and Chua (2005) studied the stigma consciousness of individuals to see how performance varies among individuals from groups vulnerable to stereotype threat. Thus, while Steele and colleagues assume the vulnerability of different groups to stereotype threat, Pinel and her colleagues study individual variation within groups. Using a measure of stigma consciousness, the researchers found that individual African Americans and Latinos who were conscious of stigma were most likely to see decreases in academic performance and academic engagement. There were some gender differences as well, with the women showing less self-esteem and academic engagement than the men. In another study, focusing on women in math, Brown and Pinel (2003) found that women who had high scores on stigma consciousness were the ones to perform less well on math tests.

In addition to stereotype threat and stigma consciousness, there is a small literature on "feeling like a fraud." First introduced by McIntosh (1985, 1989) with respect to women, this concept suggests that people who don't see themselves as "belonging" are vulnerable to feeling like a fraud; that is, they fear that because they don't belong, they will finally be discovered as not being up to the challenges of the roles they are in. In my experience with very diverse groups of doctoral students who are adults, and often women, this metaphor of feeling like a fraud is very common. The challenge, like the challenge of stereotype threat, is that it produces an internal dialogue in which the person assumes they don't have what it takes to succeed (Crocker, Major, & Steele, 1998; Koch, 2002; McIntosh, 1985, 1989).

As Steele has noted, in addition to trying to reduce the saliency of stereotype threat, one of the most useful ways to interrupt these phenomena is through the role of advisors and mentors. The strategy here is not one of reducing expectations, but rather conveying the belief that the individual can succeed through effort and with support. Mentors and advisors can also suggest that the work to be done can be learned rather than being linked to aptitude. Recently, someone in a dinner conversation told a story about the reassuring impact a Nobel Prize winner had had on a diverse group of science students when he revealed that he had gotten several Ds in his undergraduate career. Such a statement debunks the notion that innate aptitude determines success and underscores the role of effort, even for Nobel Prize winners. Institutional strategies that emphasize multiplicity of identity, develop critical mass, and create an environment of belief in students have all been found to be helpful for interrupting stereotype threat (Cohen & Steele, 2002; Rosenthal & Crisp, 2006; Tatum, 2007).

Diversity Courses and Programs

As reviewed earlier, the evidence suggests that engagement in diversity by students from a wide variety of backgrounds leads to student satisfaction and learning (Cheng & Zhao, 2006; Croteau & Kusek, 1992; Engberg, 2004; Geasler, Croteau, Heineman, & Edlund, 1995; Herbst & Malaney, 1999; Maruyama & Moreno, 2000; Smith et al., 1997). The work by Gurin and her colleagues at the University of Michigan showing a positive relationship between participation in activities and classes "with diverse others" and growth in cognitive complexity had a strong impact in the field in part because they studied outcomes beyond student satisfaction and beyond values related to diversity, such as racial tolerance.

It is not surprising, therefore, that we are now seeing the emergence of a concern for difficult dialogues and for the conditions under which such dialogues and learning can best occur. While a destabilized environment facilitates learning, it also requires that the faculty and other group leaders have the capacity to facilitate these dialogues. From the point of view of students from more marginalized groups, these experiences can be seen as indicating institutional commitment, can provide opportunities to discuss relevant topics, and can make a link between identity concerns and academic and co-curricular experiences. These efforts, particularly if they involve intergroup work, must be designed carefully so as not to disadvantage students of color in the service of educating White students.

Overarching Themes for Student Success

Critical to all of this research on special-purpose institutions, engagement in learning, diversity experiences, and student success is how students experience their education, their institution, and their own place in the process of learning. A number of themes emerge from these literatures.

· *High expectations, belief, and support are three staples of an approach to learning.* The results of all this research have implications for the institution, the classroom, and the approach to students. At the level of the institution, there would be an intentional and visible focus on student success. In the classroom, there would be attention to the climate, the culture, the pedagogy, and the assumptions about student learning. Key in the approach to students are high expectations, belief in students' capacity, resources and support, and an institutional commitment to student success.

In every study of programs or approaches that lead to student success, high expectations emerge as critical. That criterion alone would not be sufficient, however. Communicating a belief in the student's capacity to succeed is also critical. Many advanced programs or highly selective institutions have high expectations. In too many, however, there is a message—conveyed through the selection process or through informal communications—that some students can succeed and others cannot; or, as is evident in the research on stereotype threat, students bring those concerns with them. In special-purpose institutions or highly successful programs, however, there is a consistent message that the institution, the faculty, and others *believe* that students overall, and any individual student, can succeed.

The third key element is providing the resources and ethos necessary to facilitate success. In women's colleges, where women may have arrived with many issues concerning success in math and science, programs are designed to provide whatever is needed to bridge any gaps that students may come with, combined with high expectations and the belief that students can succeed. Is it any wonder that women's colleges have provided a disproportionate share of women getting PhD's in math and science? The same is true for African Americans at HBCUs. This occurs even without the institutional resources that many highly selective campuses can claim.

· *Engagement and mattering matter.* The concept of mattering, developed by Schlossberg (1989), captures much of what is suggested by the word. Schlossberg's concept of mattering aligns well with Rendón's notion of validation (1999), Hurtado and Carter's emphasis on belonging (1997), and Noddings's notion of an ethic of care (2006). Schlossberg suggests that mattering takes into account four qualities.

   · Attention. This is the sense that you are noticed by your presence or by your absence. It matters that you are in class or at a meeting, and it matters whether you missed class or a meeting.
   · Ego extension. Here the focus is on whether your failures or successes mat-

ter to others and whether they will be proud of success and saddened by failure. In special-purpose institutions, every success or failure is taken seriously by the institution and has significance for the larger community.

- Dependence. The sense that the group or others are depending on you for
something facilitates involvement, belonging, and engagement. This is one
of the key elements for successful athletic teams, where the individual's role
matters for the group's success.
- Appreciation. Mattering is manifest as well when your efforts are appreciated. If they are ignored, overlooked, or discounted (as the literature describes as often occurring for marginal groups), feelings of marginalization will be increased.

While mattering can be thought of solely in terms of individuals, it can also
be described in terms of groups. To what degree does my group matter to the institution? To what degree do I matter to a group or to the institution? Groups
can be noticed, depended on, and appreciated.

Think about being in an institution where one feels that one matters, and ask
how often that occurs. On many campuses, the opposite of mattering often occurs. If a student misses class or a meeting, nothing is said. Many students express the feeling that their ideas or the presence of their group are not appreciated. Indeed, many campuses convey this to members of racial or ethnic support
groups when they pejoratively label participation in such groups as self-segregation; yet campus groups that are White, such as fraternities and sororities, are never
accused of self-segregation. The feeling of not mattering is exacerbated when institutions want to play down LGBT activities or seem to be embarrassed by them.
And of course, if a campus is not accessible, the most fundamental form of mattering—being able to access the institution or its resources—is denied. My own
perception is that it is in racial or ethnic support groups, LGBT activities, Muslim centers, and ethnic and women's studies where students feel that they matter,
and that it is in more generic activities where students from particular identities
too often feel they don't matter.

How can institutions, faculty, mentors, and so on convey mattering in such a
way that students from particular identity groups experience inclusion? Generic
statements don't work. If the institution wishes to convey commitment to student
success in an environment in which a community does not feel included, then it
will need to be clear that the community is seen, appreciated, and valued. If a community matters, it is called on to serve an institutional purpose, it is publicly recognized, and its successes and failures are taken seriously.

I recall an incident on a campus when an Asian American student group was trying to gain access to a campus facility for an exhibition. They were stymied in their efforts and told to try other venues. Some time later, when a racist incident occurred on campus, the administration asked the group if it would help with a public performance and other events to show the institution's commitment to diversity and inclusion. All resources of time, space, and publicity were offered. The message was that the group mattered only in a time of crisis.

The institutional environment that conveys mattering is strongly related to individual interactions. Mattering, and a sense of mattering, takes place for individuals through interactions with others on campus. Being treated as if one matters by advisors, teachers, administrators, and staff persons can really make a difference. For those who are looking for signs that the institution is truly inclusive, even casual interactions can make a difference. The forgotten commitment or the rushed conversation can have greater meaning for a student of color arriving for an appointment, for example, or for a woman in science coming in to talk about her major. Groups and individuals need to experience that they matter from day to day in the ways that such groups matter in special-purpose institutions.

· *The classroom is central.* In part because of the changing nature of student attendance in college and the changing nature of students, the classroom and its related activities are increasingly the central location for a student's college experience. For part-time and adult learners, the classroom is the place where college is experienced. It is therefore appropriate to look at the prior research in the context of the classroom, the faculty who teach in that setting, and the ways in which institutional commitments and practices are communicated through what occurs there. Tinto highlighted the significance of the classroom in an article entitled "Classrooms as Communities" (1997). The importance of the classroom is true even for residential campuses, although such campuses have, of course, many additional opportunities for engagement in learning.

The core questions focus on what is taught in the classroom, how it is taught, and how success is facilitated. Increasingly, our classrooms will be the location for the difficult dialogues that higher education will need to engage for the benefit of student learning, for the institution's capacity to develop pluralistic communities that work, and ultimately for the society.

Classroom dynamics are affected not only by the interactions among students and the approaches taken by faculty. There is growing evidence that the traditional power dynamics between faculty members (who supposedly have power) and students (who do not) can be reversed in classrooms where faculty are not White or male, because of feelings of entitlement and privilege on the part of students, especially White students (Benjamin, 1997; Chesler, Lewis, & Crowfoot, 2005; Harlow, 2003; McGowan, 2000).

· *The diversity of today's students must be seen as bringing strengths and experience, not deficits.* For the sake of students and their success, as well as the learning environment, the backgrounds of students need to be seen as adding to the excellence of the campus. In the era after World War II, many campuses resisted welcoming entering veterans. They were older, often had families, and were frequently first-generation college students. The concern was that they wouldn't be focused (as if traditional-age college students are focused) or bring strong academic backgrounds. But it became clear that in fact, the motivation and commitment of veterans often set a tone of high expectations on campuses throughout the country.

This same pattern emerged when women began to push for admission to professional schools and advanced degrees. The notion at the time was that they would be distracted, drop out, or get pregnant. Today, women's success is largely undisputed. Deficit models of diversity, whether explicit or implied, undercut positive movement. Believing in the capacity of a student to achieve success and believing that diversity will bring strength are preconditions for developing an environment in which students can succeed and learn from one another.

· *Classroom environments must be both welcoming and committed.* A core aspect of success is the culture and the climate of a class. This is particularly important in the STEM fields. With more older, racially and ethnically diverse, and first-generation students, the climate and culture of a classroom communicate many messages about whether a student is likely to succeed, whether people are encouraged to work together, and whether the faculty member really believes in their capacity to succeed, with effort and support.

There was a time when colleges across the country were proud to suggest to students that at the end of four years, those sitting to their right and their left would no longer be there. There was, and perhaps still is, a certain pride in showing failure and dropout rates as a measure of excellence. Those times are fading, but many of those messages remain. If they don't come explicitly from peers or faculty, they may come from the students themselves, who often don't believe they can succeed. The presence of the literature on feeling like a fraud is not an accident. Students, especially those new to higher education or those who don't see someone like themselves as faculty, can believe that they won't or shouldn't succeed. Interrupting those messages will require explicit strategies by faculty, peers, and support services.

· *Pedagogy should be both engaging and diverse in its formats.* There is a large literature on student learning styles and a tendency to suggest that students from different cultural or ethnic backgrounds respond best to different styles of learning. At its worst, this point of view essentializes identity in a way that is not productive. However, if one sees the mandate for addressing diverse styles of learning as a call to employ different learning modalities, the result will be a classroom in which more and different kinds of students can engage and learn.

· *Out-of-class experiences that are educationally purposeful are required.* Engagement with faculty on research, service learning, community engagement, and attendance at lectures and discussions are all emerging as critically important for student success. Because so many of our campuses have extraordinary opportunities outside of class that could be educationally significant, I have come to believe that requiring participation in these opportunities and structuring classes to make use of them is vital for the institution (attendance goes up) and for education. These requirements can be structured flexibly, to accommodate a variety of schedules. But if they are required, the student is exposed to many more opportunities than he or she might otherwise be inclined to experience. Finding ways for students to take advantage of study-abroad opportunities is also important, because such study should be something more than a simply voluntary opportunity for those who can afford it.

· *Gateway courses as filters must become courses as attractive points of entry.* Many students enter college with aspirations to become doctors and other professionals but leave their dreams for something more pragmatic after encountering a gateway course that serves as a filter for so many. While some people will naturally change their goals as they experience new things or find that their goals were not appropriate, too many students make this decision because of courses on our campuses that traditionally eliminate students. From a diversity point of view, these courses often disproportionately weed out underrepresented students. If one goes to a campus, one can quickly determine, simply by asking, which these courses are. I suspect most campus practitioners would not be surprised to find such courses as introductory statistics in economics and psychology, introductory calculus in management, and organic chemistry for premed identified as gateway courses. In a community college, developmental courses in English and math might also prove to be barriers to college-level courses.

The challenge in changing this pattern is not to reduce the relevant expectations for such courses. Rather, it is clear that redesigning a course using the strategies described throughout this chapter would yield a kind of success that is also well aligned with faculty goals for excellence. Any strategy will also require reframing what it takes to succeed from the notion of aptitude to the notion of effort. Schools in the United States have done a good job of suggesting that some people have the aptitude for mathematics, for example, and some do not. In other countries, the concept of aptitude is not central—the concept of effort is (Drew, 1996; Dweck, 2000; Mueller & Dweck, 1998). Tests that correlate with socioeconomic status, gender, and ethnicity only exacerbate the deeply held beliefs about aptitude. Faculty will have to be quite intentional to undermine the belief that students hold (and which faculty may hold) about aptitude.

· *Diversifying the content of the curriculum opens many opportunities for learning.* So many fields today engage diversity as an academic endeavor. Introducing them into the curriculum and course materials creates opportunities for new learning for both faculty and students. Because diversity is about so many things, content need not be comprehensive, but it can be illustrative of how diversity affects knowledge. While it is common to suggest that the reason for diversifying courses is the diversity of the students, I believe that courses should be diversified in order to engage fully the complexity and new developments in scholarship. I am not interested in teaching the social psychology or higher education content of the 1950s. Knowledge develops over time; and in virtually all fields, content develops as well. Such diversity will have a profound impact on student learning for all students, who need to understand a broader conception of the development of scholarly thinking and need to know more about our social contexts than might have been true decades ago. Engaging class, sexual orientation, gender, race, and ethnicity is pertinent for all learners, not just those from a particular group.

Moreover, the inclusion of knowledge on diverse groups suggests that they are worth studying and knowing. This symbolic role enhances the potential for connecting to students, for facilitating the experience of mattering, and for creating a classroom culture that reflects the multidimensional aspects of diversity and identity. In STEM fields, this may need to take place through the intentional focus on students and their ability to succeed, through connecting the significance of the field to things that matter, and through bringing in diverse groups of alumni, faculty, and other members of the community to demonstrate that the field is not all White or all male.

· *Classrooms can become successful sites for difficult dialogues.* As campuses grow in diversity, so do many classrooms. As a result, classes focusing on religion, literature, sociology, psychology, history, and philosophy can be locations for essential, though difficult, conversations about equity, racism, disparities, and so on. Faculty will increasingly need help from others, such as those in student affairs or from teaching and learning centers, to negotiate the potentially volatile conversations that can emerge. The potential here is to facilitate and develop critical-thinking abilities, intergroup relationships, multiple perspectives, and the connections to social needs and concerns. When classes are also connected to service learning and civic engagement, the opportunities for good conversation grow.

· *Classrooms will increasingly become places for academic empowerment and faculty important facilitators of that development.* Classrooms, well designed, can be opportunities for students who might not have seen themselves as academically inclined, as researchers, as future faculty members, or simply as smart to see themselves differently. Students must feel that they matter, that someone believes in their ability besides themselves, and that they are engaged rather than alienated or silenced. This is especially true in fields where the diversity of participants is not robust and where students may see few people like themselves.

· *Excellence will not always look the same.* If excellence means excelling on multiple-choice tests or raising one's hand first in class, then only a few will be deemed interested or excellent. Taking a serious look at the variety of ways in which excellence can become manifest is an essential part of a pedagogy that engages diversity. This is as true in science as in philosophy.

· *Collaboration, rather than competition, is to be facilitated.* Most of the research on student success highlights the power of team approaches and peer advisors. Learning communities in a single class or among a set of classes are also emerging as potent centers for student learning and success. Any of these activities will be weakened by competition. A culture of competition in a classroom or grading on a curve will undermine the ability of students to work together. Faculty will also have to be mindful that allowing people to develop their own study groups may leave some people out and may in fact foster hierarchies of success in the class.

· *Advising—indeed, aggressive advising—will be important.* Advising from multiples sources is essential for first-generation students. Increasingly, one sees calls for proactive, even aggressive advising. More-privileged students take for granted things that first-generation students do not. I remember the first time a student sat outside my office door without knocking to let me know she was there for her appointment. Had I not walked outside to check, I would have been sitting in my office waiting and she would have been sitting outside waiting. When I asked, she said she hadn't wanted to intrude. This was in stark contrast to other students who knock, call, ask questions all the time, and think little of interrupting.

I have visited campuses where faculty and administrators describe a culture in which students who get low-grade notices are expected to make appointments with their faculty advisor but where it is not viewed as appropriate to require that the student come in and talk. Increasingly, we have to understand that the comfort with "coming in to talk" varies and that if we don't want to find ourselves at the end of a term with a failing student, assertive advising will be required.

TABLE 7.1
Guiding Questions for Diversity and Student Success

• Does the institution's mission statement convey its recognition of diversity and the significance of diversity for the institution and its success?

• Are the institution's history and legacy engaged with respect to diversity? There are numerous examples where an institution's history might not be positive but is nevertheless being used to teach about the future.

• Is the message of high expectations and belief in students' capacity conveyed in all academic and co-curricular areas? Are the necessary resources (including effective pedagogical practices) provided to foster success?

• Does the institution have, or is it moving toward having, sufficient diversity that individuals feel they can be both individuals and members of identity groups? Is that diversity present at all levels? Are there places where stereotyped roles may be operating?

• Are all faculty, staff, and administrators, regardless of their background, perceived as being committed to student success, or is that support emerging mostly from those with similar backgrounds? Is competence in being successful with diverse groups of students a requirement?

• Does the institution affirm that people matter and that their success or failure has significance for the community at large?

• Are special-purpose groups and locations perceived as "problems," or are they valued as contributing to the diversity of the institution and its educational mission?

• Are members of the alumni body and board diverse enough and visible enough to function as signifiers of success?

· *Assessment is essential for learning and for monitoring institutional progress.* While many people think of assessment as an exercise necessary to satisfy an outside agency or an academic office, good assessment is critically important in helping faculty understand what students are learning and where their approaches are being effective, and in general to monitor their own progress in facilitating student success. Whether a faculty member uses the strategies developed by Cross in her work on classroom assessment (Angelo & Cross, 1993) or other techniques, assessment can be a tool for both the faculty member and the student to monitor progress. This is especially true if it is not presented as an indication of a failure of aptitude on the part of the student, or a failure on the part of the faculty member. Assessments can also be used to see how engaged students are in the material. They can be very productive in the middle of a course and can be used to invite a conversation about learning or about the goals of the course, and to communicate that the faculty member wants to know what students think—while the course is in progress.

While each of these elements for student success might be present in a program or a single unit within an institution, it is clear from the research that successful institutions are those that create an ethos of commitment to student success, with all the intentionality that that requires. This commitment must be shared throughout the institution and built into its commitment to excellence. Translating these broad themes into practice is not simple, especially doing so throughout an institution. Table 7.1 displays a series of questions that might be used as an inventory for the success of diverse groups of students. The evidence suggests that the institutional orientation to student learning reflected in these questions will help guard against the use of background characteristics as the dominant source for predictors of student success (Kuh, Kinzie, Buckley, Bridges, & Hayek, 2006). That is to say, good education matters.

PART IV

What Will It Take?

❁

CHAPTER EIGHT

Monitoring Progress on Diversity

The previous chapters focused attention on the work of diversity. This chapter, in contrast, will focus, on whether the work of diversity—the programs, initiatives, and planning for it—has made a difference institutionally. I like to frame the question this way: *How do you know you are making progress?* As the work of diversity increases and broadens, the number of programs and initiatives grows. Without attention to the question of monitoring, many campuses inevitably find the work of diversity increasing and campus task forces becoming overwhelmed. Robert Shireman (2003) labeled this tendency "projectitis," in which diversity *activity* is equated with diversity *progress.*

I have been on many campuses where, in response to a question about progress, I have been asked to look at the campus and the diversity that is visible. Increasing numbers of diverse undergraduates, or visible diversity, does not address whether the institution's capacity at all levels is increasing and whether that diversity is present in the faculty, among graduate students, or in senior leadership. It doesn't address whether students are succeeding or thriving.

Because of the growing domains for diversity, different constituencies will use different information to answer the question about progress. Leaders will tend to look at the progress made in terms of, for example, undergraduates. Others may look at areas of diversity where less progress is evident. Some will imagine what the institution could be and see what needs to be done. Some will identify important areas where no progress is evident. These competing views tend to breed frustration on all sides. Leaders may wonder whether constructing a new building would be more satisfying, and committed activists may decide it is not worth spending time on yet another task force.

This chapter presents an approach to monitoring progress that moves diversity to the center of the institution, takes the framework described in chapter 3, builds on key indicators for change, and proposes a way to monitor progress that uses organizational learning as a tool. A caveat is in order, however, about the use of organizational learning and especially about the focus on data and systemic information. A danger inherent in discussing the use of a framework and data is that the approach to change will imply that it is rationally driven and linear. Indeed, that is not the case. As I ask people to look at key indicators of progress, many of them data-based, I do not assume that the process by which change occurs will simply flow from that. Even when boards of trustees ask for accountability on elements of diversity, the process that emerges can be neither hierarchical nor linear. A framework and data provide a way to organize a monitoring process. The approach to change, however, especially on a college campus, is a far more complex process and will no doubt build on the involvement and commitment of many people throughout the institution.

The emerging work on knowledge organizations, organizational learning, and change strongly demonstrates that being strategic and monitoring progress is not simply rational. It is practical, human, and even *aspirational*, relying as much on tacit and implicit knowledge as on positivist and concrete knowledge (Bauman, 2005; Cavaleri & Seivert, 2005; Dowd, 2005; Nonaka, 2005; Nonaka & Takeuchi, 1995; Weick & Sutcliffe, 2001). It takes knowledge of people, context, and stakeholders and an understanding of the environment to create action toward a vision that is shared and then to continue to learn and improve. However, without some manageable and overarching way to monitor progress and create a context in which to make meaning out of information, diversity efforts proliferate in ways that can obscure the lack of change in core aspects of the institution, such as climate or faculty hiring. Without an institutional approach, it is too easy to imply that the responsibility for institutional success in diversity lies with those who direct programs, rather than with the institution itself. The simultaneous use of a more "rationally" oriented *data-driven decision-making* and an orientation toward change that uses community building creates a healthy tension that, if developed, can facilitate the work of diversity.

The growing imperative for an approach to monitoring progress grows out of some of the patterns that have emerged among institutions engaged in diversity work (Musil et al., 1999; Nettles et al., 2002; Smith et al., 2000; Smith, Parker, Clayton-Pedersen, Moreno, & Teraguchi, 2006.) First, as mentioned earlier, campus reviews of diversity often consist more of information on activities than on institutional change. Second, despite general agreement that progress on institutional change, especially diversity, will require the engagement of senior leadership, we have not developed systemic ways for leaders to monitor progress.

Third, it appears that the impetus to reflect on the status of diversity often tends to be reactive, as a response to an external requirement, as a response to a call to "demonstrate" (and sometimes prove) the effectiveness of a single program in a highly politicized context, or in response to a campus incident. Fourth, though campus conversations about, and actions related to, diversity occur in a wide variety of settings throughout a college or university, there are few places where a diverse group of people from different parts of the institution can come together to discuss progress and set strategies. Finally, it appears that in most cases, work on diversity remains parallel to core institutional functions. So when a campus is doing a self-study for accreditation, for example, it is all too common that diversity is not incorporated into that effort.

Linking Diversity to Institutional Quality and Educational Effectiveness

Increasing in its centrality and urgency at both the national and local levels is an ongoing discussion of institutional accountability and educational effectiveness. It is taking place in all higher education contexts: national policy centers, the U.S. Congress, state legislatures, professional associations, accreditation agencies, grant-making foundations, and campuses. For example, the Western Association of Schools and Colleges (WASC) provides its member institutions with an inventory of educational-effectiveness indicators and describes the key elements of educational effectiveness as (1) student learning and success, (2) institutional capacity, and (3) organizational learning. For each of these, WASC requires institutions to describe both their processes for meeting the standard and the measures by which the institution assesses itself.

In this context, institutions should be able to say, for example, whether students are succeeding, what the criteria are for success, by what means success is measured, and how the institution ensures that its measures and methods are accurate and up-to-date. Second, and critical to all educational initiatives, institutions are asked to demonstrate that they have the intellectual, human, and financial resources (the capacity) to fulfill their mission with quality. And with respect to organizational learning, WASC, for example, requires institutions to show their capacity to assess themselves: How does the institution ensure that the information it collects and maintains about itself is current, accurate, and of the right kinds? How effectively does the institution assess its capacity to analyze information and use the result of such assessments for improvements?

Increasingly, institutions are being encouraged to increase their capacity to use information as the basis for evaluating effectiveness and to reformulate the culture of decision-making to incorporate data, evidence, and inquiry. For some, this is framed as *data-driven decision-making* or *organizational learning*. Others have used the concepts *culture of evidence, culture of inquiry, knowledge management,* or *knowledge creation*. Regardless of what it is called, the effort invites institutions to reflect on the status of strengths and weaknesses and to use the data to improve quality.

It encourages the use of structures in which members of the campus community can honestly reflect on successes and failures and take ownership of the process and the results. It takes into consideration both internal and external community influences, and it is reflected in the analysis of collected institutional data. It involves a holistic approach to the institution (Bensimon, 2004; Connolly, 2007; Nettles et al., 2002; W. K. Kellogg Foundation, 1998). Ideally, this approach also opens up opportunities to reflect not only on the immediate information and approaches, but also on the systems and processes of the institution that lead to these results; this requires efforts that are both deep and broad (Argyris, 2005; Astin & Astin, 2000; Clayton-Pedersen, Parker, Smith, Moreno, & Teraguchi, 2007; Eckel, Green, & Hill, 2001; Eckel, Hill, Green, & Mallon, 1999; Hill, Green, & Eckel, 2001).

Yet all too often, the diversity effort is not linked to these central initiatives in a substantial way. As long as diversity remains a separate component of institutional work, unrelated to other elements, it seems likely that it will remain marginalized and that core institutional processes will remain unaffected by diversity. In contrast, diversity is more likely to be at the center of educational practice when it is linked to effectiveness. However, it generally has been unclear how this might be done. How might the core processes link to diversity?

If we look at educational effectiveness using the WASC lens of student success, institutional capacity, and a culture of evidence, it is not hard to see how diversity and effectiveness might be linked. Access and success refers to the means by which a student is admitted to the institution and the institutional conditions that facilitate students' success once they are enrolled. Access involves asking whether the institution has the students it requires at the undergraduate, graduate, professional, or certificate level and asking about the means by which talent is identified. Success involves markers of achievement, such as grade point average, scholastic awards, leadership positions, academic major of concentration, years to degree completion, postgraduate success, and, of course, learning outcomes.

The diversity discourse becomes central when questions are asked not only about student access and success in the aggregate, but about student access and success *disaggregated*. Increasingly, campuses are being asked to explain and sometimes justify the criteria being used for admissions and who is included or excluded as a result. Campuses can ask: Who is succeeding? Are all groups of students engaged on campus? Where are they engaged? Do all groups of students perceive an institutional commitment to their success? Disaggregating the key indicators that are being used ties diversity to education in a very central way.

Because assessing institutional effectiveness involves a holistic approach to the institution, data collection and analysis cannot focus simply on students; it must also engage institutional capacity. Institutional capacity involves the governing structures and financial status of the school and its capacity to mount its educational and scholarly program. Institutional capacity involves asking questions about mission, the strategic-planning process, leadership capability (especially in upper management and the board of trustees), financial stability and long-range forecasts, and the public perceptions of the institution. One way that this is typically addressed is to look at whether the institution has fiscal and physical equilibrium, adequate personnel with appropriate credentials and experience, and operational practices that facilitate the mission. If an institution has declared that its mission is to educate all students to thrive in a diverse society and a global context, the link between diversity and effectiveness should be apparent.

If the institution's mission also includes serving the needs of the region or the world through basic and applied research, the same questions about capacity emerge, although the capacity to function as a teaching institution will be quite different than the capacity to function as a research university, medical school, or law school, or with other programs requiring specialized or advanced study. If diversity is at the core of the mission, a campus needs to ask what kind of capacity it requires to address the societal and educational issues involved. Institutional capacity operates in another way as well. Does the institution have the capacity to bring together diverse groups of people to evaluate the status of diversity, collectively engage the multiple perspectives that are likely present, and come to recommendations that can lead to substantive improvement?

In addition to looking at educational effectiveness and institutional capacity, the newer accreditation processes also ask whether the campus uses evidence to make claims and guide decisions. Increasingly, organizational learning is emerging as a means of helping institutions monitor their progress and focus strategically on improving quality by building a culture of institutional learning (Hernandez & Visher, 2001; Preskill & Torres, 1999). While there are many definitions and arguments surrounding organizational learning (Kezar, 2005; Nonaka &

Takeuchi, 1995), I am choosing to use the concept as a broad umbrella that in some way incorporates a variety of strategies, tools, and concepts, such as organizational learning itself, data-driven decision-making, knowledge management, and knowledge creation. In this way, organizational learning can highlight the importance of bringing people together to consider information, disrupt assumptions about the institution, and ultimately create a *culture of inquiry* directed to improvement.

A number of foundations, for example, have utilized an information-based, organizational-learning approach to evaluation (Brock et al., 2007; Campbell & McClintock, 2002; Dowd, 2005; Hernandez & Visher, 2001; Pew Charitable Trusts, 2001; D. G. Smith, 2004; W. K. Kellogg Foundation, 1998). The James Irvine Foundation incorporated an organizational-learning approach into its evaluation strategies. Its entire grant-making process for the Campus Diversity Initiative (CDI)—its work with twenty-eight independent colleges and universities in California from 2000 to 2005—was designed to encourage campuses to think about evaluating progress on diversity in a way that would help improve their own efforts, rather than simply to be in compliance with the reporting requirements of the foundation. In addition, regional accreditation organizations have been introducing an organizational-learning model for quality improvement (Western Association of Schools and Colleges, 2002). Many such organizations are now engaged in an effort to see whether, and how, organizational learning increases campus capacity to evaluate progress toward important institutional goals and encourages strategic decision-making (Kezar, 2005; Morest & Jenkins, 2007).

Current research on institutional change, effectiveness, and diversity suggests that organizational learning has the potential to increase a campus's capacity to evaluate the effectiveness of its diversity work in making progress toward its institutional goals. In theory, organizational learning seems well suited to higher education (Bensimon, Polkington, Bauman, & Vallejo, 2004; Boyce, 2003; Eckel, Green, & Hill, 2001; D. G. Smith, 1999; Symonette, 2006). Academic institutions are knowledge organizations. They are highly decentralized and require broad engagement in decision-making for many academic efforts, such as hiring, curricular change, and program reviews (Gilmore, Hirschhorn, & Kelly, 1999; Lipman-Blumen, 1998). Organizational learning assumes that most change will come more from the institution (and people in the institution) than from requirements through outside mandates.

In contrast to the language typically associated with outcomes assessment or evaluation, organizational learning does not necessarily imply that only highly specialized experts can engage in the evaluation process. Organizational learning asks whether thoughtful people, mindful of the institutional context and using relevant and available information, can facilitate needed change. Because diversity inevitably involves a broad range of constituents, a process that allows for—in fact, requires—widespread participation is well suited to diversity. For me, the question directing this process would be, "How do we know we are making progress?" rather than questions about "proving the impact of some program" or some other, more scientized version of evaluation. Framing the question in this way permits individuals to ask for meaningful and systemic information that would indicate change, whether positive or negative. Furthermore, it shifts the focus to a process for improvement, rather than simply a summative conclusion about outcomes.

Based on the analysis of collected institutional data (both quantitative and qualitative), organizational learning holds the promise of being more informative and usable. It encourages the use of structures in which members of the campus community can honestly reflect on successes and failures and take ownership of the process and the results. It involves a broad representation of decision-makers across the institution. It is not a process imposed from the outside but takes into consideration both internal and external community influences. Finally, it builds on the academic discourse of educational effectiveness that is already familiar to institutional leaders. In the end, it is also likely to provide better information on which to judge the overall impact.

At the same time, there is sufficient evidence that organizational learning, developing a culture of inquiry, and being guided by data-driven decision-making are not easy to institutionalize or operationalize in general, and especially with respect to diversity (Argyris, 2005; Argyris & Schön, 1996; Cameron, 2005; Friedman, Lipshitz, & Overmeer, 2001; Kezar, 2005; Senge, 2000; Trower & Honan, 2002). The challenges of interrupting parallel initiatives, considering whether organizational learning is the work of individuals or institutions, using data, developing processes, providing continuity, engaging institutional culture and mission, and sharing information must be addressed.

Parallel Initiatives

Introducing organizational learning to colleges and universities can be a challenge, because it actually interrupts typical campus practices at almost every point. Bringing together campus constituents across institutional boundaries, accessing campus data systems to obtain usable information, creating meaningful dialogue among diverse constituencies, and finding ways to mount strategies that bring many departments together are essential to the process of organizational learning, and not typical on many campuses. Diversity work also interrupts the usual—in considering admissions standards, faculty-hiring processes, definitions of good practice, and so on. Thus, these two intense processes—diversity work and organizational learning—often run on parallel courses. Intentionally linking them is one of the most important lessons that has emerged from the work going on nationally.

Organizational Learning as the Work of Individuals or Institutions

Even though organizational learning focuses on institutional-level change, individuals and teams of individuals do the work. However, the institutional context in which individuals and teams work either enhances or complicates organizational learning and diversity. Efforts across the country that have utilized organizational learning (Bensimon, 2004; Clayton-Pedersen, Parker, Smith, Moreno, & Teraguchi, 2007) have highlighted a number of factors that strongly influence the effectiveness of individual or team efforts and the ultimate impact they have on institutional indicators. These factors include the potentially dramatic turnover in personnel; the culture of the institution in relation to the use of data; the role of senior leadership at all levels, who either foster and encourage organizational learning or discourage it; the presence or absence of effective and capable institutional researchers; and the purpose of the institution (Clayton-Pedersen, Parker, Smith, Moreno, & Teraguchi, 2007).

Using Data

For all too many campuses, relevant data is not as accessible as one might think it should be, and there is little experience in the use of data to inform decisions. There are exceptions, of course; in finance, advancement, and even admissions offices, data are required and used. In academic areas, this is less often the case. Even obvious data, such as longitudinal information on graduation and retention disaggregated by race and ethnicity, often have to be developed or found.

Moreover, while openness to data is part of academic culture, sharing institutional data may generate controversy for the leadership or the reputation of the institution. It is hard to overcome the desire to want to make the campus look good or avoid making information too public. This is particularly true where diversity has been the object of intense political and legal challenges. Furthermore, the wide range of opinions on campuses and the diffusion of leadership mean that conversations about diversity can be contentious and difficult to engage.

Keeping focused on institutional goals is particularly important for diversity work (Clayton-Pedersen, Parker, Smith, Moreno, & Teraguchi, 2007; Nettles et al., 2002). The success or failure of a diversity effort does not rest solely with a program. Knowing how many underrepresented students are served by a program is no doubt important. But the key issue (an institution-wide issue, for which a program may be one strategy) is whether underrepresented students are being retained at the institution. If so, are they doing well academically? Are they attaining a degree? Are they thriving? What is the length of time from first enrollment to completion for these students? Is it comparable to the average for other student cohorts? Are they going on to graduate school after completion at a rate nearly the same as that of other students? When the focus is merely on what a program does or does not accomplish, institutions can miss critical information that helps discern progress and problems in reaching institutional goals. Moreover, information about a specific program is better evaluated in the larger context of the success (or lack thereof) of underrepresented students. Thus, the use of basic, disaggregated institutional data is fundamental to monitoring and discussing progress.

Finally, while there can be resistance to using data, people may also become intrigued with it; requests for data may proliferate unmanageably, hampering the ability to develop and use it. Starting with existing information rather than generating a new survey, for example, ensures that the data provided are well used and increases the likelihood of sustaining the effort beyond one year.

A Process for Meaning-Making and Decision-Making

While data are important, creating a process that builds shared knowledge and shared ownership of decision-making is also a challenge. Decision-making is not an immediate outcome of new information (Garvin & Roberto, 2001). It is a process that requires, in most cases, a collaboration of diverse groups and individuals. Who is sitting at the table and whether the group can truly engage the difficult conversations that may be required are open issues on many campuses. When decision-making is facilitated well, however, what can emerge is a real understanding of where the campus is, what assumptions and myths have been guiding past efforts, and what strategies might be employed for improvement (Argyris, 2005; Kezar & Eckel, 2002b; Weick, 2005).

Continuity

Lack of continuity and turnover in key leadership have emerged as surprisingly powerful challenges in maintaining continual progress. In some of the CDI work with campus teams, we found significant turnover in a one- or two-year period. Some turnover is a function of normal institutional transitions. Some is a function of burnout, when long-standing diversity leaders cannot bring themselves to go through the diversity planning stage again without some reassurance that this time it might make a difference (Clayton-Pedersen, Parker, Smith, Moreno, & Teraguchi, 2007). Intentional efforts to maintain continuity are critical to facilitate the engagement of new participants and to facilitate familiarity with past diversity work and organizational history. Use of key documents developed for a diversity initiative, such as an institutional overview, a proposal to a foundation, or interim reports, has proven to be an important strategy for maintaining continuity through transition.

Linking Diversity to Mission and Culture

All too often, the conversations about diversity and success appear almost identical, whether one is at a community college, a research university, or a liberal arts college. While all institutions should find evidence on student success, engagement, and learning to be relevant, what indicators might be relevant for a research university or a science institution?

Because there is an important relationship between organizational culture and diversity work (Aleman & Salkever, 2003; Ibarra, 2000; Kezar & Eckel, 2002a), linking diversity initiatives to institutional mission and overall educational effectiveness is essential for campuses to reach their institutional goals. Different types of institutions and different campus cultures will facilitate organizational learning and the work of diversity differently, or to different degrees. For example, institutions with social-justice missions tend to address diversity directly, although they may or may not facilitate the use of data to monitor progress. Other campuses find the use of data common and have created processes for making meaning from the data. Understanding culture and mission is important in monitoring progress, as it is for diversity work overall.

Sharing Among and Between Institutions

In part because of turnover, individuals and groups often begin to reinvent the wheel. Little knowledge exists among faculty about the extensive and important resources available nationally. Assumptions go unexamined and may drive policy decisions. Organizational learning is buttressed by opportunities for institutions and intracampus teams to come together to question, to inquire, and to share best practices and strategies for overcoming challenges. Bringing together units across the campus for workshops within or across disciplines or for attendance at national conferences, such as the Diversity and Learning conferences of the Association of American Colleges and Universities, provides faculty and staff with the scholarship on diversity. Not only do such opportunities provide useful information, they also create a sense of community. This is particularly significant for campus leaders, who often feel isolated and marginalized in their diversity work. In addition, national resources such as Diversity Web and national conferences are very significant in facilitating change.

Building Institutional Capacity for Organizational Learning and Diversity

Despite its limits and complexities, at a conceptual level, using *organizational learning* in *learning organizations* seems to make sense. Can one take issue with the notion that "intentionality and thoughtfulness should be the hallmarks of change in the academy"? (Eckel, Hill, Green, & Mallon, 1999). Moreover, as with other domains already discussed, we are confronted today mostly with an absence of information. As a result, myths and rhetoric often substitute for reality. Perhaps what is needed instead is a form of organizational learning, a culture of inquiry lite—the appropriate use of information, both quantitative and qualitative, that will ensure the institution's credibility in discussions of progress, the ability to identify institutional strengths and weaknesses, and the capacity to make strategic decisions concerning progress and success.

Using data and systematic information for organizational learning and placing diversity at the center of regular institutional processes would seem to have strong potential to build institutional capacity for greater success on diversity and excellence. Moreover, creating a manageable and coherent approach to monitoring progress on diversity aligns with the political and educational imperative for higher education to become more effective in its capacity for diversity, and it also accords with good practice in general.

In chapter 3, I described how thinking about technology might help illuminate the position of diversity in the institution. It might be helpful to use another parallel—a mental model of the budget process—to illustrate the use of a framework and indicators to monitor progress. The process of managing the budget on a college campus relies on several key elements, including a generally agreed-upon accounting framework, a set of indicators, and a regular reporting structure. College presidents and chief finance officers do not make reports on the budget in terms of specific expenditures or line-by-line descriptions of where resources are being spent. Large categories for expenses and revenues, combined with the ability to report progress in terms of past, present, and future indicators, suffice to provide the institution, its board, and its leadership with a snapshot, a "dashboard," of how the institution is doing financially. These can be gross indicators, such as operating surplus or deficit figures, or more refined indicators, such as the debt-to-asset ratios or endowment-to-student ratio developed by the National Association of College and University Business Officers. This framework and its relevant indicators are accompanied by a regular reporting structure and report mechanism.

Monitoring finances has developed so that it is manageable and fairly reflective of what most people would consider institutional fiscal health and progress. Moreover, parallel approaches exist within most units of the campus, from the development office to student-affairs offices to academic departments, with more nuanced and comprehensive information being shared as the budget information is localized. While some indicators may vary in their centrality to different areas (for example, fund-raising is more central to the development office, and balanced budgets to the student-affairs office), the general indicators are similar and in alignment with the institution. I understand that in accounting, the indicators that are used to monitor an institution's financial condition and processes are considered *intelligent metrics* that make sense, rather than being precise measures. That is a useful way, I believe, to think about these diversity indicators.

Similarly, a manageable and coherent approach to monitoring progress in diversity in higher education that includes a set of principles, a framework for organizing the effort, and a set of indicators that can guide the collection and analysis of data is appropriate and, I would argue, urgent. Each of these components forms a conceptual structure that is discussed in detail below. While the overall approach can be generalized, clearly the particulars must be developed to align with the specific institutional mission, culture, and context. However, caution must be used to make sure that data do not become removed from context or used to make the issues so complex that no meaning can be developed. Data and data requests can also get out of control and proliferate to the point of meaninglessness (Trower & Honan, 2002). That is why it is important to agree on simple indicators and to seek more nuanced data only if it is clear that it is important.

Principles

The approach to monitoring progress needs to include a number of principles that reflect common sense and lessons learned from research and practice. These principles emphasize the development of information that is *manageable*, that is *relevant* to the needs of the particular institution, and that generates an *ongoing process geared to change*. The principles have great relevance for campuses attempting to approach diversity using organizational learning. They are as follows:

- Embed the framework and indicators in the context of the particular institution.
- Approach information from an organizational-learning point of view, to help the entire institution be better informed, to monitor progress, to identify successes and challenges, and to make strategic decisions.
- Make sure the approach is manageable for the campus and capable of being maintained. How many times do campus constituents or even institutional research people develop an approach that is simply not sustainable?
- Monitor key elements and trends rather than taking a comprehensive approach to every program or practice.
- Focus on institutional change, not simply project-specific issues. The purpose of the framework is to monitor *institutional* progress. If a goal is to increase retention for all racial and ethnic groups, then the indicators would relate to retention. Focusing on institutional change makes it clear that the responsibility is an institutional one. In contrast, if retention is monitored in the context of a program review of a student-success program, it suggests that student success is the sole responsibility of the program.
- Develop an appropriate process for making meaning out of the information and for communication to the community.

A Three-Pronged Process for Monitoring Progress

Not unlike many program reviews or accreditation processes, a three-pronged process for engaging diversity on campus might be imagined. For any campus interested in taking a strategic approach to diversity, three elements can be quite useful, even essential: (1) establishing the context and background for diversity at the campus; (2) developing an approach for monitoring progress with a relevant framework and indicators; and (3) developing a mechanism for reporting and sharing information and a time and place to discuss progress and make necessary changes.

CONTEXT AND BACKGROUND

First, one might examine, in a self-study or a report, the status of diversity on the campus in the context of the institution's history and mission. A good first step is a review of previous reports (on most campuses there are usually many reports, often developed in response to a crisis and in which similar recommendations are made), along with the gathering of available information using the framework suggested here. A self-study can also provide a context for what stage the campus is in (García, Hudgins, Musil, Nettles, & Sedlacek, 2001; Kezar, 2007; Valverde, 1998). Is the campus just beginning its diversity efforts? Is it restarting something? Is it trying to move to another level? Only when the campus has identified its greatest areas of need and its prior accomplishments and failures is it appropriate to begin to develop strategic recommendations and strategies. Sadly, a review of twenty or thirty years' worth of reports on many campuses would show little continuity and much redundancy in recommendations.

INSTITUTIONAL FRAMEWORK AND INDICATORS

Second, the campus should develop a framework with a set of indicators that will facilitate the answer to the question, how can we know if we are making progress? This question is significant because it does not emphasize the usual language of evaluation but, rather, asks educated people in an institutional context to determine how they might come to know whether or not they are making progress on student success, faculty hiring, curriculum change, and so on.

An institutional framework (as described below) that is established at the beginning of the diversity initiative becomes a conceptual model to facilitate discussion and monitor change in a manageable way. It provides an institutional map that guides leaders toward institutional goals and prevents side excursions from supplanting those goals. Moreover, an institutional framework enables leaders to see how their programs contribute toward reaching the institutional goal, rather than being isolated activities. Rather than getting paralyzed by discussions of the definition of diversity, an institution could employ the framework described in chapter 3, which has proven useful in capturing both diversity work and its relevant indicators. Figure 8.1 (identical to fig. 3.1) reminds us of that framework.

REPORTING

Third, the institution should develop a means of regular reporting on an interim basis to the campus. Annually may be sufficient, but the frequency of reports

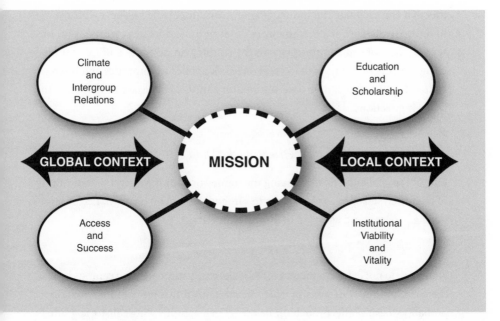

Figure 8.1. A framework for diversity

should certainly be discussed. Connected to a reporting process should be an understanding of where and how a diverse group of people will gather to make meaning from the data and make recommendations based on the data. The reports are intended to be learning-organization tools drawing upon available data, as well as updates on the formative process of campus diversity work.

When an institution gathers manageable and relevant information about the progress of the campus toward its goals and supports a process of monitoring and discussing progress, information becomes available that is centrally relevant to the campus community (as well as to any outside funders or constituencies).

The Framework for Diversity and Relevant Indicators

Discussions of diversity on college campuses typically occur in many locations and from different perspectives. Conversations thus cannot look at diversity from an integrated, strategic point of view. Without a structure by which the conversations can be defined and framed, they are likely to be frustrating and useless. The framework described in chapter 3 and here (in fig. 8.1) lends itself to indicators that can facilitate the monitoring of institutional effectiveness with respect to diversity. As part of the framework, a set of indicators has evolved from observing the work of campuses across the country on diversity and institutional change. Some of the ways that the framework applies to campuses and the relevant indicators that can be used to monitor campus efforts are described in the following sections.

Orienting the Data

One of the challenges in developing the framework among a diverse community of interested stakeholders is to come to some agreement on benchmarks for monitoring progress and agreeing to disaggregate data.

BENCHMARKING

Numbers do not exist in a vacuum. If I say the graduation rate on a campus is 70%, there are a number of ways to make meaning from this piece of information; it probably doesn't reflect much on its own. On a campus whose historic graduation rate was around 50% until ten years ago, a current rate of 70% would mark significant improvement. If this rate was for Asian American students and stood in contrast to an overall graduation rate of 85%, we might not feel as good about it. Monitoring progress might mean looking at all these things; there might be progress in relation to some comparators, and decline or concern in comparison to others. By taking a multidimensional approach, it is possible for a campus community to be in agreement on areas where progress has been made and areas where more progress is needed. For example, in chapter 5, some key indicators for faculty were suggested, including overall demographic change, new hires, and turnover. These can be efficiently used to monitor progress.

Implicit in these examples are five approaches to progress that are useful to consider.

Change over time. Data on change over time would allow an institution to chart progress made in terms of its own goals. How often do campuses report the rate of faculty hiring and the diversity of new hires in a single year but fail to report how the overall faculty diversity information has changed over time?

Change in relation to some criterion or criteria. Data on change according to specified criteria would allow an institution to evaluate whether its efforts were adequate in terms of some yardstick. The analysis of faculty turnover reported in chapter 5 suggests that having nearly three out of five new URM hires, on average, simply replace those who have left is too high a ratio to make substantial progress. Some campuses have tried to develop goals as part of the benchmarking progress. This can all too often degenerate into arguments about the goals, rather than an agreement to make progress. Consequently, goal statements that include specific targets must be developed cautiously.

Change in comparison to national, statewide, or peer institutional data. It is a common practice for campuses to compare themselves to other institutions on many fronts, but this is rarely done within the context of diversity. In part this is because institutions vary widely and because many institutions are reluctant to publicly share information on this topic. Moreover, with diversity work there is a danger that doing as well as a group of peers would give license to an institution to remain static. This is certainly true for faculty hiring, where peer-group comparisons can provide a sense that the campus is doing as well as others—when in fact no one is doing well.

Change in comparison to outstanding performers. Using true benchmarks—that is, outstanding performers, rather than common peer groups—can provide encouragement toward progress, even if an institution is not likely to match such performance. Looking at comparable institutions that do not have achievement gaps among racial/ethnic groups (as was discussed in chapter 4) could provide rich information and strategies.

Change in comparison to groups or sectors within the campus. Comparisons of outstanding performance by different units in an institution can be a powerful way to show what can be done within the same context. If the physics department is graduating a higher percentage of Latino PhD's than the biology and chemistry departments, one might ask why. Comparing the persistence rates between physics and chemistry might help provide information, in the institution's own context, of the variation in approaches. The same would be true for increasing diversity from one academic unit to the next.

DISAGGREGATION

The key to linking diversity to effectiveness is to answer the questions posed here, not only by regularly collecting and analyzing detailed data on students, faculty, and staff, but by *disaggregating* the data by race, ethnicity, gender, and economic class, among other variables desired by the school. Whereas many institutions gather data on their students, few consistently disaggregate such data or look at all survey questions in a disaggregated manner. The indicators for student success, for example, can include the National Survey of Student Engagement, GPA, time to degree, graduation rates, and success in STEM fields.

Disaggregating these data will tell an important story about who is engaged on campus, who is succeeding, and for whom the institution is successful. So, for example, an institutional survey that seeks to assess the level of student satisfaction with campus life and academic engagement may include some questions about discrimination or satisfaction with ethnic studies courses. When only the diversity questions are disaggregated, it appears that the only significant indicators are diversity-related. However, the institution is losing very valuable information by not disaggregating the other questions to learn whether there are differences by relevant groups. Through the use of disaggregated data, schools can begin to address whether they are making progress toward their institutional goals for the diverse communities they are serving. The NCAA's requirement that schools publish graduation rates by race/ethnicity established the significance of studying student success by group, rather than in the aggregate. If the analyses in chapter 7 revealed anything, it was the importance of considering which intersections, such as race and gender, are critically important for such assessments.

Indicators Associated with the Dimensions-of-Diversity Framework

Below, I describe each of the dimensions in the diversity framework (fig. 8.1) and the kind of indicators that might be associated with it. Some of these indicators are more qualitative in nature, while others are basic quantitative indicators that can provide snapshots of the institution over time.

INSTITUTIONAL VIABILITY

The dimension of institutional viability provides a sample of indicators focusing on building institutional capacity (fig. 8.2). A core aspect of increasing institutional capacity for diversity now centers on diversifying leadership on campus. In particular, many campuses are addressing the hiring and retention of faculty of color, especially African American, Latino, and American Indian faculty. Key indicators here can look at the diversity of faculty and staff, and their retention and success as well. As discussed in chapter 5, key indicators for faculty might include change in demographics over time, new hires, and the turnover quotient. In addition, the indicators can be disaggregated by schools or fields. These indicators can apply to staff, board members, and administrative leadership as well. Perceptions of the institution by constituencies inside and outside and the centrality of diversity as evidenced by its inclusion in core documents and processes, such as strategic planning and accreditation, can be key indicators. Reviewing such core documents can suggest whether diversity is central or peripheral to the institution. The existence of and knowledge of policies that facilitate the perceptions

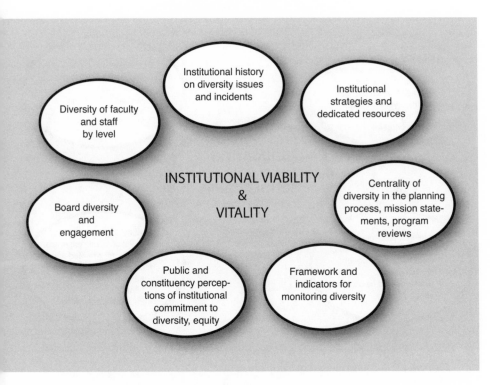

Figure 8.2. Institutional viability and vitality indicators

of commitment for different groups are relevant here. These can include domestic-partner benefits, Americans with Disabilities Act compliance and outreach, tuition policies for undocumented students, family-leave approaches, outreach to local tribal communities, and so on.

While this dimension could be called by many different names, I have chosen to use "institutional viability and vitality" in order to capture the ways in which the dimension reflects capacity-building, links to vitality, and for many institutions continued viability in the pluralistic contexts in which they exist.

EDUCATION AND SCHOLARSHIP

As with the first generations of diversity efforts, most campuses are still working with faculty on curricular transformation. A few campuses have begun to address student learning directly, but most are working on increasing the range of courses and departments that include the scholarship on diversity. As part of that effort, campuses are also offering opportunities to faculty to work in scholarly

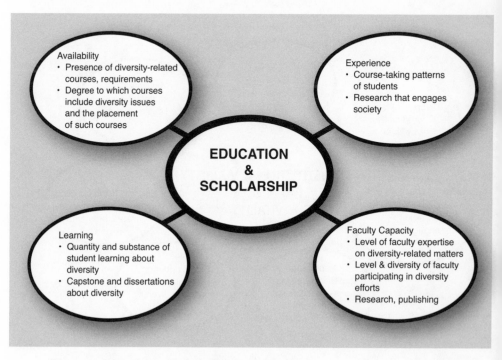

Figure 8.3. Education and scholarship indicators

areas related to diversity. Virtually all campuses have begun to link the work in this dimension to their institutional mission of preparing students for leadership in a diverse society. While this generic mission is present to a greater or lesser degree across virtually all campuses, many campuses have made specific links to more unique aspects of their mission. For some, a commitment to social justice is prominent. For others, intentionality with respect to leadership development is emphasized.

The indicators in this dimension are organized around four elements—availability of curricular offerings, experience with the opportunities available (for example, course-taking patterns), student learning, and the depth of faculty capacity (fig. 8.3). From an undergraduate perspective, these indicators work reasonably well. However, for a graduate institution or a research university, some key indicators might also include dissertation topics related to diversity, engagement with diversity in the disciplines, and the percentage of faculty who engage in research linked to diversity in the social sector. In this dimension, diversity can be quite inclusive, addressing the complexity of society, social stratification, and identities.

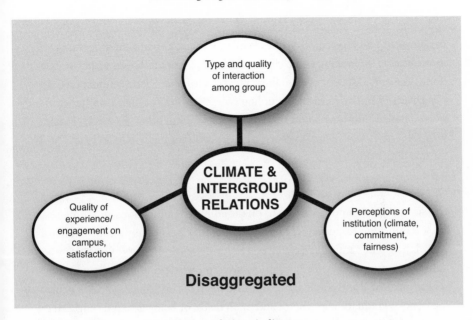

Figure 8.4. Climate and intergroup relations indicators

CLIMATE AND INTERGROUP RELATIONS

Many, if not most, institutions are working to improve campus climate through programmatic efforts and discussions about institutional commitment. Approaches such as those funded by the Ford Foundation (2005a) to increase the opportunities to engage in difficult dialogues suggest some indicators that describe where these conversations are occurring and whether they are effective. While much of the work in higher education focuses on undergraduates, it is clear to me that indicators monitoring climate and intergroup efforts should include faculty, staff, the board, and graduate students. For graduate students going into faculty positions, building their competence and experience in guiding difficult dialogues should be important. Many campus teaching and learning centers are working with faculty to increase faculty capacity to address conflict, for example. This dimension also provides a context in which other questions related to sexual orientation, gender, or religious differences can be engaged.

The indicators in this dimension provide data on interactions among groups, engagement on campus, satisfaction, and perceptions about how people are treated (fig. 8.4). Disaggregation of the data by race, ethnicity, gender, and, where possible, class is common. Campus surveys and focus groups are frequent means of collecting these data. For example, surveys can gather information about the experiences of religious communities, while focus groups and interviews may be more feasible for looking at the climate for groups from different sexual orientations. A resource kit developed in the context of the James Irvine Foundation Campus Diversity Initiative, available online (www.aacu.org/irvinediveval), provides more detailed information on surveys, indicators, and other resources. In addition, Diversity Web (www.diversityweb.org) includes many resources and tools for this dimension.

ACCESS AND SUCCESS

Classic indicators for diversity focus on the admitted populations and some basic success indicators, especially for undergraduates. It is especially important in this regard that some campuses have moved beyond basic indicators of success (graduation, retention, and GPA) and are focused on whether students from underrepresented racial and ethnic groups are *thriving* at the institution—that is, achieving honors, graduating in science and math fields, or being generally engaged on campus. While virtually all campuses would in this dimension use data focusing on the access and success of historically underrepresented populations (African Americans, Latinos, and American Indians), more and more campuses are also engaging the experiences of different Asian American populations, as well as first-generation students from lower economic backgrounds.

Concentrating on groups that have been historically significant while paying attention to every group is an important development in current diversity initiatives and can be achieved by disaggregating data thoughtfully. Using a category of students of color in the aggregate is not likely to be adequate, as it overlooks important issues within groups. Similarly, looking at access and success by the intersection of race and gender will emerge as very important, to the extent that it has not already. Addressing diversity within graduate and professional populations would bring attention to STEM fields, demographic indicators, and success indicators such as time to degree and graduation rates (fig. 8.5).

Learning and Reporting

What has emerged most clearly is the necessity for campuses to have a mechanism to create opportunities to review data and link the data to relevant decision-making. The process of reporting on a regular basis creates the opportunity for campuses to collect and review data and other information on the indicators and provides a mechanism to institute corrective actions as needed. An overarching

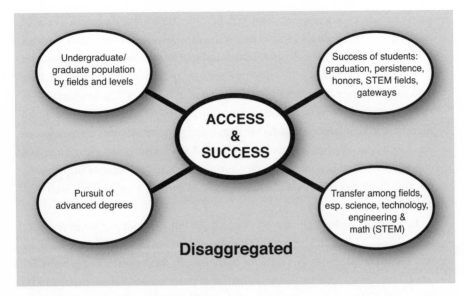

Figure 8.5. Access and success indicators

intent of this process is to prompt campuses to look holistically and reflectively at their progress and to look longitudinally at disaggregated data on a regular basis.

Diversity work cuts across the entire campus. A good reporting process can provide an opportunity for people from multiple levels and perspectives to come together to talk about progress and issues. This process can interrupt the isolation and lack of communication and sharing that often occurs. One campus, for example, noticed that after a year of successful progress in diversifying the faculty, the progress had not continued in the second and third years. Even as it relished its new reputation as being at the forefront of successful faculty diversity efforts, the campus was surprised that its strategies had been successful for only one out of three years. On another campus, after an initial self-study, it was discovered that significant achievement gaps existed among different racial groups at the institution. It became clear that many of the strategies developed to address diversity were not in fact designed to address student success. Consequently, redesign followed.

On yet another campus, the president, who often placed progress on diversity as the highest of priorities, used the diversity framework described here to provide an opportunity for an annual discussion among diverse groups on campus about diversity progress. This discussion validated the hard work of those who bore the greatest responsibility for diversity, because it became clear that others, such as deans of schools, had responsibility too. The conversations also created an opportunity for schools within universities to examine the success of students in particular fields and in specific courses and to strategize about needed changes.

It is clear, however, that developing the capacity to generate, present, and use data for institutional purposes does not always come easily. The tendency is for staff who are already busy, and often overburdened, to prepare and submit interim reports in a compliance mode rather than using them to facilitate campus learning. Central to whether this process is handled as a learning opportunity or as a compliance task is how much the institutional culture facilitates or impedes the use and sharing of data, as well as how the role of the institutional research officer is defined.

In addition, we have all seen reports that are framed from particular perspectives. One can imagine a report on diversity progress in which someone needs to share only the good news or only the bad news. In the report of the Irvine CDI work, it became apparent that in preparing reports, consideration needed to be given to "*who shapes the story, who tells the story, who hears the story,* and *who validates the story*" (Clayton-Pedersen, Parker, Smith, Moreno, & Teraguchi, 2007, pp. 52–53). Thinking about these questions is very important. In a context in which such reports are not required, it is clear that some other structure, probably initiated by institutional leaders, will be necessary if the campus is to make the time for reflection on information and formulation of decisions regarding implementation adjustments. A key issue for campuses in general is how to make the process of data collection and analysis a manageable part of institutional practice.

If the diversity framework and indicators outlined above (or others developed by the campus) are used by the leadership to provide an audit of campus progress, in much the same way that a financial audit provides a regular glimpse of financial progress and health, campuses would make much more sustainable efforts toward institutional change. How much information is to be shared, beyond core institutional indicators, would, of course, differ with the audience or constituency and its role. Members of the board of trustees would receive regular reports on these key indicators in much the same way that they receive reports on fiscal well-being and progress. Presidents and provosts would presumably receive more refined data that might be disaggregated by the relevant units of the campus, such as schools and departments. Deans would be expected to know much more about the progress of their schools and be involved in the recommendations about needed changes in strategy. And program directors and staff should be in a position to have a much deeper and richer contextual knowledge of what is occurring and where there are positive gains or challenges to be addressed. A key element, then, is how this information is integrated vertically as well as horizontally to create coherence and a collaborative understanding for change.

❁

With an institution-wide process for monitoring progress that centers on the mission of the campus, institutional effectiveness, and involvement of all constituencies, campuses have the opportunity to become the institutions they seek to be. Linking diversity to core indicators of excellence and institutional capacity has the potential to move organizations to reexamine and reformulate institutional success. The three-pronged process of self-study of institutional diversity, implementation of a framework with indicators, and interim reports encourages campuses to look at themselves holistically and in context in order to promote intentionality in monitoring progress over time.

While it is likely that this model can yield meaningful and sustainable progress on diversity, the supposition that organizational learning is a "natural" for higher education institutions is not necessarily true (Senge, 2000). However, it seems to be the most likely process to keep an institution focused on monitoring progress toward greater institutional capacity for diversity.

NOTE

This chapter is drawn from Smith & Parker, 2005; Smith, Parker, Clayton-Pedersen, Moreno, & Teraguchi, 2006; and Clayton-Pedersen, Parker, Smith, Moreno, & Teraguchi, 2007.

CHAPTER NINE

Making Diversity Work

Recommendations and Conclusions

For higher education—as for our society—diversity is not only its challenge but also its future. When we look over the past forty years, two conclusions emerge. Diversity represents an expanding and deepening set of issues. At the same time, there is a huge amount of unfinished and urgent business that remains. We are at a pivotal time. Changing demographics are touching all parts of the country in ways that are real, not just abstract projections. Moreover, there is serious tension and reaction to the changes in all corners of society.

Ironically, while our campuses often look more diverse because of increases in diversity among undergraduates, that appearance is misleading and can camouflage the concerns that emerge as one looks deeper into the institution. The objective of this book has been to reframe diversity as central to the mission of higher education and our society and to suggest that our fundamental imperative at this time is to build the capacity of higher education for diversity through strategic change.

Reframing Diversity

A number of themes have emerged from the previous chapters that can serve to integrate the issues developed in chapter 1 on the overall context for diversity and the important elements for building institutional capacity to fulfill the aspirations for excellence in higher education.

Framing the Issues of Diversity as Central to the Mission

It should be clear by now that diversity in the national and global context today is framed as being central to an *institution's capacity* to excel and function in society to fulfill its mission. Much like technology, diversity is seen as central, not something that develops in parallel to normal institutional functioning. In that sense, while diversity will require change, this change will be in the service of the institution and will increase capacity and excellence. We thought that technology and the technological revolution would change everything. Some said that as a result of technology, higher education as we knew it would no longer exist. My own interpretation of the changes related to technology is that although many things have indeed changed, institutions as we know them continue to exist. Certainly, new institutions have developed, and new ways of doing business have evolved. Nonetheless, the wave of technology that early users predicted has been both revolutionary and nonrevolutionary. I suspect that this will be true of diversity as well.

At its core, embedding diversity at the center of the institution's mission has the potential to serve the future of society in ways that are healthy and essential. Embedding diversity in this way creates the opportunity for vitality, for new ways of thinking, and for new kinds of knowledge. The transitional states, as was true with technology, may not be easy. However, clarifying core values and purposes can facilitate the decision-making required. What this means is that the rationale for diversity in each of the dimensions must be deeply understood and formulated so that it rings true in the context of any given campus.

Diversity as Inclusive and Differentiated

Conceptually, as we have seen, diversity as related to identities will grow in complexity. A more comprehensive understanding, as described in chapter 2, must include consideration for the kinds of identity being discussed, the multiplicity and intersections of identity, the need to see identity in context, the need to consider power and asymmetry in understanding identity in an institutional context, and the fact that identities themselves do not fully describe an individual. The paradox of identity is that as its complexity grows, the essential meaning of any one aspect is much harder to grasp. At the same time, the significance of identities that are salient for the society remains visible and central. Dismissing the centrality of identity by pointing to its complexity will only increase its salience for people and groups that continue to deal with inequity.

The strategy of creating lists of identities can be replaced by consideration of how specific identities, in all their complexity, challenge the campus. The framework for diversity and its dimensions of *access and success* for underrepresented students, *campus climate and intergroup relations, education and scholarship,* and *institutional viability and vitality* presented in chapter 3 has proven helpful in a number of settings. While the identities associated with diversity are many, they are differentiated in how they intersect. Thus, they can be engaged quite practically in ways that are integral to a healthy institution and consistent with its mission. Creating spaces and ways of incorporating and acknowledging multiplicity of identity and ensuring that individuals and groups matter is essential. It also opens up the possibility that institutions will become healthier. Improving morale, crossing group boundaries, working together effectively, and increasing creativity are likely if mattering and multiplicity are incorporated effectively into institutional functioning. Effective integration of identities also builds the capacity of many people on campus to engage and participate in diversity efforts, regardless of their own background.

Identifying Talent by Interrupting the Usual

Throughout the previous chapters, the imperative of identifying talent was invoked in relation to student access and success, faculty hiring, research, and leadership. In a new era, what forms of intelligence and what kinds of talents and capacities will be required? Central to identifying talent is articulating what is needed for the particular context, institution, or discipline—the rationale. Numerous books in the fields of management and psychology echo the institutional need for multiple kinds of intelligence and a broad variety of skills. Implicit in so much of the organizational-behavior literature, the diversity literature, and the literature on epistemology is the recognition that excellence, intelligence, and leadership are not unidimensional phenomena, nor are they fixed across different contexts. Rather, they are multidimensional and are very much framed by context. Creative thinking, recognizing new patterns, and interpersonal skills for working on teams are all competencies that are now important and will continue to be so in the future (Davis, 2002; Lipman-Blumen, 1998; Pink, 2006). Emotional intelligence is important and can be learned (Goleman, 2005, 2006).

In the management literature today, there is a great deal written about leadership skills that focus on building connections, listening, and tolerating the kind of complexity and ambiguity that are ubiquitous in organizations and in society. While logic and rationality will no doubt remain important, invention, empathy, and understanding the big picture are becoming essential (Weick and Sutcliffe, 2001). In addition, the ability to connect across communities, to work for social justice, and to create coalitions is also important (Blackwell, Kwoh, & Pastor, 2002).

Creating a multidimensional understanding of talent has implications for education, admissions, hiring, and selection of leadership throughout the institution. It also has profound implications for the leadership development of college presidents, student body leaders, and department chairs. Figuring out how to identify and develop them will be important. Recognizing the multidimensionality of talent will necessarily bring about changes in criteria for selection, processes for evaluating candidates, and the metrics that are used. Discerning how the new will both invigorate and preserve the traditional is one of the core challenges of any change. Central to that will be having enough diversity around the table to make those judgments and to develop those processes. At the present time, the homogeneity around most tables renders institutions at risk for not making the appropriate changes. Whether seen through the lens of postmodernism, chaos theory, practical leadership, knowledge management, studies of intelligence, or diversity, our institutions will benefit from understanding and validating the value of multidimensionality throughout the institution (Aguirre & Martinez, 2007; Blackwell, Kwoh, & Pastor, 2002; Gardner, 1983; Goleman, 2005, 2006; Lipman-Blumen, 1998; Pink, 2006; Sternberg, 1985; Sternberg & Grigorenko, 2004; Wheatley, 2006).

Supporting People and Groups and Building Human Capacity

The concept of mattering—and belonging—is important to healthy institutions. It will reverberate throughout the institution, positively or negatively. It will also affect retention at every level. Building human capacity must touch all constituencies and programs, including staff and students, leadership development, orientation, and the hiring and retention practices with diverse groups. It must consider whether people are thriving. Parker Palmer (2002) captures this sense of mattering: "It seems I am in community when I feel seen, known and respected . . . when I am taken seriously and appreciated, not just for the function I perform, but for who I am as a person. Community is about power and rewards and relationships and meaning . . . and there will always be imbalances among us in those regards. But we can go a long way toward community by understanding that imbalances in one area can often be corrected, or at least relieved" (p. 183).

The process of building institutional capacity for diversity must and will benefit from the ideas and the perspectives of individuals and groups throughout the campus and at all levels. Those who have expertise, perspective, and resources related to diversity can be an enormous resource to a campus. Including people who bring diverse perspectives into decision-making is not always easy in an institution with little diversity. However, reaching out and including them is vital. To the degree that individuals can participate in ways that are meaningful, the human capital of the institution will be developed in fundamental ways. Including such people also helps to build a commitment to the institution, in part because it suggests that the institution is committed to them. This does not require endless meetings or committees, but it does suggest the capacity to listen and to act on information and perspectives that may need to be linked to discussions occurring at other locations on campus.

Debunking Myths

Part of the process of any specific domain of diversity will be to ensure that myths, when they are voiced, will be debunked. Myths emerge from assumptions that individuals or groups believe are true. Whether the myths are associated with students and their ability to succeed or with faculty hiring, institutional turnover, or any other topic, it is important to identify them and engage them. Myths really do become self-fulfilling prophecies that impede change. They also signal to those who see the assumptions as myths that the campus is not serious about change.

Synergy

As diversity inevitably becomes more complex and pressing, there will be more and more initiatives, programs, projects, and individual work throughout a campus. This is all to the good. But at present, the lack of awareness of and connection between these efforts means that they are less likely to build on one another, support one another, and create opportunities for strategic use of resources—human, fiscal, and physical. As the multiplicity of and intersectionality among identities increase, this will become more and more important. Ensuring that there is a reasonable degree of alignment between the vision, the strategies in place, and the indicators being used can help build synergy without being overly controlling.

Intentionality and Institutional Commitment

Many of the strategies outlined in the previous chapters will not emerge naturally, nor will they be sustained without effort. Diversity efforts (indeed, any deep changes) require intentionality if, for example, diversity is to be linked to core institutional processes or if monitoring progress on diversity and excellence is to be sustained. Institutional commitment is essential and will only be achieved if there is a perception among a variety of constituencies that the institution is committed, and committed over the long term. Indeed, as we saw in chapters 6 and 7, perceptions of institutional commitment have emerged as a critical factor in the context for student success and intergroup relations. We know little yet about how an institution can ensure that people will perceive it as committed, but it is clear that it matters for individual and institutional success.

Asymmetry

A significant theme that emerges throughout the large literatures reviewed is the importance of recognizing asymmetry. The experience of people and groups and the response of the institution to them are related to position and location in the institution and to its structure, history, and values. Positionality really does matter. The perspectives of those in a dominant position in a given identity can be quite different from those of people in subordinate positions. Perceptions about mattering and power can be experienced quite differently from a position of privilege. How the work of diversity is perceived from particular vantage points is critical for leadership. Asymmetry emerges in any intergroup context, in allocation of resources, and in perceptions of the institution and affects the effectiveness of efforts.

As one grapples with the multiplicity of identity, it becomes clear that one might be in the dominant position with respect to one identity (e.g., male) and subordinate with respect to another (e.g., ethnicity). As a result, one of the related challenges in all diversity domains is whether people who might be in a position of privilege based on a particular identity will stand up for others. Having understood sexism, can White women be counted on to engage racism? Having encountered racism, can groups of color be counted on to engage homophobia? I am reminded here of the powerful message of the Reverend Martin Luther King, Jr., who said in his letter from the Birmingham jail (April 16, 1963), "Injustice anywhere is a threat to justice everywhere." The future of change will rely on allies, and on working across difference.

Beyond Affirmative Action toward Mission and Excellence

It is probably apparent by now that this book was not written to respond to current legal and policy challenges to affirmative action. While the challenges have been very destructive of diversity efforts in many ways, focusing on them without fundamentally reframing the diversity agenda creates a very narrow space for making what appear to be only marginal changes with respect to diversity. Indeed, before the recent challenges, one could make the case that progress on diversity was not all that robust. Reframing diversity to be central to the institution creates the potential for change that is essential to the institution, inextricably links excellence to diversity, and considers building social equity a core element of an institution's capacity to thrive.

Good Education Matters

One of the indicators of institutional success will be the degree to which students at all levels and from all backgrounds are succeeding and thriving—when background recedes and effective educational practices take its place. By using disaggregated data, an institution can assess its success for students with respect to diversity. As described in chapter 7, research has demonstrated that good education, excellent teaching, and a supportive institutional ethos can facilitate student success, regardless of background or K–12 preparation.

A Process for Monitoring Progress and Learning

The three-step process for monitoring progress described in chapter 8 provides a conceptual scheme for beginning and sustaining a diversity effort. A self-study creates an opportunity to look at the history of diversity at the institution, the current status of efforts, and the strategic directions required. Developing and agreeing on a framework such as the one used throughout this book, with a relevant and limited set of indicators, provides a way to monitor progress and to learn what is working and what is not. The third prong is a reporting and meaning-making process that can open up opportunities to be more public about diversity efforts and to share information across the campus and the many silos on it.

It is worth underscoring the notion that the apparent paradox between using a data-driven approach to monitoring progress and recognizing the necessity of using community-based approaches to change inherent in many campuses creates an important and healthy tension that can facilitate change. Change can occur in ways consistent with organizational learning and an organized anarchy. I do not see any way for an institution to keep track of diversity, let alone bring a wide variety of constituencies together for strategically focused decision-making, without a framework and a set of indicators for monitoring progress. In this effort, the role of institutional research and people who are skilled in facilitating a meaning-making process will be central.

Strategic Change

Many capacities are needed in order to create change. It takes knowledge of people, stakeholder participation, familiarity with the local and larger contexts, and understanding of the environment to create action toward a vision and then to continue to learn and improve. There are a number of literatures, not only those related to diversity, that are quite relevant and well aligned with the numerous ideas presented in the preceding chapters that can facilitate the understanding of what happens on campuses and also of strategic ways to proceed. Just as thinking about technology as a parallel imperative suggested ways to frame diversity in higher education, some of the new literatures on leadership and change in higher education are instructive. In addition, the literature on leadership and diversity is also helpful (see, e.g., Aguirre & Martinez, 2007; Moses, 1997).

Disequilibrium

In reviewing all of the research summarized in this book related to diversity and institutional change, perhaps one of the first observations I would make is about the potentially important role for disequilibrium. Although this concept initially arose from Lewin's early research on change (1951), it is extremely relevant to diversity efforts. If one studies the reasons campuses begin a serious engagement of diversity efforts, what emerges is that in most cases, whatever the source, there is something creating disequilibrium that prompts the institution to act or react. It can be a crisis, an external pressure, or a gap between the reality and the expectations (Hill, Green, & Eckel, 2001). In the results of a W. K. Kellogg Foundation project on transformational change in higher education, Eckel, Hill, Green, and Mallon (1999) note that "successful change leaders recognize windows of opportunity created by everyday events and capitalize on serendipity" (p. 5). In the early decades of diversity efforts, student and faculty activists trying to address concerns about access and then success for students generated much of the disequilibrium. Activism remains an episodic but powerful force on many campuses.

Campuses, regardless of prior efforts, continue to experience racist or other incidents that trigger outrage and inevitably call the campus's commitment and progress on diversity into question. There is a common scenario that follows. Even if the leadership on campus takes all appropriate steps to respond to a hate incident, the incident invariably prompts a discussion or a protest about the elements of diversity outlined in the framework I have described. Students and others will raise issues related to the diversity of the student body, the climate on campus, the degree to which students are being educated to engage diversity, the diversity of the faculty and staff, the institutional commitment to diversity, the commitment of the board, and community-related concerns. For campuses that have been seriously addressing diversity, these incidents can provide important opportunities to make even greater progress. At campuses that have not been working on diversity consistently, the leadership is often put on the defensive and pushed to make commitments for change. The problem when disequilibrium is prompted by incidents is that the campus response is often reactive and not reflective. It might also be superficial.

Concerns about enrollment at tuition-driven institutions or concerns about relationships with a nearby community can also create disequilibrium. Case studies of campuses suggest that issues of enrollment or tuition in contexts with changing demographics can link diversity to viability in the most fundamental way. Survival is a powerful motivator for change. Accreditation processes and national concerns about graduation rates of URM students might trigger some efforts to improve student success and institutional capacity. A board of trustees or public-policy mandate can create the need to address issues of diversity. These can be a powerful force for change, if the institution acts strategically.

The point about disequilibrium is that it can come from many different places and can provide the opportunity for beginning or restarting the change process. It can be prompted externally or driven by internal events. It can be economic, political, educational, strategic, or philosophical in orientation. It can be linked to institutional viability and vitality, education and scholarship, climate and intergroup relations, and/or access and success of URM students. Looking for disequilibrium and connecting it to diversity efforts is one way that a campus can generate greater commitment and involvement. The question is, will the change, especially if done under pressure, be sustainable and strategic in the best sense? In any case, as some recent research on change suggests, incidents and pressures provide opportunity. But strategic change needs to be anchored in the institution, so that it is not just a temporary response to a crisis.

Vision and Mission

A key element of a strategic approach to change emerges in much of the organizational, leadership, and diversity literatures: developing a theme that can focus people's attention on the initiative and that emerges out of institutional values and mission. In higher education, that vision needs to reflect the academic core of a specific institution. The Kellogg project noted that "to make progress on a change initiative, an institution develops ways to operate paradoxically: changing its culture in ways congruent with its culture" (Eckel, Hill, Green, & Mallon, 1999, p. 7).

The notion of connecting change to something that can coalesce many of the disparate efforts of a campus is common to much of the literature on change and makes sense (Eckel, Hill, Green, & Mallon, 1999). "For change to happen, leaders need to get people's attention and active help" (Hirschhorn & May, 2000, p. 30). Culture can be a source of strength as well as an impediment to change; but an important role for the vision as well as for leadership is to impart "a strong sense of what is enduring across discontinuity so people can cope with change by having some sense of stability" (Gilmore, Hirschhorn, & Kelly, 1999, p. 12). In Hirschhorn and May's discussion of strategic change in higher education, they invoke the notion of a campaign strategy (as in a capital campaign) to mobilize scarce resources to implement deep change. Because diversity can be about so much and can occur in all corners of the institution, I find their way of framing an approach to change as if it were a capital campaign quite useful. They suggest that the future is already in the institution: "The important leadership skill is seeing the emergent in the present. . . . Your aim is to look for vivid, specific ways that external forces and trends are taking hold in your own institution" (p. 31).

They also emphasize the need to create a vision that takes advantage of relevant embedded activities and people who are passionate, that mobilizes others to join, and that builds an appropriate infrastructure so that the vision can be sustained. This body of literature also suggests that the best vision is one in which different segments of the campus can see themselves and the relevant work they are doing, rather than a vision that is something entirely new. Understanding the mission, context, and history provides an anchor in which visions can flourish. Thus, linking the vision to excellence, current efforts, and values already in the institution is a common strategy (Collins, 2005; Gardner, Csikszentmihalyi, & Damon, 2001; Schein, 1999; Sturm, 2007; Wheatley, 2006). The vision must be clear and empowering and must be repeated; it must capture people's attention; and it must resonate with the institution's culture and mission. Wheatley, in *Leadership and the New Science* (2006), suggests that in creating a vision, one is creating a force in the institution for change. There is a gift in being able to take information from the campus and to craft language that can be shared—to create a narrative or a metaphor that goes to the heart of the institution and its purpose.

In this way, the effort has visibility and resources and builds on the community's own ongoing work. It also underscores the importance of *sensemaking*, an important concept in the change and organizational-learning literature imply-ing a *process* that "allows people to craft, understand, and accept new conceptu-alizations of the organization" (Kezar & Eckel, 2002b, p. 314). This approach to vision and sensemaking seems highly relevant to the diversity initiatives. It pro-vides synergy, validates and builds on work being done, and locates diversity cen-trally, at the core of the institution's mission, vitality, and viability. A campus's vi-sion for diversity must be a shared sense of how diversity is related to its highest aspirations for research, for teaching, and for service—for excellence in a plural-istic society (Kezar & Eckel, 2002b; Lakoff & Johnson, 2003).

But the vision must be more than words, and it must matter. It must be lived. Wheatley (2006) urges, "We must say what we mean and seek for a much deeper level of integrity in our words and acts than ever before" (p. 57). With every di-versity initiative, with every response to crisis, those who have been working on diversity for years inevitably hold their breath waiting to see if the effort is real, inclusive, and structured to ensure that a campus will "walk the talk."

Because many campuses do not already have sufficient diversity at decision-making levels, it is very important to make sure that the vision-making process is a *process*, not a pronouncement. Engaging people who are already hard at work on diversity to contribute to the vision is likely to improve the vision and vali-date their efforts. The process of articulating the vision, along with the efforts to build on work already begun, has the effect of announcing to the entire commu-nity the importance of diversity efforts to the institution and also serves to invite others to participate.

Leadership That Is Distributed

The role of leadership cannot be underestimated in creating change for diversity. Often, however, when people talk about leadership, they assume this means pres-idential leadership. What seems clear from the field and from research on leader-ship, management, and diversity is that presidential or senior leadership is essen-tial but not sufficient. Nonetheless, having senior leadership that is committed and knowledgeable is vital (Bennis, 1989; Eckel, Green, & Hill, 2001; Heifetz, 1994). Leadership can make a dramatic difference to whether and how diversity is built into the institution's understanding of itself or whether it is merely a series of pro-grams or initiatives that run parallel to the core elements of the campus.

In a recent conversation with staff and faculty on a campus with a new presi-dent, I asked about the difference he was making with respect to diversity. This president, like the previous one, is deeply committed to diversity. Unlike the previous president, whose rhetoric was wonderful, this one combines rhetoric with a day-to-day effort that made the campus, in his first six months, feel quite differently about its diversity efforts. The chair of the faculty diversity committee senses that the efforts of the committee might now make a difference. The staff people directing a variety of diversity efforts now believe they are being seen as important to the future of the institution. Under the previous leader, they were often disappointed by the lack of change institutionally and were increasingly cynical, though they continued to work because of their concern for students. Thus, leadership at the top can make a significant difference in helping to focus, sustain, and energize the effort.

However, that kind of leadership is not enough. Building institutional capacity for diversity is a multidimensional effort and exists in many different locations in the institution—all requiring leadership. We know that faculty hiring requires the leadership of deans and department chairs. Student-affairs functions are critical to how diversity is framed and how diversity efforts are delivered and experienced by students. The campus police set a tone for how people will be treated. Many different departments and many different people throughout the institution help create the overall culture and climate of the campus. Sturm (2007) describes the critical role for campus catalysts who mobilize knowledge and people for change. Decisions related to diversity are made in every location on campus. Decisions are made in the moment, and, while often quite particular, they can facilitate diversity or create a crisis. In this sense, leadership is and must be distributed. Moreover, change can occur when a critical mass of people begin to work together (Rendón, 2005).

An important set of resources for building institutional capacity are the people, programs, scholarship, and curricular developments that emerge from, among other places, ethnic studies and ethnic student-affairs centers, women's studies and women's centers, LGBT programs, multicultural student centers, and on and on. Most campuses have an incredible array of talent related to diversity in many locations. These resources are central for campuses as they move forward. These resident experts, too, have an opportunity to model and develop capacity for engaging the multiple identity issues that emerge within and across groups. They can also provide resources for curriculum transformation, dialogue efforts, linkages to communities, and research development. Collaborations with and among people and groups is inspirational and vital.

A board of trustees that expresses commitment and asks for regular reports on progress for diversity, using a framework, creates a context in which diversity and accountability for diversity matter. An academic senate that also expresses commitment and works to ensure that search committees and departments build diversity into searches, program-review processes, curriculum development, research initiatives, and the mission of the institution provides the academic legitimacy that any president or provost needs in order to deeply engage diversity. Student body leaders who create opportunities for students to work together across boundaries and who see multiplicity of identities can facilitate discussions on campus. Students who monitor and describe their experiences and who think about the ways the institution is building their individual and collective capacity to engage diversity can help bring topics to the fore, provide pressure where it is needed, and give energy and support to institutional change. The institutional research office on many campuses is becoming critical, not only in assisting in the collection of data, but in facilitating a process for making meaning out of the data (Bauman, Bustillos, Bensimon, Brown, & Bartee, 2005; Brock et al., 2007; Clayton-Pedersen, Parker, Smith, Moreno, & Teraguchi, 2007).

One of the challenges, however, is to create a sense that these disparate pockets on our campuses are working together and creating change that is larger than the particulars—that they are working to "sing better." Clearly, any process that allows for discussion, dialogue, and sensemaking will facilitate this effort. Because of the diffusion of diversity efforts, this is one place where a chief diversity officer (CDO) who is empowered to develop and coordinate all these elements can make a huge difference, both to the senior leadership and to the efforts of many people on campus. On a number of campuses where a CDO has been hired, there has been concern among people in areas related to diversity that their own efforts would be either reorganized "under" this person or not valued. A clear mandate for anyone assuming the CDO mantle is to bring together a coalition to empower and encourage cross-unit conversations. Building relationships, not restructuring, is probably a first order of business.

Capacities associated with successful leadership throughout the literature on diversity resonate with themes in the more general organizational literature. Successful leadership communicates a powerful and ennobling vision that also honors local autonomy, coalesces and energizes people throughout the institution, monitors progress toward real change and results, and supports a multiplicity of divergent efforts to build success. Nonaka (2005), writing in the context of the knowledge organization, adds that successful leaders draw people to them and have the ability to energize the emotional and spiritual resources of people. Cavaleri and Seivert (2005), also addressing the kind of leadership needed in a knowledge organization, emphasize balance between traditional data sources and pragmatic or intuitive knowledge that is gleaned from people. Note in these descriptions the important role of both nonrational and rational capacities.

Blackwell, Kwoh, and Pastor (2002) suggest that leadership for diversity, in particular, requires competencies in crossing borders and boundaries across sectors; building one's own ability to see multiple perspectives, especially multiracial and multiethnic perspectives; a commitment to justice for all; and a commitment to keep learning. Their work in cities demonstrates that in pluralistic communities, coalitions built on relevant and salient identity groups are important for building equity and capacity. All of these skills produce something vital to the future of diversity—resiliency in the organization (Gilmore, Hirschhorn, & Kelly, 1999; Wheatley, 2006). As we have seen, diversity requires substantive and deep change. Building capacity that will continue beyond the presence of any one person and that will also create capacity to survive setbacks is critical.

Ideally, then, leadership at all levels really matters. This is especially true, however, when the identity of the president or provost places this person in a token position. It is a delicate task to lead an institution when one's identity is in contrast to the historical identity of the institution (Aguirre & Martinez, 2007; Bush & Bridges, 2007; Evans & Chun, 2007). Most frequently today, this difference is in gender, race, class, or sexuality. Religion and nationality have also been relevant in this context. When the leader is in a token position, it is important to be mindful of the dynamics that can occur, although this does not often happen. The community has a strategic role in facilitating successful leadership (Bligh, Pillai, & Uhl-Bien, 2007).

Indeed, some emerging and sobering evidence suggests that communities from which the leader has come can add to the tension by asking for evidence that the individual is committed to diversity and has not "sold out." Aguirre and Martinez (2007) suggest that "diverse communities in higher education often expect more from diverse leadership in higher education than it can deliver" (p. 83). Leaders can hope that they are trusted and seen as committed to their own history even as they have to show that they are not committed *just* to that community. Finding the right balance is a challenge for leadership. It also requires that the community support and engage diversity efforts more vigorously, so that the person in the leadership position is not isolated from social and informational networks. This is not blind followership, but deeply engaged followership (Bligh, Pillai, & Uhl-Bien, 2007; Cavaleri & Seivert, 2005). Finding the right balance also requires that everyone understand that the complexity and multidimensionality of diversity will require engagement, and the recognition that there will be varying views and agendas within and among groups. The board plays a critical role as well in supporting the person and the campus in their efforts (Yoshino, 1999).

What becomes very clear in looking at diversity in leadership is that no matter how senior the leader, or who the leader is, leaders are always in the middle (Gilmore, 1997; Hill, Green, & Eckel, 2001). They are negotiating on behalf of the institution among many constituencies and among the stakeholders above (such as boards), those outside in the community (in government or foundations, for example), and those within the institution. For those committed to diversity, it is so easy to imagine that when a leader representing diversity is chosen, the path to change will be easy. However, although a deep commitment to diversity may be clear, the leader's path to success may be more challenging. While being in the middle is true of all leaders, people in token positions must negotiate the many challenges of being visible as a representative and invisible as an individual. Such persons are often heavily scrutinized, and mistakes that might be easily tolerated in others could be viewed as evidence of a fundamental mismatch or incompetence. With being a token comes stress, the threat of burnout, and the constant need to stay true to oneself while negotiating many competing demands.

Conflict and Difficult Dialogues

As many of the issues related to diversity have become more contentious around the world, learning how to deal with conflict and to craft solutions for the benefit of the campus is becoming more and more urgent. It does not happen easily. As described in chapter 6, programs that foster conflict resolution, mediation, and dialogues are emerging in communities as well as on college campuses. However, fostering difficult dialogues cannot be just the function of a program, or something centered on student learning. It is about the institution and how it deals with conflict (Sturm & Gadlin, 2007).

Creating an institutional culture in which difficult dialogues can be engaged well, with learning and respect, would go a long way toward building environments that many people would see as healthier and more productive than those that exist on many campuses today. Paradoxically, the imperative of building capacity for diversity creates an urgency concerning the improvement of core processes on campus that have needed improvement for a long time—including the ability to have difficult discussions and to have discussions across new and traditional academic boundaries.

Communication and Building Networks

Because of the complexity of institutions and the multidimensional nature of diversity, building institutional capacity to effectively communicate about diversity is emerging as important. Indeed, good communication is critical to any change strategy, as it is to any successful leader (Eckel, Green, & Hill, 2001). Diversity efforts live in departments, in schools, in administrative offices, in the cafeteria, and throughout the institution. Developing a credible and honest process for sharing information and challenges will become increasingly important. Because turnover is a normal part of institutional life and an issue in many change efforts, good communication provides a means of giving new members of the community an opportunity to catch up and jump in on current efforts, which facilitates the ability to sustain momentum beyond the work of any one individual (Clayton-Pedersen, Parker, Smith, Moreno, & Teraguchi, 2007; Eckel, Green, & Hill, 2001).

One of the important opportunities that diversity presents is the opportunity to broaden and deepen the participation of people who may have formerly been on the outside. This does not mean that everyone in an academic community will agree on any one effort. Nonetheless, as we have seen with technology and earlier in this chapter, a vision that provides an opportunity for people to see themselves in the future will be more effective than one that suggests that only some people matter. Perhaps one of our greatest failings in diversity thus far has been our lack of attention to clarifying what will need to change and what does not need to change—what will maintain the soul and standards of the institution and what will impede its improvement. For example, when a discussion takes place about admissions or persistence, high standards of excellence should be explicitly maintained as important, even as the standards by which excellence is judged necessarily become less exclusive and more equitable. By framing diversity in ways that suggest that multiplicity of identity matters, we include many people who can begin to see how their own future will be enriched by an institution that manifests diversity.

Good communication requires thinking through both the informal and the formal networks that are available. Any campus is full of information, both accurate and inaccurate, that gets shared. Facilitating the use of active networks can be powerful. Making sure the messages are clear and available is important. When I speak on campuses, I am often told that I am preaching to the choir; however, my instinct has been that unless we are clear about the diversity effort—framing it in ways that link to the mission of the campus and to excellence, and suggesting that serving diversity is actually moving the institution to a more vital and viable level—we will not serve our commitments to diversity as well as we might. Wheatley (2006) reinforces that notion when she writes, "From witnessing how networks can communicate around the world with information they deem essential, I've come to believe that 'preaching to the choir' is exactly the right thing to do. If I can help those who already share certain beliefs and dreams sing their song a little clearer, a little more confidently, I know they will take that song back to their networks. . . . We gain courage from learning we are part of a choir. We sing better when we know we are not alone" (pp. 151–152).

Because those engaged in diversity work on a campus are often not associated with traditional sources of power, this quotation takes on even greater significance. The stress, alienation, and anger that come with trying to create environments that are truly equitable, let alone simply trying to survive when one is in a token position, make Wheatley's description for a collaborative vision of networking very powerful. Another consequence of effective networking is that there will be greater shared ownership and implementation of solutions.

Concluding Thoughts

We know some of what must be done. Yet it is also clear that diversity requires more change and faster change. The reality, however, is that few of us have been in the truly diverse environments that we envision for colleges and universities— especially ones that work. As is the case with technology, we are building institutional capacity as we go. In the long term, we will need to be more articulate about what equity will look like in each of our institutions. But asking this question is a little like asking what health or institutional effectiveness looks like; illness and incompetence are much easier to identify. Similarly, inequity is clearer. Cultures that alienate rather than engage are more palpable. We are still at the place of overcoming the barriers to equity.

What *is* clear is that we need to create campuses in and for the twenty-first century that function well in a pluralistic society, that create the leadership for that society, that help engage the issues of that society, and, perhaps, that model what thriving, diverse communities look like. If not on our campuses, where? Do we have a better chance of creating those thriving communities in Los Angeles or New York than on our campuses? And if not now, when?

We can learn the hard way by watching what happens around the world and doing nothing locally. But higher education has an extraordinary opportunity—an imperative, especially given the increasing diversity of the society—to live up to its promise for learning, for research, and for the aspirations of a democratic community.

Adams, M. (2001). Core processes of racial identity development. In C. L. Wijeyesinghe & B. W. Jackson III (Eds.), *New perspectives on racial identity development: A theoretical and practical anthology* (pp. 209–243). New York: New York University Press.

Adams, V. H., Rand, K. L., Kahle, K., Snyder, C. R., Berg, C., King, E. A., et al. (2003). African Americans' hope and coping with racism stressors. In R. Jacoby & G. Keinan (Eds.), *Between stress and hope: From a disease-centered to a health-centered perspective* (pp. 235–249). New York: Greenwood.

Adelman, C. (2006). *The Toolbox revisited: Paths and degree completions from high school through college.* Washington, DC: U.S. Department of Education.

Adkins, G. Y. (2003). *Diversity beyond the numbers: Business vitality, ethics and identity in the 21st century.* Long Beach, CA: GDI Press.

Advisory Committee on Student Financial Assistance. (2006, September). *Mortgaging our future: How financial barriers to college undercut America's global competitiveness.* Washington, DC: Author.

Agars, M. D. (2004). Reconsidering the impact of gender stereotypes for the advancement of women in organizations. *Psychology of Women Quarterly, 28*(2), 103–111.

Aguirre, A. (1995). A Chicano farmworker in academe. In R. Padilla & R. Chavez (Eds.), *The leaning ivory tower: Latino professors in American universities* (pp. 17–28). Albany: State University of New York Press.

Aguirre, A. (2000). Women and minority faculty in the academic workplace: Recruitment, retention, and academic culture. *ASHE-ERIC Higher Education Report, 27*(6). San Francisco: Jossey-Bass.

Aguirre, A., Jr., & Martinez, R. O. (2007). Diversity leadership in higher education. *ASHE-ERIC Higher Education Report, 32*(3). San Francisco: Jossey-Bass.

Aguirre, F. P. (2005). Mendez v. Westminster School District: How it affected Brown v. Board of Education. *Journal of Hispanic Higher Education, 4*(4), 321–332.

Aldefer, C. P. (1992). Changing race relations embedded in organizations. In S. E. Jackson and associates (Eds.), *Diversity in the workplace: Human resources initiatives* (pp. 138–166). New York: Guilford Press.

Aleman, A. M. M., & Salkever, K. (2003). Mission, multiculturalism, and the liberal arts college: A qualitative investigation. *Journal of Higher Education, 74*(5), 563–596.

Alger, J. R. (2000). How to recruit and promote minority faculty: Start by playing fair. *Black Issues in Higher Education*, 17(20), 160–163.

Alger, J. R. (2005a, Fall). *As the workplace turns: Affirmative action in employment.* Unpublished paper, State University of New Jersey, Rutgers.

Alger, J. R. (2005b, October 24). *Building a diverse pipeline.* Unpublished paper, State University of New Jersey, Rutgers.

Ali, S. (2003). *Mixed-race, post-race: Gender, new ethnicities and cultural practices.* Oxford: Berg Publishers.

Allen, W. R. (1992). The color of success: African-American college student outcomes at predominantly white and historically black public colleges and universities. *Harvard Educational Review*, 62(1), 26–44.

Allen, W. R., Epps, E. G., & Haniff, N. Z. (Eds.). (1991). *College in black and white: African American students in predominantly White and in historically Black public universities.* Albany: State University of New York Press.

Allen, W., Epps, E., Suh, S., & Stassen, M. (2002). Outsiders within: Race, gender and faculty status in U.S. higher education. In W. A. Smith, P. G. Altbach, & K. Lomotey (Eds.), *The racial crisis in American higher education: Continuing challenges for the twenty-first century* (Rev. ed., pp. 189–220). Albany: State University of New York Press.

Allport, G. (1954). *The nature of prejudice.* Reading, MA: Addison-Wesley.

Alon, S., & Tienda, M. (2007). Diversity, opportunity and the shifting meritocracy in higher education. *American Sociological Review*, 72(4), 487–511.

Altbach, P. G., Berdahl, R. O., & Gumport, P. J. (Eds.). (2005). *American higher education in the twenty-first century: Social, political and economic challenges* (2nd ed.). Baltimore: Johns Hopkins University Press.

American Association of State Colleges and Universities/National Association of State Universities and Land-Grant Colleges Task Force on Diversity. (2005). *Now is the time: Meeting the challenge for a diverse academy.* New York: Author.

American Bar Association. (2006). *Visible invisibility: Women of color in law firms.* Retrieved September 21, 2006, from http://www.abanet.org.

American Council on Education. (2005). *College students today: A national portrait.* Washington, DC: Author.

American Council on Education. (2007). *The American college president.* Washington, DC: Author.

American Council on Education. (2008a). *Broadening the leadership spectrum: Advancing diversity in the American college presidency.* Washington, DC: Author.

American Council on Education. (2008b). *On the pathway to the presidency.* Washington, DC: Author.

American Council on Education, Center for Policy Analysis. (2006, February). *Missed opportunities revisited: New information on students who did not apply for financial aid* (ACE Issue Brief). Washington, DC: Author.

American Educational Research Association. (2006). Do the math: Cognitive demand makes a difference. *Research Points*, 4(2).

American Indian Higher Education Consortium, Institute for Higher Education Policy, & Sallie Mae Education Institute. (2000). *Creating role models for change: A survey of tribal college graduates.* Alexandria, VA: Author.

Anderson, E., & Kim, D. (2006). *Increasing the success of minority students in science and technology.* Washington, DC: American Council on Education.

Anderson, W. W., & Lee, R. G. (Eds.). (2005). *Displacements and diasporas: Asians in the Americas.* New Brunswick, NJ: Rutgers University Press.

Angelo, T. A., & Cross, K. P. (1993). *Classroom assessment techniques: A handbook for college teachers* (2nd ed.). San Francisco: Jossey-Bass.

Antonio, A. L. (2001a). Diversity and the influence of friendship groups in college. *Review of Higher Education, 25*(1), 63–89.

Antonio, A. L. (2001b). The role of interracial interaction in the development of leadership skills and cultural knowledge and understanding. *Research in Higher Education, 42*(5), 593–617.

Antonio, A. L. (2002). Faculty of color reconsidered. *Journal of Higher Education, 73*(5), 582–602.

Antonio, A. L. (2004). The influence of friendship groups on intellectual self-confidence and educational aspirations in college. *Journal of Higher Education, 75*(4), 446–471.

Antonio, A. L., Astin, H. S., & Cress, C. M. (2000). Community service in higher education: A look at the nation's faculty. *Review of Higher Education, 23*(4), 373–398.

Antonio, A. L., Change, M. J., Hakuta, K., Kenny, D., Levin, S., & Milem, J. (2004). Effects of racial diversity on complex thinking in college students. *Psychological Science, 15*(8), 507–510.

Anzaldúa, G. E. (2002, October 11). Beyond traditional notions of identity. *Chronicle of Higher Education, 49*(7), B11.

Argyris, C. (2005). Double loop learning in organizations: A theory of action perspective. In K. G. Smith & M. A. Hitt (Eds.), *Great minds in management: The process of theory development* (pp. 261–279). Oxford: Oxford University Press.

Argyris, C., & Schön, D. (1996). *Organizational learning II.* Reading, MA: Addison-Wesley.

Aronson, E., & Patnoe, S. (1997). *The jigsaw classroom.* New York: Longman.

Aronson, J. (2002). Stereotype threat: Contending and coping with unnerving expectations. In J. Aronson (Ed.), *Improving academic achievement: Impact of psychological factors on education* (pp. 279–301). San Diego, CA: Academic Press.

Asante, M. K., & Min, E. (Eds.). (2000). *Socio-cultural conflict between African American and Korean American.* Lanham, MD: University Press of America.

Astin, A. W. (1993a). Diversity and multiculturalism on the campus: How are students affected? *Change, 25,* 44–49.

Astin, A. W. (1993b). *What matters in college? Four critical years revisited.* San Francisco: Jossey-Bass.

Astin, A. W. (2002). Creating a bridge to the future: Preparing new faculty to face changing expectations in a shifting context. *Review of Higher Education, 26*(2), 119–144.

Astin, A. W., & Astin, H. S. (2000). *Leadership reconsidered: Engaging higher education in social change.* Battle Creek, MI: W. K. Kellogg Foundation.

Astin, A. W., & Oseguera, L. (2005). *Degree attainment rates at American colleges and universities* (Rev. ed.). Los Angeles: Higher Education Research Institute, University of California, Los Angeles.

Atkinson, R. C., & Pelfrey, P. A. (2006, November). *Opportunity in a democratic society: Race and economic status in higher education* (Research and Occasional Paper Series, CSHE.18.06). Berkeley: University of California, Berkeley, Center for Studies in Higher Education.

Baez, B. (2000). Diversity and its contradictions. *Academe, 86*(5), 43–47.

Baez, B. (2002, April 21–23). "Race" work and faculty of color: Changing the academy from within. *Conference Proceedings from the Keeping Our Faculties Conference* (pp. 47–51). St. Paul: University of Minnesota.

Baez, B. (2003). Outsiders within. *Academe, 89*(4), 41–45.

Banks, J. (1997). *Educating citizens in a multicultural society.* New York: Teachers College Press.

Barkan, E. (2000). *The guilt of nations: Restitution and negotiating historical injustices.* New York: Norton.

Barkan, E. (2005). History on the line: engaging history, managing conflict and reconciliation. *History Workshop Journal, 59*, 301–308.

Barnhardt, C. (1994). Life on the other side: Native student survival in a university world. *Peabody Journal of Education, 69*, 115–139.

Baugh, S. G., & Graen, G. B. (1997). Effects of team gender and racial composition on perceptions of team performance in cross-functional teams. *Group and Organizational Studies, 22*(3), 366–383.

Baum, R. (2006). *The rise and fall of the Caucasian race: A political history of racial identity.* New York: New York University Press.

Bauman, G. L. (2005). Promoting organizational learning in higher education to achieve equity in educational outcomes. In A. Kezar (Ed.), *Organizational learning in higher education* (New Directions for Higher Education, No. 131, pp. 23–35). San Francisco: Jossey-Bass.

Bauman, G. L., Bustillos, L. T., Bensimon, E. M., Brown, C. M. II, & Bartee, R. D. (2005). *Achieving equitable outcomes with all students: The institution's roles and responsibilities.* Washington, DC: Association of American Colleges and Universities.

Bean, D., & Stevens, G. (2003). *American newcomers and the dynamics of diversity.* New York: Russell Sage Foundation.

Beatty, A., Greenwood, M. R. C., & Linn, R. L. (Eds.). (1999). *Myths and tradeoffs: The role of tests in undergraduate admissions.* Washington, DC: National Research Council.

Beatty, J. E., & Kirby, S. L. (2006). Beyond the legal environment: How stigma influences invisible identity groups in the workplace. *Employee Responsibilities and Rights Journal, 18*(1), 29–44.

Beckham, E. F. (Ed.). (2000). *Diversity, democracy, and higher education: A view from three nations.* Washington, DC: Association of American Colleges and Universities.

Beckham, E. F. (Ed.). (2002). *Global collaborations: The role of higher education in diverse democracies (India, South Africa, the United States).* Washington, DC: Association of American Colleges and Universities.

Bell, D. (2004). *Silent covenants: Brown v. Board of Education and the unfulfilled hopes for racial reform.* Oxford: Oxford University Press.

Benjamin, L. (1997). *Black women in the academy: Promises and perils.* Gainesville: University Press of Florida.

Bennett, D. (Ed.). (1998). *Multicultural states: Rethinking difference and identity.* New York: Routledge.

Bennis, W. (1989). *On becoming a leader.* Reading, MA: Addison-Wesley.

Bensimon, E. M. (2004). The diversity scorecard: A learning approach to institutional change. *Change, 36*(1), 45–52.

Bensimon, E. M., Polkington, D. E., Bauman, G., & Vallejo, E. (2004). Doing research that makes a difference. *Journal of Higher Education, 75*(1), 104–126.

Berger, J. B. (2002). The influence of the organizational structures of colleges and universities on college student learning. *Peabody Journal of Education, 77*(3), 103–119.

Bertrand, M., & Mullainathan, S. (2004). Are Emily and Greg more employable than Lakisha and Jamal? A field experiment on labor market discrimination. *American Economic Review, 94*(4), 991–1014.

Beutel, A. M., & Nelson, D. J. (2005). Gender and race-ethnicity of faculty in top science and engineering research departments. *Journal of Women and Minorities in Science and Engineering, 11*, 389–403.

Beutel, A. M., & Nelson, D. J. (2006). Gender and race-ethnicity of faculty in top social science research departments. *Social Science Journal, 43*, 111–125.

Bikson, T. K. (1996). Educating a globally prepared workforce: New research on college and corporate perspectives. *Liberal Education, 82*(2), 12–19.

Bikson, T. K., & Law, S. A. (1994). *Global preparedness and human resources.* Santa Monica, CA: RAND Institute.

Blackwell, A. G., Kwoh, S., & Pastor, M. (2002). *Searching for the uncommon common ground: New dimensions on race in America.* New York: Norton.

Blake, J. H. (1985). Approaching minority students as assets. *Academe, 71*(6), 19–21.

Blake, J. H., & Moore, E. L. (2004). Retention and graduation of Black students: A comprehensive strategy. In I. M. Duranczyk, J. L. Higbee, & D. B. Lundell (Eds.), *Best practices for access and retention in higher education* (pp. 63–72). Minneapolis: Center for Research on Developmental Education and Urban Literacy, General College, University of Minnesota.

Blank, R. M. (2001). An overview of trends in social and economic well-being, by race. In N. J. Smelser, W. J. Wilson, & F. Mitchell (Eds.), *America becoming: Racial trends and their consequences,* Vol. 1 (National Research Council, Commission on Behavioral and Social Sciences and Education, pp. 21–39). Washington, DC: National Academy Press.

Blau, F. D., Brinton, M. C., & Grusky, D. B. (Eds.). (2006). *The declining significance of gender?* New York: Russell Sage Foundation.

Blau, P. M. (1977). *Inequality and heterogeneity: A primitive theory of social structure.* New York: Free Press.

Bligh, M., Pillai, R., & Uhl-Bien, M. (2007). The social construction of a legacy: Summarizing and extending follower-centered perspectives on leadership. In B. Shamir,

R. Pillai, M. Bligh, & M. Uhl-Bien (Eds.), *Follower-centered perspectives on leadership* (pp. 265–278). Greenwich, CT: Information Age.

Boisjoly, J., Duncan, G. J., Kremer, M., Levy, D. M., & Eccles, J. (2006). Empathy or antipathy? The impact of diversity. *American Economic Review*, 96(5), 1890–1905.

Bonsangue, M. V., & Drew, D. E. (1995). Increasing minority students' success in calculus. In J. Gainen & E. W. Williamson, *Fostering student success in quantitative gateway courses* (New Directions for Teaching and Learning, No. 61, pp. 23–33). San Francisco: Jossey-Bass.

Borrego, S. E. (2004). Class in the academy. *The Academic Workplace* (New England Resource Center for Higher Education), 15(2), 1–7.

Bowen, H. R., & Schuster, J. H. (1986). *American professors: A national resource imperiled*. Fair Lawn, NJ: Oxford University Press.

Bowen, W. G., & Bok, D. (1998). *The shape of the river: Long-term consequences of considering race in college and university admissions*. Princeton, NJ: Princeton University Press.

Bowen, W. G., Kurzweil, M. A., & Tobin, E. M. (2005). *Equity and excellence in American higher education*. Charlottesville: University of Virginia Press.

Bowen, W. G., & Sosa, J. A. (1989). *Prospects for faculty in the arts and sciences: A study of factors affecting demand and supply, 1987–2012*. Princeton, NJ: Princeton University Press.

Boxer, M. J. (2001). *When women ask the questions: Creating women's studies in America*. Baltimore: Johns Hopkins University Press.

Boyce, M. E. (2003). Organizational learning is essential to achieving and sustaining change in higher education. *Innovative Higher Education*, 28(2), 119–136.

Boyer, P. (1997). *Native American colleges: Progress and prospects*. Princeton, NJ: Carnegie Foundation for the Advancement of Teaching.

Brewer, M. B. (1996). When contact is not enough: Social identity and intergroup cooperation. *International Journal of Intercultural Relations*, 20, 291–303.

Brewer, M. B. (1997). The social psychology of intergroup relations: Can research inform practice? *Journal of Social Issues*, 53, 197–211.

Brewer, M. B. (2000). Reducing prejudice through cross-categorization: Effects of multiple social identities. In S. Oskamp (Ed.), *Reducing prejudice and discrimination* (pp. 165–184). Mahwah, NJ: Erlbaum.

Brewer, M. B., & Brown, R. J. (1998). Intergroup relations. In D. T. Gilbert & S. T. Fiske (Eds.), *The handbook of social psychology* (4th ed., Vol. 2, pp. 554–594). Boston: McGraw-Hill.

Bridges, B., Cambridge, B., Kuh, G. D., & Leegwater, L. H. (2005). Student engagement at minority-serving institutions: Emerging lessons from the BEAMS project. In G. H. Gaither (Ed.), *Minority retention: What works?* (New Directions for Institutional Research, No. 125, pp. 25–43). San Francisco: Jossey-Bass.

Brock, T., Jenkins, D., Ellwein, T., Miller, J., Gooden, S., Martin, K., MacGregor, C., & Pih, M. (2007). Building a culture of evidence for community college student success: Early progress in the Achieving the Dream Initiative. Retrieved June 14, 2007. http://www.mdrc.org/publications/452.html.

Brodkin, K. (2004). *How Jews became White folks and what that says about race in America* (Rev. ed.). New Brunswick, NJ: Rutgers University Press.

Bronstein, P., Rothblum, E. D., & Solomon, S. E. (1993). Ivy halls and glass walls: Barriers to academic careers for women and ethnic minorities. *New Directions for Teaching and Learning,* 53, 17–31.

Brown, H. A. (2006). *Graduate enrollment and degrees: 1986 to 2005.* Washington, DC: Council of Graduate Schools.

Brown, R. P., & Pinel, E. C. (2003). Stigma on my mind: Individual differences in the experience of stereotype threat. *Journal of Experimental Social Psychology,* 35, 626–633.

Brown, S. V. (1988). *Increasing minority faculty: An elusive goal.* Princeton, NJ: Princeton University Press.

Brown, W. (2006). *Regulating aversion: Tolerance in the age of identity and empire.* Princeton, NJ: Princeton University Press.

Burton, N. W., & Wang, M. (2005). *Predicting long-term success in graduate school: A collaborative validity study* (GRE Board Research report, 99–14R). Princeton, NJ: Educational Testing Service.

Busenberg, B. E., & Smith, D. G. (1997). Affirmative action and beyond: The woman's perspective. In M. García (Ed.), *Affirmative action's testament of hope: Strategies for a new era in higher education* (pp. 149–180). Albany: State University of New York.

Bush, V. B., & Bridges, B. K. (2007). *Keeping balance on a very thin line: African American presidents of predominantly-White institutions.* Unpublished manuscript.

Butler, J. E., & Walter, J. C. (1991). *Transforming the curriculum: Ethnic studies and women's studies.* Albany: State University of New York Press.

Caldwell-Colbert, A. T., et al. (1996). *How to recruit and hire ethnic minority faculty* (Commission on Ethnic Minority Recruitment, Retention, and training in Psychology, Workgroup on Faculty Recruitment and Retention). Washington, DC: American Psychological Association.

Cameron, K. (2005). Organizational effectiveness: Its demise and re-emergence through positive organizational psychology. In K. G. Smith & M. A. Hitt (Eds.), *Great minds in management: The process of theory development* (pp. 304–330). Oxford: Oxford University Press.

Campbell, M., & McClintock, C. (2002). Shall we dance? Program evaluation meets OD in the nonprofit sector. *OD Practitioner,* 34(4), 3–7.

Campbell, T. A., & Campbell, D. E. (1997). Faculty/student mentor program: Effects on academic performance and retention. *Research in Higher Education,* 38(6), 727–742.

Carey, K. (2005). *One step from the finish line: Higher college graduation rates are within our reach.* Washington, DC: The Education Trust.

Carnegie Foundation for the Advancement of Teaching. (1989). *Tribal colleges: Shaping the future of Native America.; a special report.* Lawrenceville, NJ: Princeton University Press.

Carnevale, A. P., & Rose, S. J. (2004). Socioeconomic status, race, and selective college admissions. In R. D. Kahlenberg (Ed.), *America's untapped resource: Low-income students in higher education* (pp. 101–156). New York: Century Foundation.

Carney, C. M. (1999). *Native American higher education in the United States.* New Brunswick, NJ: Transaction Publishers.

Carter, D. J., & O'Brien, E. M. (1993). *Employment and hiring patterns for faculty of color* (Research Briefs 4[6]). Washington, DC: Division of Policy Analysis and Research, American Council on Education.

Carter, R. (2008). *Multiplicity: The new science of personality, identity, and the self.* New York: Little, Brown.

Carver, M. R., Jr., & King, T. E. (1994). An empirical investigation of the MBA admission criteria for nontraditional programs. *Journal of Education for Business,* 70(2), 95–98.

Castellanos, J., & Jones, L. (Eds.). (2003). *The majority in the minority: Expanding the representation of Latina/o faculty, administrators, and students in higher education.* Sterling, VA: Stylus.

Catalyst. (2004). *The bottom line: Connecting corporate performance and gender diversity.* New York: Author.

Cavaleri, S., & Seivert, S. (2005). *Knowledge leadership.* Burlington, MA: Elsevier.

Ceci, S. J., & Williams, W. M. (Eds.). (2007). *Why aren't more women in science? Top researchers debate the evidence.* Washington, DC: American Psychological Association.

Champagne, D. (2005). Rethinking native relations with contemporary nation states. In D. Champagne, K. J. Torjesen, & S. Steiner (Eds.), *Indigenous people and the modern state* (pp. 3–23). Walnut Creek, CA: Alta Vista Press.

Champagne, D., Torjesen, K. J., & Steiner, S. (Eds.). (2005). *Indigenous people and the modern state.* Walnut Creek, CA: Alta Vista Press.

Chan, T. W., & Goldthorpe, J. H. (2007). Class and status: The conceptual distinction and the empirical evidence. *American Sociological Review,* 72(4), 512–533.

Chang, M. J. (1999). Does racial diversity matter? The educational impact of a racially diverse undergraduate population. *Journal of College Student Development,* 40, 377–395.

Chang, M. J., Astin, A. W., & Kim, D. (2004). Cross-racial interaction among undergraduates: Some causes and consequences. *Research in Higher Education,* 45(5), 527–551.

Chang, M. J., & DeAngelo, L. (2002). Going Greek: The effects of racial composition on white students' participation patterns. *Journal of College Student Development,* 43(6), 809–823.

Chang, M. J., Denson, N., Saenz, V., & Misa, K. (2006). The educational benefits of sustaining cross-racial interaction among undergraduates. *Journal of Higher Education,* 77(3), 431–455.

Chang, M. J., & Kiang, P. N. (2002). New challenges of representing Asian American students in U.S. higher education. In W. A. Smith, P. G. Altbach, & K. Lomotey (Eds.), *The racial crisis in American higher education: Continuing challenges for the twenty-first century* (Rev. ed., pp. 137–158). Albany: State University of New York Press.

Chang, M. J., Park, J. J., Lin, M. H., Poon, O. A., & Nakanishi, D. T. (2007). *Beyond myths: The growth and diversity of Asian American college freshmen, 1971–2005.* Los Angeles: Higher Education Research Institute.

Chang, M. J., Witt, D., Jones, J., & Hakuta, K. (Eds.). (1999). *Compelling interest: Examining the evidence on racial dynamics in higher education.; a report of the AERA Panel on Racial Dynamics in Colleges and Universities.* Stanford, CA: Center for Comparative Studies in Race and Ethnicity, Stanford University.

Chapa, J. (2006). Preparing a future professoriate to successfully teach California's and the nation's Latino and African American students. In P. Gándara, C. Horn, & G. Orfield (Eds.), *Expanding opportunities in higher education* (pp. 243–264). New York: State University of New York Press.

Cheng, D. X., & Zhao, C. (2006). Cultivating multicultural competence through active participation, multicultural activities, and multicultural learning. *NASPA Journal,* 43(4), 13–38.

Chesler, M., Lewis, A., & Crowfoot, J. (2005). *Challenging racism in higher education: Promoting justice.* Oxford: Rowman & Littlefield.

Chin, J. L. (Ed.). (2000). *Relationships among Asian American women.* Washington, DC: American Psychological Association.

Chubin, D. E., & Malcolm, S. M. (2006). The new backlash on campus. *College and University Journal,* 81(4), 67–70.

Clair, J. A., Beatty, J. E., & MacLean, T. L. (2005). Out of sight but not out of mind: Managing invisible social identities in the workplace. *Academy of Management Review,* 30(1), 78–95.

Clayton-Pedersen, A. R., Parker, S., Smith, D. G., Moreno, J. F., & Teraguchi, D. H. (2007). *Making a real difference with diversity: A guide to institutional change.* Washington, DC: Association of American Colleges and Universities.

Clery, S., & Solórzano, B. (2006, November/December). Developmental math students and college-level coursework. *Data Notes* (Achieving the Dream, Lumina Foundation).

Cloete, N., Cross, M., Muller, J., & Pillay, S. (1999). Culture, identity and the role of higher education in building democracy in South Africa. In M. Cross, N. Cloete, E. F. Beckham, A. Harper, J. Indiresan, & C. M. Musil (Eds.), *Diversity and unity: The role of higher education in building democracy* (pp. 20–48). Cape Town, South Africa: Maskew Miller Longman.

Cloete, N., Muller, J., Makgoba, M. W., & Ekong, D. (Eds.). (1997). *Knowledge, identity, and curriculum transformation in South Africa.* Cape Town, South Africa: Maskew Miller Longman.

Cloke, K. (2006). *The crossroads of conflict.* Calgary, Alberta: Janis Publications.

Clotfelter, C. T., Ehrenberg, R. G., Getz, M., & Siegfried, J. J. (Eds.). (1991). *Economic challenges in higher education.* Chicago: University of Chicago Press.

Cohen, G. L., & Steele, C. M. (2002). A barrier of mistrust: How negative stereotypes affect cross-race mentoring. In J. Aronson (Ed.), *Improving academic achievement:*

Impact of psychological factors on education (pp. 303–327). San Diego, CA: Academic Press.

Cohen, L. L., & Swim, J. K. (1995). The differential impact of gender ratios on women and men: Tokenism, self-confidence, and expectations. *Personality and Social Psychology Bulletin*, 21(9), 876–884.

Cole, D. (2007). Do interracial interactions matter? An examination of student-faculty contact and intellectual self-concept. *Journal of Higher Education*, 78(3), 249–281.

Cole, D. G., Bennett, C., Thompson, J. (2003). Teacher education in a collaborative multicultural classroom: Implications for critical-mass-minority and all-minority classes at a predominantly White institution. *Journal of Classroom Interaction*, 38(1), 17–28.

Cole, J. B., & Guy-Sheftall, B. (2003). *Gender talk: The struggle for women's equality in African American communities*. New York: One World Books.

Cole, S. J., & Barber, E. (2003). *Increasing faculty diversity: The occupational choices of high-achieving minority students*. Cambridge, MA: Harvard University Press.

Colella, A. (2001). Coworker distributive fairness judgments of the workplace accommodation of employees with disabilities. *Academy of Management Review*, 26, 100–116.

College Board. (1997, June). Common sense about SAT score differentials and test validity. *Research Notes* (RN-01).

Collins, J. (2005). *Good to great and the social sectors: Why business thinking is not the answer*. Boulder, CO: Jim Collins.

Collins, P. H. (1990). *Black feminist thought: Knowledge, consciousness, and the politics of empowerment*. New York: Routledge.

Collins, P. H. (2000). Toward a new vision: Race, class and gender as categories of analysis and connection. In M. Adams et al. (Eds.), *Readings for diversity and social justice* (pp. 457–462). New York: Routledge.

Collins, R. W., & Johnson, J. A. (1990). One institution's success in increasing the number of minority faculty: A provost's perspective. *Peabody Journal of Education*, 66(1), 71–76.

Colquitt, J. A., Greenberg, J., & Scott, B. (2005). Organizational justice: Where do we stand? In J. Greenberg & J. A. Colquitt (Eds.), *Handbook of organizational justice* (pp. 589–619). Mahwah, NJ: Erlbaum.

Combs, G. M. (2002). Meeting the leadership challenge of a diverse and pluralistic workplace: Implications of self-efficacy for diversity training. *Journal of Leadership and Organizational Studies*, 8(4), 1–16.

Committee on National Statistics. (2004). *Measuring racial discrimination* (Report brief, Division of Behavioral and Social Sciences and Education). Washington, DC: National Academies Press.

Congressional Commission on the Advancement of Women and Minorities in Science, Engineering and Technology Development. (2000). *Land of plenty: Diversity as America's competitive edge in science, engineering and technology*. Washington, DC: National Science Foundation.

Conley, D. (1999). *Being Black, being in the red: Race, wealth and social policy in America*. Berkeley, CA: University of California Press.

Connolly, P. M. (2007). *Deeper capacity building for greater impact* (James Irvine Foundation briefing paper). San Francisco: James Irvine Foundation.

Cook, B. J., & Córdova, D. L. (2006). *Minorities in higher education: Twenty-second annual status report*. Washington, DC: American Council on Education.

Cooper, J. E., & Stevens, D. D. (Eds.). (2002). *Tenure in the sacred grove: Issues and strategies for women and minority faculty*. Albany: State University of New York Press.

Cornell, S., & Hartmann, D. (1998). *Ethnicity and race: Making identities in a changing world*. Thousand Oaks, CA: Pine Forge Press.

Cortés, C. (2002). *The making and remaking of a multiculturalist*. New York: Teachers College Press.

Cox, T. H., Jr. (1993). *Cultural diversity in organizations: Theory, research, and practice*. San Francisco: Berrett-Koehler.

Cox, T. H., Jr. (2001). *Creating the multicultural organization: A strategy for capturing the power of diversity*. San Francisco: Jossey-Bass.

Cox, T. H., Jr., & Blake, S. (1991). Managing cultural diversity: Implications for organizational competitiveness. *Academy of Management Executive*, 5, 45–56.

Cox, T. H., Jr., Lobel, S. A., & McLeod, P. L. (1991). Effects of ethnic group cultural differences on cooperative and competitive behavior on a group task. *Academy of Management Journal*, 34, 827–847.

Crisp, R. J., & Hewstone, M. (2007). Multiple social categorization. In M. P. Sanna (Ed.), *Advances in experimental social psychology* (Vol. 39, pp. 163–254). Orlando, FL: Academic Press.

Crisp, R. J., Hewstone, M., & Rubin, M. (2001). Does multiple categorization reduce intergroup bias? *Personality and Social Psychology Bulletin*, 27(1), 76–89.

Crisp, R. J., Stone, C. H., & Hall, N. R. (2006). Categorization and subgroup identification: Predicting and preventing threats from common ingroups. *Personality and Social Psychology Bulletin*, 32(2), 230–243.

Crisp, R. J., Walsh, J., & Hewstone, M. (2006). Crossed categorization in common ingroup contexts. *Personality and Social Psychology Bulletin*, 32(9), 1204–1218.

Crocker, J., & Garcia, J. A. (2006). Stigma and the social basis of the self: A synthesis. In S. Levin & C. van Laar (Eds.), *Stigma and group inequality* (pp. 287–308). Mahwah, NJ: Erlbaum.

Crocker, J., Major, B., & Steele, C. M. (1998). Social stigma. In D. T. Gilbert, S. T. Fiske, & G. Linzey (Eds.), *Handbook of Social Psychology* (4th ed., pp. 504–553). Boston: McGraw-Hill.

Cross, M., Cloete, N., Beckham, E. F., Harper, A., Indiresan, J., & Musil, C. M. (Eds.). (1999). *Diversity and unity: The role of higher education in building democracy*. Cape Town, South Africa: Maskew Miller Longman.

Cross, M., Mikwanazi-Twala, Z., & Klein, G. (Eds.). (1998). *Dealing with diversity in South African education*. Kenwyn, South Africa: Juta.

Cross, T. (1994). Black faculty at Harvard: Does the pipeline defense hold water? *Journal of Blacks in Higher Education*, 4, 42–46.

Croteau, J. M., & Kusek, M. T. (1992). Gay and lesbian speaker panels: Implementation and research. *Journal of Counseling and Development*, 70, 396–401.

Crouse, J., & Trusheim, D. (1998). *The case against the SAT*. Chicago: University of Chicago Press.

Crutcher, R. A. (2006, Summer). Spiraling the glass ceiling: Seven critical lessons for negotiating a leadership position in higher education. *Liberal Education*, 92(3), 14.

Cummings, J. N. (2004). Work groups, structural diversity and knowledge sharing in a global organization. *Management Science*, 50(3), 352–364.

Cuyjet, M. J. (2006). African American college men. In M. Cuyjet and associates, *African American men in college* (pp. 3–23). San Francisco: Jossey-Bass.

Dale, R. (2004). Comments on chapters 9 and 10. In A. H. Eagly, R. M. Baron, & V. L. Hamilton (Eds.), *The social psychology of group identity and social conflict: Theory, application, and practice* (pp. 189–192). Washington, DC: American Psychological Association.

Dalton, S. (1976). A decline in the predictive validity of the SAT and high school achievement. *Educational and Psychological Measurement*, 36, 445–448.

Darder, A. (1991). *Culture and power in the classroom: A critical foundation for bicultural education*. New York: Bergin & Garvey.

Darder, A., & Torres, R. D. (2003). Shattering the "race" lens: Toward a critical theory of racism. In A. Darder, M. Baltodano, & R. D. Torres (Eds.), *The critical pedagogy reader* (pp. 245–263). New York: Routledge.

Dar-Nimrod, I., & Heine, S. J. (2006). Exposure to scientific theories affects women's math performance. *Science*, 314, 435.

Davies, P. G., Spencer, S. J., Quinn, D. M., & Gerhardstein, R. (2002). Consuming images: How television commercials that elicit stereotype threat can restrain women academically and professionally. *Personality and Social Psychology Bulletin*, 28, 1615–1628.

Davis, L. R. (2002). Racial diversity in higher education: Ingredients for success and failure. *Journal of Applied Behavioral Science*, 38(2), 137–155.

Dayton, B., Gonzalez-Vasquez, N., Martinez, C. R., & Plum, C. (2004). Hispanic-serving institutions through the eyes of students and administrators. In A. M. Ortiz (Ed.), *Addressing the unique needs of Latino American students*. (New Directions for Student Services, No. 80, pp. 31–41). San Francisco: Jossey-Bass.

Deitch, E. A., Barsky, A., Butz, R. A., Chan, S., Brief, A. P., & Bradley, J. C. (2003). Workplace discrimination and race. *Human Relations*, 56(11), 1299–1324.

de la Luz Reyes, M., & Halcon, J. J. (1991). Practices of the academy: Barriers to access for Chicano academics. In P. G. Altbach & K. Lomotey (Eds.), *The racial crisis in American higher education* (pp. 167–186). Albany: State University of New York Press.

Delgado, R., Stefancic, J., & Lindsley, J. N. (2000). Symposium: Race and the law at the turn of the century; California's racial history and constitutional rationales for race-conscious decision making in higher education. *UCLA Law Review*, 47, 1521.

Delgado-Romero, E. A., Manlove, A. N., Manlove, J. D., & Hernandez, C. A. (2007).

Controversial issues in the recruitment and retention of Latino/a faculty. *Journal of Hispanic Higher Education,* 6(1), 34–51.

Devine, P. G., & Elliot, A. J. (1995). Are racial stereotypes really fading? The Princeton Trilogy revisited. *Personality and Social Psychology Bulletin,* 21(11), 1139–1150.

DiversityInc. (2003). *The business case for diversity* (4th ed.). New Brunswick, NJ: Allegiant Media.

DiversityInc. (2006). *The business case for diversity* (5th ed.). New Brunswick, NJ: Allegiant Media.

Dixon, J., Durrheim, K., & Tredoux, C. (2005). Beyond the optimal contact theory. *American Psychologist,* 60(7), 697–711.

Dobbin, F., & Kalev, A. (2007). The architecture of inclusion: Evidence from corporate diversity programs. *Harvard Journal of Law and Gender,* 30, 279–301.

Donovan, M. S., Bransford, J. D., & Pelligrino, J. W. (Eds.). (1999). *How people learn: Bridging research and practice.* Washington, DC: National Academies Press.

Douglass, J. A. (2007). *The conditions for admission: Access, equity, and the social contract of public universities.* Stanford, CA: Stanford University Press.

Douglass, J. A., Roebken, H., & Thomson, G. (2007). *The immigrant university: Assessing the dynamics of race, major, and socioeconomic characteristics at the University of California* (Research and Occasional Paper Series, CSHE.19.07). Berkeley: University of California, Berkeley, Center for Studies in Higher Education.

Dovidio, J. F., Gaertner, S. L., Isen, A. M., & Lowrance, R. (1995). Group representations and intergroup bias: Positive affect, similarity, and group size. *Personality and Social Psychology Bulletin,* 21(8), 856–865.

Dovidio, J. F., Gaertner, S. L., & Validzic, A. (1998). Intergroup bias: Status, differentiation, and a common in-group identity. *Journal of Personality and Social Psychology,* 75(1), 109–120.

Dovidio, J. F., Kawakami, K., & Gaertner, S. L. (2000). Reducing contemporary prejudice: Combating explicit and implicit bias at the individual and intergroup level. In S. Oskamp (Ed.), *Reducing prejudice and discrimination* (pp. 137–164). Mahwah, NJ: Erlbaum.

Dowd, A. C. (2005). *Data don't drive: Building a practitioner-driven culture of inquiry to assess community college performance.* Indianapolis, IN: Lumina Foundation.

Dowd, A. C. (2007). Community colleges as gateways and gatekeepers: Moving beyond the access "saga" toward outcome equity. *Harvard Educational Review,* 77(4), 407–418.

Drew, D. (1996). *Aptitude revisited: Rethinking math and science education for America's next century.* Baltimore: Johns Hopkins University Press.

Drewry, H. N., & Doermann, H. (2001). *Stand and prosper: Private Black colleges and their students.* Princeton, NJ: Princeton University Press.

Drucker, P. F. (1993). *Post-capitalist society.* New York: Harper.

Dudziak, M. L. (2000). *Cold war civil rights: Race and the image of American democracy.* Princeton, NJ: Princeton University Press.

Duran, R. P. (1986). Prediction of Hispanics' college achievement. In M. Olivas (Ed.), *Latino college students* (pp. 221–245). New York: Teachers College Press.

Duster, T. (1992). *The diversity project: Final report.* Berkeley: University of California, Berkeley, Institute for the Study of Social Change.

Dweck, C. S. (2000). *Self theories: Their role in motivation, personality, and development.* Philadelphia: Psychology Press.

Dweck, C. S. (2007). Is math a gift? Beliefs that put females at risk. In S. J. Ceci & W. M. Williams (Eds.), *Why aren't more women in science? Top researchers debate the evidence* (pp. 47–56). Washington, DC: American Psychological Association.

Eagly, A. H., Baron, R. M., & Hamilton, V. L. (Eds.). (2004). *The social psychology of group identity and social conflict.* Washington, DC: American Psychological Association.

Eckel, P., Green, M., & Hill, B. (2001). *On change V—Riding the waves of change: Insights from transforming institutions.* Washington, DC: American Council on Education.

Eckel, P., Hill, B., Green, M., & Mallon, B. (1999). *On change—Reports from the road: Insights on institutional change.* Washington, DC: American Council on Education.

Ehrenberg, R. G., & Rothstein, D. S. (1994). Do historically Black institutions of higher education confer unique advantages on Black students? In R. G. Ehrenberg (Ed.), *Choices and consequences: Contemporary policy issues in education* (pp. 89–137). Ithaca, NY: ILR Press.

Eisenhardt, K., Kahwajy, J., & Bourgeois, L. (1997). Conflict and strategic choice: How top management teams disagree. *California Management Review, 39,* 42–62.

Eisenmann, L. (2006). *Higher education for women in postwar America, 1945–1965.* Baltimore: Johns Hopkins University Press.

Elliott, J. R., & Smith, R. A. (2004). Race, gender and workplace power. *American Sociological Review, 69*(3), 365–386.

Ellwood, D. T., & Kane, T. J. (2000). Who is getting a college education? Family background and the growing gaps in enrollment. In S. Danziger & J. Waldfogel (Eds.), *Securing the future: Investing in children from birth to college* (pp. 283–324). New York: Russell Sage Foundation.

Ely, R. (1994). The effects of organizational demographics and social identity on relationships among professional women. *Administrative Science Quarterly, 39,* 203–238.

Ely, R. J., & Thomas, D. A. (2001). Cultural diversity at work: The effects of diversity perspectives on work group processes and outcomes. *Administrative Science Quarterly, 46*(2), 229–273.

Engberg, M. E. (2004). Improving intergroup relations in higher education: A critical examination of the influence of educational interventions on racial bias. *Review of Educational Research, 74*(4), 473–524.

Ensher, E. A., & Murphy, S. E. (2005). *Power mentoring: How successful mentors and proteges get the most out of their relationships.* San Francisco: Jossey-Bass.

Erikson, E. H. (1997). *The life cycle completed.* New York: Norton.

Eschbach, K. (1993). Changes in self-identification of American Indians and Alaska Natives. *Demography, 30,* 635–652.

Espiritu, Y. L. (1997). *Asian American women and men.* Thousand Oaks, CA: Sage.

Evans, A., & Chun, E. B. (2007). *Are the walls really down? Behavioral and organiza-*

tional barriers to faculty and staff (ASHE Higher Education Report, Vol. 33, No. 1). San Francisco: Jossey-Bass.

Fagenson, E. A. (1993). Is what's good for the goose also good for the gander? On being white and male in a diverse workforce. *Academy of Management Executive, 7*(4), 80–82.

Falk, D., & Aitken, L. P. (1984). Promoting retention among American Indian college students. *Journal of American Indian Education, 23*, 24–31.

Farley, R., & Haaga, J. (Eds.). (2005). *The American people: Census 2000.* New York: Russell Sage Foundation.

Feagin, J. R. (2006). *Systemic racism: A theory of oppression.* New York: Routledge.

Feagin, J. R., & McKinney, K. (2003). *The many costs of racism.* Lanham, MD: Rowman & Littlefield.

Feng, Y. (2003). *Democracy, governance, and economic performance.* Boston: MIT Press.

Ferdman, B. M. (1997). Values about fairness in an ethnically diverse workplace. *Business and the Contemporary World, 9*, 191–208.

Ferdman, B. M., & Gallegos, P. I. (2001). Racial identity development and Latinos in the United States. In C. L. Wijeyesinghe & B. W. Jackson III (Eds.), *New perspectives on racial identity development: A theoretical and practical anthology* (pp. 32–66). New York: New York University Press.

Fitzgerald, B. K. (2006). Lowering barriers to college access: Opportunities for more effective coordination of state and federal student aid policies. In P. Gándara, C. Horn, & G. Orfield (Eds.), *Expanding opportunities in higher education* (pp. 53–74). New York: State University of New York Press.

Fitzgerald, B. K., & Delaney, J. A. (2002). Educational opportunity in America. In D. E. Heller (Ed.), *Condition of access: Higher education for lower income students* (pp. 3–24). Washington, DC: American Council on Education.

Fleming, J. (1984). *Blacks in college: A comparative study of students' success in Black and White institutions.* San Francisco: Jossey-Bass.

Fleming, J., & Manning, C. (1998). Correlates of the SAT in minority engineering students: An exploratory study. *Journal of Higher Education, 69*(1), 91–108.

Florida, R. (2006). The flight of the new creative class. *Liberal Education, 92*(3), 22–29.

Florida, R., Gates, G., Knudsen, B., & Stolarick, K. (2006). *The university and the creative economy.* Retrieved August 18, 2006, from http://www.creativeclass.com/richard_florida.

Ford Foundation. (2005a). *Difficult dialogues: Promoting pluralism and academic freedom on campus* (A Letter from Higher Education Leaders and Susan Beresford to College and University Presidents). Retrieved June 20, 2005, from http://ford found.org/news/more/dialogues/05_difficult_dialogues_letter.pdf.

Ford Foundation. (2005b). *Ford Foundation "Difficult Dialogues Initiative" grantee profiles.* Retrieved July 7, 2007, from http://fordfound.org/news/more/dialogues/05_difficult_dialogues_profiles.pdf.

Forman, T. (2003). The social-psychological costs of racial segmentation in the workplace: A study of African Americans' well-being. *Journal of Health and Social Behavior, 44*(3), 332–352.

Fox, M. J. T., Lowe, S. C., & McClellan, G. (Eds.). (2005). *Serving Native American students* (New Directions for Student Services, No. 109). San Francisco: Jossey-Bass.

Frable, D. E. S. (1997). Gender, racial, ethnic, sexual, and class identities. *Annual Review of Psychology*, 48, 139–162.

Frankenberg, R. (1993). *White women, race matters: The social construction of Whiteness*. Minneapolis: University of Minnesota Press.

Freeman, C. E. (2004). *Trends in education equity of girls and women: 2004* (NCES 2005–016). Washington, DC: U.S. Department of Education, Institute of Education Sciences.

Frey, W. H. (1999). Immigration and demographic balkanization: Toward one America or two? In J. W. Hughes & J. J. Seneca (Eds.), *America's demographic tapestry: Baseline for the new millennium* (pp. 78–100). New Brunswick, NJ: Rutgers University Press.

Friday, S. S., Moss, S. E., & Friday, E. (2004). Socioethnic explanations for racial and ethnic differences in job satisfaction. *Journal of Management Development*, 23(2), 152–168.

Fried, J. (1995). *Shifting paradigms for student affairs: culture, context, teaching, and learning*. Alexandria, VA: American College Personnel Association.

Friedkin, N. E. (2004). Social cohesion. *Annual Review of Sociology*, 30, 409–425.

Friedman, T. L. (2005). *The world is flat: A brief history of the twenty-first century*. New York: Farrar, Straus & Giroux.

Friedman, V. J., Lipshitz, R., & Overmeer, W. (2001). Creating conditions for organizational learning. In A. Antal, M. Dierkes, J. Child, & I. Nonaka (Eds.), *Handbook of organizational learning and knowledge* (pp. 757–774). Oxford: Oxford University Press.

Frierson, H. T., Jr. (1990). The situation of black educational researchers. *Educational Researcher*, 19(2), 12–17.

Fries-Britt, S., & Turner, B. (2002). Uneven stories: Successful Black collegians at a black and a white campus. *Review of Higher Education*, 25(3), 315–330.

Gaertner, S. L., Dovidio, J. F., Nier, J. A., Ward, C. M., & Banker, B. S. (1999). Across cultural divides: The value of superordinate identity. In D. A. Prentice & D. T. Miller (Eds.), *Cultural divides: Understanding and overcoming group conflict* (pp. 173–212). New York: Russell Sage Foundation.

Gainen, J., & Boice, R. (Eds.). (1993). *Building a diverse faculty*. San Francisco: Jossey-Bass.

Gallacher, J., & Osborne, M. (2005). *A contested landscape: International perspectives on diversity in mass higher education*. Leicester, UK: National Institute of Adult Continuing Education.

Gándara, P. (1999). Staying in the race: The challenges for Chicanos/as in higher education. In J. F. Moreno (Ed.), *The elusive quest for equality: 150 years of Chicano/Chicana education* (pp. 169–196). Cambridge, MA: Harvard Educational Review.

Gándara, P., & Contreras, F. (2009). *The Latino education crisis: The consequences of failed social policy*. Cambridge, MA: Harvard University Press.

Gándara, P., Orfield, G., & Horn, C. C. (Eds.). (2006). *Expanding opportunity in higher education: Leveraging promise.* Albany: State University of New York Press.

García, E. (2002). *Student cultural diversity: Understanding and meeting the challenge* (3rd ed.). Boston: Houghton Mifflin.

Garcia, H. (2007). [A content analysis of diversity in higher education journals]. Unpublished raw data.

García, M. (Ed.). (2000). *Succeeding in an academic career: A guide for faculty of color.* Westport, CT: Greenwood Press.

García, M. (2007). Seeing through the eyes of difference: The strength of women's multicultural alliances. *On Campus with Women, 36*(1), 1–3. Retrieved June 20, 2007, from http://www.aacu.org/ocww/volume35_1/.

García, M., Hudgins, C. A., Musil, C. M., Nettles, M. T., & Sedlacek, W. E. (2001). *Assessing campus diversity initiatives.* Washington, DC: Association of American Colleges and Universities.

Gardenswartz, L., & Rowe, A. (2003). *Diverse teams at work: Capitalizing on the power of diversity.* Alexandria, VA: Society for Human Resource Management.

Gardner, H. (1983). *Frames of mind: The theory of multiple intelligences.* New York: Basic Books.

Gardner, H., Csikszentmihalyi, M., & Damon, W. (2001). *Good work: When excellence and ethics meet.* New York: Basic Books.

Garibaldi, A., Dawson, H. G., Jr., & English, R. A. (2001). The continuing and expanding role of historically Black colleges and universities in an era of affirmative action and diversity in higher education. In B. Lindsay & M. J. Justiz (Eds.), *The quest for equity in higher education* (pp. 183–208). Albany: State University of New York Press.

Garvin, D. A., & Roberto, M. A. (2001, September). What you don't know about making decisions. *Harvard Business Review,* pp. 108–116.

Garza, H. (1988). The barrioization of Hispanic faculty. *Educational Record, 68*(4), 122–124.

Garza, H. (1992). Academic power, discourse, and legitimacy: Minority scholars in U.S. universities. In M. Romero & C. Candelaria (Eds.), *Community empowerment and Chicano scholarship. Selected Proceedings from the 1989 NACCS 17th Annual Conference* (pp. 35–52). San Jose, CA: National Association for Chicana and Chicano Studies.

Garza, H. (1993). Second class academics: Chicano/Latino faculty in U.S. universities. In J. Gainen & R. Boice (Eds.), *Building a diverse faculty.* San Francisco: Jossey-Bass.

Gasman, M. (2007). *Envisioning black colleges: A history of the United Negro College Fund.* Baltimore: Johns Hopkins University Press.

Geasler, M. J., Croteau, J. M., Heineman, C. J., & Edlund, C. J. (1995). A qualitative study of students' expression of change after attending panel presentations by lesbian, gay, and bisexual speakers. *Journal of College Student Development, 36,* 483–492.

Geiser, S., & Santelices, M. V. (2006). The role of advanced placement and honors courses in college admissions. In P. Gándara, C. Horn, & G. Orfield (Eds.), *Expanding opportunities in higher education* (pp. 75–114). New York: State University of New York Press.

Geiser, S., & Santelices, M. V. (2007). *Validity of high-school grades in predicting student success beyond the freshman year: High-school record vs. standardized tests as indicators of four-year college outcomes* (Research & Occasional Paper Series, CSHE.6.07). Berkeley: University of California, Berkeley, Center for Studies in Higher Education.

Gerstle, G., & Mollenkopf, J. (Eds.). (2001). *E pluribus unum: Contemporary and historical perspectives in immigrant political incorporation.* New York: Russell Sage Foundation.

Gilmore, T. N. (1997). *Leaders as middles.* Philadelphia: Center for Applied Research.

Gilmore, T. N., Hirschhorn, L., & Kelly, M. (1999). *Challenges of leading and planning in higher education.* Philadelphia: Center for Applied Research.

Giroux, H. A. (1998). The politics of national identity and the pedagogy of multiculturalism in the USA. In D. Bennett (Ed.), *Multicultural states: Rethinking difference and identity* (pp. 178–194). New York: Routledge.

Glaeser, E. L., Laibon, D., Scheinkman, J. A., & Soutter, C. L. (1999). *What is social capital? The determinants of trust and trustworthiness* (Working paper 7216). Cambridge, MA: National Bureau of Economic Research.

Goffman, E. (1963). *Stigma: Notes on the management of spoiled identity.* Englewood Cliffs, NJ: Prentice-Hall.

Goldberg, E. L., & Alliger, G. M. (1992). Assessing the validity of the GRE for students in psychology: A validity generalization approach. *Educational and Psychological Measurement, 52*(4), 1019–1027.

Golde, C., & Walker, G. E. (Eds.). (2006). *Envisioning the future of doctoral education: Preparing stewards of the discipline.* San Francisco: Jossey-Bass.

Goldin, C., Katz, L. F., & Kuziemko, I. (2006). The homecoming of the American college women: The reversal of the college gender gap. *Journal of Economic Perspectives, 20*(4), 133–156.

Goldman, C. A., & Massy, W. F. (2001). *The PhD factory.* Boston: Anker.

Goleman, D. (2005). *Emotional intelligence: Why it matters more than IQ* (10th anniversary ed.). New York: Bantam.

Goleman, D. (2006). *Social intelligence: The new science of human relationships.* New York: Bantam.

Gomez, M. N. (2006). Inquiry, respect and dissent. *Academe, 92*(4), 55–57.

Gonzalez, A. (2006). *The racial manipulation of Asian Americans and the discourse of denial of success.* Unpublished manuscript, Claremont Graduate University.

González, C., & Gándara, P. (2005). Why we like to call ourselves Latinas. *Journal of Hispanic Higher Education, 4*(4), 392–398.

Goodman, D. J. (2001). *Promoting diversity and social justice: Educating people from privileged groups.* Thousand Oaks, CA: Sage.

Gough, H. G., & Hall, W. B. (1975). The prediction of academic and clinical performance in medical school. *Research in Higher Education, 3*, 301–314.

Graduate Employees and Students Organization. (2005). *The (Un)changing face of the Ivy League.* Retrieved March 20, 2005, from http://www.yaleunions.org/geso/geso_reports.html.

Greenberg, J., & Colquitt, J. A. (Eds.). (2005). *Handbook of organizational justice.* Mahwah, NJ: Erlbaum.

Greene, M. (2003). In search of a critical pedagogy. In A. Darder, M. Baltodano, & R. D. Torres (Eds.), *The critical pedagogy reader* (pp. 97–114). New York: Routledge.

Gregory, S. T. (2001). Black faculty women in the academy: History, status and future. *Journal of Negro Education,* 70(3), 124–138.

Greisdorf, K. E. (2001). An honest conversation on race, reconciliation, and responsibility: Hope in the cities. In D. L. Schoem & S. Hurtado (Eds.), *Intergroup dialogue: Deliberative democracy in school, college, community, and workplace* (pp. 151–165). Ann Arbor: University of Michigan.

Gruenfeld, D. H., Thomas-Hunt, M., & Kim, P. (1998). Cognitive flexibility, communication strategy, and integrative complexity in groups: Public vs. private reactions to majority and minority status. *Journal of Experimental Social Psychology,* 34, 202–206.

Grutter v. Bollinger, 539 U.S. 306 (2003).

Guarasci, R., Cornwell, G. H., & associates (Eds.). (1997). *Democratic education in an age of difference.* San Francisco: Jossey-Bass.

Gudeman, R. H. (2000). College missions, faculty teaching, and student outcomes in a context of low diversity. In *Does diversity make a difference? Three research studies on diversity in college classrooms* (pp. 37–60). Washington, DC: American Council on Education and American Association of University Professors. Available at http://www.acenet.edu/about/programs/access&equity/omhe/diversity-report /home.html.

Guinier, L., Fine, M., & Balin, J. (1997). *Becoming gentlemen: Women, law and institutional change.* Boston: Beacon Press.

Guinier, L., & Torres, G. (2002). *The miner's canary: Enlisting race, resisting power, transforming democracy.* Cambridge, MA: Harvard University Press.

Gupta, A. (2006, June). *Affirmative action in higher education in India and the US: A study in contrasts* (Research and Occasional Paper Series, CSHE.10.06). Berkeley: University of California, Berkeley, Center for Studies in Higher Education.

Gurin, P. (1999a). Expert report of Patricia Gurin. In Gratz et al. v. Bollinger et al., *The compelling need for diversity in higher education,* No. 97–75231 (E.D. Mich.), and Grutter et al. v. Bollinger et al., No. 97–75928 (E.D. Mich.). Ann Arbor: University of Michigan. Available at http://www.umich.edu/~newsinfo/Admission/Expert /gurintoc.html.

Gurin, P. (1999b). New research on the benefits of diversity in college and beyond: An empirical analysis. *Diversity Digest,* 3(3). Available at http://www.inform.umd .edu/DiversityWeb/Digest.

Gurin, P., Dey, E., Hurtado, S., & Gurin, G. (2002). Diversity and higher education: Theory and impact on educational outcomes. *Harvard Educational Review,* 72, 330–366.

Gurin, P., Peng, T., Lopez, G., & Nagda, B. R. (1999). Context, identity, and intergroup relations. In D. Prentice & D. Miller (Eds.), *Cultural divides: The social psychology of intergroup contact* (pp. 133–170). New York: Russell Sage Foundation.

Gutman, A. (2003). *Identity in democracy*. Princeton, NJ: Princeton University Press.

Gutman, A., & Thompson, D. (2004). *Why deliberative democracy?* Princeton, NJ: Princeton University Press.

Hagedorn, L. S. (Ed.). (2000). *What contributes to job satisfaction among faculty and staff?* San Francisco: Jossey-Bass.

A half century of progress of Black students in medical schools. (2000–2001, Winter). *Journal of Blacks in Higher Education*, 30, 28–31.

Hall, M. L., & Allen, W. R. (1989). Race consciousness among African-American college students. In G. L. Berry & J. K. Asamen (Eds.), *Black students: Psychosocial issues and academic achievement* (pp. 172–197). Newbury Park, CA: Sage.

Hall, S. (1996). New ethnicities. In S. Hall, D. Morely, & K. Chen (Eds.), *Stuart Hall: Critical dialogues in cultural studies* (pp. 441–449). New York: Routledge.

Harding, A. (2005, November 7). Disability is not a handicap. *The Scientist.* Retrieved March 16, 2009, from http://www.the-scientist.com/2005/11/07/s22/1.

Harding, S. (1986). *The science question in feminism*. Ithaca, NY: Cornell University Press.

Harlow, R. (2003). Race doesn't matter, but: The effect of race on professors' experiences and emotion management in the undergraduate classroom. *Social Psychology Quarterly*, 66(4), 348–363.

Harper, S. (2006). *Black male students at public flagship universities in the U.S.: Status, trends, and implications for policy and practice*. Washington, DC: Joint Center for Political and Economic Studies.

Harris, L. M. (2006). (Re)writing the history of race at Emory. *Academe*, 92(4), 31–34.

Harrison, D. A., Price, K. H., & Bell, M. P. (1998). Beyond relational demography: Time and the effects of surface- and deep-level diversity on work group cohesion. *Academy of Management Journal*, 41, 96–107.

Hartenian, L. S., & Gudmundson, D. E. (2000). Cultural diversity in small business: Implications for firm performance. *Journal of Developmental Entrepreneurship*, 5(3), 209–219.

Hartman, A. (2006). Language as oppression. In C. Hartman (Ed.), *Poverty and race in America* (pp. 29–37). Lanham, MD: Lexington Books.

Harvey, W. B., & Anderson, E. L. (2005). *Minorities in higher education: Twenty-first annual status report*, 2003–4. Washington, DC: American Council on Education.

Harvey, W. B., & Scott-Jones, D. (1985). We can't find any: The elusiveness of Black faculty members in American higher education. *Issues in Education*, 3, 68–76.

Hawley, W. D., & Jackson, A. W. (Eds.). (1995). *Toward a common destiny: Improving race and ethnic relations in America*. San Francisco: Jossey-Bass.

Haycock, K. (2006, August). *Promise abandoned: How policy choices and institutional practices restrict college opportunities*. The Education Trust.

Hayles, R. (2003, May). *Why proactively seek diversity?* Cultural Diversity at Work Online.com. Retrieved July 15, 2007, from http://www.diversitycentral.com.

Hayles, R., & Russell, A. M. (1997). *The diversity directive*. New York: McGraw-Hill.

HeavyRunner, I., & DeCelles, R. (2002). Family education model: Meeting the student retention challenge. *Journal of American Indian Education*, 41(2), 29–37.

Hehir, T. (2005). *New directions in special education: Eliminating ableism in policy and practice.* Cambridge, MA: Harvard Education Press.

Heifetz, R. (1994). *Leadership without easy answers.* Cambridge, MA: Harvard University Press.

Heller, D. E. (Ed.). (2002). *Condition of access: Higher education for lower income students.* Washington, DC: American Council on Education.

Helms, J. E. (2006). Fairness is not validity or cultural bias in racial-group assessment: A quantitative perspective. *American Psychologist, 61*(8), 845–859.

Herbst, S., & Malaney, G. D. (1999). Perceived value of a special interest residential program for gay, lesbian, bisexual, and transgender students. *NASPA Journal, 36,* 106–119.

Herek, G. M., & Capitanio, J. P. (1996). "Some of my best friends": Intergroup contact, concealable stigma, and heterosexuals' attitudes toward gay men and lesbians. *Personality and Social Psychology Bulletin, 22,* 412–424.

Hernandez, G., & Visher, M. (2001). *Creating a culture of inquiry: A James Irvine Foundation report.* San Francisco: James Irvine Foundation.

Herring, C. (2006). *Does diversity pay? Racial composition of firms and the business case for diversity.* Unpublished manuscript, University of Illinois at Chicago and Institute of Government and Public Affairs, University of Illinois.

Hersch, J. (2007). *Profiling the new immigrant worker: The effects of skin color and height.* Unpublished manuscript, Vanderbilt University, Nashville, TN.

Hersh, R. H., & Merrow, J. (Eds.). (2005). *Declining by degrees: Higher education at risk.* New York: Palgrave Macmillan.

Hewstone, M. (1994). Revision and change of stereotypic beliefs: In search of the elusive subtyping model. In W. Stroebe & M. Hewstone (Eds.), *European Review of Social Psychology, 5*(1), 69–109.

Hewstone, M., Rubin, M., & Willis, H. (2002). Intergroup bias. *Annual Review of Psychology, 53*(1), 575–604.

Higginbotham, E. (1993). Sociology and the multicultural curriculum: The challenges of the 1990s and beyond. *Race, Sex, and Class, 1,* 13–24.

High-ranking colleges and universities show little progress in increasing their enrollments of low-income students. (2006, Autumn). *Journal of Blacks in Higher Education, 53,* 50–58.

Hill, B., Green, M., & Eckel, P. (2001). *On Change IV—What governing boards need to know about institutional change.* Washington, DC: American Council on Education.

Hirschhorn, L., & May, L. (2000). The campaign approach to change: Targeting the university's scarcest resources. *Change, 32*(3), 30–37.

Hispanics and the future of America. (2006). In M. Tienda & F. Mitchell (Eds.), *Panel on Hispanics in the United States* (National Research Council, Committee on Population, Division of Behavioral and Social Sciences and Education). Washington, DC: National Academies Press.

Holland, D., Lachicotte, Q., Jr., Skinner, D., & Cain, C. (1998). *Identity and agency in cultural worlds.* Cambridge, MA: Harvard University Press.

Hollinger, D. A. (1995). *Postethnic America: Beyond multiculturalism*. New York: Basic Books.

Holzer, H. J., & Neumark, D. (2006). Affirmative action: What do we do now? *Journal of Policy Analysis and Management*, 25(2), 463–490.

hooks, b. (2000). *Where we stand: Class matters*. New York: Routledge.

hooks, b. (2003). Reflections on race and sex. In A. Darder, M. Baltodano, & R. D. Torres (Eds.), *The critical pedagogy reader* (pp. 238–245). New York: Routledge.

Hopkins, N. (2006). Diversification of a university faculty: Observations on hiring women faculty in the Schools of Science and Engineering at MIT. *MIT Faculty Newsletter*, 18(4). Retrieved March 14, 2009, from http://web.mit.edu/fnl/volume/184.html.

Horn, L., & Bobbitt, L. (1999). *Students with disabilities in postsecondary education: A profile of preparation, participation and outcomes* (NCES 1999-187). Washington, DC: U.S. Department of Education, National Center for Education Statistics.

Hornsey, M. J., & Hogg, M. A. (2000). Subgroup relations: A comparison of mutual intergroup differentiation and common ingroup identity models of prejudice reduction. *Personality and Social Psychology Bulletin*, 26, 242–256.

Horse, P. G. (2001). Reflections on American Indian identity. In C. L. Wijeyesinghe & B. W. Jackson III (Eds.), *New perspectives on racial identity development: A theoretical and practical anthology* (pp. 91–107). New York: New York University Press.

House, J. D. (1989). Age bias in prediction of graduate grade point average from Graduate Record Examination scores. *Educational and Psychological Measurement*, 49, 663–666.

Hrabowski, F. A. III, Maton, K. I., Greene, M. L., & Greif, G. L. (2002). *Overcoming the odds: Raising academically successful African American young women*. Oxford: Oxford University Press.

Hrabowski, F. A. III, Maton, K. I., & Greif, G. L. (1998). *Beating the odds: Raising academically successful African American males*. Oxford: Oxford University Press.

Hubbard, D. (2006). The color of our classroom, the color of our future. *Academe*, 92(6), 27–29.

Hubbard, E. (Ed.). (1998). *Best practices in institutional planning for diversity*. Boulder, CO: Western Interstate Commission on Higher Education (WICHE).

Huber, J., & Form, W. (1973). *Income and ideology*. New York: Free Press.

Hu-DeHart, E. (1994). PC and the politics of multiculturalism. In S. Gregory & R. Sanjek (Eds.), *Race* (pp. 243–256). New Brunswick, NJ: Rutgers University Press.

Hu-DeHart, E. (1995). Ethnic studies in U.S. higher education: History, development and goals. In J. A. Banks (Ed.), *Handbook of research on multicultural education* (pp. 696–707). New York: Macmillan.

Hughes, J. W., & Seneca, J. J. (Eds.). (1999). *America's demographic tapestry: Baseline for the new millennium*. New Brunswick, NJ: Rutgers University Press.

Hull, G. T., Scott, P. B., & Smith, B. (Eds.). 1982. *All the women are white, all the Blacks are men, but some of us are brave: Black women's studies*. Old Westbury, NY: Feminist Press.

Humphreys, D. (1997). *General education and American commitments: A national re-*

port on diversity courses and requirements. Washington, DC: Association of American Colleges and Universities.

Hune, S. (1995). Opening the American mind and body: The role of Asian American studies. In D. T. Nakanishi & T. Y. Nishida (Eds.), *The Asian American educational experience.* New York: Routledge.

Hune, S. (2002). Demographics and diversity of Asian American college students. In M. K. McEwen, C. M. Kodama, A. N. Alvarez, S. Lee, & C. T. H. Liang (Eds.), *Working with Asian American College Students* (New Directions for Student Services, No. 97, pp. 11–20). San Francisco: Jossey-Bass.

Hune, S. (2003). Through "our eyes": Asian Pacific Islander American women's history. In S. Hune & G. M. Nomura (Eds.), *Asian Pacific Islander American Women* (pp. 1–12). New York: New York University Press.

Hune, S., & Chan, K. S. (1997). Special focus: Asian Pacific American demographic and educational trends. In D. J. Carter & R. Wilson (Eds.), *15th Annual Status Report on Minorities in Higher Education* (pp. 39–63). Washington, DC: American Council on Education.

Hurtado, A. (1996). *The color of privilege.* Ann Arbor: University of Michigan Press.

Hurtado, S. (1992). The campus racial climate: Contexts for conflict. *Journal of Higher Education, 63*(5), 539–568.

Hurtado, S. (1994a). Graduate school racial climates and academic self-concept among minority graduate students in the 1970s. *American Journal of Education, 102,* 330–351.

Hurtado, S. (1994b). The institutional climate for talented Latino students. *Research in Higher Education, 35,* 21–41.

Hurtado, S. (1996). How diversity affects teaching and learning: A climate of inclusion has a positive effect on learning outcomes. *Educational Record, 66,* 27–29.

Hurtado, S. (2000). Linking diversity with educational purpose: How diversity impacts the educational environment and student development. In G. Orfield (Ed.), *Diversity challenged: Legal crisis and new evidence.* Cambridge, MA: Harvard Education Publishing Group.

Hurtado, S. (2001a). Linking diversity and educational purpose: How diversity affects the classroom environment and student development. In G. Orfield & M. Kurlaender (Eds.), *Diversity challenged: Evidence on the impact of affirmative action* (pp. 187–203). Cambridge, MA: Harvard Education Publishing Group.

Hurtado, S. (2001b). Research and evaluation on intergroup dialogue. In D. L. Schoem & S. Hurtado (Eds.), *Intergroup dialogue: Deliberative democracy in school, college, community, and workplace* (pp. 22–38). Ann Arbor: University of Michigan.

Hurtado, S. (2002). Creating a climate of inclusion: Understanding Latina/o college students. In W. A. Smith, P. G. Altbach, & K. Lomotey (Eds.), *The racial crisis in American higher education: Continuing challenges for the twenty-first century* (Rev. ed., pp. 121–136). Albany: State University of New York Press.

Hurtado, S. (2006). Linking diversity with the educational and civic missions of higher education. *Review of Higher Education, 30*(2), 185–196.

Hurtado, S., & Carter, D. F. (1997). Effects of college transition and perceptions of the campus racial climate on Latino college students' sense of belonging. *Sociology of Education*, 70, 324–345.

Hurtado, S., Carter, D. F., & Spuler, A. (1996). Latino student transition to college: Assessing difficulties and factors in successful college adjustment. *Research in Higher Education*, 37(2), 135–157.

Hurtado, S., Milem, J. F., Clayton-Pedersen, A. R., & Allen, W. R. (1998). Enhancing campus climates for racial/ethnic diversity: Educational policy and practice. *Review of Higher Education*, 21, 279–302.

Ibarra, R. A. (2000). *Beyond affirmative action: Reframing the context of higher education*. Madison: University of Wisconsin Press.

Ibarra, R. A. (2003). Latina/o faculty and the tenure process in cultural context. In J. Castellanos & L. Jones (Eds.), *The majority in the minority: Expanding the representation of Latina/o faculty, administrators, and students in higher education* (pp. 207–219). Sterling, VA: Stylus.

Institute for Higher Education Policy. (2007). *College access for the working poor: Overcoming barriers to succeed in higher education*. Washington, DC: Author.

Institute of Medicine of the National Academies. (2004). *In the nation's compelling interest: Ensuring diversity in the health-care workforce*. Washington, DC: National Academies Press.

Inzlicht, M., & Ben-Zeev, T. (2000). A threatening intellectual environment: Why females are susceptible to experiencing problem-solving deficits in the presence of males. *Psychological Science*, 11, 365–371.

Inzlicht, M., & Good, C. (2006). How environments can threaten academic performance, self-knowledge, and sense of belonging. In S. Levin & C. van Laar (Eds.), *Stigma and group inequality* (pp. 129–150). Mahwah, NJ: Erlbaum.

Iwata, K. (2004). *The power of diversity: 5 essential competencies for leading a diverse workforce*. Petaluma, CA: Global Insights Publishing.

Jacobs, L. R., & Skocpol, T. (Eds.). (2005). *Inequality and American democracy: What we know and what we need to learn*. New York: Russell Sage Foundation.

Jacobson, J. F. L. (2006). Hiring practices of African American males. *Teachers College Record*, 108(2), 316–338.

Jaeger, D. A., & Page, M. E. (1996). Degrees matter: New evidence on sheepskin effects in returns to education. *Review of Economic Statistics*, 78, 733–740.

Jayne, M. E. A., & Dipboye, R. L. (2004). Leveraging diversity to improve business performance: Research findings and recommendation for organizations. *Human Resource Management*, 43(4), 409–424.

Johnson, A. G. (2001). *Privilege, power, and difference*. Boston: McGraw-Hill.

Johnson, D. W., & Johnson, R. T. (1987). The three C's of reducing prejudice and discrimination. In S. Oskamp & S. Spacapan (Eds.), *Interpersonal processes: Claremont symposium on applied social psychology* (pp. 239–268). Newbury Park, CA: Sage.

Johnsrud, L. K., & Rosser, V. (2002). Faculty members' morale and their intention to leave: A multicultural explanation. *Journal of Higher Education*, 73(4), 518–542.

Johnsrud, L. K., & Sadao, K. C. (1998). The common experience of "otherness": Ethnic and racial minority faculty. *Review of Higher Education*, 21(4), 315–342.

Johnston, W. B., & Packer, A. H. (1987). *Workforce 2000: Work and workers for the 21st century*. Indianapolis, IN: Hudson Institute.

Johnstone, B. (2005). Financing higher education: Who should pay? In P. G. Altbach, R. O. Berdahl, & P. J. Gumport (Eds.), *American higher education in the twenty-first century: Social, political and economic challenges* (2nd ed., pp. 369–392). Baltimore: Johns Hopkins University Press.

Jones, T., & Young, G. S. A. (1997). Classroom dynamics: Disclosing the hidden curriculum. In A. I. Morey & M. K. Kitano (Eds.), *Multicultural course transformation in higher education: A broader truth* (pp. 89–103). Boston: Allyn & Bacon.

Jordan, D. (2006). *Sisters in science*. West Lafayette, IN: Purdue University Press.

Judy, R. W., & D'Amico, C. (1999). *Workforce 2020: Work and workers in the 21st century*. Indianapolis, IN: Hudson Institute.

Kahlenberg, R. D. (Ed.). (2004). *America's untapped resource: Low-income students in higher education*. New York: Century Foundation Press.

Kalbfleisch, P. J., & Davies, A. B. (1991). Minorities and mentoring: Managing the multicultural institution. *Communication Education, 40*, 266–271.

Kanter, R. M. (1977). Some effects of proportions on group life: Skewed sex ratios and responses to token women. *American Journal of Sociology, 5*, 965–990.

Katznelson, I. 2005. *When affirmative action was white: An untold history of racial inequality in twentieth-century America*. New York: Norton.

Kendall, F. E. (2006). *Understanding white privilege: Creating pathways to authentic relationships across race*. New York: Routledge.

Kessler, R. C., Mickelson, K. D., & Williams, D. R. (1999). The prevalence, distribution, and mental health correlates of perceived discrimination in the United States. *Journal of Health and Social Behavior, 40*(3), 208.

Kezar, A. (Ed.). (2005, Fall). *Organizational learning in higher education* (New Directions for Higher Education, No. 131). San Francisco: Jossey-Bass.

Kezar, A. (2007). Tools for time and place: Phased leadership strategies to institutionalize diversity. *Review of Higher Education, 30*(4), 413–440.

Kezar, A., & Eckel, P. D. (2002a). The effect of institutional culture on change strategies in higher education. *Journal of Higher Education, 73*(4), 435–460.

Kezar, A., & Eckel, P. D. (2002b). Examining the institutional transformation process: The importance of sensemaking, interrelated strategies, and balance. *Research in Higher Education, 43*(3), 295–328.

Kezar, A., & Eckel, P. D. (2005). *Leadership strategies for advancing campus diversity: Advice from experienced presidents*. Washington, DC: American Council on Education.

Kilian, C. M., Hukai, D., & McCarty, C. E. (2005). Building diversity in the pipeline to corporate leadership. *Journal of Management Development, 24*(2), 155–168.

Kimmel, M. (2000). *"What about the boys?" What the current debates tell us, and don't tell us about boys in school*. Paper, sixth annual gender-equity conference, January 12, 2000. Wellesley, MA: Wellesley College, Center for Research on Women.

King, J. (2006). *Gender equity in higher education: 2006*. Washington, DC: American Council on Education, Center for Policy Analysis.

Kirkman, B. L., Tesluk, P. E., & Rosen, B. (2004). The impact of demographic heterogeneity and team leader–team member demographic fit on team empowerment and effectiveness. *Group and Organization Management,* 29(3), 334–368.

Kirsch, I., Braun, H., Yamamoto, K., & Sum, A. (2007). *America's perfect storm: Three forces changing our nation's future.* Princeton, NJ: Educational Testing Service.

Klitgaard, R. (1985). *Choosing elites.* New York: Basic Books.

Knapp, L. G., Kelly-Reid, J. E., Ginder, S. A., & Miler, E. (2008). *Enrollment in postsecondary education institutions, fall, 2006 and graduation rates, 2000 and 2003 cohorts; financial statistics, fiscal year 2006* (NCES 2008-173). Washington, DC: U.S. Department of Education, National Center for Education Statistics.

Knefelkamp, L., & Schneider, C. (1997). Education for a world lived in common with others. In R. Orrill (Ed.), *Education and democracy: Re-imagining liberal learning in America* (pp. 327–344). New York: College Board.

Knowles, M., & Harleston, B. (1997). *Achieving diversity in the professoriate: challenges and opportunities.* Washington, DC: American Council on Education.

Koch, J. (2002). Coping with feelings of fraudulence. In J. Cooper & D. D. Stevens (Eds.), *Tenure in the sacred grove: Issues and strategies for women and minority faculty* (pp. 107–117). Albany: State University of New York Press.

Kochan, T., Bezruka, K., Ely, R., Jackson, S., Joshi, A., & Jehn, K., et al. (2003). The effects of diversity on business performance: Report of the Diversity Research Network. *Human Resources Management,* 42(1), 3–21.

Konrad, A. (2003). Defining the domain of workplace diversity scholarship. *Group and Organizational Management,* 28(1), 4–17.

Konrad, A. M., & Gutek, B. (1987). Theory and research on group composition: Applications to the status of women and ethnic minorities. In S. Oskamp & S. Spacapan (Eds.), *Interpersonal processes: Claremont symposium on applied social psychology* (pp. 85–121). Newbury Park, CA: Sage.

Kramer, V., Konrad, A., & Erkut, S. (2006). *Critical mass on corporate boards: Why three or more women enhance governance* (Report no. 781 283-2510). Wellesley, MA: Wellesley Centers for Women.

Krieger, N., Rowly, D., Herman, A., Avery, B., & Phillips, M. (1993). Racism, sexism, and social class: Implications for studies of health, disease, and well-being. *American Journal of Preventative Medicine,* 9, 82–122.

Krueger, A., Rothstein, J., & Turner, S. (2006). *Race, income, and college in 25 years* (Research and Occasional Paper Series, CSHE.19.06). Berkeley: University of California, Berkeley, Center for Studies in Higher Education.

Kuh, G. D. (1993). In their own words: What students learn outside the classroom. *American Educational Research Journal,* 30(2), 277–304.

Kuh, G. D. (2003). What we're learning about student engagement from NSSE: Benchmarks for effective educational practice. *Change,* 35(2), 24–32.

Kuh, G. D., & Hu, S. (2001). The effects of student-faculty interaction in the 1990s. *Review of Higher Education,* 24(3), 309–332.

Kuh, G. D., Kinzie, J., Buckley, J. A., Bridges, B. K., & Hayek, J. C. (2006, July). *What matters to student success: A review of the literature.* National Postsecondary Education Cooperative.

Kuh, G. D., Kinzie, J., Buckley, J. A., Bridges, B. K., & Hayek, J. C. (2007). *Piecing together the student success puzzle* (ASHE Higher Education Report, 3[5]). San Francisco: Jossey-Bass.

Kuh, G. D., Kinzie, J., Schuh, J. H., Whitt, E. J., & associates. (2005). *Student success in college: Creating conditions that matter.* San Francisco: Jossey-Bass.

Kuh, G. D., Nelson Laird, T. F., & Umbach, P. D. (2004). Aligning faculty activities and student behavior: Realizing the promise of greater expectations. *Liberal Education, 90*(4), 24–31.

Kuh, G. D., Schuh, J. H., & Whitt, E. J. (1991). *Involving colleges.* San Francisco: Jossey-Bass.

Kulis, S., Chong, Y., & Shaw, H. (1999). Discriminatory organizational contexts and Black scientists on postsecondary faculties. *Research in Higher Education, 40*(2), 115–148.

Kulis, S., & Shaw, H. (1996). Racial segregation among postsecondary workers. *Social Forces, 75*(2), 575–591.

Ladson-Billings, G. (2006). From the achievement gap to the education debt: Understanding achievement in U.S. schools. *Educational Researcher, 35*(7), 3–12.

La Duke, W. (2005). *Recovering the sacred: The power of naming and claiming.* Cambridge, MA: South End Press.

Laird, T. F. N. (2005). College student experiences with diversity and their effects on academic self-confidence, social agency, and disposition toward critical thinking. *Research in Higher Education, 46*(4), 365–387.

Laird, T. F. N., Engberg, M. E., & Hurtado, S. (2005). Modeling accentuation effects: Enrollment in a diversity course and the importance of social action engagement. *Journal of Higher Education, 76*(4), 448–476.

Lakoff, G., & Johnson, M. (2003). *Metaphors we live by.* Chicago: University of Chicago Press.

Langer, E. (1997). *The power of mindful learning.* Cambridge, MA: Da Capo Press.

Langhout, R. D., Rosselli, F., & Feinstein, J. (2006). Assessing classism in academic settings. *Review of Higher Education, 30*(2), 145–184.

Lardner, J., & Smith, D. A. (Eds.). (2005). *Inequality matters: The growing economic divide in America and its poisonous consequences.* New York: New Press.

Lawler, A. (1999). Scientific community: Tenured women battle to make it less lonely at the top. *Science, 286*(5443), 1272–1278.

Lawry, S., Laurison, D., & Van Antwerpen, J. (2006). *Liberal education and civic engagement.* New York: Ford Foundation.

Layer, G. (Ed.). (2005). *Closing the equity gap: The impact of widening participation strategies in the UK and USA.* Leicester, UK: National Institute of Adult Continuing Education.

Lederach, J. P. (1997). *Building peace.* Washington, DC: U.S. Institute of Peace Press.

Lee, J., & Bean, F. D. (2004). America's changing color lines: Immigration, race/ethnicity and multiracial identification. *Annual Review of Sociology, 30*, 221–242.

Lee, S. J. (1996). *Unraveling the "model minority" stereotype: Listening to Asian American youth.* New York: Teachers College Press.

Levin, S. (2003). Social psychological evidence on race and racism. In M. J. Chang, D. Witt, J. Jones, & K. Hakuta (Eds.), *Compelling interest: Examining the evidence on racial dynamics in colleges and universities* (pp. 97–125). Stanford, CA: Stanford University Press.

Levin, S., & van Laar, C. (Eds.). (2006). *Stigma and group inequality*. Mahwah, NJ: Erlbaum.

Levin, S., van Laar, C., & Foote, W. (2006). Ethnic segregation and perceived discrimination in college: Mutual influences and effects on social and academic life. *Journal of Applied Social Psychology, 36*(6), 1471–1501.

Levin, S., van Laar, C., & Sidanius, J. (2003). The effects of ingroup and outgroup friendships on ethnic attitudes in college: A longitudinal study. *Group Processes and Intergroup Relations, 6*(1), 76–92.

Levinson, S. (2003). *Wrestling with diversity*. Durham, NC: Duke University Press.

Lewin, K. (1951). *Field theory in social sciences*. New York: Harper & Row.

Light, P. (1994). Diversity in the faculty "not like us": Moving barriers to minority recruitment. *Journal of Policy Analysis and Management, 13*(1), 163–186.

Lindsay, B. (2001). Forging new university initiatives in the twenty-first century: Women executives and equity. In B. Lindsay & M. J. Justiz (Eds.), *The quest for equity in higher education* (pp. 229–256). Albany: State University of New York.

Lipman-Blumen, J. (1998). Connective leadership: What business needs to learn from academe. *Change, 30*(1), 49–53.

Lipset, S. M. (1959). Some social requisites of democracy: Economic development and political legitimacy. *American Political Science Review, 53*, 69–105.

Loden, M., & Rosener, J. B. (1991). *Workforce America: Managing employee diversity as a vital resource*. Homewood, IL: Business One Irwin.

Lopez, G., Gurin, P., & Nagda, B. R. (1998). Education and understanding structural causes of group inequalities. *Political Psychology, 19*, 305–329.

López, I. F. H. (1996). *White by law: The legal construction of race*. New York: New York University Press.

Lott, J. T. (1998). *Asian Americans: From racial categories to multiple identities*. Walnut Creek, CA: Alta Mira Press.

Lowe, E. Y., Jr. (Ed.). (1999). *Promise and dilemma: Perspectives on racial diversity and higher education* (pp. 135–142). Princeton, NJ: Princeton University Press.

Lowman, R. P., & Spuck, D. W. (1975). Predictors of college success for the disadvantaged Mexican-American. *Journal of College Student Personnel, 16*(1), 40–48.

Luna de la Rosa, M. (2005). *Making a difference: Diverse college faculty and factors influencing student engagement*. Unpublished dissertation, Claremont Graduate University, Claremont, CA.

Luna de la Rosa, M., & Tierney, W. G. (2006). *Breaking through the barriers to college*. Los Angeles: University of Southern California, Center for Higher Education Policy Analysis.

MacDonald, V., Botti, J. M., & Clark, L. H. (2007). From visibility to autonomy: Latinos in higher education in the U.S., 1965–2005. *Harvard Educational Review, 77*(4), 474–504.

MacDonald, V., & García, T. (2003). Historical perspectives on Latino access to higher education. In J. Castellanos & L. Jones (Eds.), *The majority in the minority: Expanding the representation of Latina/o faculty, administrators, and students in higher education* (pp. 15–43). Sterling, VA: Stylus.

Macedo, D., & Gounari, P. (Eds.). (2006). *The globalization of racism.* Boulder, CO: Paradigm Publishers.

MacLachlan, A. (2006). *Developing graduate students of color for the professoriate in science, technology, engineering and mathematics (STEM)* (Research and Occasional Paper Series, CSHE.6.06). Berkeley: University of California, Berkeley, Center for Studies in Higher Education.

Maher, F. A., & Tetrault, M. K. T. (2007). *Privilege and diversity in the academy.* New York: Routledge.

Major, B., & O'Brien, L. T. (2005). The social psychology of stigma. *Annual Review of Psychology, 56,* 393–421.

Mangan, K. S. (2002, December 19). Law-school council considers plan to de-emphasize test scores and rankings that use them. *Chronicle of Higher Education.* Retrieved March 17, 2009, from http://chronicle.com/daily/2002/12/2002121901n.htm.

Marable, M. (1995). *Beyond black and white: Transforming African-American politics.* New York: Verso.

Maramba, D. (2008). Immigrant families and the college experience: Perspectives of Filipina Americans. *Journal of College Student Development, 49*(4), 336–350.

Marcus, H. R., Steele, C. M., & Steele, D. M. (2002). Color blindness as a barrier to inclusion: Assimilation and nonimmigrant minorities. In R. A. Shweder, M. Minow, & H. R. Marcus (Eds.), *Engaging cultural differences.* New York: Russell Sage Foundation.

Marcus-Newhall, A. M., Miller, N., Holtz, R., & Brewer, M. B. (1993). Cross-cutting category membership with role assignment: A means of reducing bias. *British Journal of Social Psychology, 32,* 125–146.

Margolis, E. (2001). *The hidden curriculum in higher education.* New York: Routledge.

Margolis, J., & Fisher, A. (2002). *Unlocking the clubhouse: Women in computing.* Cambridge, MA: MIT Press.

Margulies, J. (2002). Lead plaintiff against Michigan still hopes for a spot at its law school. *Chronicle of Higher Education, 49*(16), A23.

Marin, P. (2000). The educational possibility of multi-racial / multi-ethnic college classrooms. In *Does diversity make a difference? Three research studies on diversity in college classrooms* (pp. 61–83). Washington, DC: American Council on Education and American Association of University Professors.

Marschke, R., Laursen, S., Nielsen, J. M., & Rankin, P. (2007). Demographic inertia revisited: An immodest proposal to achieve equitable gender representation among faculty in higher education. *Journal of Higher Education, 78*(1), 1–26.

Martin, J. R. (2000). *Coming of age in the academy: Rekindling women's hopes and transforming the academy.* New York: Routledge.

Martin, R. G. (2005). Serving American Indian students in tribal colleges: Lessons for mainstream colleges. In M. J. T. Fox, S. C. Lowe, & G. McClellan (Eds.), *Serving*

Native American students (New Directions for Student Services, No. 109, pp. 79–86). San Francisco: Jossey-Bass.

Maruyama, G., & Moreno, J. F. (2000). University faculty views about the value of diversity on campus and in the classroom. In *Does diversity make a difference? Three research studies on diversity in college classrooms* (pp. 9–35). Washington, DC: American Council on Education and American Association of University Professors.

Marx, A. W. (1998). *Making race and nation: A comparison of South Africa, the United States, and Brazil.* Cambridge: Cambridge University Press.

Marx, D., & Roman, J. S. (2002). Female role-models: Protecting women's math test performance. *Personality and Social Psychology Bulletin, 28,* 1183–1193.

Massey, D. S., Charles, C. Z., Lundy, G. F., & Fischer, M. J. (2003). *The source of the river: The social origins of freshmen at America's selective colleges and universities.* Princeton, NJ: Princeton University Press.

Massey, D. S., Mooney, M., Torres, K. C., & Charles, C. Z. (2007). Black immigrants and Black natives attending selective colleges and universities in the United States. *American Journal of Education, 111,* 243–271.

Maton, K. I., & Hrabowski, F. A. (2004, September). Increasing the number of African American PhDs in the sciences and engineering. *American Psychologist, 59*(6), 547–556.

McCoy, M., & McCormick, M. A. (2001). Engaging the whole community in dialogue and action: Study Circles Resource Center. In D. L. Schoem & S. Hurtado (Eds.), *Intergroup dialogue: Deliberative democracy in school, college, community, and workplace* (pp. 137–150). Ann Arbor: University of Michigan.

McDonough, P. M. (2002). Resisting common injustice: Tenure politics, department politics, gay and lesbian politics. In J. E. Cooper & D. D. Stevens (Eds.), *Tenure in the sacred grove: Issues and strategies for women and minority faculty* (pp. 122–147). Albany: State University of New York Press.

McGinley, A. C. (1997). The emerging cronyism defense and affirmative action: A critical perspective on the distinction between colorblind and race-conscious decision making under Title VII. *39 Arizona Law Review 1003.*

McGlone, M. S., Aronson, J., & Kobrynowicz, D. (2006). Stereotype threat and the gender gap in political knowledge. *Psychology of Women Quarterly, 30*(4), 393–398.

McGowan, J. M. (2000). African American faculty classroom teaching experiences in predominantly white colleges and universities. *Multicultural Education, 8*(2), 11–22.

McGuire, W. J., McGuire, C. V., Child, P., & Fujioka, T. (1978). Salience of ethnicity in the spontaneous self-concept as a function of one's ethnic distinctiveness in the social environment. *Journal of Personality and Social Psychology, 36*(5), 511–520.

McIntosh, P. (1983). *Interactive phases of curriculum re-vision: A feminist perspective* (Working paper series, No. 124). Wellesley, MA: Wellesley College, Center for Research on Women.

McIntosh, P. (1985). *Feeling like a fraud* (Paper no. 18). Wellesley College, The Stone Center.

McIntosh, P. (1989). *Feeling like a fraud: Part Two* (Paper no. 37). Wellesley College, The Stone Center.

McIntosh, P. (2008). White privilege: Unpacking the invisible knapsack. In P. Rothenberg (Ed.), *White privilege: Essential readings on the other side of racism* (3rd ed., pp. 123–128). New York: Worth.

McLaurin, I. (Ed.). (2001). *Black feminist anthropology: Theory, praxis, and poetics.* New Brunswick, NJ: Rutgers University Press.

McMillan-Capehart, A. (2006). Heterogeneity or homogeneity: Socialization makes the difference in firm performance. *Performance Improvement Quarterly*, 19(1), 83–98.

Mendoza-Denton, R., Page-Gould, E., & Pietrak, J. (2006). Mechanisms for coping with status-based rejection expectations. In S. Levin & C. van Laar (Eds.), *Stigma and group inequality* (pp. 151–170). Mahwah, NJ: Erlbaum.

Menges, R. J., & Exum, W. H. (1983). Barriers to the progress of women and minority faculty. *Journal of Higher Education*, 54(2), 122–143.

Merisotis, J. P., & Phipps, R. A. (2000). Remedial education in colleges and universities: What's really going on? *Review of Higher Education*, 24(1), 67–85.

Merritt, D. J., & Resken, B. F. (1997). Sex, race and credentials: The truth about affirmative action in law faculty hiring. *97 Columbia Law Review 199*, 206–230.

Merrow, J. (2007). Community colleges: The (often rocky) path to the American Dream. *Change*, 39(6), 14–21.

Merton, R. K. (1988). The Matthew Effect in science, II. *ISIS*, 79, 606–623.

Mickelson, R. A., & Oliver, M. L. (1991). Making the short list: Black candidates and the faculty recruitment process. In P .G. Altbach & K. Lomotey (Eds.), *The racial crisis in American higher education* (pp. 149–166). Albany: State University of New York Press.

Milem, J. F. (2001). Increasing diversity benefits: How campus climate and teaching methods affect student outcomes. In G. Orfield & M. Kurlaender (Eds.), *Diversity challenged: Evidence on the impact of affirmative action* (pp. 233–249). Cambridge, MA: Harvard Education Publishing Group.

Milem, J. F., & Astin, H. S. (1993). The changing composition of the faculty: What does it really mean for diversity? *Change*, 25(2), 21–27.

Milem, J. F., Chang, M. J., Antonio, A. L. (2005). *Making diversity work on campus: A research-based perspective.* Washington, DC: Association of American Colleges and Universities.

Milem, J. F., Dey, E. L., & White, C. B. (2004). Diversity considerations in health professions education. In B. D. Smedley, A. S. Butler, & L. R. Bristow (Eds.), *In the nation's compelling interest: Ensuring diversity in the healthcare workforce* (pp. 345–390). Washington, DC: National Academies Press.

Miller, F. A., & Katz, J. H. (2002). *The inclusion breakthrough: Unleashing the real power of diversity.* San Francisco: Berrett-Koehler.

Miller, L. S. (1995). *An American imperative: Accelerating minority educational attainment.* New Haven, CT: Yale University Press.

Miller-Bernal, L., & Poulson, S. L. (2004). *Going coed: Women's experiences in formerly men's colleges and universities, 1950–2000.* Nashville, TN: Vanderbilt University Press.

Milliken, F. J., & Martins, L. L. (1996). Searching for common threads: Understanding the multiple effects of diversity in organizational groups. *Academy of Management Review*, 21, 402–433.

Min, P. G. (2002). *The second generation: Ethnic identity among Asian Americans*. New York: Alta Mira Press.

Minnich, E. K. (2005). *Transforming knowledge* (2nd ed.). Philadelphia: Temple University Press.

Minnich, E., O'Barr, J., & Rosenfeld, R. (Eds.). (1988). *Reconstructing the academy: Women's education and women's studies*. Chicago: University of Chicago Press.

Mintz, B., & Rothblum, E. (1997). *Lesbians in academia: Degrees of freedom*. New York: Routledge.

Misra, J., Kennelly, I., & Karides, M. (1999). Employment chances in the academic job market in sociology: Do race and gender matter? *Sociological Perspectives*, 42(2), 215–247.

Moffatt, G. K. (1993, February). *The validity of the SAT as a predictor of grade point average for nontraditional college students*. Paper presented at the Annual Meeting of the Easter Educational Research Association at Clearwater Beach, FL. (ERIC Document Reproduction Service No. ED356252)

Monroe, K. R., Hankin, J., & Van Vechten, R. B. (2000). The psychological foundations of identity politics. *Annual Review of Political Science*, 3, 419–447.

Monzon, R. I. (2003). *Integration and persistence of Filipino college students: The mediating effects of family obligation and reputation*. Unpublished doctoral dissertation, Claremont Graduate University, Claremont, CA.

Moody, J. (2004). *Faculty diversity: Problems and solutions*. New York: RoutledgeFalmer.

Moore, L. C. (2007). *The career choices of underrepresented doctoral recipients*. Unpublished doctoral dissertation, Claremont Graduate University, Claremont, CA.

Moran, J., Yengo, L., & Algier, A. (1994). Participation in minority oriented cocurricular organizations. *Journal of College Student Development*, 35, 143.

Moreno, J. F. (Ed.). (1999). *The elusive quest for equality: 150 years of Chicano/Chicana education*. Cambridge, MA: Harvard Educational Review.

Moreno, J., Smith, D. G., Clayton-Pedersen, A. R., Parker, S., & Teraguchi, D. H. (2006). *The revolving door for underrepresented minority faculty in higher education*. San Francisco: The James Irvine Foundation, http://www.irvine.org/assets/pdf/pubs/education/insight_Revolving _Door.pdf.

Moreno, J., Smith, D. G., Parker, S., Clayton-Pedersen, A. R., & Teraguchi, D. H. (2006). *Using multiple lenses: An examination of the economic and racial/ethnic diversity of college students*. San Francisco: The James Irvine Foundation, http://www.irvine.org/assets/pdf/pubs/education/insight_Multiple_Lenses.pdf.

Morest, V. S., & Jenkins, D. (2007). *Institutional research and the culture of evidence at community colleges* (Culture of Evidence Series, report no. 1). New York: Community College Research Center, Teachers College, Columbia University.

Morey, A. I., & Kitano, M. K. (Eds.). (1997). *Multicultural course transformation in higher education*. Boston: Allyn & Bacon.

Morrison, A. M. (1992). *The new leaders: Guidelines on leadership diversity in America*. San Francisco: Jossey-Bass.

Morrison, T., & Morrison, M. (1995). A meta-analytic assessment of the predictive validity of the quantitative and verbal components of the Graduate Record Examination with graduate grade point average representing the criterion of graduate success. *Educational and Psychological Measurement*, 55(2), 309–317.

Mortensen, T. G. (1999). Where are the boys? The growing gender gap in higher education. *College Board Review*, 188, 8–17.

Moses, R. P., & Cobb, C. E. (2001). *Radical equations: Math literacy and civil rights*. Boston: Beacon Press.

Moses, Y. T. (1997). Black women in academe: Issues and strategies. In L. Benjamin (Ed.), *Black women in academe: Promises and perils* (pp. 23–38). Gainesville: University Press of Florida.

Mowday, R. T., & Colwell, K. A. (2003). Employee reactions to unfair outcomes in the workplace: The contributions of equity theory to understanding work motivation. In L. W. Porter, G. A. Bigley, & R. M. Steers (Eds.), *Motivation and work behavior* (pp. 65–113). Boston: McGraw-Hill Irwin.

Mueller, C. M., & Dweck, C. S. (1998). Praise for intelligence can undermine children's motivation and performance. *Journal of Personality and Social Psychology*, 75(1), 33–52.

Mukhopadhyay, C. C., Henze, R., & Moses, Y. T. (2007). *Race, culture, and biology: An educator's sourcebook*. New York: Rowman & Littlefield.

Musil, C. M., García, M., Hudgins, C. A., Nettles, M. T., Sedlacek, W. E., & Smith, D. G. (1999). *To form a more perfect union: Campus Diversity Initiatives*. Washington, DC: Association of American Colleges and Universities.

Musil, C. M., García, M., Moses, Y. T., & Smith, D. G. (1995). *Diversity in higher education: A work in progress*. Washington, DC: Association of American Colleges and Universities.

Myrdal, G. (1944). *An American dilemma: The Negro problem and modern democracy*. New York: Harper & Row.

Nagda, B. A., Gurin, P., Sorensen, N., Gurin-Sands, C., & Osuna, S. (2009, March 5). From separate corners to dialogue and action. *Race and Social Problems*. Retrieved March 17, 2009, from http://www.springerlink.com.

Nagda, B. A., Gurin, P., Sorensen, N., & Zúñiga, X. (2009). Evaluating intergroup dialogue: Engaging diversity for personal and social responsibility. *Diversity and Democracy*, 12(1), 4–6.

Nakanishi, D. T. (1993). Asian Pacific Americans in higher education: Faculty and administrative representation and tenure. In J. Gainen & R. Boice (Eds.), *New Directions for Teaching and Learning*, 53, 51–59.

Nakanishi, D. T. (2001). Political trends and electoral issues of the Asian Pacific American population. In N. J. Smelser, W. J. Wilson, & F. Mitchell (Eds.), *America becoming: Racial trends and their consequences*, Vol. 2 (National Research Council, Commission on Behavioral and Social Sciences and Education, pp. 170–199). Washington, DC: National Academy Press.

Nakanishi, D. T., & Nishida, T. Y. (Eds.). (1995). *The Asian American educational experience*. New York: Routledge.

Nardi, P., & Schneider, B. E. (Eds.). (1998). *Social perspectives in gay and lesbian studies*. New York: Routledge.

National Association of State Student Grant and Aid Programs. (2006). *37th annual survey report on state-sponsored student financial aid, 2005–2006*. Washington, DC: Author.

National Center for Education Statistics (NCES). (1996–2007). Data retrieved from http://www.nces.ed.gov/programs/digest/2007menu_tables.asp.

National Center for Education Statistics. (2000). *Postsecondary students with disabilities*. Washington, DC: Author.

National Research Council. (1997). *Building a diverse work force: Scientists and engineers in the office of Naval Research*. Washington, DC: Author.

National Research Council. (2006). *Hispanics and the future of America*. Washington, DC: National Academy Press.

National Science Foundation Advance Project. (2002). *Advance: Assessing the academic work environment for women scientists and engineers*. Ann Arbor: University of Michigan, Institute for Research on Women and Gender.

National Science Foundation Survey of Earned Doctorates. (2005–6). Available from http://webcaspar.nsf.gov.

National Science Foundation Survey of Earned Doctorates. (2008). Report tables retrieved March 13, 2009, from http://norc.org/SED/SED=Tables.htm.

Nelson, D., & Rogers, D. C. (2004). *A national analysis of diversity in science and engineering faculties at research universities*. Retrieved June 15, 2007, from http://www.now.org/issues/diverse/diversity_report.pdf.

Nemeth, C. J. (1994). The value of minority dissent. In S. Moscovici, A. Mucchi-Faina, & A. Maass (Eds.), *Minority influence* (pp. 3–15). Chicago: Nelson-Hall.

Nettles, M. T., & Millet, C. M. (2006). *Three major letters: Getting to the PhD*. Baltimore: Johns Hopkins University Press.

Nettles, M. T., Sedlacek, W., Smith, D., Musil, C., Hudgins, C., & García, M. (2002). *Assessing diversity on college and university campuses*. Washington, DC: Association of American Colleges and Universities.

Nieli, R. (2004). *The changing shape of the river*. Unpublished paper, Princeton University, Princeton, NJ.

Niemann, Y. F. (1999). The making of a token: A case study of stereotype threat, racism, and tokenism in academe. *Frontiers*, 20(1), 111–134.

Noddings, N. (2006). Educating whole people: A response to Jonathan Cohen. *Harvard Educational Review*, 76(2), 238–242.

Nonaka, I. (2005). Managing organizational knowledge: Theoretical and methodological foundations. In K. G. Smith & M. A. Hitt (Eds.), *Great minds in management: The process of theory development* (pp. 373–394). Oxford: Oxford University Press.

Nonaka, I., & Takeuchi, H. (1995). *The knowledge-creating company*. Oxford: Oxford University Press.

Nora, A., & Cabrera, A. (1996). The role of perceptions of prejudice and discrimination on the adjustment of minority students to college. *Journal of Higher Education*, 67, 119–148.

Nussbaum, M. C. (2003). Women's education: A global challenge. *Signs*, 29(2), 325–355.

Ogbu, J. U. (2003). *Black American students in an affluent suburb: A study of academic disengagement.* Mahwah, NJ: Erlbaum.

Okamura, J. Y., & Agbayani, A. R. (1997). Pamantasan: Filipino American higher education. In M. P. P. Root (Ed.), *Filipino Americans: Transformation and identity* (pp. 183–197). Thousand Oaks, CA: Sage.

Olivas, M. A. (Ed.). (1986). *Latino college students.* New York: Teachers College Press.

Olivas, M. A. (1994). The education of Latino lawyers: An essay on crop cultivation. *Chicano-Latino Law Review*, 14, 117–138.

Olivas, M. A. (1999). Higher education admissions and the search for one important thing. *University of Arkansas at Little Rock Law Review*, 993–1024.

Olivas, M. A. (2005). The legal environment: The implementation of legal change on campus. In P. G. Altbach, R. O. Berdahl, & P. J. Gumport (Eds.), *American higher education in the twenty-first century: Social, political and economic challenges* (2nd ed., pp. 226–252). Baltimore: Johns Hopkins University Press.

Oliver, M., & Shapiro, T. (1997). *Black wealth, White wealth.* New York: Routledge.

Oliver, M. L., & Shapiro, T. M. (2001). Wealth and racial stratification. In N. J. Smelser, W. J. Wilson, & F. Mitchell (Eds.), *America becoming: Racial trends and their consequences*, Vol. 2 (National Research Council, Commission on Behavioral and Social Sciences and Education, pp. 222–251). Washington, DC: National Academy Press.

Omi, M. A. (2001). The changing meaning of race. In N. J. Smelser, W. J. Wilson, & F. Mitchell (Eds.), *America becoming: Racial trends and their consequences*, Vol. I (National Research Council, Commission on Behavioral and Social Sciences and Education, pp. 243–263). Washington, DC: National Academy Press.

Omi, M., & Winant, H. (1994). *Racial formation in the United States.* New York: Routledge.

O'Neill, R. M. (2006). The difficult dialogues initiative. *Academe*, 92(4), 29–30.

Opp, R. D. (1994). Minority versus White administrators' perceptions of the recruitment and retention of minority faculty in two-year colleges. *Journal of Applied Research in the Community College*, 1(2), 85–99.

Opp, R. D., & Smith, A. (1994). Effective strategies for enhancing minority faculty recruitment. *Community College Journal of Research and Practice*, 10, 147.

O'Reilly, C., Williams, K., & Barsade, S. (1997). Group demography and innovation: Does diversity help? In E. Mannix & M. Neale (Eds.), *Research in the management of groups and teams* (Vol. 1, pp. 77–140). Greenwich, CT: JAI Press.

Orfield, G. (Ed.). (2004). *Dropouts in America.* Cambridge, MA: Harvard Education Press.

Orfield, G., & Kurlaender, M. (Eds.). (2001). *Diversity challenged: Evidence on the impact of affirmative action.* Cambridge, MA: Harvard Education Publishing Group.

Orfield, G., Marin, P., & Horn, C. (Eds.). (2005). *Higher education and the color line.* Cambridge, MA: Harvard Education Press.

Orfield, G., & Whitla, D. (1999). *Diversity and legal education: Student experiences in leading law schools.* Cambridge, MA: The Civil Rights Project, Harvard University.

Padilla, F. M. (1997). *The struggle of Latino/Latina university students: In search of a liberating education.* New York: Routledge.

Padilla, R. V. (2004). *Unity and diversity in an ethnomorphic society.* San Antonio: University of Texas.

Page, S. E. (2007). *The difference: How the power of diversity creates better groups, firms, schools and societies.* Princeton, NJ: Princeton University Press.

Palmer, P. (2002). The quest for community in higher education. In W. McDonald & associates, *Creating campus community: In search of Ernest Boyer's legacy* (pp. 179–192). San Francisco: Jossey-Bass.

Parekh, B. (2008). *A new politics of identity: Political principles for an interdependent world.* New York: Palgrave Macmillan.

Parker, S. (2007). *Diversity as praxis for institutional transformation in higher education.* Unpublished dissertation, University of Auckland, Auckland, NZ.

Pascarella, E. T., Edison, M., Nora, A., Hagedorn, L. S., & Terenzini, P. T. (1996). Influences on students' openness to diversity and challenge in the first year of college. *Journal of Higher Education, 67*(2), 174–195.

Pascarella, E. T., & Terenzini, P. T. (1991). *How college affects students: Findings and insights from twenty years of research.* San Francisco: Jossey-Bass.

Pascarella, E. T., & Terenzini, P. T. (2005). *How college affects students: A third generation of research.* San Francisco: Jossey-Bass.

Pavel, M., Swisher, K., & Ward, M. (1994). Special focus: American Indian and Alaska Native demographic and educational trends. *Minorities in Higher Education, 13*, 33–56.

Peat, F. D. (2002). *Blackfoot physics.* Grand Rapids, MI: Phanes Press.

Perez, W. (2009). *We are Americans: Undocumented students pursuing the American dream.* Sterling, VA: Stylus.

Perez, W., Coronado, H., & Ramos, K. (2007). *Civic engagement patterns of undocumented Latino immigrant youth: Model citizens at the margins of society.* Poster paper at the Bi-annual Society for Research on Child Development, Boston.

Perkins, L. (1983). The impact of the "cult of true womanhood" in the education of Black women. *Journal of Social Issues, 39*(3), 17–28.

Perlmann, J., & Waters, M. C. (Eds.). (2002). *The new race question: How the census counts multiracial individuals.* New York: Russell Sage Foundation.

Perna, L. W. (2004). Understanding the decision to enroll in graduate school: Sex and racial/ethnic group differences. *Journal of Higher Education, 75*(5), 487–527.

Perna, L. W., & Titus, M. A. (2005). The relationship between parental involvement as social capital and college enrollment. *Journal of Higher Education, 76*(5), 485–519.

Pettigrew, T. F. (1998a). Intergroup contact theory. *Annual Review of Psychology, 49*, 65–85.

Pettigrew, T. F. (1998b). Prejudice and discrimination on the college campus. In J. L. Eberhardt & S. T. Fiske (Eds.), *Confronting racism: The problem and the response* (pp. 263–279). Thousand Oaks, CA: Sage.

Pettigrew, T. F., & Tropp, L. R. (2000). Does intergroup contact reduce prejudices? Recent meta-analytic findings. In S. Oskamp (Ed.), *Reducing prejudice and discrimination* (pp. 93–114). Mahwah, NJ: Erlbaum.

Pew Charitable Trusts. (2001). *Returning results: Planning and evaluation at the Pew Charitable Trusts.* Philadelphia: Author.

Pfeffer, J. (1985). Organizational demography: Implications for management. *California Management Review*, 28, 67–81.

Phinney, J. S. (1990). Ethnic identity in adolescents and adults: Review of research. *Psychological Bulletin*, 10, 499–514.

Phinney, J. S. (1996). When we talk about American ethnic groups, what do we mean? *American Psychologist*, 51(9), 918–927.

Pike, G. R., & Kuh, G. D. (2005). First and second-generation college students: A comparison of their engagement and intellectual development. *Journal of Higher Education*, 76(3), 276–300.

Pike, G. R., & Kuh, G. D. (2006). Relationships among structural diversity, informal peer interactions and perceptions of the campus environment. *Review of Higher Education*, 29(4), 425–450.

Pike, G. R., Kuh, G. D., & Gonyea, R. M. (2003). The relationship between institutional mission and students' involvement and educational outcomes. *Research in Higher Education*, 44(2), 241–261.

Pinel, E. C., Warner, L. R., & Chua, P. (2005). Getting there is only half the battle: Stigma consciousness and maintaining diversity in higher education. *Journal of Social Issues*, 61(3), 481–506.

Pink, D. H. (2006). *A whole new mind: Why right brainers will rule the future.* New York: Riverhead Books.

Polzer, J. T., Milton, L. T., & Swann, W. B. (2002). Capitalizing on diversity: Interpersonal congruence in small work groups. *Administrative Science Quarterly*, 47, 296–324.

Pope, J., & Joseph, J. (1997). Student harassment of female faculty of African descent in the academy. In L. Benjamin (Ed.), *Black women in academe: Promises and perils* (pp. 252–260). Gainesville: University Press of Florida.

Preskill, H., & Torres, R. T. (1999). *Inquiry for learning in organizations.* Thousand Oaks, CA: Sage.

Pressman, J. L., & Wildavsky, A. (1984). *Implementation* (3rd ed.). Berkeley: University of California Press.

Preves, S. E. (2005). *Intersex and identity.* New Brunswick, NJ: Rutgers University Press.

Price, D. V. (2004). *Borrowing inequality: Race, class and student loans.* Boulder, CO: Lynne Rienner Publishers.

Pryor, J. H., Hurtado, S., Saenz, V. B., Santos, J. L., & Korn, W. S. (2007). *The American freshman: Forty-year trends.* Los Angeles: Higher Education Research Institute, University of California, Los Angeles.

Puraskin, L., & Lee, J. (2004). *Raising the graduation rates of low-income students.* Washington, DC: Pell Institute for the Study of Opportunity in Higher Education.

Putnam, R. D. (2007). *E pluribus unum*: Diversity and community in the twenty-first century. *Scandinavian Political Studies*, 30(2), 137–174.

Quinn, D. M. (2006). Concealable versus conspicuous identities. In S. Levin & C. van Laar (Eds.), *Stigma and group inequality* (pp. 83–104). Mahwah, NJ: Erlbaum.

Ragins, B. R. (1995). Diversity, power, and mentorship in organizations: A cultural, structual, and behavioral perspective. In M. Chemers, S. Oskamp, & M. Costanza (Eds.), *Diversity in organizations* (pp. 91–132). Newbury Park, CA: Sage.

Ramirez, M., & Castañeda, A. (1991). Toward a cultural democracy. In B. Murchand (Ed.), *Higher education and the practice of democratic politics: A political education reader* (pp. 115–121). Dayton, OH: Kettering Foundation.

Rankin, S. (2003). *Campus climate for gay, lesbian, bisexual, and transgendered people.* Washington, DC: Policy Institute of the National Gay and Lesbian Task Force.

Raskin, P. M. (2002). Identity in adulthood: Reflections on recent theory and research. *Identity,* 2(1), 101–108.

Rauscher, L., & McClintock, M. (1997). Ableism and curriculum design. In M. Adams, L. A. Bell, & P. Griffen (Eds.), *Teaching for diversity and social justice* (pp. 198–231). New York: Routledge.

Rendón, L. I. (1992). From the barrio to the academy: Revelations of a Mexican American scholarship girl. In L. S. Zwerling & H. B. London (Eds.), *First-generation students: Confronting the cultural issues* (New Directions for Community Colleges, No. 80, pp. 55–64). San Francisco: Jossey-Bass.

Rendón, L. I. (1999). Toward a new vision of the multicultural community college for the next century. In K. M. Shaw, J. R. Valdez, & R. A. Rhoades (Eds.), *Community colleges as cultural contexts: Qualitative explorations of organizations and student culture* (pp. 195–204). Albany: State University of New York Press.

Rendón, L. I. (2005). Recasting agreements that govern teaching and learning:An intellectual and spiritual framework for transformation. *Religion and Education,* 32(1), 79–108.

Rendón, L. I., & Hope, R. (Eds.). (1996). *Educating a new majority.* San Francisco: Jossey-Bass.

Rich, A. (1986). *Blood, bread, and poetry.* New York: Norton.

Richard, O. C. (2000). Racial diversity, business strategy, and firm performance: A resource-based review. *Academy of Management Journal,* 43(2), 164–177.

Richard, O. C., Kochan, T. C., & McMillan-Capehart, A. (2002). The impact of visible diversity on organizational effectiveness: Disclosing the contents in Pandora's black box. *Journal of Business and Management,* 8(3), 1–26.

Riordan, C. M. (2000). Relational demography within groups: Past developments, contradictions, and new directions. *Research in Personnel and Human Resource Management,* 19, 131–173.

Riordan, C. M., & Shore, L. M. (1997). Demographic diversity and employee attitudes: An empirical examination of relational demography within work units. *Journal of Applied Psychology,* 82, 342–358.

Rodriguez, C. E. (1994). Challenging racial hegemony: Puerto Ricans in the U.S. In S. Gregory & R. Sanjek (Eds.), *Race* (pp. 131–145). New Brunswick, NJ: Rutgers University Press.

Rojas, F. (2007). *From Black power to Black studies: How a radical social movement became an academic discipline.* Baltimore: Johns Hopkins University Press.

Root, M. P. P. (Ed.). (1997). *Filipino Americans: Transformation and identity.* Thousand Oaks, CA: Sage.

Rosenthal, H. E. S., & Crisp, R. J. (2006). Reducing stereotype threat by blurring intergroup boundaries. *Personality and Social Psychology Bulletin, 32*(4), 501–511.

Rosser, P. (1992). *Sex bias in college admissions tests: Why women lose out* (14th ed.). Cambridge, MA: National Center for Fair and Open Testing.

Rosser, S. (Ed.). (1995). *Teaching the majority: Breaking the gender barrier in science, mathematics, and engineering.* New York: Teachers College Press.

Rouhana, N. (2004). Identity and power in the reconciliation of national conflict. In A. H. Eagly, R. M. Baron, & V. L. Hamilton (Eds.), *The social psychology of group identity and social conflict: Theory, application, and practice* (pp. 173–187). Washington, DC: American Psychological Association.

Rowe, M. P. (1990). Barrier to equality: The power of subtle discrimination to maintain unequal opportunity. *Employee Responsibility and Rights Journal, 3*(2), 153–163.

Sachs, A. (1999). Foreword to M. Cross, N. Cloete, E. F. Beckham, A. Harper, J. Indiresan, & C. M. Musil (Eds.), *Diversity and unity: The role of higher education in building democracy* (p. v). Cape Town, South Africa: Maskew Miller Longman.

Sackett, P. R., Borneman, M. J., & Connelly, B. S. (2008). High-stakes testing in higher education and employment. *American Psychologist, 63*(4), 215–227.

Sacks, P. (1999). *Standardized minds: The high price of America's testing culture and what we can do to change it.* New York: Perseus Publishing.

Sagaria, M. A. D. (2002). An exploratory model of filtering in administrative searches: Toward counter-hegemonic discourses. *Journal of Higher Education, 73*(6), 677–710.

Sanchez, G. (2004). *Crossing Figueroa: The tangled web of diversity and democracy* (Position paper no. 4, Imagining America). Ann Arbor: University of Michigan.

Sander, R. (2004, November). A sytemic analysis of affirmative action in American law schools. *Stanford Law Review, 57*(2), 367–484.

Sandler, B. (1983). *The chilly climate for women.* Washington, DC: Association of American Colleges and Universities.

Sanjek, R. (1994). The enduring inequalities of race. In S. Gregory & R. Sanjek (Eds.), *Race* (pp. 1–17). New Brunswick, NJ: Rutgers University Press.

Santiago, I. S. (1996). Increasing the Latino leadership pipeline: Institutional and organizational strategies. In R. C. Bowen & G. H. Muller (Eds.), *Achieving administrative diversity* (New Directions for Community Colleges, No. 94, pp. 25–38). San Francisco: Jossey-Bass.

Saunders, H. H. (1999). *A public peace process: Sustained dialogue to transform racial and ethnic conflicts.* New York: St. Martin's Press.

Schein, E. H. (1999). *The corporate culture survival guide.* San Francisco: Jossey-Bass.

Schiebinger, L. (2006). *Nature's body: Gender in the making of modern science.* New Brunswick, NJ: Rutgers University Press.

Schiebinger, L. (2008). Getting more women into science and engineering—knowledge issues. In L. Schiebinger (Ed.), *Gendered innovations in science and engineering* (pp. 1–21). Stanford, CA: Stanford University Press.

Schlossberg, N. K. (1989). Marginality and mattering: Key issues in building community. In D. C. Roberts (Ed.), *Designing campus activities to foster a sense of community* (New Directions for Student Services, No. 48, pp. 5–15). San Francisco: Jossey-Bass.

Schmitz, B., Butler, J. E., Rosenfelt, D., & Guy-Sheftall, B. (1995). Women's studies and curriculum transformation. In J. A. Banks (Ed.), *Handbook of research on multicultural education* (pp. 708–728). New York: Macmillan.

Schoem, D. L., & Hurtado, S. (Eds.). (2001). *Intergroup dialogue: Deliberative democracy in school, college, community, and workplace*. Ann Arbor: University of Michigan.

Schoem, D. L., Hurtado, S., Sevig, T., Chesler, M., & Sumida, S. (2001). Intergroup dialogue: Democracy at work in theory and practice. In D. L. Schoem & S. Hurtado (Eds.), *Intergroup dialogue: Deliberative democracy in school, college, community, and workplace* (pp. 1–21). Ann Arbor: University of Michigan.

Schrader, W. B. (1978). *Admissions test scores as predictors of career achievement in psychology*. Princeton, NJ: Educational Testing Service. (ERIC Document Reproduction Service No. ED241563)

Schuster, J. H. (2003). The faculty makeover: What does it mean for students? In E. Benjamin (Ed.), *Exploring the role of contingent instructional staff in undergraduate learning* (New Directions for Higher Education, No. 123, pp. 15–22). San Francisco: Jossey-Bass.

Schuster, J. H., & Finkelstein, M. J. (2006). *The American faculty: The restructuring of academic work and careers*. Baltimore: Johns Hopkins University Press.

Schwan, E. S. (1988). MBA admissions criteria: An empirical investigation and validation study. *Journal of Education for Business*, 63, 158–162.

Sedlacek, W. (1998). Admissions in higher education: Measuring cognitive and noncognitive variables. In D. Wilds & R. Wilson (Eds.), *Minorities in higher education* (pp. 47–71). Washington, DC: American Council on Education.

Sedlacek, W. E. (1999). Black students on white campuses: 20 years of research. *Journal of College Student Development*, 40(5), 538–550.

Sen, A. F. (2006). *Identity and violence: The illusion of destiny*. New York: Norton.

Senge, R. M. (2000). The academy as learning community: Contradiction in terms or realizable goal? In A. F. Lucas & associates, *Leading academic change* (pp. 275–300). San Francisco: Jossey-Bass.

Seymour, E., & Hewitt, N. (1997). *Talking about leaving: Why undergraduates leave the sciences*. Boulder, CO: Westview Press.

Shireman, R. (2003, August 15). 10 questions college officials should ask about diversity. *The Chronicle Review*, 49(49), B10. Available at http://chronicle.com/prm/weekly/v49/i49/49b01001.htm.

Short, D. (2003). Reconciliation, assimilation, and the indigenous peoples of Australia. *International Political Science Review*, 24(4), 491–513.

Sidanius, J., Levin, S., van Laar, C., & Sears, D. O. (2008). *The diversity challenge: Social identity and intergroup relations on the college campus*. New York: Russell Sage Foundation.

Sidanius, J., Levin, S., van Laar, C., & Sinclair, S. (2004). Ethnic enclaves and the dynamics of social identity on the college campus: The good, the bad and the ugly. *Journal of Personality and Social Psychology*, 87(1), 96–110.

Sidanius, J., & Pratto, F. (1999). *Social dominance*. Cambridge: Cambridge University Press.

Simpson, J. (2003). *'I have been waiting': Race and U.S. higher education*. Toronto: University of Toronto Press.

Skerry, P. (2002). Beyond sushiology: Does diversity work? *Brookings Review*, 20, 2023.

Slaughter, J. B. (2004). *Diversity and equity in higher education: A new paradigm for institutional excellence*. Speech given November 1, 2004, Johns Hopkins University, Baltimore.

Slavin, R. E., & Cooper, R. (1999). Improving intergroup relations: Lessons learned from cooperative learning programs. *Journal of Social Issues*, 55(4), 647–663.

Sleeter, C. E., & Grant, C. A. (1988). A rationale for integrating race, gender, and social class. In L. Weis (Ed.), *Class, race, and gender in American education* (pp. 126–143). Albany: State University of New York.

Smart, J. B. (1990). A causal model of faculty turnover intentions. *Research in Higher Education*, 31(5), 405–424.

Smedley, A., & Smedley, B. (2005). Race as biology is fiction: Racism as social problem is real. *American Psychologist*, 60(1), 16–26.

Smelser, N. J., Wilson, W. J., & Mitchell, F. (Eds.). (2001). *America becoming: Racial trends and their consequences*, Vols. 1 & 2 (National Research Council, Commission on Behavioral and Social Sciences and Education). Washington, DC: National Academy Press.

Smith, D. G. (1990). Women's colleges and coed colleges: Is there a difference for women? *Journal of Higher Education*, 61, 181–195.

Smith, D. G. (1995). Organizational implications of diversity. In M. Chemers, S. Oskamp, & M. Costanza (Eds.), *Diversity in organizations* (pp. 220–244). Newbury Park, CA: Sage.

Smith, D. G. (1997). How diversity influences learning. *Liberal Education*, 83(2), 42–47.

Smith, D. G. (1999). Strategic evaluation: An imperative for the future of campus diversity. In M. Cross, N. Cloete, E. F. Beckham, A. Harper, J. Indiresan, & C. M. Musil (Eds.), *Diversity and unity: The role of higher education in building democracy*. Cape Town, South Africa: Maskew Miller Longman.

Smith, D. G. (2004). *The James Irvine Foundation Campus Diversity Initiative: Current status, anticipating the future*. http://www.irvine.org/publications/by_topic/education.shtml.

Smith, D. G. (2005). The challenge of diversity: Involvement or alienation in the academy (reprinted with an introduction by D. G. Smith and L. Wolf-Wendel). *ASHE Higher Education Report*, 31(1).

Smith, D. G., García, M., Hudgins, C. A., Musil, C. M., Nettles, M. T., & Sedlacek, W. E. (2000). *A diversity research agenda*. Washington, DC: Association of American Colleges and Universities.

Smith, D. G., & Garrison, G. (2005). The impending loss of talent: An exploratory study challenging assumptions about testing and merit. *Teachers College Record*, 107(4), 629–653.

Smith, D. G., Gerbick, G. L., Figueroa, M., Watkins, G. H., Levitan, T., Moore, L. C., et al. (1997). *Diversity works: The emerging picture of how students benefit.* Washington, DC: Association of American Colleges and Universities.

Smith, D. G., Moreno, J. F., Clayton-Pedersen, A. R., Parker, S., & Teraguchi, D. H. (2005). *Unknown students on college campuses: An exploratory analysis.* San Francisco: James Irvine Foundation.

Smith, D. G., Morrison, D. E., & Wolf-Wendel, L. E. (1994). Is college a gendered experience? *Journal of Higher Education*, 65, 696–725.

Smith, D. G., & Parker, S. (2005). Organizational learning: A tool for diversity and institutional effectiveness. In A. Kezar (Ed.), *Organizational learning in higher education* (New Directions for Higher Education, No. 131, pp. 113–125). San Francisco: Jossey-Bass.

Smith, D. G., Parker, S., Clayton-Pedersen, A. R., Moreno, J. F., & Teraguchi, D. H. (2006). *Building capacity: A study of the impact of the James Irvine Foundation Campus Diversity Initiative.* San Francisco: James Irvine Foundation.

Smith, D. G., Turner, C. S., Osei-Kofi, N., & Richards, S. (2004). Interrupting the usual: Successful strategies for hiring diverse faculty. *Journal of Higher Education*, 75(2), 133–160.

Smith, D. G., Wolf, L. E., Busenberg, B., & associates. (1996). *Achieving faculty diversity: Debunking the myths.* Washington, DC: Association of American Colleges and Universities.

Smith, D. G., Wolf-Wendel, L. E., & Morrison, D. E. (1995). How women's colleges facilitate the success of their students. *Journal of Higher Education*, 66, 245–266.

Smith, K. G., Smith, K. A., Olian, J. D., Sims, H. P., O'Bannon, D. P., & Scully, J. A. (1994). Top management team demography and process: The role of social integration and communication. *Administrative Science Quarterly*, 39, 412–438.

Smith, L. D., Best, L. A., Stubbs, D. A., Archibald, A. B., & Roberson-Nay, R. (2002). Constructing knowledge: The role of graphs and tables in hard and soft psychology. *American Psychologist*, 57(10), 749–761.

Smith, L. T. (1999). *Decolonizing methodologies: Research and indigenous peoples.* London: Zed Books.

Smith, P. (2004). *The quiet crisis: How higher education is failing America.* Boston: Anker.

Smith, W. A., Altbach, P. G., & Lomotey, K. (Eds.). (2002). *The racial crisis in American higher education: Continuing challenges for the twenty-first century* (Rev. ed.). Albany: State University of New York Press.

Smith, W. A., Yosso, T. J., & Solórzano, D. G. (2006). Challenging racial battle fatigue on historically White campuses: A critical race examination of race-related stress. In C. A. Stanley (Ed.), *Faculty of color: Teaching in predominantly White colleges and universities* (pp. 299–328). Boston: Anker.

Sobol, M. G. (1984). GPA, GMAT, and scale: A method for quantification of admissions criteria. *Research in Higher Education*, 20(1), 77–88.

Soldatenko, M. (2001). Radicalism in higher education. In E. Margolis (Ed.), *The hidden curriculum in higher education* (pp. 193–232). New York: Routledge.

Solórzano, D. G. (1993). *The road to the doctorate for California's Chicanas and Chicanos: A study of Ford Foundation minority fellows.* Berkeley: The Regents of the University of California. (ERIC Document Reproduction Service No. ED374-941)

Solórzano, D. G. (1995). The doctorate production and baccalaureate origins of African Americans in the sciences and engineering. *Journal of Negro Education*, 64(1), 15–32.

Solórzano, D. G., Ceja, M., & Yosso, T. (2000). Critical race theory, racial microaggressions, and campus racial climate. *Journal of Negro Education*, 69(1), 60–73.

Sommers, S. R. (2006). On racial diversity and group decision making: Identifying multiple effects of racial composition in jury deliberations. *Journal of Personality and Social Psychology*, 90(4), 597–612.

Sonnenschein, W. (1999). *Diversity toolkit.* New York: McGraw-Hill.

Sparber, C. (2009). Racial diversity and aggregate productivity in U.S. industries: 1980–2000. *Southern Economic Journal*, 75(3), 829–865.

Spencer, S. J., Steele, C. M., & Quinn, D. M. (1999). Stereotype threat and women's math performance. *Journal of Experimental Social Psychology*, 35, 4–28.

Stanley, C. A. (Ed.). (2006). *Faculty of color: Teaching in predominantly White colleges and universities.* Boston: Anker.

Stanton-Salazar, R. D. (2001). *Manufacturing hope and despair.* New York: Teachers College Press.

Staples, R. (1984). Racial ideology and intellectual racism: Blacks in academia. *Black Scholar*, 15, 2–17.

Steele, C. M. (1997). A threat in the air: How stereotypes shape intellectual identity and performance. *American Psychologist*, 52, 613–629.

Steele, C. M., & Aronson, J. (1995). Stereotype threat and the intellectual performance of African Americans. *Journal of Personality and Social Psychology*, 69, 797–811.

Steers, R. M., & Porter, L. W. (1979). *Motivation and work behavior* (2nd ed.). New York: McGraw-Hill.

Stein, V. W., & Malcolm, S. (1998). *Talking about disability: The education and work experiences of graduates and undergraduates with disabilities in science, mathematics, and engineering majors.* Washington, DC: American Association for the Advancement of Science.

Steinpreis, R. E., Anders, K. A., & Ritzke, D. (1999). The impact of gender on the review of the curricula vitae of job applicants and tenure candidates: A national empirical study. *Sex Roles*, 41(7/8), 509–528.

Stephan, W. G., & Stephan, C. W. (2001). *Improving intergroup relations.* Thousand Oaks, CA: Sage.

Sternberg, R. J. (1985). *Beyond IQ: A triarchic theory of intelligence.* Cambridge: Cambridge University Press.

Sternberg, R. J., & Grigorenko, E. L. (2002). *Dynamic testing: The nature and measurement of learning potential.* New York: Cambridge University Press.

Sternberg, R. J., & Grigorenko, E. L. (Eds.). (2004). *Culture and competence: Contexts of life success*. Washington, DC: American Psychological Association.

Sternberg, R. J., & Williams, W. M. (1997). Does the Graduate Record Examination predict meaningful success in the graduate training of psychologists? *American Psychologist*, 52(6), 630–641.

Sturm, S. (2007). Gender equity as institutional transformation. In A. J. Stewart, J. E. Malley, & D. La Veque-Manty (Eds.), *Transforming science and engineering: Advancing academic women* (pp. 262–279). Ann Arbor: University of Michigan Press.

Sturm, S., & Gadlin, H. (2007). Conflict resolution and systemic change. *Journal of Dispute Resolution*. Retrieved August 2008 from http://www.law.virginia.edu/pd /work shops/0607/sturm.pdf.

Sue, D. W., Capodilupo, C. M., Torino, G. C., Bucceri, J. M., Holder, A. M. B., & Nadal, K. L., et al. (2007). Racial microaggressions in everyday life. *American Psychologist*, 62(4), 271–286.

Sumida, S., & Gurin, P. A. (2001). Celebration of power. In D. L. Schoem & S. Hurtado (Eds.), *Intergroup dialogue: Deliberative democracy in school, college, community, and workplace* (pp. 280–293). Ann Arbor: University of Michigan.

Summers, M. F., & Hrabowski, F. A. (2006, March 31). Preparing minority scientists and engineers. *Science*, 311, 1870–1871.

Sunstein, C. R. (1997). *Free markets and social justice*. Oxford: Oxford University Press.

Sunstein, C. R. (2004). *The second bill of rights*. New York: Basic Books.

Swail, W. S., Cabrera, A., & Lee, C. (2004). *Latino youth and the pathway to college*. Washington, DC: Educational Policy Institute.

Swail, W. S., Cabrera, A., Lee, C., & Williams, A. (2005). *Latino students and the educational pipeline, Part III*. Washington, DC: Educational Policy Institute.

Swail, W. S., Redd, K. E., & Perna, L. (2003). Retaining minority students in higher education: A framework for success. *ASHE-ERIC Higher Education Report*, 30(2). San Francisco: Jossey-Bass.

Swinton, S. S. (1987). *The predictive validity of the restructured GRE with particular attention to older students*. Princeton, NJ: Educational Testing Service.

Swoboda, M. J. (1993). Hiring women and minorities. In R. H. Stein & S. J. Trachtenberg (Eds.), *The art of hiring in America's colleges and universities* (pp. 123–136). Buffalo, NY: Prometheus Books.

Symington, A. (2004, August). Intersectionality: A tool for gender and economic justice. *Women's rights and economic change* (Association for Women in Development), No. 9.

Symonette, H. (2006). *Striving to get diversity grounded in assessment right: Looking back and leaping forward in the University of Wisconsin system*. Paper presented at the annual meeting of the American Evaluation Association, November 1–4, Portland, OR.

Tafoya, S. M., Johnson, H., & Hill, L. E. (2005). Who chooses two? In R. Farley & J. Haaga (Eds.), *The American people: Census 2000* (pp. 332–335). New York: Russell Sage Foundation.

Tajfel, H. (1978). Social categorization, social identity, and social comparison. In H.

Tajfel (Ed.), *Differentiation between social groups: Studies in the social psychology of intergroup relations*. London: Academic Press.

Takagi, D. (1998). *The retreat from race: Asian Americans and racial politics*. New Brunswick, NJ: Rutgers University Press.

Takaki, R. (1993). *A different mirror: A history of multicultural America*. New York: Little, Brown.

Tanaka, G., Bonous-Hammarth, M., & Astin, A. W. (1998). An admissions process for a multiethnic society. In G. Orfield & E. Miller (Eds.), *Chilling admissions* (pp. 123–130). Cambridge, MA: Harvard University Press.

Tatum, B. D. (1997). *"Why are all the Black kids sitting together in the cafeteria?" and other conversations about race*. New York: Basic Books.

Tatum, B. D. (2007). *Can we talk about race? and other conversations in an era of resegregation*. Boston: Beacon Press.

Taylor, C., & associates. (1994). *Multiculturalism: Examining the politics of recognition*. Princeton, NJ: Princeton University Press.

Teranishi, R. T. (2002). Asian American Pacific Americans and critical race theory: An examination of school racial climate. *Equity and Excellence in Education*, 35(2), 144–154.

Teranishi, R. T., Ceja, M., Antonio, A. L., Allen, W. R., & McDonough, P. (2004). The college choice process for Asian Pacific Americans: Ethnicity, socioeconomic class in context. *Review of Higher Education*, 27(4), 527–555.

Terenzini, P. T., Springer, L., Pascarella, E. T., & Nora, A. (1995). Academic and out-of-class influences on students' intellectual development. *Review of Higher Education*, 19(1), 23–44.

Thacker, A. J., & Williams, R. E. (1974). The relationship of the Graduate Record Examination to grade point average and success in graduate school. *Educational and Psychological Measurement*, 34, 939–944.

Thelin, J. (2004). *A history of American higher education*. Baltimore: Johns Hopkins University Press.

Thiederman, S. (2003). *Making diversity work: Seven steps to defeating bias in the workplace*. Chicago: Dearborn Trade.

Thomas, D. A. (2001). The truth about mentoring minorities: Race matters. *Harvard Business Review*, 79(4), 99–107.

Thomas, D., & Ely, R. (1996, September/October). Making differences matter: A new paradigm for managing diversity. *Harvard Business Review*, 79–91.

Thomas, G. D., & Hollenshead, C. (2002). Resisting from the margins: The coping strategies of Black women and other women of color faculty members at a research university. *Journal of Negro Education*, 70(3), 166–175.

Thomas, R. R., Jr. (1990). From affirmative action to affirming diversity. *Harvard Business Review*, 90(2), 107–117.

Thomas, R. R., Jr. (2006). *Building on the promise of diversity*. New York: AMACOM Books.

Thomas, S. L. (2000). Ties that bind: A social network approach to understanding student integration and persistence. *Journal of Higher Education*, 71(5), 591–615.

Thompson, G. L. (2007). *Up where we belong: Helping African American and Latino students rise in school and life.* San Francisco: Jossey-Bass.

Thompson, G. L., & Louque, A. C. (2005). *Exposing the "culture of arrogance" in the academy.* Sterling, VA: Stylus.

Thompson, M., Sekaquaptewa, P. (2002). When being different is detrimental: Solo status and the performance of women and racial minorities. *Analysis of Social Issues and Public Policy,* 2, 183–203.

Tidball, M. E. (1976). Of men and research: The dominant themes in higher education include neither teaching nor women. *Journal of Higher Education,* 47, 373–389.

Tidball, M. E. (1980). Women's colleges and women achievers revisited. *Signs: Journal of Women in Culture and Society,* 5, 504–517.

Tidball, M. E. (1986). Baccalaureate origins of recent natural science doctorates. *Journal of Higher Education,* 57, 606–620.

Tidball, M. E., Smith, D. G., Tidball, C. S., & Wolf-Wendel, L. E. (1999). *Taking women seriously: Lessons and legacies for educating the majority.* Phoenix, AZ: American Council on Education & Oryx Press.

Tierney, W. G. (1993). *Building communities of difference: Higher education in the twenty-first century.* Westport, CT: Bergin & Garvey.

Tierney, W. G. (1997). *Academic outlaws: Queer theory and cultural studies in the academy.* Thousand Oaks, CA: Sage.

Tierney, W. G., & Bensimon, E. M. (1996). *Promotion and tenure: Community and socialization in academe.* Albany: State University of New York Press.

Tilley, C. *Durable inequality.* (1998). Berkeley: University of California Press.

Tinto, V. (1997). Classrooms as communities: Exploring the educational character of student persistence. *Journal of Higher Education,* 68(6), 599–623.

Tippeconnic, J. W. III. (2002, April 21–23). American Indians and Alaska Native faculty in academe: The good, the bad and the ugly. In *Conference proceedings from the Keeping our Faculties conference* (pp. 53–59). St. Paul: University of Minnesota.

Tiven, L. (2001). Student voices: The ADL's A World of Difference. In D. L. Schoem & S. Hurtado (Eds.), *Intergroup dialogue: Deliberative democracy in school, college, community, and workplace* (pp. 59–73). Ann Arbor: University of Michigan.

Tobias, S. (1990). *They're not dumb, they're different.* Tucson, AZ: Research Corp.

Tobin, K., & Roth, W. M. (Eds.). (2007). *The culture of science education.* New Directions in Mathematics and Science Education. Rotterdam, Netherlands: Sense Publishers.

Tomás Rivera Policy Institute. (2006, November). *College scholarships for Latino students: Are opportunities being missed?* Los Angeles: Author.

Tonso, K. L. (2001). Plotting something dastardly: Hiding a gender curriculum in engineering. In E. Margolis (Ed.), *The hidden curriculum in higher education* (pp. 155–174). New York: Routledge.

Torres, V., Howard-Hamilton, M. F., & Cooper, D. L. (2003). Identity development of diverse populations: Implications for teaching and administration in higher education. *ASHE-ERIC Higher Education Report,* 29(6). San Francisco: Jossey-Bass.

Towers, S. (2008). *A case study of gender bias at the postdoctoral level in physics, and its resulting impact on the academic career and advancement of females.* Retrieved April 19, 2008, from http://export.arxiv.org/abs/0804.2026.

Treisman, U. (1992). Studying students studying calculus: A look at the lives of minority mathematics students in college. *College Mathematics Journal, 23*(5), 362–372.

Treviño, J. (2001). Voices of discovery: Intergroup dialogues at Arizona State University. In D. L. Schoem & S. Hurtado (Eds.), *Intergroup dialogue: Deliberative democracy in school, college, community, and workplace* (pp. 87–98). Ann Arbor: University of Michigan.

Triandis, H. C., Kurowski, L. L., & Gelfand, M. J. (1994). Workplace diversity. In H. C. Triandis & M. D. Dunnette (Eds.), *Handbook of industrial and organizational psychology* (2nd ed., Vol. 4, pp. 769–827). Palo Alto, CA: Consulting Psychologists Press.

Trix, F., & Psenka, P. (2003). Exploring the color of glass: Letters of recommendation for female and male medical faculty. *Discourse and Society, 14*(2), 191–220.

Tropp, L. R. (2006). Stigma and intergroup contact among members of minority and majority status groups. In S. Levin & C. van Laar (Eds.), *Stigma and group inequality* (pp. 171–192). Mahwah, NJ: Erlbaum.

Trower, C. A., & Chait, R. P. (2002, March/April). Faculty diversity: Too little for too long. *Harvard Magazine*, pp. 33ff.

Trower, C. A., & Honan, J. (2002). How might data be used. In R. P. Chait, *The questions of tenure* (pp. 271–308). Cambridge, MA: Harvard University Press.

Tsikata, D. (n.d.). *Progressing with truth and integrity? Gender, institutional cultures and the career trajectories of faculty of the University of Ghana.* Draft chapter for A. Mama & T. Barnes (Eds.), *Gender and institutional cultures in African universities.* Forthcoming.

Tuan, M. (2005). *Forever foreigners or honorary whites? The Asian ethnic experience today* (Rev. ed.). New Brunswick, NJ: Rutgers University Press.

Turner, C. S. V. (1999). Addressing the recruitment and retention of faculty of color in higher education: Promoting business as unusual. *Keeping our Faculties: Symposium proceedings for plenary sessions* (pp. 1–42). University of Minnesota: Office of the Associate Vice President for Multicultural and Academic Affairs.

Turner, C. S. V. (2002a). *Diversifying the faculty: A guidebook for search committees.* Washington, DC: American Association of Colleges and Universities.

Turner, C. S. V. (2002b). Women of color in academe: Living with multiple marginality. *Journal of Higher Education, 73*(1), 74–93.

Turner, C. S. V. (2003). Incorporation and marginalization in the academy: From border towards center for faculty of color? *Journal of Black Studies, 34*(1), 112–125.

Turner, C. S. V. (2007). Pathways to the presidency: Biographical sketches of women of color firsts. *Harvard Educational Review, 77*(1), 1–38.

Turner, C. S. V., & Myers, S. L. (1997). Faculty diversity and affirmative action. In M. Garcia (Ed.), *Affirmative action's testament of hope: Strategies for a new era in higher education* (pp. 131–148). Albany: State University of New York Press.

Turner, C. S. V., & Myers, S. L. (2000). *Faculty of color in academe: Bittersweet success.* Needham Heights, MA: Allyn & Bacon.

Turner, S. E., & Bound, J. (2003). Closing the gap or widening the divide: The effects of the GI Bill and World War II on the educational outcomes of Black Americans. *Journal of Economic History*, 63(1), 145–177.

Tushman, M., & O'Reilly, C. (1996). The ambidextrous organization: Managing evolutionary and revolutionary change. *California Management Review*, 38, 1–23.

Tusmith, B., & Reddy, M. T. (Eds.). (2002). *Race in the college classroom: Pedagogy and politics*. New Brunswick, NJ: Rutgers University Press.

Twine, F. W. (2005). *Racism in a racial democracy: The maintenance of White supremacy in Brazil*. New Brunswick, NJ: Rutgers University Press.

Umbach, P. D. (2006). The contributions of faculty of color to undergraduate education. *Research in Higher Education*, 47(3), 317–345.

Umbach, P. D. (2007). How effective are they? Exploring the impact of contingent faculty on undergraduate education. *Review of Higher Education*, 30(2), 91–123.

Umbach, P. D., & Kuh, G. D. (2006). Student experiences with diversity at liberal arts colleges: Another claim for distinctiveness. *Journal of Higher Education*, 77(1), 169–192.

Umbach, P. D., & Wawrzynski, M. R. (2005). Faculty do matter: The role of college faculty in student learning and engagement. *Research in Higher Education*, 46(2), 153–184.

Valencia, R. R. (2008). *Chicano students and the courts: The Mexican American legal struggle for educational equity*. New York: New York University Press.

Valenzuela, A. (1999). *Subtractive schooling: U.S.-Mexican youth and the politics of caring*. Albany: State University of New York Press.

Valian, V. (2000). *Why so slow? The advancement of women*. Cambridge, MA: MIT Press.

Valian, V. (2005). Beyond gender schemas: Improving the advancement of women in academia. *Hypatia*, 20(3), 198–213.

Valverde, L. A. (1998). Future strategies and actions: Creating multicultural higher education campuses. In L. A. Valverde & L. A. Casenell (Eds.), *The multicultural campus: Strategies for transforming higher education* (pp. 13–29). Walnut Creek, CA: Alta Mira Press.

Van Der Vegt, G. S., Bunderson, J. S., & Oosterhof, A. (2006). Expertness diversity and interpersonal helping in teams: Why those who need the most help end up getting it least. *Academy of Management Journal*, 49(5), 877–893.

van Laar, C., Levin, S., Sinclair, S., & Sidanius, J. (2005). The effect of university roommate contact on ethnic attitudes and behavior. *Journal of Experimental Social Psychology*, 41, 329–354.

Vea, B. (2008). *The college experiences of Filipina/o Americans and other AAPI subgroups: Disaggregating the data*. Unpublished doctoral dissertation, Claremont Graduate University, Claremont, CA.

Villalpondo, O., & Delgado Bernal, D. (2002). A critical race theory analysis of barriers that impede the success of faculty of color. In W. A. Smith, P. G. Altbach, & K. Lomotey (Eds.), *The racial crisis in American higher education: Continuing challenges for the twenty-first century* (Rev. ed., pp. 243–269). Albany: State University of New York Press.

Vincent, F. (2005, June). *No merit in these scholarships*. Policy Perspectives. Washington, DC: Educational Policy Institute.

W. K. Kellogg Foundation. (1998). *Evaluation handbook*. Battle Creek, MI: Author.

Wainer, H., & Steinberg, L. (1992). Sex differences in performance on the mathematics section of the Scholastic Aptitude Test: A bidirectional validity study. *Harvard Educational Review, 62*, 323–336.

Wallach, M. A. (1976). Tests tell us little about talent. *American Scientist, 64*, 57–63.

Walser, N. (2006). "R" is for resilience. *Harvard Education Letter, 22*(5), 1–3.

Washington, S. (2007). Fostering women's multicultural alliances as an academic administrator. *On Campus with Women, 36*(1), 1–2. Retrieved June 20, 2007, from http://www.aacu.org/ocww/volume36_1/national.cfm.

Washington, V., & Harvey, W. (1989). Affirmative rhetoric, negative action: African American and Hispanic faculty at predominantly White institutions. *ASHE-ERIC Report No. 2*. Washington, DC: School of Education and Human Development, George Washington University.

Watson, S. W., Cabrera, A. F., Lee, C., & Williams, A. (2005). *Latino students and the educational pipeline*. Stafford, VA: Educational Policy Institute. Available at http://www.educationalpolicy.org.

Watson, W. E., Johnson, L., & Merritt, D. (1998). Team orientation, self-orientation, and diversity in task groups: Their connection to team performance over time. *Group and Organization Management, 23*, 161–188.

Watson, W. E., Kumar, K., & Michaelson, L. K. (1993). Cultural diversity's impact on interaction process and performance: Comparing homogeneous and diverse work groups. *Academy of Management Journal, 36*, 590–602.

Watts, D. J. (2004). The "new" science of networks. *Annual Review of Sociology, 30*, 243–270.

Wegner, J. W. (2006). The view from Chapel Hill: Addressing the underlying conflicts between faith and reason in the wake of violence. *Academe, 92*(4), 46–49.

Weick, K. (2005). The experience of theorizing: Sensemaking as topic and resource. In K. G. Smith & M. A. Hitt (Eds.), *Great minds in management: The process of theory development* (pp. 394–416). Oxford: Oxford University Press.

Weick, K. E., & Sutcliffe, K. M. (2001). *Managing the unexpected: Assuring high performance in an age of complexity*. San Francisco: Jossey-Bass.

Weinberg, S. L. (2008). Monitoring faculty diversity. *Journal of Higher Education, 79*(4), 365–387.

West, M. E. (2000). Faculty women's struggle for equality at the University of California. *UCLA Women's Law Journal, 10*(2), 259–319.

Western Association of Schools and Colleges. (2002). *A guide to using evidence in the accreditation process*. Oakland, CA: Author.

Wharton, A. S. (1992). The social construction of gender and race in organizations: A social identity and group mobilization perspective. *Research in Sociology of Organizations, 10*, 55–84.

Wheatley, M. J. (2006). *Leadership and the new science: Discovering order in a chaotic world* (3rd ed.). San Francisco: Berrett-Koehler.

White, J. A. (1989). The engineering faculty pipeline: An NSF perspective. *Engineering Education*, 79(5), 547–549.

Whitt, E. J. (2005). *Promoting student success: What student affairs can do* (Occasional Paper No. 5). Bloomington: Center for Postsecondary Research, Indiana University.

Wightman, L. F. (1997). The threat to diversity in legal education: An empirical analysis of the consequences of abandoning race as a factor in law school admissions decisions. *New York University Law Review*, 72(1).

Wightman, L. F. (1998). *NSAL longitudinal bar passage study* (LSAC Research Report Series). Newtown, PA: Law School Admissions Council.

Wightman, L. (2000). Standardized testing and equal access: A tutorial. In M. Chang, D. Witt, J. Jones, & K. Hakuta (Eds.), *Compelling interest: Examining the evidence on racial dynamics in higher education* (pp. 84–125). Stanford, CA: AERA Panel on Racial Dynamics in Colleges and Universities.

Wijeyesinghe, C. L., & Jackson, B. W. III (Eds.). (2001). *New perspectives on racial identity development: A theoretical and practical anthology*. New York: New York University Press.

Williams, A., & Swail, W. S. (2005). *Is more better? The impact of postsecondary education on the economic and social well-being of American society*. Washington, DC: Educational Policy Institute.

Williams, D. A., Berger, J. B., & McClendon, S. A. (2005). *Toward a model of inclusive excellence and change in postsecondary education*. Washington, DC: Association of American Colleges and Universities.

Williams, K. C. (1994). Mapping the margins: Intersectionality, identity politics, and violence against women of color. In M. A. Fineman & R. Mylitiuk (Eds.), *The public nature of private violence* (pp. 93–118). New York: Routledge.

Williams, K. Y., & O'Reilly, A. (1998). Demography and diversity in organizations: A review of 40 years of research. In B. W. Shaw & L. L. Cummings (Eds.), *Research in Organizational Behavior*, 20, 77–140. Greenwich, CT: JAI Press.

Wilson, A. (1996). How we find ourselves: Identity development and Two-Spirit people. *Harvard Educational Review*, 66(2), 303–317.

Wilson, R. (1995a). *Affirmative action: Yesterday, today, and beyond*. Washington, DC: American Council on Education.

Wilson, R. (1995b, June 2). Hiring of black scholars stalls at some major universities. *Chronicle of Higher Education*, A16.

Winborne, W., & Smith, A. (2001). Not just dialogue for dialogue's sake: The National Conference for Community and Justice. In D. L. Schoem & S. Hurtado (Eds.), *Intergroup dialogue: Deliberative democracy in school, college, community, and workplace* (pp. 166–177). Ann Arbor: University of Michigan.

Winston, A. S. (Ed.). (2004). *Defining difference: Race and racism in the history of psychology*. Washington, DC: American Psychological Association.

Wise, T. (2006). Whites swim in racial preferences. In C. Hartman (Ed.), *Poverty and race in America* (pp. 3–6). Oxford: Lexington Books.

Wittig, M. A., & Molina, L. (2000). Moderators and mediators of prejudice reduction in multicultural education. In S. Oskamp (Ed.), *Reducing prejudice and discrimination* (pp. 295–318). Mahwah, NJ: Erlbaum.

Wolf-Wendel, L. E. (1998). Models of excellence: The baccalaureate origins of successful European American women, African American women, and Latinas. *Journal of Higher Education,* 69, 141–186.

Wolf-Wendel, L. E. (2000). Women-friendly campuses: What five institutions are doing right. *Review of Higher Education,* 23(3), 319–345.

Wolf-Wendel, L. E., Baker, B. D., & Morphew, C. C. (2000). Dollars and sense: Institutional resources and baccalaureate origins of women doctorates. *Journal of Higher Education,* 71(2), 165–186.

Wolf-Wendel, L. E., Ward, K., & Kinzie, J. (2007, November). *The tangled web we weave: The overlap and unique contribution of involvement, engagement and integration.* Paper presented at the meeting of the Association for the Study of Higher Education, Louisville, KY.

Wood, E. M. (1995). *Democracy against capitalism.* Cambridge: Cambridge University Press.

Woodrow Wilson Foundation. (2005). *Diversity and the PhD.* Princeton, NJ: Author.

Woodward, K. (Ed.). (2000). *Questioning identity: Gender, class, nation.* London: Routledge.

Worchel, S., & Austin, W. G. (Eds.). (1986). *Psychology of intergroup relations.* Chicago: Nelson-Hall.

Wright, B., & Head, P. W. (1990). Tribally controlled community colleges: A student outcomes assessment of associate degree recipients. *Community College Review,* 18, 28–33.

Wright, B., & Tierney, W. G. (1991). American Indians in higher education: A history of cultural conflict. *Change,* 23(2), 11–20.

Wright, P., Ferris, S. P., Hiller, J. S., & Kroll, M. (1995). Competitiveness through management of diversity: Effects on stock price valuation. *Academy of Management Journal,* 38(1), 272–287.

Xavier University: The nesting place for Black doctors. (1996, Autumn). *Journal of Blacks in Higher Education,* 13, 48–49.

Yale University. (1990). Report on the committee on recruitment and retention of minority group members on the faculty at Yale. *Minerva,* 28(2), 217–247.

Yoder, J. D. (2002). Context matters: Understanding tokenism processes and their impact on women's work. *Psychology of Women Quarterly,* 26, 1–8.

Yoder, J. D., Adams, J., Grove, S., & Priest, R. F. (1985). To teach is to learn: Overcoming tokenism with mentors. *Psychology of Women Quarterly,* 9, 119–131.

Yoder, J. D., & Schleicher, T. L. (1996). Undergraduates regard deviation from occupational gender stereotypes as costly for women. *Sex Roles,* 35, 389–400.

Yoshino, K. F. (1999). American college presidents on social justice: The intersection of personal and community values (Doctoral dissertation, Claremont Graduate University, 1999). *Dissertation Abstracts International,* AAT9917991.

Yoshino, K. (2006). *Covering: The hidden assault on our civil rights.* New York: Random House.

Young, J. W. (1994). Differential prediction of college grades by gender and by ethnicity: A replications study. *Educational and Psychological Measurement, 54*(4), 1022–1029.

Zandy, J. (1996). Decloaking class: Why class identity and consciousness count. *Race, Gender, & Class, 5*(1), 7–23.

Zandy, J. (Ed.). (2001). *What we hold in common: An introduction to working-class studies.* New York: Feminist Press.

Zavella, P. (1994). Reflections on diversity among Chicanas. In S. Gregory & R. Sanjek, *Race* (pp. 199–212). New Brunswick, NJ: Rutgers University Press.

Zúñiga, X., & Nagda, B. R. (2001). Design considerations in intergroup dialogue. In D. L. Schoem & S. Hurtado (Eds.), *Intergroup dialogue: Deliberative democracy in school, college, community, and workplace* (pp. 306–327). Ann Arbor: University of Michigan.

Zúñiga, X., Nagda, B. R., Chesler, M., & Cytron-Walker, A. (2007). Intergroup dialogue in higher education: Meaningful learning about social justice. *ASHE Higher Education Report, 32*(4). San Francisco: Jossey-Bass.

Zúñiga, X., & Sevig, T. D. (1997). Bridging the "us/them" divide through intergroup dialogue and peer leadership. *Diversity Factor, 6*(2), 23–28.

Zwick, R. (2007). *College admissions testing.* Washington, DC: National Association for College Admissions Counseling.

Page numbers in *italics* indicate figures and tables.